PURBASA: EAST MEETS EAST

Synergising the North-East and Eastern India with the Indo-Pacific

PURBASA: EAST MEETS EAST

Synergising the North-East and Eastern India with the Indo-Pacific

Editors

Lalit Mansingh

Anup K. Mudgal

Udai Bhanu Singh

PENTAGON PRESS LLP

PURBASA: EAST MEETS EAST

Synergising the North-East and Eastern India with the Indo-Pacific

Editors: Lalit Mansingh, Anup K. Mudgal, Udai Bhanu Singh

First Published in 2019

ISBN 978-93-86618-64-1

Disclaimer: The views expressed in this book are those of the authors and do not necessarily reflect those of the Kalinga International Foundation (KIF), or the Government of India.

Published by

PENTAGON PRESS LLP
206, Peacock Lane, Shahpur Jat
New Delhi-110049
Phones: 011-64706243, 26491568
Telefax: 011-26490600
email: rajan@pentagonpress.in
website: www.pentagonpress.in

Printed at Aegean Offset Printers, Greater Noida, U.P.

Contents

Preface

The Kalinga International Foundation (KIF) believes that the eastern and north-eastern regions of India are a seamless, homogeneous sub-region of India, sharing historical and cultural ties over centuries with the Indo-Pacific region.

This was the impulse behind the KIF's flagship conference PURBASA, a word with rich shades of meaning implying the rise of the east, the hopes from the east and the message from the east.

At PURBASA: EAST MEETS EAST, diplomats and scholars representing fifteen countries of the Indo-Pacific region engaged in an intensive dialogue on a wide spectrum of bilateral and regional issues with a galaxy of experts from India, including Ministers, MPs, academics, corporate leaders, former diplomats and military leaders.

The conclave was held, appropriately, in Bhubaneswar, the capital of ancient Kalinga—currently, of the state of Odisha. It was from Kalinga that some of the earliest maritime contacts were made with the Indo-Pacific. The Act East Policy of India has rejuvenated these historic linkages and spurred new initiatives to establish closer linkages with the region through three Cs: Connectivity, Commerce and Culture.

This publication brings out some of the presentations by the experts at the conference and attempts to share the flavour of this remarkable confluence of East with East.

It will be our endeavour to continue the PURBASA dialogue in the times to come.

October 8, 2018

Amb Lalit Mansingh
Chairman
Kalinga International Foundation (KIF)

Kalinga International Foundation

The Kalinga International Foundation (KIF) is an independent, non-partisan think tank which seeks to analyse and propose solutions to pressing issues relating to international and national security, international trade, India's foreign policy and regional co-operation. Its vision is for peace and prosperity in the region with the mission to build consensus on solutions for fulfilling these goals. It specialises in the ability to establish strong institutional relationships with experts, academics and concerned citizens and further to network with decision-makers.

KIF brings together, for the first time, the eastern and north-eastern region of India with their proximate neighbours—Bangladesh, Bhutan, Nepal, Sri Lanka and beyond, with the ASEAN nations and the wider Indo-Pacific region. The States located in India's north-east—Arunachal Pradesh, Assam, Manipur, Meghalaya, Mizoram, Nagaland, Sikkim and Tripura and in the east—Andhra Pradesh, Bihar, Chhattisgarh, Jharkhand, Odisha and West Bengal and Andaman and Nicobar in the south-east, have strong common ties of history, culture, language and customs and traditions from early times. Sailors, merchants, farmers, scholars and artisans from this region travelled overseas and established linkages with the people of South East Asia dating back to the fourth Century BCE. The pioneers among them were the *Sadhavas*, the sailor-merchants of Kalinga, a powerful empire straddling the eastern sea coast of India. The great poet, Kalidasa, in the 5th century CE described the King of Kalinga as *Mahodadhipati*, i.e. the Lord of the Oceans.

The *Sadhavas* acted as the messengers of peace and couriers of culture between eastern India and the Indo-Pacific region. Indians to this day, are referred to as *Klings*, *Kalings* or *Kelangs* in South East Asia. Kalinga has, therefore, been used as a metaphor for the historic ties that bind this wider region together.

While drawing inspiration from the past, the focus of the KIF will be on the potential for developing new and robust partnerships between India and the countries of the region. India's eastern region is richly endowed with natural and human resources. It is also a vast repository of rich cultural and spiritual heritage. The potential for trade, investments, tourism and joint ventures is enormous.

Since the Look East Policy was announced in 1992, India has concluded strategic partnerships not only with individual member states but collectively with ASEAN. Under the current 'Act East Policy', a new dynamism and vigour has been introduced in India's foreign policy towards the Indo-Pacific region.

The KIF aspires to play a catalytic role in creating valuable linkages within the region. It will work collaboratively with the Central and State Governments, Chambers of Commerce and Industry, with India's missions abroad and foreign diplomatic missions in India and other think tanks and institutions that share its objectives.

Our dialogues with partner countries will revolve around five major clusters of issues:

1. Political cooperation
2. Trade and investments
3. Strategic cooperation
4. Energy security ; and
5. Cultural connectivity and heritage tourism

Over the coming months, the Foundation proposes to organise seminars, conferences and outreach programmes in New Delhi, in State capitals and in selected venues abroad.

As we launch this new endeavour, I seek your valued co-operation and support for the success of our mission.

Amb Lalit Mansingh
Chairman - Kalinga International Foundation

Introduction

The Indo-Pacific presents many possibilities and challenges today. India's East and Northeast has had a civilisational connect with other cultures both overland and through the India n Ocean and the Pacific Ocean for centuries. India's Act East Policy, has extended India's vision beyond ASEAN to the larger Indo-Pacific region which consolidates the Indian Ocean Region (IOR) and the Western Pacific Region (WP) into a singular regional construct. How should the relationship between India and countries of the region develop in this period of geopolitical flux in the wider Indo Pacific?

The Indo-Pacific which accounts for over 3 billion of the world's population and almost 50 per cent of the global GDP features prominently in India's foreign policy. India, especially its eastern seaboard overlooking the Bay of Bengal, seeks to achieve peace and security through the promotion of the 3Cs—Commerce, Connectivity and Culture.

The ASEAN-India Commemorative Summit (January 25, 2018) themed 'Shared Values, Common Destiny' was attended by the ten Association of South East Asian Nations (ASEAN) Heads of State or Government. Earlier, all South Asian Association for Regional Cooperation (SAARC) leaders had been invited by Prime Minister Modi at the swearing-in ceremony in May 2014. In an article published in Straits Times (Singapore) on the theme of Shared Values, Common Destiny he wrote, "We have a common vision for the future, built on commitment to inclusion and integration, belief in sovereign equality of all nations irrespective of size, and support for free and open pathways of commerce and engagement."

The Commemorative Summit issued the 36-para Delhi Declaration. It captures India's commitment to work closely with ASEAN to uphold respect for international law, primacy of United Nations Convention on the Laws of the Seas (UNCLOS), freedom of navigation and overflights in the region, peaceful resolution of disputes and an early conclusion of the Code of Conduct (CoC) in the South China Sea.

India's Look East Policy (LEP) enunciated in 1992 under Prime Minister Narasimha Rao's leadership matured over the years with India's deepening engagement with the ASEAN process. India first became a sectoral dialogue partner and went on to become a full dialogue partner of ASEAN (before China did). In 2012 the ASEAN India Vision Statement raised the partnership to the strategic level. The structural foundation (laid in the LEP phase) was hampered by tardy implementation. It was at the 12th India-ASEAN Summit in Naypyitaw in November 2014 that Prime Minister Narendra Modi declared that India's Look East policy had been upgraded to an Act East policy. India now has a dedicated mission to ASEAN (in Jakarta) and the ASEAN India Centre (in New Delhi). The ASEAN leaders were given an assurance that the projects on the India-Myanmar border would be speeded up and trade policy improved. At the Global Investors' Summit- 'Advantage Assam' in Guwahati in February 2018, Mr Modi said "We created the Act East Policy and the Northeast is at the heart of it." Besides, Bangladesh became the first country to open a consulate in Guwahati and Bhutan the second. India has emphasised engagement with the immediate and extended neighbourhood. There were high level visits to Myanmar, Vietnam, Singapore, Japan, Australia and Fiji. PM Modi had said: "India's Act East starts with Bangladesh". This was further buttressed by India's engagement with the Bay of Bengal Initiative for Multi-Sectoral Technical and Economic Cooperation (BIMSTEC), and the Ganga-Mekong Cooperation Initiative. In addition, India brought together the Pacific islands at the 2nd Forum for India-Pacific Islands Cooperation (FIPIC) Summit, Jaipur in August 2015.

India sees a role for itself in shaping the emerging Security and Economic Architecture, including forums like the East Asia Summit (EAS), the ASEAN Defence Ministers' Meeting-Plus (ADMM-Plus) and the Council for Security Cooperation in the Asia Pacific (CSCAP) — evident in the India-US Joint Strategic Vision for the Asia-Pacific and Indian Ocean Region (January, 2015). However, India's involvement in the RCEP process and the ADMM Plus is yet to be fully exploited.

The first part of the book includes chapters pertaining to the Inaugural Session, held on the first day of the Conference (March 16, 2018) at Mayfair

Lagoon, Bhubaneswar, Odisha. The session began with Welcome Remarks by Ambassador Lalit Mansingh (Chairman of the Kalinga International Foundation). Second, a detailed Report of Proceedings captures the highlights of the session that included speeches (by Assam Minister Mr C.M. Patowary, Union Minister Mr Dharmendra Pradhan and the Minister of Buddha Sasana of Sri Lanka, Hon. Gamini Jayawickrama Perera) and a cultural extravaganza in the form of a dance-ballet. Finally, the glittering session concluded with the Vote of Thanks by Ms. Shreerupa Mitra.

The second part of the book is devoted to the proceedings of the Academic Sessions. It included separate sessions on Economic Cooperation; Maritime Connectivity and Security in the Indo-Pacific, Regional Connectivity (two sessions); Energy Cooperation; Connecting Women, Youth and Civil Society; Tourism, Culture, Buddhism; India's Bilateral Relations with Sri Lanka, Myanmar, Indonesia and ASEAN in general, and Japan: Valedictory which included speeches by Lalit Mansingh and Ajarn Sulak Sivaraksa and finally the Valedictory Address by the Governor of Odisha, His Excellency Dr. S.C. Jamir. The book concludes with 'The Purbasa Conference: A Critical Evaluation' by Ambassador Rajiv Bhatia.

Economic Cooperation

India and ASEAN have a combined population of 1.8 billion or one-fourth of the world's population and a combined GDP which exceeds $4.5 trillion. Yet, China had a decisive edge in the Indo-Pacific with its $12 trillion economy and $450 billion trade with ASEAN and its Belt and Road Initiative (BRI). China has a growing economic and political presence in the Pacific islands too. This is marked by a perceived US withdrawal from the region and its abandonment of the Trans-Pacific Partnership (TPP). That inevitably puts the focus on the Regional Comprehensive Economic Partnership (RCEP). The 16 RCEP negotiating parties who are working towards concluding their negotiations have to narrow their differences on competition, intellectual property rights and rules of origin; and table revised offers for services and investment. But given the Chinese influence in the region, there is also a tacit acceptance of China's leadership role in the Regional Comprehensive Economic Partnership (RCEP).

PM Modi at World Economic Forum (WEF) Davos (January 2018) spoke against the trend towards protectionism. China's BRI uses ASEAN as a market for its exports and investment. By 2025 India will be the fifth largest consumer market and ASEAN will have 163 million strong Middle Class. By 2020 India could potentially reap the demographic dividend when it will become the world's youngest country (with an average age of 29). India's fast growing internet user base and a growing digital economy could indicate a role for India in the Indo-Pacific.

At the summit level, relations with ASEAN have been growing since 2002. The ASEAN-India Free Trade Area, which went into effect in 2010, promises to increase trade between the two sides to $200 billion by 2022. A new milestone in the relationship has been the India-ASEAN Agreement on Trade in Services and Agreement on Investment. ASEAN is India's fourth largest trade partner, India is ASEAN's seventh. Although India-ASEAN trade has grown 25 times in as many years, at $70 billion (2016-17) the potential is yet to be fully exploited. The current record of investment is less than adequate. India accounts for only 1.8 per cent of FDI inflows into ASEAN during 2010-2016. In fact, the Prime Minister of Singapore urged ASEAN and India to redouble efforts to promote trade and investment.

The Academic Sessions began with the session on Economic Cooperation, highlighting the key role economics has come to play in international relations. V.S. Seshadri explores some aspects of India's trade cooperation with East and South East Asia. He also points out some of key steps India needs to take to derive benefit from the FTAs. Ton Sinh Thanh (Ambassador of Vietnam) strikes a note of caution as he flags the challenges that stand in the way of improved cooperation between the two regions. Anil Wadhwa notes that development of the North East India is required for an alternative model to China's Belt and Road Initiative to be crafted. Palitha Kohona concludes that greater economic cooperation in the Indian Ocean Region including through China's BRI could be a force for the good. Prabir De while discussing Indo Pacific connectivity, emphasizes the need for a bottoms-up approach of developing regional supply chains rather than a top-down approach imposed by governments, as a more effective way to regional integration.

Maritime Connectivity and Security in the Indo-Pacific

In considering Maritime Connectivity, Trade and Security are but two sides of the same coin. Session II devoted to Maritime Connectivity and Security in the Indo-Pacific addressed the concerns of all those countries of the region whose very economic sustainability depends on secure sea lanes of communications and in devising common strategies to deal with potential threats and instability.

From India's perspective, security is a prerequisite for internal cohesion, economic development, and consolidation. India's primary interest is to create an enabling external environment for the economic progress of the country. Unless there is regional security, economic development cannot be envisaged.

It is in this context that New Delhi's emphasis on the potential of the Blue Economy becomes relevant. The Blue Economy includes economic activities pertaining to sustainable development of resources and assets in the oceans, related rivers, water bodies and coastal regions in a manner that ensures equity, inclusion, innovation and modern technology. Prime Minister Modi in fact likened the blue chakra or wheel in India's national flag to the potential of Blue Revolution or the Ocean Economy in the coastal areas organically linked to the hinterland and the PM's vision of 'Security And Growth for All in the Region' (SAGAR). The Indian Ocean Rim Association (IORA) and the Bay of Bengal Initiative for Multi-Sectoral Technical and Economic Cooperation (BIMSTEC) can be effective mediums for pursuing the vision of the Blue Economy.

China's military and economic rise is being closely monitored in the region. When China rejected the Permanent Court of Arbitration (PCA) ruling of July 2016 which went against it in the Philippine-China dispute in the South China Sea, it was seen as a blow to the rules-based global order. India remains concerned as the bulk of its trade is via maritime routes and thus requires freedom of navigation and the security of sea lanes of communication. Even though India is not a party to any of the disputes in the South China Sea, it has a significant stake in the stability of the region because any conflict would disrupt the flow of trade and supplies. In contrast, in a similar maritime dispute between India and Bangladesh, in July 2014 when the court awarded Bangladesh 19,467 square kilometers of sea area in the Bay of Bengal, New Delhi readily accepted the decision.

To address challenges in the maritime domain, the Indian Navy has stepped up its activities in regional waters. The Indian Navy released its maritime security strategy *Ensuring Secure Seas: Indian Maritime Security Strategy* at the Naval Commanders' Conference in October 2015, which replaced and updated the 2007 strategy. India was a founding member of the Indian Ocean Rim Association (IORA). It also founded the Indian Ocean Naval Symposium (IONS) in 2009, which provides a forum to discuss issues that have a bearing on maritime security in the Indian Ocean region. Moreover, the Indian Navy has adopted a proactive approach to maritime security by organizing the 2016 International Fleet Review (its second ever) and the latest March 2018 Milan ("confluence") exercises in the Bay of Bengal.

Non Traditional Security challenges in the Indian Ocean region require joint defence responses to the common problems of environmental degradation/ climate change, and resource wars (especially over food and water). While bilateral agreements help in mitigating these challenges, due to the trans-border nature of most of these problems often resort to multilateral agreements and regimes is more effective. India's business links have a glorious past which is best exemplified by the fact that the Kalingas traded with the East some 2000 years ago.

R.K. Dhowan in his opening remarks introduces India's essentially maritime character while emphasizing the need for synergy in waterways connectivity, maritime security, in the Indo-Pacific region. He also advocates freedom of navigation, adherence to international law, peace, safety and security of the waterways. P.K. Singh highlightes the security challenges of maritime connectivity in the context of China's grand design for dominance through its Belt and Road Initiative. The Sri Lankan view on maritime security has been articulated by Jayanath Colombage who sees Indian Ocean become increasingly a place for strategic competition wherein a maritime cold war is unfolding. He supports a maritime 'code of conduct' and a greater role for existing organisations like IORA and BIMSTEC in building a rule based order. Aruna Gopinath of Malaysia brings out the element of security cooperation between India and ASEAN especially through ASEAN-led mechanisms. Vietnam's Vo Xuan Vinh explaines the Indo-Pacific concept, India' perception of it, and the place of South China in it. Myanmar's Naing Swe Oo highlightes Myanmar Navy's role in the rapidly changing maritime security scenario in the Indian Ocean. Dhruv Jaishankar traces the maritime history to highlight robust sea based trade and the change that the arrival of the Europeans brought about to the security and the economic architecture of the region. With exponentially growing challenges, India is emerging as a security provider in the Indian Ocean region. In a Closing Remarks the chariman refers to Indian initiatives for development of the maritime domain (through SAGAR and Project Mausam) by harnessing the Blue Economy.

Regional Connectivity

The future of the Indo-Pacific region is going to be greatly impacted by the enlarged connectivity. Hence, the Challenges of Regional Connectivity deserve greater attention. Two important projects on the Indo-Myanmar border nearing completion are: the Kaladan Multimodal Transit Transport Project and the India-Myanmar Thailand Trilateral Highway. Great potential exists for border trade through the Northeast region. Four Northeastern States: Arunachal Pradesh, Manipur, Mizoram and Nagaland share 1,643 kms of border with Myanmar. At present the existing Land Customs Station (LCS) between India and Myanmar suffers from lack of infrastructure, when compared with Myanmar's other border points - such as the Sino-Myanmar and Thai-Myanmar. Rail connectivity through the Trans-Asian Railway (TAR) network once the missing links on the Myanmar and Indian sides are completed, would bring an immense improvement in connectivity. Air connectivity through the major cities of the region, to Eastern India is still inadequate. Digital connectivity could be India's USP given India's experience.

Given the importance of Regional Connectivity two separate sessions were devoted to it—chaired by S.D. Muni and Baladas Ghoshal respectively. Arvinder Lamba underlines the fact that connectivity of India's Northeast with the region would be a gamechanger. Rajiv Bhatia concerns the challenge of regional connectivity with a focus on a two decade old—BIMSTEC. Rizal Abdul Kadir's paper provides a sharp critique of India's Look East/Act East policy from a Malaysian perspective and suggests the way forward. Sonu Trivedi enumerates in some detail the connectivity corridors designed as development corridors between Northeast India and Myanmar.

The second part of Regional Connectivity focuses on the role perceptions play in developing connectivity, or ideational connectivity. It deals with the response of countries to the emerging security scenario and the evolving geopolitical and structural changes. Baladas Ghoshal opined that ideational connectivity is the key to linking the regions, peoples, values and cultures.

Udai Bhanu Singh then carries the discussion further by providing an Indian perspective on regional security challenges and connectivity. Mustafizur Rahman emphasises the importance to Bangladesh's economy of connecting to India's North East. Shankari Sundararaman argues how connectivity would help overcome some of the security challenges. Connectivity and enhanced economic cooperation would be aided by the communication revolution. Yet challenges will continue to persist. Harsh Pant indictes that India's geopolitical and economic interests in the region can be best served by reimagining a role for itself and engaging with different nations.

Energy Cooperation

Energy cooperation has become important for the Indo-Pacific in the face of exponential rates of energy consumption, the declining hydro-carbon reserves and the uncertain security situation in West Asia. States seek to secure multiple energy sources and identify multiple sources of supply. For instance, although India sources its oil and gas primarily from West Asia, it is looking to Vietnam, Myanmar and other sources in the Indo-Pacific. The session on Energy Cooperation addresses regional cooperation in both conventional and non-conventional sectors. According to Prabhat Singh we have entered a 'Golden Age of Gas'. Govind Pokhrel on the other hand emphasises the need for tapping the renewable hydro-potential resource.

Women, Youth and Civil Society

People to People connectivity is an important part of India's ties with the region. It is in this context that the session on 'Connecting Women, Youth and Civil Society' assumed significance. The two important sectors which could play an important role in this are- promoting health and education along the India-Myanmar border. In addition, significantly, India has a six million strong diaspora in the ASEAN region alone. This somewhat complex, multidimensional subject has been put across ably by three women panelists representing the two regions. Mary Teresita Daza (Ambassador of the Philippines to India) provides a twin perspective on the role of women: the Philippines' perspective and the ASEAN perspective. Alana Golmei sees an opportunity in the Act East Policy which could provide better connectivity to the people of the North East to link with the people of South East Asia as they share common interest, culture and beliefs. Finally, Lopamudra Maitra Bajpai's paper studies

Divine Feminine deities (Durga, Tara, Sophia and others) from India to Southeast Asia and beyond that are revered in diverse religious and folk cults. She attempts to highlight this diversity through oral tradition and mark its relevance in contemporary times.

Tourism, Culture, Buddhism

There was a tremendous intermingling of India and the Pacific region civilisationally which was primarily commercial and cultural. The session on Tourism; Culture; Buddhism delves in to the common civilisational strands which serve to both bind us and provide the richness of diversity. Kalidas Nag wrote a book on India and the Pacific World (1941) while Jawaharlal Nehru had foreseen the decline of the Atlantic in his Discovery of India in 1944. The Kalinga and Chola influence is still visible in Southeast Asia- the earliest beginning of India's Look East Policy. But, the cultural connect between India and the Indo-Pacific is not limited to the past. In the contemporary period the exchange has been a two way process, whether through the Bollywood cinema, social media and the internet, the books or the Universities although it is yet to be fully documented.

The Indian mainland was the source of successive waves - of Hinduism, Buddhism and Islam- footprints of which are visible even today in Southeast Asia. Imprints of these influences can be seen today in Borobudur, Angkor Vat and equally in the intangible cultural heritage. These cultures adopted Hindu icons while continuing to follow the principal tenets of Islam. It is the spread of Buddhism from India that has had the most lasting influence in the region where it blossomed into a living faith. Buddhism continues to play a major role in linking the region. Tourism, culture and Buddhism are closely interwined in the Indo-Pacific. Paramjit S. Sahai with many years' diplomatic experience has laid out clearly the steps to carry out cultural diplomacy and promote people to people relations. Benudhar Patra shows how maritime history of Kalinga is preserved in South East Asian traditions and makes a case study of Kalinga and Java in Indonesia. Lopamudra Maitra Bajpai (her second paper in this book) attempts to document the connectivity across intangible cultural traditions of South and Southeast Asia. Finally, Jatin Das provides an artist's view of the cultural similarities that exist between Odisha and Bali and bring the regions close together.

Bilaterals: India's Most Favoured Nations

The most crucial yet the most difficult relationships are the bilateral relationships India has with its immediate neighbours. V. Suryanarayan reminds us that we can choose our friends but not our neighbours. He points to the shared heritage of India and Sri Lanka relations, and the need to build mutual trust and understanding. Sidharto S. Suryodipuro welcomes the crescendo in India-Indonesia bilateral relations but also warns that we must learn from past mistakes and avoid indifference. Pinak Chakravarty, having served in Bangladesh as India's High Commissioner and in Thailand as India's Ambassador, is most suitably placed to comment on India's relations with these two countries. In his paper on India-Bangladesh ties he point out that there are over 50 bilateral institutional mechanisms in place. But, as the two countries head for elections in 2018 and 2019 respectively, domestic issues could come to the forefront and affect bilateral ties (especially the issue of illegal migration and the National Register of Citizens in Assam; and the sharing of river waters). Pinak Chakravarty's second paper, on India-Thailand relations points out that Thailand is India's natural ally given the rapidly evolving geo-strategic scenario in which China's influence in the neighbourhood is increasing. Moe Kyaw Aung, Ambassador of Myanmar in India, feels that while his country stands as a bridge between South and Southeast Asia, trading volume between India and Myanmar was below potential.

Deepa G Wadhwa, India's former Ambassador to Japan points to the synergy that exists between India's Act East Policy and Japan's Free and Open Pacific strategy although there is still considerable distance to be covered. Chitranganee Wagiswara, High Commissioner of Sri Lanka to India, while acknowledging ancient cultural ties with India, notes that it is China which plays an important role in Sri Lanka's economic development.

The penultimate chapter Valedictory Session includes the Special Address by Lalit Mansingh, the Valedictory Message by Ajan Sulak Sivaraksa and the Valedictory Address by the Governor of Odisha, Dr SC Jamir.

The final chapter 'The Purbasa Conference: A Critical Evaluation' by Rajiv Bhatia analyses the outcome of the three day deliberation in Bhubaneswar from a critical perspective and concludes that the mission, for peace and prosperity in the region, undertaken by Kalinga International Foundation (KIF) is aptly served through the process of consensus building in such dialogues.

The views expressed in the papers are those of the participants in the Conference (and not necessarily to the institution to which they belong) and have been reproduced without any significant change. We compliment them for their contribution. We must thank the four Rapporteurs during the Conference: Mr Jayadev Parida, Dr Mathew Sinu Simon, Ms. Divisha Srivastava and Mr Pfokrehrii Pekosii for their valuable contribution.

Bhubaneswar, provided the right setting and ambience for issues that were at times contentious, to be discussed and debated in a frank yet relaxed manner. We thank the Chairpersons of the eight sessions: Prof Rajat Nag (Session I), Admiral RK Dhowan (Session II), Prof SD Muni (Session III), Prof Baladas Ghoshal (Session IV), Amb Neelam Deo (Session V), Mr Sabyasachi Dutta (Session VI), Amb Lalit Mansingh (Session VII), and Amb Pinak Chakravarty (Session VIII). Our gratitude to Ms. Preeti Singh, who copyedited the manuscript at short notice. Finally, a word of thanks to Mr. Rajan Arya and his team in the Pentagon Press for their professional efficiency in bringing out this book.

1

Welcome Address

Lalit Mansingh, Chairman, Kalinga International Foundation

16 March 2018

The Hon. Minister for Petroleum and Natural Gas, Skill Development, and Entrepreneurship, Shri Dharmendra Pradhan ji; Hon. Minister of Buddha Sasana, Sustainable Development and Wildlife of Sri Lanka, Mr. Gamini Jayawickrama Perera; Hon. Minister for Industry & Tourism of Assam, Shri Chandra Mohan Patowary; Excellencies, Ladies and Gentlemen,

As the Chairman of the Kalinga International Foundation and as a proud son of the soil of Odisha, it is my privilege to extend to all of you a welcome to Bhubaneswar.

As the ancient capital of Kalinga, Bhubaneswar has seen the rise of many empires. It has also witnessed events that have changed the course of history. A few kilometres away lies a small hill from where Emperor Ashoka, in the 3rd Century BC saw the magnitude of human suffering caused by his invasion of Kalinga, and took a momentous decision to renounce war and embrace Buddhism. This, in turn, has influenced the history and culture of many of the countries whose distinguished representatives are here with us.

At 6 o'clock in the morning, when the first rays of the sun fall on the statue of the Sun God in the Konarka temple, it will be 6.30 in Dhaka, 7.00 in Yangon, 7.30 in Bangkok, Jakarta and Hanoi, and 9.30 am in Tokyo. The sixteen countries represented at the PURBASA Conference are, indeed, the sunrise States of the Indo-Pacific which come to life when the rest of the world is still asleep. In terms of geo-politics and geo-economics, the centre of gravity of the world is in the process of shifting from the Euro-Atlantic to the Indo-Pacific. This is the new hub of human activity in the 21st Century.

Also represented in this Conference are fourteen provinces from the North East and Eastern regions of India. The Kalinga International Foundation believes that the East and the North East should be seen as a homogeneous cultural and economic region of India, which will play a crucial role in the India's Act East Policy. The region is marked by an abundance of natural resources, a rich cultural heritage, and a talented population which is producing a new generation of well-educated, tech-savvy youth with superior skills.

The Kalinga International Foundation is pleased that, for the first time, the North East and Eastern regions of India will be in a dialogue with the friendly neighbours on India's eastern periphery: Nepal, Bhutan, Bangladesh, and Sri Lanka, with ASEAN partners, and beyond with Japan and Australia. The title of the dialogue is aptly named PURBASA, meaning the rise of the East, the hopes from the East, and the message from East.

To Prime Minister Abe of Japan goes the credit of giving the Indo-Pacific a geo-political connotation. In August 2007, while addressing the Indian Parliament, Prime Minister Abe referred to a 'Confluence of the Indian and Pacific Oceans'. As strategic partners, India and Japan have assumed the role of the sentinels protecting and ensuring the security of the Indo-Pacific region.

Our ties with South East Asia go back to the beginnings of history. The Look East Policy may have been announced by Prime Minister Narasimha Rao in 1992, but the merchant sailors of Kalinga (called the Sadhabas) were sailing to Sri Lanka, Thailand, Java, Sumatra, Bali, and other distant destinations as early as the 4th Century BCE. For the people of the Kalinga region, the Look East is not a new policy, but a part of their historical heritage. They were the pioneers who brought India in contact with the people of the Indo-Pacific. Our challenge today is to revive the connectivity we had with the region over the thousand years also.

Sri Lanka ranks amongst the closest neighbours and strategic partners of India. Meeting here in Bhubaneswar, once the capital of imperial Kalinga, it is relevant to recall that Kalinga and Sri Lanka have had inseparable histories. Sri Lanka's history begins with the arrival of Prince Vijaya of Kalinga in the 6th Century BC. It is from Kalinga that the Bodhi tree and sacred tooth relic of Lord Buddha were transported to Sri Lanka.

We feel specially privileged to receive the Hon. Gamini Jayawickrama Perera, Minister of Buddha Sasana, of Sri Lanka. To the Hon. Minister Sir, may I say 'Ayubhowan' and extend to you a warm welcome to the land of your ancestors. We consider your visit an important landmark for the people of this State.

I also wish to extend a special welcome to Shri Chandra Mohan Patowary, Minister of Industry and Tourism of Assam. He brings to this forum the elevated presence of the North East, which Prime Minister Modi has described as 'the heart of the Act East Policy'. Thank you, Minister, for joining us at the inauguration. We look forward to your support for holding our forthcoming conferences in the North East.

To their Excellencies, the Ambassadors, High Commissioners, and other high representatives of friendly partner countries, may I also extend a very warm welcome? Most of you had joined us at our earlier conference on 13 December 2017 in New Delhi, when we celebrated twenty five years of India-ASEAN Partnership. I am grateful for the support and commitment to our cause, and seek your continued involvement in our efforts to bring your countries closer to India.

In the next two days, the leading experts from India and abroad, along with the high dignitaries and Heads of diplomatic missions, will engage in intense discussions on the entire gamut of India's relations with its eastern neighbourhood. The agenda for discussions has followed Prime Minister Modi's mantra of the Three Cs: Commerce, Connectivity, and Culture. Following the historic India-ASEAN Commemorative Summit of 15 January 2018, we are pursuing the theme of 'Shared Values, Common Destiny'.

We look forward to a stimulating dialogue in the coming days, a dialogue that will be carried forward in other centres in the region, like Shillong, Guwahati, Gangtok, Kolkata, Patna, and other places.

I am pleased to note that the cream of Odisha's intelligentsia and thought leaders have assembled at this inaugural event. I invite you to join us at this session of the Conference which, I promise you, will be intellectually rewarding. PURBASA will close in the evening of 18th March, with a valedictory function with the Hon. Governor of Odisha, His Excellency Dr. S.C. Jamir as the Chief Guest.

Before I conclude, I would like to offer my sincere thanks to the high dignitaries on the stage, especially our distinguished Guests of Honour: His

Excellency, Mr Gamini Jayawickrama Perara, Minister of Buddha Sasana; and Shri Chandra Mohan Patowary, Hon. Minister of Industry and Tourism of Assam. Above all, we owe an enormous debt of gratitude to our Chief Guest, Shri Dharmendra Pradhan, Minister of Petroleum and Natural Gas, Skill Development, and Entrepreneurship. The Kalinga International Foundation has been privileged to receive his support, and we seek your blessings and guidance for our activities in the days to come.

To all of you, Excellencies, Ladies, and Gentlemen, a very warm welcome, once again, to the inauguration of PURBASA.

2

Inaugural Programme: Summary Report on the Proceedings

Kalinga International Foundation (KIF) organised a three-day conference (16–18, March 2018). The theme of the conference was *Purbasa: East meets East—Synergising the North-East and Eastern India with the Indo-Pacific* at Mayfair Lagoon, Bhubaneswar, Odisha. The conference was inaugurated by the Chief Guest, Shri Dharmendra Pradhan, Honorable Minister for Petroleum and Natural Gas, Skill Development and Entrepreneurship, on March 16.

In lighting the lamp, the Union Minister was joined by the Guest of Honor, Shri C.M. Patowary, Honorable Minister for Industry, Commerce, Transport, Parliamentary Affairs, and Act East Policy Affairs, Government of Assam; the Guest of Honour, Gamini Jayawickrama Perera, Minister of Buddha Sasana, Sustainable Development and Wildlife, Sri Lanka; H.E. Mr. Sidharto Reza Suryodipuro, Ambassador of Indonesia; H.E. Mr. Moe Kyaw Aung, Ambassador of Myanmar; H.E. (Ms.) Maria Teresita C. Daza, Ambassador of Republic of the Philippines; H.E. Mr. Chutintorn Gongsakdi, Ambassador of Thailand; H.E. Mr. Ton Sinh Thanh, Ambassador of Vietnam; H.E. Mr. Syed Muazzem Ali, High Commissioner of Bangladesh; H.E. (Mrs.) Chitraganee Wagiswara, High Commissioner of Sri Lanka; and Mr. Kenko Sone, Economic Minister, Embassy of Japan. The above dignitaries were presented Angavastrams and souvenirs by Ambassador Lalit Mansingh, Chairman, Kalinga International Foundation (KIF).

In his welcome remarks, Ambassador Lalit Mansingh stated that the sixteen countries as represented in the Purbasa conference are the 'sunrise states' of the Indo-Pacific. In terms of geo-politics and geo-economics, the centre of gravity is slowly churning away from the Euro-Atlantic towards the Indo-Pacific, therein making it a hub for human activity in the 21st century. He reminded the august audience of the geo-strategic importance attached to the Indo-Pacific as brought out by Japan's Prime Minister Abe in his address to the Indian parliament in August 2007. He also observed the participation of fourteen provinces from the east and northeast India. The KIF believes that the East and the Northeast should be seen as a homogenous cultural and economic region of India that is playing a crucial role in India's Act East policy. This region is marked by an abundance of natural resources, a rich cultural heritage, and a young talented tech-savvy population. The title of the East-Northeast India dialogue with India's eastern neighbourhood was aptly named as *Purbasa* being the rise of the east, hopes, and message from the east.

As the Guest of Honour, Shri C.M. Patowary, Honourable Minister for Industry, Commerce, Transport, Parliamentary Affairs, Skill Development, and Act East Policy Affairs, Government of Assam called for the need to revitalize the energy requirements of Assam and India through the mode of regional connectivity. He also stressed on the growing geopolitical significance of Assam and the Northeast to the ASEAN and the Indo-Pacific region. He reiterated that indeed the northeast is at the heart of India's Act East policy. He credited the present ruling dispensation at the Centre for improving inter-state connectivity. This was evident with the connection of Assam gas pipeline to the national grid.

Also addressing the audience was the Guest of Honour, Gamini Jayawickrama Perera, Honorable Minister of Buddha Sasana, Sustainable Development and Welfare, Sri Lanka. He talked about the potentialities and opportunities with regional connectivity, socio-economic, cultural, and religious connections among South Asia, Southeast Asia and Indo-Pacific. ASEAN is a powerful regional body, with the purpose of promoting cooperation on all fronts. Speaking on the historical linkages between the regions, he remarked that the spread of Buddhism with its espousal of non-violence, has played a vital role in uniting the people, the cultures, and the economy.

A Memorandum of Understanding (MoU) was signed between Ambassador Lalit Mansingh, Chairman, Kalinga International Foundation (KIF) and Admiral Jayanath Colombage, Pathfinder Foundation of Sri Lanka.

The Kalinga Saraswati Samman was awarded to Professor V. Suryanarayan and Shri Sudip Sen for their notable academic works, *Together in struggle: India and Indonesia (1945–49)* and *Pride and Glory of Balijata*, respectively. The Chief Guest complimented the works of awardees, and called for further research on matters connecting India to her east and the Indo-Pacific.

While delivering the inaugural address, the Union Minister, Dharmendra Pradhan, elaborated upon Odisha's connections with the Indo-Pacific. In his keynote address, the Minister emphasised the rich, cultural, religious, and linguistic commonalities shared by Odisha with India's eastern neighbourhood. Citing the shared cultural, Buddhist heritage, and ancestral maritime trade with Sri Lanka, the Sanchi Stupa's architectural similarities with the Torana gate in Malaysia, the local celebrations of the Bali Jatra festival, its involvement with the Angkor Wat temple restoration works in Cambodia, Odisha has indeed been a gateway for India to meet Southeast Asia and the Indo-Pacific.

While addressing the gathering, the Minister stated that India's Look East policy received a further impetus and an upgrade with Prime Minister Narendra Modi's initiative to Act East. The ASEAN-India Commemorative Summit themed 'Shared Values, Common Destiny' in January 2018 further signals India's deepening engagement with the ASEAN process. The Act East Policy envisages the development of the Northeast region with adequate infrastructure and human resource capital in order to facilitate people to people contacts, connectivity, and commerce. At the Global Investors' Summit—'Advantage Assam' in Guwahati in February 2018—Prime Minister Modi said "We created the Act East Policy and the Northeast is at the heart of it." He further added that India's Act East Policy starts with Bangladesh. India's growing engagement with its immediate and extended neighbourhood is evident by Bangladesh and Bhutan opening their Consulates in Assam.

Delving further into the Petroleum Ministry initiatives, the Minister stated that India's engagements with the ASEAN region in the hydrocarbon sector are noteworthy. Last year, India imported 6 million metric ton of crude oil from Malaysia, Brunei, and Indonesia. India also imported 1.5 million metric ton of LNG from Singapore and Malaysia. India has exported 12.2 million metric ton of petroleum products to the region, accounting for 18.8 per cent of its total exports for the same period. India has recently dispatched the first consignment of high-speed diesel to Myanmar. India is working with PTT Exploration Production, Thailand as well as with PETRONAS, Malaysia. India is, however, yet to reach the full potential of cooperation with robust Indo-Pacific engagement as a region.

Ms. Shreerupa Mitra, Trustee KIF, proposed the vote of thanks. The inaugural ceremony of PURBASA signals the meeting of minds and hearts towards a greater resolution of connectivity across the regions.

Highlights of the Inaugural Ceremony

- The title of East-Northeast India dialogue with India's eastern neighbourhood was aptly named PURBASA: the rise of the east, hopes, and the message from the east.
- Prime Minister Narendra Modi's mantra of connectivity, commerce, and culture has added impetus to India's Act East Policy.
- The Look East policy is not a new policy, but a part of Odisha's rich, cultural, historical heritage, with seafaring travels to the east.
- Northeast India is at the heart of India's Act East policy.

3

Vote of Thanks at the Kalinga International Foundation: Inaugural Session

Shreerupa Mitra, Member of the Steering Group, KIF

Excellencies, distinguished dignitaries, honoured guests, supporters and well-wishers of KIF, friends, ladies and gentlemen.

It is my privilege to propose a Vote of Thanks.

I rise to do so with a mix of joy and pride at what the Kalinga International Foundation has achieved today by bringing together distinguished political dignitaries, intellectuals and scholars, and activists for two exciting days of reflections, deliberations, friendship, and networking. This young and dynamic institution is committed to the promotion of closer ties of cooperation in the Indo-Pacific region. Tonight, we embark on an exciting journey to make our own pioneering contribution to help our polity achieve the national goal of 'acting East'.

On behalf of KIF, I wish to thank a number of people.

First of all, we are grateful to all the political dignitaries who took part in our inaugural session this evening. Our special thanks and gratitude go to Shri Dharmendra Pradhan, Hon. Minister for Petroleum & Natural Gas and Skill Development & Entrepreneurship, not only for his inspiring address but also for his unstinting support to KIF.

We are particularly grateful to Shri Gamini Jayawicrama Perera, Minister of Buddha Sasana in Sri Lanka for taking the time to visit Odisha to participate in our event. We are, indeed, honoured, Sir. Like our Hon'ble Minister

Shri Pradhan just said, we have many Buddhist sites in the State, and we do hope you have the time to visit some of them.

We are also thankful to the Shri Chandra Mohan Patowary, Cabinet Minister for Transport, Parliamentary Affairs, Industry and Commerce, Government of Assam, for his presence today. We hope that this conference is successful in its object of bringing the east and the north-east closer to its eastern neighbours.

The presence of ambassadors and diplomats of several ASEAN member-states and from the larger Indo-Pacific region amidst us is a testimony to the strength and the potential of this region to galvanise the international community. In particular, we thank the Ambassadors of Indonesia, Myanmar, Philippines, Thailand, and Vietnam, the High Commissioners of Bangladesh and Sri Lanka and the Minister (Economic) in the Japanese embassy in New Delhi, who are with us on the podium today.

Our chairs and panel lists will offer important intellectual perspectives to look into issues of mutual interest, both bilaterally and as a region. We thank them in advance for their time in participating in the event and their contribution over the next two days. We are confident that they shall stay engaged in our future endeavours.

An event of this nature requires resources and assistance. These have been largely provided by Petronet, GAIL, ONGC, and Indian Oil. We are grateful to them, particularly to Shri Prabhat Singh, CEO-MD Petronet, who will participate in one of our technical sessions.

It is heartening to note and acknowledge the presence of numerous representatives of our media organisations. We sincerely thank them for their interest and support.

The idea of the Kalinga International Foundation has been conceptualized, crafted, and choreographed by an outstanding personality: the former Foreign Secretary, Shri Lalit Mansingh, our Chairman. The high respect he enjoys all around made it possible for us to move quickly and effectively from the stage of conception to the inaugural evening today. In this task, the esteemed Members of our Steering Group have also played a sterling role. We applaud them. We are also grateful to our band of young volunteers who have come from various parts of the city to help us execute this event.

Finally, dear friends, KIF is most grateful to you all—our audience. By your presence here, you have given us your unflinching support and blessings that are greatly appreciated. You have given us tremendous energy and inspiration. As we begin this conference, KIF re-dedicates itself to creating a powerful momentum to strengthen the east-east friendship in all relevant domains.

I thank you for your attention.

ECONOMIC CO-OPERATION

4

India's Economic Cooperation with East and Southeast Asia

V.S. Seshadri

I would like to thank the organisers of this important conference, in particular Ambassador Lalit Mansingh, for inviting me to be a panellist. I will briefly explore a few aspects of India's trade cooperation with East and South East Asia. Let me, however, say that these are my personal views, and not of any organisation.

1. The first is regarding India's trade and trading framework, and how well they are working. After India's FTA with Singapore in 2005, India also entered into an FTA with ASEAN as a whole on goods, as well as more comprehensive CEPA agreements with Korea and Japan and a bilateral one with Malaysia. All of these came into effect during the years 2010 and 2011.
2. India's trade with ASEAN countries showed momentum in the initial years after the signing of the India-ASEAN FTA. India's exports to ASEAN as a whole peaked in 2011–12 when they reached US $ 36.7 billion. However, it still has to get back to the same level after the steep decline it saw in the following years. While 2016–17 was good, when India's exports to ASEAN revived after the global slowdown and went up by 23 per cent, they climbed in the first six months of this financial year 2017–18 by another 22.6 per cent. However, it is still doubtful if, at the end of 2017–18, India's exports will reach the level of 2011–12.
3. The trend is similar in the case of imports from ASEAN even though they are somewhat higher. They reached a peak of US $ 44.7 billion in

2014–15; but the following two years saw decline and stagnation. There has been a strong revival in the first six months of this year (2018), with an increase of almost 19 per cent. But they are still below the peak level of 2014–15.

4. The situation is not very different in the case of India's exports to Korea and Japan; but imports from Korea and Japan have fared somewhat better. On a single indicator, India's export to Korea was 1.49 per cent of India's overall exports in 2010–11. After six years of CEPA implementation, it was only 1.54 per cent in 2016–17. On the other hand, Korea did somewhat better. Its share in India's imports went up from 2.83 per cent to 3.27 per cent.
5. In the case of Japan, the record is somewhat disappointing. The share of India's exports to Japan of all of its global exports declined from 2.03 per cent in 2010–11 to 1.39 per cent in 2016–17. On the other hand, Japan's share in India's imports has gone up from 2.33 per cent to 2.53 per cent.
6. The point to note is that India's exports to ASEAN or Korea or Japan have not done as well as one would have expected in the aftermath of an FTA. However, one could say that while India's partners have done better, they have done *only somewhat* better. On the other hand, even without an FTA, China has enhanced its market share in India from 11.75 per cent in 2010–11 to 15.94 per cent in 2016–17.
7. If India is looking to enhance economic cooperation with East and South East Asia, it needs to examine how to promote trade in a sustainable manner—and in both directions. Having examined the implementation of some of these FTAs, the reasons for the inadequate increase lie in a combination of the following factors:
    - Lack of adequate awareness, particularly among SMEs in India, that is also seeing relatively lower levels of utilisation;
    - Diminishing competitiveness of Indian exports, particularly the labour intensive ones—despite increased market access, we could not enhance our export of garments, for example, to Japan;
    - There have also been supply constraints on some items which were doing well, such as iron ore, soya bean, meal, etc.;
    - All our partner countries have entered into more FTAs which have diminished India's access in those markets to some extent; while

we, on the other hand, have not joined any more FTAs since 2011;

- The non-tariff barriers in our partner countries, including in the areas of agriculture products, pharma items where India has proven strengths, have certainly been restraining factors;
- Equally, the fact that Indian exports have predominantly been in raw material or processed items in a more primary form. Several examples include: raw cotton and cotton yarn rather than fabrics and made ups; cut and sawn granite rather than polished granite; iron ore and ferro manganese rather than higher end steel; refined copper rather than copper wires and plates; aluminium ingots rather than aluminium sheets and foils; raw shrimps rather than processed and value added (breaded or skewered) shrimps, etc.;
- In East Asian markets, distribution channels work more comfortably with local partners—almost in a protective manner—preferring local products even if they are not price competitive. Global Indian IT companies have offices in these countries; but they have not been able to secure much local business;
- There is also the need for Indian businesses to imbibe the East Asian culture of doing business where local commercial presence and the building of mutual trust are very important elements. This is, of course, not just one way. Our East and South East Asian partners have to understand us better. An article in *The Hindu* analysing how India-Japan relations have been underwhelming, quoted Mr. Tomofumu Nishizawa (of JETRO's overseas research department) as saying the greatest challenge is cultural.[1]

8. There are three key aspects on which India needs to take urgent action to derive greater benefits from the FTAs: improve its competitiveness, work on value addition on its export products; and work on trade facilitation and investment facilitation to attract investment. These involve actively pursuing the Make in India, the Sagarmala India, the Skills India programmes. Also, there is need to have more special economic zones in States like Odisha that are geographically well placed to connect with the East. Indian businesses also need to better strategise and build trust based relationships with these markets. Events such as this conference could also sensitise India's business persons in this regard.
9. Even as India faces the issue about inadequate deliverance by its FTAs,

it is already negotiating a more comprehensive RCEP involving 16 countries: the ten ASEAN countries and their six dialogue partners—Australia, China, India, Japan, Korea and New Zealand. It is no secret that there is some discomfort in the Indian industry about how they may get impacted by such FTAs, particularly in the context of India having a large trade imbalance with China. While China has a 16 per cent share overall in India's imports, the share is much greater in certain manufactured sectors. In electronics, it is 57 per cent; in machinery it is 35 per cent; in organic chemicals it is 36 per cent; in furniture and lighting it is 60 per cent; in steel products it is 36 per cent; and in toys over 80 per cent. In certain specific products, it is even more. And, all this without even an FTA.

10. The key aspect that needs to be pointed out is that the Indian industry may need some time before it can stand up to such competition. While India can be in RCEP, it may have to be permitted only minimal commitments until 2025 by which time the Make in India programme would have made significant headway. Further, tariff liberalisation could take place thereafter through back-loaded tariff reduction commitments extending up to ten or fifteen years beyond 2025. Meanwhile, in the next couple of years, India will need to work hard on trade and investment facilitation, as well as on attracting foreign investment to join the domestic effort in consolidating its domestic capacities and embarking on value added manufacturing. Promoting a sound infrastructure and reducing transaction costs will also be essential. If India can co-opt ASEAN in this effort, mutual benefit can be derived from what today is still only a potentially a large Indian market to what can become a truly large Indian market.

11. Another important aspect that needs to be stressed is promoting trade in the neighbourhood. Border trade has a great deal of potential, particularly trade between India and Bangladesh, and India and Myanmar. Somehow, border transit and trade facilitation needs at land borders as well as logistical linkages behind the border have not delivered to the extent they could have.

12. However, the prospects do appear bright now, thanks to the three or four connectivity projects under implementation between India and Myanmar that may be getting completed by 2020 to 2022. The India

Myanmar Thailand trilateral highway project; the renovation of the 60 odd bridges on the TKK road; the Kaladan multi modal project and the Rhi-Tiddim project are some examples. Similarly, indications are that a number of highway and broad gauge railway projects leading up to the border in north east India may also be ready by this time line. No doubt a great number of supply or production chain arrangements could happen if all these are completed in a coordinated manner, in which case such production chains can then feed into the larger trade liberalisation undertaking in the Asia Pacific region.

13. It will be important to put in place the software of the connectivity, including speedy and single window clearances at the border; easy payment arrangements; behind the border logistic facilitation; and agreements for freer vehicular movements; cross border movement of trade and businesspersons; and arrangements for the efficient operation and maintenance of the connectivity assets created. Many of these need to be taken up bilaterally with Myanmar and Bangladesh. Some of them can also be complemented through BIMSTEC—such as a motor vehicle agreement and another agreement for promoting coastal shipping.
14. This three to five year period could also be used to attract investors in India, Myanmar, and third countries by leveraging the prospective connectivity that will open up a wider market, thus making also more economic projects viable. Connectivity is only an enabler, and timely efforts are necessary to transform the connectivity corridor into a development corridor. This will help in making the North East as one of the arrow heads for further developing India's Act East policy.

NOTE

1. 'Pallavi Aiyar, 'Far Short of the Potential', *The Hindu*, 15 March 2018.

5

Remarks by Ambassador of Vietnam

Ton Sinh Thanh

Dr Rajat Nag, Chair of this panel, Excellencies, ladies and gentlemen.

First of all, I would like to appreciate Kalinga International Foundation for organising this Conference which is very timely. India is accelerating the Act East Policy as well as economic cooperation between East and Northeast India with Southeast Asia, which has become the highlight of the day in the context of the Indo-Pacific Region. And, the venue of this Conference is also very meaningful as Odisha is now emerging as the development hub of East India, and has great potential for cooperation with other countries in Southeast Asia. In any discussion about economic cooperation between East and Northeast India with South East Asian countries, we have to look at the status of economic cooperation between the two regions. Economic cooperation between this part of India and Southeast Asia has made quite a lot of progress. We have doubled the trade between the two regions after one decade. Now, with US $76 billion plus last year, India has become the fourth largest trade partner of ASEAN, and ASEAN the seventh largest trading partner of India.

However, it must be pointed out that this is not up to potential—especially if we compare with trade and investment of ASEAN and India with other partners, especially China. I am optimistic of seeing growing economic cooperation between ASEAN and East and Northeast India. First of all, this part of India (East and Northeast India) compared with other areas of India is very close in geostrategic terms to Southeast Asia. This becomes very clear when you take a flight from Northeast India or Odisha to Southeast Asia. This part of India also shares both land and sea border with Southeast Asian countries.

Moreover, the East and Northeast India have very close traditional and cultural bonds with Southeast Asia. We have a long list of cultural, religious, and commercial interactions. The Northeast India, especially, has many similarities in lifestyle, culture, and even ethnic identities with many countries in Southeast Asia, including Myanmar, Thailand, and Vietnam. It is not too difficult to find music, melodies, and dance in Southeast Asia which are similar to those in Northeast India. Historically, the eastern part of India, particularly Odisha itself, has strong cultural and civilisational links with countries in Southeast Asia.

It is said that people from eastern India, travelled along the coast of the Bay of Bengal to Indo-China, and introduced elements of their culture to the residents of Southeast Asia. According to some sources, around 2000 years ago, people from Odisha travelled by boat to Vietnam and even set up a Hindu Kingdom in Vietnam. Today, we can find many Hindu relics in Vietnam, like temples, music, melodies, and dances. This is true also of Cambodia and Thailand. Even the name of the Champa Kingdom in Vietnam was named after some village in Odisha. These similarities emphasise the close links between the two regions.

The bright prospects of Northeast India, East India, and Southeast Asia are also based on the fact that both India and Southeast Asian countries are growing fast. India is growing at 7 per cent; Southeast Asia is growing at 5 per cent, and is expected to grow faster next year. This will undoubtedly bring many opportunities for expanding cooperation between our two great regions. Secondly, both India and ASEAN are very determined to promote their economic cooperation. ASEAN sees India as a natural and reliable partner, while India considers ASEAN as a key pillar in the region. Over the past 25 years, cooperation between India and ASEAN has expanded to many areas—to nearly 30 mechanisms. Moreover, the Indian government is attaching great importance to developing the Northeast and the East Indian region, and considers this area as a gateway to Southeast Asia. Prime Minister Modi has many times stated that Northeast is the heart of India's Act East Policy. In fact, the Indian Government has invested a large amount of money and effort in developing the Northeast and Eastern Indian States to make them more connected to the Southeast Asian States.

However, some challenges remain, and have to be tackled to improve cooperation between Northeast and East India with Southeast Asian nations.

First, we must see that, in comparison with other States of India, Northeast India and Eastern India are less developed, with a lack of infrastructure and connectivity. All this limits the advantages of this region in doing business with Southeast Asia. Secondly, since connectivity has not improved much, connectivity infrastructure must be improved first. There is also need to improve peace and security in both the regions, especially maritime and aviation safety, without which economic cooperation between the two regions would be impossible.

The tension in the South China Sea, which constitutes one of the most serious obstacles to trade, should draw the attention of not only ASEAN but all other partners, including India. In short, there is huge potential for economic cooperation between East/Northeast India with Southeast Asia Toturn the potential into opportunities and realities, more efforts need to be made by both regions for developing connectivity and infrastructure, as also develop peace and maintain security in the Indo-Pacific region. I wish the Conference a great success.

6

Economic Engagement and Connectivity between India's North East and the Indo-Pacific

*Anil Wadhwa**

The presence of all ten Heads of State from ASEAN countries in New Delhi on the occasion of the 69th Republic day of India (2018) as joint Chief Guests was an unprecedented event, significant in many respects. Although the ostensible occasion was to commemorate the 25th anniversary of the India ASEAN engagement, geopolitics played a big role in all of them coming together to the Indian capital at the same time. The second Forum for India Pacific Islands Cooperation (FIPIC) Heads of States meeting in Delhi in 2015 also attracted representatives from all the Pacific Island States, where development cooperation was high on the agenda. The Bay of Bengal Initiative for Multi-Sectoral Technical and Economic Cooperation (BIMSTEC); the Bangladesh, Bhutan, India, Nepal (BBIN); and the Mekong Ganga Cooperation frameworks have all emphasised India's engagement with its neighbours in multiple spheres, and economics is at the heart of this process. The rise of China and its aggressive posture in the South China Sea has also been a parallel development over the past few years. In fact, the scale and speed of land reclamation, militarisation, and their population and administration by a determined Chinese State—which took place in the background of a reluctant engagement of the United States in the Pacific—has left the ASEAN and its partners stunned and helpless. China has managed to divide the ASEAN by offering lucrative economic incentives and liberal lines of credit to the less developed ASEAN countries

* Ambassador Anil Wadhwa has served as Secretary (East) in the Ministry of External Affairs, and has been the Indian Ambassador to Italy, Thailand, Poland, and Oman.

(like Laos and Cambodia) and using them to block consensus on conference outcomes stressing the centrality of ASEAN and a combined ASEAN stand opposing the militarisation and occupation of the disputed islands in the South China Sea.

With China looming large with its actions in the South China Sea, its Belt and Road Initiative, and its forays in the Indian Ocean—which is changing the geo strategic landscape of the Indo-Pacific—India has a full agenda of cooperation of its own in mind. At the heart of the Indo Pacific strategy and the Act East policy of India is the ASEAN with whom India's trade figures have been lacklustre—$71 billion last year compared to a whopping $450 billion trade which China has with the Asean. The balance of trade has more or less been in favour of ASEAN in this equation. A few countries, like Singapore, Malaysia, and Thailand, have emerged major export destinations for India. There are also trade complementarities with ASEAN. Indian investments into ASEAN have been merely US $ 40 billion from 2000 to 2017. India received US$ 514 billion in ASEAN investments from 2000 to 2015, of which US$ 13.8 billion was received in 2015–16. Singapore accounts for a major chunk of these investments. A framework agreement on comprehensive economic cooperation between India and ASEAN was signed in Bali in October 2003, which was expected to eliminate tariff barriers among all the members, another was signed in Bangkok in 2009 to eventually establish a free trade area in goods; and another agreement on services and investments was signed in New Delhi in 2015.

However, not all barriers have yet been removed. While the FTA on trade in goods is in force, two ASEAN countries are yet to ratify the FTA on services and investment. If the FTA on services and investment enters into force in the near future, this could open up new vistas of cooperation. Bilateral agreements with various other members of ASEAN, such as Thailand, Singapore, and Malaysia, have also been signed, all of them aimed at deepening economic integration with the region. In a related and significant development, on 23 January 2018 in Tokyo, 11 negotiating partners of the Trans-Pacific Partnership (TPP), minus the USA, agreed to go ahead and sign this agreement which will create a powerful trade block. Many ASEAN countries are part of this agreement, requiring higher standards in trade and manufacturing. India has not been in the TPP negotiations, but has been taking part in the Regional

Comprehensive Economic Partnership (RCEP) negotiations, alongside all ten ASEAN countries, China, Australia, New Zealand, Japan and the Republic of Korea. In these negotiations, India has been unsuccessfully trying to gain concessions in services, bring in phased liberalisation in tariffs, and has been accused of slowing down the negotiations. The TPP signature on 11 March 2018 should spur Indian negotiators to rethink strategy on the RCEP. Staying away from the RCEP in the light of developments on TPP could create difficulties for Indian exports.

At a recent Ministerial meeting in Singapore, it was agreed that two chapters—on economic and technical cooperation and small and medium enterprises—will soon be added to the draft RCEP, as major negotiations start in April 2018. Compromises are being sought on issues like transition period and capacity building. All efforts will be made to keep the aspiration of the negotiating countries to come up with a good, commercially meaningful RCEP agreement which will meet the participative states commitment to achieve a modern, comprehensive, high quality and mutually beneficial economic partnership agreement. RCEP will cover trade in goods, services, investment, economic and technical cooperation, intellectual property, competition, e commerce, dispute settlement and other trade issues.

Regional value chains expand market access, and integration with value chains leads to benefits, like reduced costs of manufacturing and trading. A range of policy measures, including trade facilitation, liberalisation of goods, services and capital, competition policy, and infrastructure quality, promote value chain integration. The free trade in goods agreement signed with ASEAN in 2009 has also facilitated the development of supply chains and production networks in many products, such as electronics and automobiles, including vehicle and component manufacturing. However, there remain certain challenges to establishing a supply chain, such as non tariff barriers, poor connectivity, and quality of infrastructure, among others.

In the important issue of maritime cooperation and security, which is closely linked to economic engagement, India has stressed upon its interest in the Indo-Pacific as an increasingly connected pathway where much of the world's trade passes. India wants the Indo Pacific to be kept free from traditional and non traditional threats to security so that the free movement of goods, people and ideas can take place. In this context, India is cooperating with ASEAN in developing a blue economy, coastal surveillance, and information sharing for increased maritime domain awareness.

Connectivity with ASEAN is most important in order to ensure that India and ASEAN walk in tandem in the journey of mutual economic development and prosperity. At this stage, Indian flag ship projects with ASEAN—like the Trilateral Highway, the Kaladan Multimodal Project, and the Rhi-Tidim Road, which will help in the development of develop development of India's North Eastern States that have suffered due to time lags. Along the trilateral highway, there are two border crossings, four customs check points, three international time zones, three customs posts, two different motor vehicle driving standards, and three different motor vehicle laws. The challenge is to reach convergence in standards and procedures along the corridor. 2020 is the projected timeline. Connectivity from India to ASEAN will be also helped by the Kaladan multi-model transport project, which will link Kolkata to Sittwe port in Myanmar, as also Mizoram by the river and land route. At present, the road from Paletwa to Zorinpui on the India-Myanmar border is being constructed, and will take upto 2020. The Tiddim-Rih project starts from the Zokhawtar land customs station in Mizoram in India to Rih in Myanmar. The 80 km road is being built by IRCON, but could also take a few years.

There are few takers for the US $1 billion line of credit announced by Prime Minister Modi in 2015 for physical and digital connectivity with ASEAN. Indeed, there is need to introspect and to tweak the terms of lending if required. India's Quick Impact projects of lesser amounts have been a big success across the CMLV countries and Asean. India and ASEAN would do well to finalise a Maritime Cooperation pact which could result in joint ventures in shipping and transhipment initiatives. Serious consideration must be given to connect India's eastern seaboard ports with Dawei in Myanmar as well as others in Thailand, to cut down on time and costs of delivery. Air connectivity needs to be improved, with direct flights to Indonesia, Laos, Cambodia, and the Philippines which are still reached from India via some other destinations. India has opened up its skies to ASEAN in 18 Tier 2 cities, and ASEAN airlines, could exploit these routes successfully. Indian tourism to ASEAN has increased by leaps and bounds; but ASEAN tourists to India only account for 3 percent of the total tourists into India. India needs to strengthen infrastructure at the 6 important sites in Uttar Pradesh and Bihar for Buddhist tourism, create comfortable infrastructure and facilities as well as strengthen the connectivity with Buddhist tourist sites in Andhra Pradesh, Maharashtra, and Madhya Pradesh. Prime Minister Modi has proposed that India and ASEAN celebrate 2019 as the year of tourism. He has also proposed the use of India's digital capabilities for connecting the rural areas in ASEAN.

However, connectivity projects like the four lane India-Myanmar-Thailand trilateral highway, which will be later extended to Laos, Cambodia, and Vietnam, can only be sustained through the movement of goods and economic activity along the route through Myanmar, and hence the growing importance of our North East. For this, it is important to focus on development and connectivity in India's North East itself, with the building of new road and rail links, opening up multi-modal transport including river navigation, the setting up of industrial corridors and economic activities like "haats" or local markets, with emphasis on agriculture, horticulture, handlooms, handicrafts, and processed foods. This will allow India to export its produce through this link rather than become a net importer of cheap Chinese goods.

The North East of India, home to 3.8 per cent of the national population, occupies about 8 per cent of India's total geographical area, and is strategically important with over 5300 kms of international borders. The four North east States of Arunachal Pradesh, Manipur, Mizoram, and Nagaland share 1643 kms of border with Myanmar. A narrow chicken's neck corridor connects it with the rest of India, and infrastructure connectivity with the main land as well as the bordering countries needs upgradation for which large investments are needed.

India plans to spend Rs 45,000 crores for the development of the region bordering China, Bhutan, Bangladesh, and Myanmar. Some recent decisions to enhance the economic development of the North East are: a 4000 km long ring road connecting the states; expediting a railway project connecting all the state capitals by 2020, and extending to 15 new destinations; border last mile rail connectivity with Myanmar; and restoring rail connectivity with Bangladesh. Work is on full swing in the 15 km stretch between Agartala and Akhura in Bangladesh, which will not only be a part of the Trans Asian Railway network but will substantially shorten the rail distance between Agartala and Kolkata via Bangladesh. 20 port townships are to be developed along the Brahmaputra and Barak river systems to enhance intra-regional connectivity. Prime Minister

Modi has also proposed the augmentation of air connectivity to and from the region which will help business ties with the ASEAN. At least 50 economic integration and development nodes are to be set up across the region, in tandem with transport corridors to boost manufacturing. Infrastructure is also being upgraded in the border areas for strategic purposes, with highways and a development plan approved for Arunachal Pradesh, Nagaland, and Manipur, including a four lane highway between Dimapur and Kohima. A recent Research and Information System for Developing Countries (RIS) study notes that the Kaladan project and the Trilateral Highway are both going to have a positive economic impact in the region.

The development of the North East is also essential if India and other countries of the Quad, including Japan, have to come up with a viable alternative model to China's Belt and Road initiative (BRI) which is often fraught with sovereign and financial risks for the partner countries who borrow for these projects from China, but are then unable to pay back the loans extended, and end up losing sovereign territory to the Chinese—as has happened in the case of the Hambantota port in Sri Lanka. There is need for investors to bridge the gaps in state funding. Japan has emerged as the obvious partner in India's efforts for the development of the North East and connectivity to ASEAN. The Indian projects under its Act East Policy can be aligned to create synergies for supply chains in the ASEAN. At the Africa Development Bank meeting in May 2017, there was an attempt to spell out a strategy called the Asia Africa Growth Corridor which would link economies, industries, and institutions of Africa and Asia in an inclusive fashion. This will not be a state funded enterprise, but will be led by the private sector drawing on existing links that both countries have with the region. A vision document has been prepared by three leading think tanks of India, Japan, and ASEAN. Towards this end, the Japan India Act East Forum has been set up, which will seek synergies between India's Act East Policy and with Japan's "Free and Open Indo-Pacific Strategy" for which it will use its ODA. North East India has sought and received assistance from Japan in areas such as road connectivity, power, water supply and sewage, skill development, food processing, and tourism. Transformational policies and supportive governments in the North East states could enable the government at the centre to roll out development schemes and infrastructure projects quickly, as has been the case with Assam. It might help to develop a collective focus on inter-state boundary disputes and other ethnic conflicts with the North East

States, and also a common approach towards enhancing connectivity, and trade facilitation with ASEAN.

At the same time, it is important to build effective institutional connectivity by harmonising trade, investment, and financial policies between India and ASEAN in particular, and South East Asia in general. Physical connectivity (transportation and soft infrastructure requirements such as telecommunications) have to be built in tandem with proper institutional arrangements to achieve cross regional connectivity. Due to the lack of adequate physical and institutional infrastructure between India and South East Asia, energy trading for one remains under-utilised. The presence of non tariff barriers and restrictive institutional arrangements hinder the movement of goods and services. Trade facilitation measures to reduce the volume of documentation required—and thereby the time of transit—is necessary to improve economic exchanges between India and South East Asian countries.

The Bay of Bengal Initiative for Multi Sectoral Technical and Economic Cooperation (BIMSTEC) includes 7 nations: Bangladesh, India, Myanmar, Sri Lanka, Thailand, Bhutan, and Nepal. 14 priority sectors of cooperation have been identified, and several BIMSTEC centres have been established in these areas. A free trade agreement among the countries is under negotiation. The projects that the group is working on are road and rail Look East connectivity projects, coastal shipping and power grid interconnection, all of which will help economic development.

Under the rubric of the BBIN (Bangladesh, Bhutan, India, Nepal) sub regional grouping which works on projects in areas such as water resources management and connectivity of power transport and infrastructure, India has approved US $1.08 billion for the construction and upgradation of 558 km long roads that will join Bangladesh, Bhutan, and Nepal. The project will receive 50 per cent funding from the ADB, and it is estimated that the project will increase regional trade by 60 per cent. While a far reaching motor vehicles agreement has been signed by all four states, it is yet to be ratified by all to go into force.

The Mekong Ganga Cooperation (MGC) comprises 6 countries: India, Thailand, Myanmar, Cambodia, Laos, and Vietnam. The four main areas of cooperation include enhancing transportation. At its last ministerial meeting held in July 2016, the grouping agreed on trade enhancement, investments in projects, and maritime connectivity, amongst other initiatives.

The Forum for India Pacific Islands Cooperation (FIPIC) was set up between India and 14 Pacific island states. They met in 2014 in Fiji, and in 2015 in India. India is cooperating on multiple issues which include a blue economy (ocean based economy), oil and natural gas, mining, IT, health care, SME cooperation, cooperation in solar projects, fishing and marine research, and space cooperation. In 2017, FIPIC held a sustainable development conference in Fiji to enhance cooperation between India and the Pacific island states.

One more corridor which has been proposed is the Bangladesh-China-India-Myanmar economic corridor (BCIM-EC). This route encompasses Kolkata in India to Kunming in China's Yunnan province, passing through Bangladesh and Myanmar. It also links Ledo in Assam through the old Stilwell road. A large part of this route overlaps with the trilateral highway, and follows Asian highways in Myanmar. Link routes connecting other nodes in the North East region, such as Shillong, Dimapur, Aizawl, Agartala, Nagaon, and Dibrugarh, may also be established. These cities could become major economic nodes along the BCIM-EC. Four national reports have been prepared and have to be synthesised into a common report. The future of BCIM–EC, however, is under a cloud due to the disagreement between India and China on OBOR projects due to the Chinese CPEC project which passes through Indian territory in Pakistan Occupied Kashmir. India also has other doubts over OBOR which it has conveyed and expressed clearly.

The ADB and India are collaborating to build a 2,500 km long East Coast Economic Corridor which will be a boon for India's Make in India policy, as well as for India's Act East Policy by integrating the Indian economy with Asia's dynamic global production networks.

7

Economic Cooperation in the Indian Ocean Region and the BRI: Threat or Opportunity?

Palitha Kohona

The Indian Ocean region is experiencing a much anticipated luxury. Almost every one of the economies of the region is expanding at a rate which gives hope to the entire region, especially to its poor and marginalised. The promise of prosperity, enthusiastically made at the time of independence from colonial rule so many decades ago, may at last become a reality. India is powering ahead, and now leads China. Still, the region continues to be confronted by an inexcusably massive burden of poverty, literacy deficits, malnutrition, and deprivation. South Asia has the dubious distinction of being home to the largest concentration of the poor in the world. Inadequate policy frameworks, corruption, military rivalries, and internal conflicts, among others, drain resources which could be devoted to economic advancement. Some internal conflicts are also funded from outside.

Encouragingly, the countries of the region are beginning to collaborate with each other in economic matters, having recognised that there is much to be gained through cooperation rather than through rivalry; however, they seem to be doing so ever so slowly, and in fits and starts. There is still much more progress that can be achieved through cooperative efforts.

The South Asian Association for Regional Cooperation (SAARC) countries have concluded the agreement on the South Asian Free Trade Area (SAFTA) covering over 1.5 billion people, and the South Asian Agreement on Trade in Services which tends to follow the GATS model. For a variety of reasons, including political tensions, religious rivalries, internal conflicts, age old suspicions, externally generated unease, colonial hang ups, etc, these agreements have not realised their intended potential. Sadly, political rivalries have held back SAARC, and many feel that the organisation created in 1987 by idealists could have achieved more in the 30 years of its existence. The Bay of Bengal countries are a part of the Bay of Bengal Initiative for the Multi-Sectoral Technical and Economic Cooperation (BIMSTEC). This agreement, too, could generate better results, if methodically implemented. The region has too much in common that can be easily marshalled for mutual benefit.

Sri Lanka has concluded free trade agreements with India and Pakistan, and is in the process of negotiating a far reaching Economic and Trade Cooperation Agreement (ETCA) with India. Exports from India to Sri Lanka have boomed. Sri Lanka's exports to India have also grown, but not at the same pace. This disparity has given rise to suspicions and opposition to the proposed ETCA. Serious perceptional and practical issues remain to be addressed.

The South Asia region, as a unity, is still to secure international acceptability. Its leaders need to be more imaginative and ambitious. Against this background, Chinese President Xi Jinping's One Belt One Road (OBOR) initiative, also known as the Belt and Road Initiative (BRI), unveiled in 2013, has provided the countries of the wider region with a new challenge as well as a unique opportunity to fast track their economies along the path to development. An investment bonanza is being made available under the OBOR or BRI, especially for the countries in the Maritime Silk Road. Carefully managed and sensitively implemented, the OBOR initiative could revive the glorious days of the ancient Silk Route. Sitting at the hub of the ancient Silk Route, Sri Lanka has embraced this concept.

It has been said that China's OBOR investment ambitions, focused on cooperative infrastructure and connectivity enhancement, have the potential to make a greater impact than the post World War US Marshall Plan. The Marshall Plan provided financial assistance to the war devastated economic giants of Europe, and was a major factor in their quick recovery. But the funds available under the OBOR make the Marshall Plan pale into insignificance. The Marshall plan provided over US $140 billion (at 2017 dollar values) to assist the West European economies. The OBOR expects to make available a stunning US$ 4–8 trillion. While the Marshall Plan achieved much, the OBOR funds are expected to achieve substantially much more by creating a vast region of shared prosperity, the clear beneficiaries being a large number of developing countries. The Marshall Plan allowed the USA to export its currency. The US dollar was used to provide subsidies, while European countries purchased US goods with their own currencies. Over time, the US dollar became a tool for stability; funds provided by the plan created the basis for future frequent easing of trade restrictions.

Adding strength to the OBOR initiative, the Chinese Yuan has now been recognised as a reserve currency by the IMF, and China appears to be moving increasingly towards international payments in Yuan. The IMF elevated the Yuan, also known as the renminbi, or 'people's money', on the same day that the Communist Party celebrated the founding of the People's Republic of China in 1949. The Yuan joins the US dollar, the Euro, the Yen, and the British Pound in the IMF's special drawing rights (SDR) basket, which determines currencies that countries can receive as part of IMF loans. This would be the first time that a new currency has been added since the Euro was launched in 1999. It is an impressive achievement, as the Yuan had very little or no credibility as recently as thirty years ago. Today, China is the world's largest economy by purchasing power parity. This is a massive leap from less than US$ 200 per capita GDP in 1970. Sri Lanka's per capita GDP is around US$ 3800 (US$ 270 in 1980).

The outward looking Belt and Road initiative could have a massively transformative impact on the economies of the vast Asian and African regions, encompassing 68 countries with over 65 per cent of the world's population. It will be a closely related factor as Sri Lanka seeks to realise its own Vision 2025. Vision 2025 provides the development blueprint for the country for the next seven years. The OBOR goal, backed by China's substantial economic clout, including through the Asian Infrastructure Investment Bank (AIIB) which claims 61 state members at present, possesses the potential to create significant opportunities for the entire region.

It is against this background that the successful Sri Lanka Economic and Investment Conclave (SEIC) 2017 was organised in Colombo, Sri Lanka, in November 2017. The objective was to highlight Sri Lanka as a trading centre and an investment destination. A significant number of the participants at SEIC 2017 came from overseas, especially from China. Others came from Wall Street, London, Geneva, Dubai, India, Hong Kong, Singapore, and Amsterdam.

Historically, traders and casual visitors have recognised Sri Lanka's potential both as a destination to visit and a trading hub. Ibn Battuta, the Moor from Tangiers, who visited the island in the 14th century, was not wrong when he observed that this was the most beautiful island on earth, and was only 40 leagues from paradise. This paradise must be preserved despite the race to modernize, and achieve a higher level of sustainable prosperity for the people of the country as they seek to climb up the development ladder.

The copious writings of the fifth century scholar monk Fa Xian from China, who spent a number of years in the ancient capital Anuradhapura, after a long sojourn in northern India, tell a tale of the bygone prosperity and complex international diplomatic and trading relations. Fa Xian carried a ship load of religious texts from Sri Lanka to China. Sri Lanka, like other countries of South Asia, had developed important relations—religious, trading and social—with the Middle Kingdom from early days. The OBOR initiative invokes memories of the multitude of traders who visited Sri Lanka in the past, and contributed to its prosperity. Already, Chinese largesse is impacting a swathe of countries and regions.

Pakistan, has been promised US$ 54 billion for investments in infrastructure. The Bangladesh-India-China-Myanmar (BCIM) corridor links China with the Bay of Bengal.

Africa is reaping the benefits of China's investments, and many African economies are prospering for the first time in years. According to the China Africa Research Initiative at Johns Advanced International Studies in Washington, by 2014, Chinese investments in Africa had risen more than 20-fold to US $220 billion. Certain reservations concerning Chinese investments have also emerged. It is likely that Chinese investments in resource rich Africa will accelerate as China also learns from experience, and responds more to the aspirations of the people of the continent.

Since 2000, Ethiopia where the African Union is headquartered, has been a major recipient of Chinese loans, with financing for dams, roads, railways, and manufacturing plants worth more than US $12.3 billion—more than twice the amount loaned to oil-rich Sudan and mineral-rich Congo. While raising some concerns, the OBOR concept, especially among the former colonial powers who ruthlessly ravaged Africa and Asia when they had the opportunity, can be used by countries of the Indian Ocean region and beyond to enhance their mutual prosperity without being constrained by the fears and suspicions inculcated by the colonial past. More importantly, they can do this without territorial occupation, racial discrimination, and the forced alteration of cultures.

Further East, Australia received AU$ 15.4 billion in Chinese investments involving 103 deals. Australia has been a major destination for Chinese investments, after the USA and Europe and investors grabbed hotel assets, real estate, agri businesses, vineyards, health care, infrastructure, etc., giving rise to a latent xenophobic anti-Asian and anti-Chinese sentiment. The port of Melbourne is now controlled by a Hong Kong-Chinese concern.

A significant share of Chinese investments is also headed to Europe. The EU, whose second largest trading partner is China, received EUR 35 billion in Chinese investments in 2016 alone. Iconic facilities, such as the Toulouse Blagnac airport where the Airbus 380 is assembled (which has been sold to the Shandong Hi-Speed Group and a Hong Kong investment firm while Emanuel Macron was the Finance Minister), Volvo (which has been sold to Geely), the AC Milan football club, the Piraeus harbour (now owned 70 per cent by COSCO), the German robot manufacturer Kuka (now owned by a Chinese company), not to mention a number of historic vineyards and buildings, are now in Chinese hands. Chinese companies are building the rail link between the Piraeus harbour, Serbia, and Hungary. Trains carrying East Asian products now travel through the Euro-Asian land mass, the modern Silk Route, to European capitals, including London, and also link up with Tehran.

The Asian Railways Network, sponsored by the Economic and Social Commission for the Asia Pacific (ESCAP), also provides South Asia the opportunity to link up with the European network through Central Asia. Tremendous trade opportunities could open up with a high speed railway linking South Asia with Europe. Natural gas from Central Asia flows along four pipelines to China. The USA has received US$ 90 billion since 2007. In New York, the Waldorf Astoria has been acquired by Chinese interests.

However, China has also tightened overseas investments, especially in real estate, hotels, film and entertainment, and sports clubs, to reduce excessive capital outflows and foreign exchange risks. Those countries seeking to benefit from the Chinese gravy train should be conscious of this development.

The expansion of China's economic and political reach has caused more than a few adverse reactions in certain international circles, especially among powers which have been used to dominating the world stage. France, Germany, and Italy are leading an initiative to require the EU to scrutinise Chinese investments in Europe more carefully. Recently, it has been said that America's focus on terrorism as the main threat has now shifted to Russia and China. According to a new Pentagon strategy released recently by Defence Secretary, Jim Mattis, the USA must build up its military to prepare for the possibility of a conflict with Russia and China. The USA persists in viewing the world in terms of hostile competitors.

Given that China and the USA are closely intertwined in a complex economic embrace, the use of such terminology is curious. The USA is China's major trading partner. The bilateral trade in 2016 was worth US$ 579 billion while the US trade deficit was over US$ 379 billion. And, China is the main lender to the US and also holds over US$ 1.2 trillion in US securities. China is also the biggest market for many US agricultural products, and millions of Chinese tourists visit the USA annually, not to mention the thousands of Chinese students who study there. Any conflict between the two countries, including a trade war, would do irreparable damage to both, not to mention the rest of the world. The two countries have a unique opportunity in history to get away from historical power based competition to cooperate for the common good. Cooperation cannot be managed in a hurry; but the opportunity is there. Many aspects of East Asian culture, including food, eating habits, traditional health care, yoga, Zen meditation, and mindfulness, martial arts, dress, philosophy have been seeping into Western and American life over the years.

The USA has been an inspiration in the liberal ideas of democracy, transparency, legal propriety, management style, sports, music, film, etc. However, these ideas will not be adopted by the East overnight. Nor will the Eastern style of living, religion, or doing business be adopted lock stock and barrel by the West any time soon. It will take time. There are clear opportunities for the two teaching each other. Instead of breast thumping and posturing, it would serve humanity's interests better in the long run if the giants of the world, both Eastern and Western, could cooperate for mutual betterment.

Similarly, a major concern is India's sensitivities regarding China's outreach. The facts that the two countries fought a border war in 1962, and have occasionally skirmished along a disputed colonial border, have not been forgotten. But, India's natural concerns and sensitivities have impacted the decision makers of the smaller countries of the Indian Ocean region. India has developed a considerable naval presence in the Indian Ocean. India's growing relationship with the USA has clear military implications. The USA has recently agreed to sell Guardian drones to India for maritime surveillance. While strengthening its naval capabilities in the Andaman and Nicobar Islands, India has also quietly developed strategic relations with Australia and Japan, participating in regular joint naval exercises. India maintains a base on one of the islands in the Seychelles, and has just concluded an agreement to build an airstrip and a sophisticated "monitoring station" at the cost of US$ 45 million. India has also signed a Bilateral Agreement for Navy Cooperation with Singapore that provides Indian Navy ships temporary deployment facilities and logistics support at Singapore's Changi naval base, which is near the disputed South China Sea. Indian military strength in the Indian Ocean region is formidable. It seems unlikely that China, even if it wished, would be able to challenge nuclear armed India in the Indian Ocean for decades to come. India enjoys overwhelming military superiority in the Indian Ocean.

Furthermore, the USA maintains a mammoth base on Diego Garcia to the south of Sri Lanka. It is highly improbable that Chinese policymakers would consider challenging the existing power arrangements in the Indian Ocean any time soon, if ever. They have not done so since Admiral Zheng He's flotilla entered the Indian Ocean in 1405, and paid a few visits till 1433. To over extend in order to meet a possible challenge from China would result in expending scarce resources for a confrontation that is unlikely to happen.

As a small neighbour, Sri Lanka is eager to ascend the development ladder in the shortest possible time; but is caught between the sensitivities of our closest neighbour and the need to develop stronger economic relations with another. There is little doubt that as a long time friend and a country that has been the source of much of Sri Lanka's religious and cultural inspiration, Sri Lanka must create and maintain an environment that makes India comfortable. India has been a major source of investment and the flow of tourists to Sri Lanka. The big neighbour must feel the reassurance that the small island to the south will not pose a strategic threat, even in collusion with any other country. It should not become someone else's large aircraft carrier! Sri Lanka's own interests will be served well with a reliable relationship with India. This does not mean subservience or a one way approach, dominated by hectoring and gratuitous advice. The relationship, if it is to be comfortable and sustainable, must be one between two proud sovereign nations. India has a positive role to play as the bigger neighbour to the north. India's burgeoning economy could provide an outlet for Sri Lankan businesses to expand. However, the over-zealous and rash opening up of our economic doors with no comparable reciprocity would certainly create unease.

Sri Lanka must seek its own development path. This might mean seeking to collaborate with whoever it likes, including China. Sri Lanka has maintained excellent relations, particularly economic, with Japan, Korea, Malaysia, Singapore, Thailand, etc. China, coincidentally, is India's major trading partner. Both Chinese and Indian leaders have made explicit overtures to each other, with repeated references to historical, religious, cultural, and trading links. Both recognise the opportunities presented by cooperation rather than by confrontation. A prosperous and stable Sri Lanka will be an asset to India; an unhappy and resentful neighbour to its south will not be. Sri Lanka's prosperity, including through participation in the OBOR initiative, will be to India's advantage as well. India could also benefit extensively from a proactive engagement with the OBOR initiative.

8

Indo-Pacific Cooperation: Some Thoughts on Connectivity

*Prabir De**

Introduction

The world has been witnessing a new wind of change—a change that has been driven by India's pro-active foreign policy. India actively pursued the Look East—Act East strategy to enhance economic integration with Southeast and East Asian countries.[1] Today, India conducts over 1/4th of India's global trade with the East Asia Summit (EAS) countries, and is a member of the Regional Comprehensive Economic Partnership (RCEP), which is being negotiated.[2]

Three important developments have been observed in recent years: First, the Look East-Act East Policy has paid well. India has developed strong bilateral relations (for example with Bangladesh, Myanmar, and Sri Lanka); is driving a sub-regional programme (for example the BBIN); and working with several regional initiatives (for example with ASEAN, BIMSTEC, and IORA). Second, connectivity is central to most of the regional cooperation initiatives in which India participates. Third, the India-Japan strategic partnership has reached new heights, which underscores the importance of Indo-Pacific cooperation.

This paper presents some thoughts on Indo-Pacific connectivity against

* The author is Professor, Research and Information System for Developing Countries (RIS), New Delhi, and also Coordinator, ASEAN-India Centre (AIC), RIS. An earlier version of the paper was presented at the Kalinga International Foundation (KIF) Conference 'PURBASA: East meets East: Synergizing the North-East and Eastern India with the Indo-Pacific', held at Bhubaneswar, on 16–18 March 2018.Views are personal.

the backdrop of the region's recent advancements in geo-economic and geo-strategic cooperation.

Ocean, the Prime Connector

The Indo-Pacific is an emerging concept, and there is no fixed definition of the region as yet.[3] Countries falling in the direct hinterland of the vast Indian and Pacific oceans can be termed as the Indo-Pacific. The motivation for a larger bloc always comes from the sheer size and resources it owns, and the scope and size of the economies of scale. The Indo-Pacific region comprises 38 countries, shares 44 percent of world surface area, 65 percent of world population, contributes up to 62 percent of world GDP, and 46 percent of world merchandise trade (Table 1).[4] Apparently, it has all the ingredients to generate regional trade and investment opportunities, thereby benefitting the consumers. The ocean is the common thread that connects this vast Indo-Pacific.

Table 1: The Indo-Pacific's Share in the World, 2017

Indicators	*Share in World (%)*
Surface Area	44
Population	65
Economic Size (GDP)	62
Economic Size (GDP PPP)	66
Merchandise Trade	46

Source: Author's calculation based on WDI, the World Bank.

The prime focus of Indo-Pacific is centred around the ocean, where India occupies an important strategic position in the Indian Ocean. India is primarily a maritime nation, having a rich and glorious history of maritime trade. It is the ocean that connects India with her major trade partners. Over 70 percent of India's merchandise trade per annum is carried out by the ocean. India has been witnessing a steady growth in commercial and subsistence activities at sea, relating to trade and transportation, resource exploitation, and the leisure industry. These activities are indispensable for any country's economic development, and generating better opportunities for livelihood.

Given the economic potential of the Indo-Pacific region, a number of countries are investing enormous financial, technological, and human capital to develop maritime economies, and are striving to leverage their unique strengths. Many countries have announced initiatives and action plans to promote the Blue Economy or the Ocean Economy. For example, Indian Prime Minister Modi has endorsed the Blue Economy as a new pillar of economic activity in the coastal areas and linked hinterlands through the sustainable tapping of oceanic resources. He has also announced his vision for the seas through Security and Growth for All in the Region (SAGAR). The maiden Maritime India Summit 2016 in Mumbai witnessed investment commitments of nearly US$ 13 billion in the shipping, ports, and allied sectors. The Indian government plans to invest US$ 190 billion over the next ten years to develop 27 industrial clusters, and to improve connectivity with ports through new rail and road projects.[5]

There is a growing realisation that a secure maritime environment in India's neighbourhood is an essential prerequisite for development and prosperity. Efficient and improved maritime connectivity is of critical importance for expanding India's regional and global trade. Greater maritime connectivity between India and her trade partners across the world is, therefore, an imperative for Indo-Pacific connectivity. In his Keynote Address at the Shangri La Dialogue on 1 June 2018 at Singapore, Prime Minister Modi reaffirmed India's key role in maritime security and cooperation, leading to strengthening the Indo-Pacific[6].

Focus on Maritime Cooperation

Maritime security and cooperation is a necessary element in both foreign and security policy frameworks. The maintenance of peace, stability, and security on and over the seas; unimpeded lawful commerce; freedom of navigation; over-flight and other internationally lawful uses of the airspace; and the protection and preservation of marine resources, as well as a sustainable and responsible fishery framework are very important to building a regional consensus on maritime security and cooperation.[7]

In the Indo-Pacific, maritime cooperation between India and Southeast Asian countries is one of the important aspects of the India-ASEAN strategic partnership. At the recently held ASEAN-India Commemorative Summit held in Delhi in January 2018, leaders underlined the need to provide lower logistics costs for increasing trade.[8] To protect the oceans and connect the countries, maritime cooperation is the most convincing option. Indo-Pacific countries may undertake collective efforts to address three aspects of the maritime commons: connectivity, security, and cooperation. For example, closer cooperation amongst the Early Warning Centres, including for tsunami warnings, could be supplemented with Humanitarian Assistance and Disaster Relief (HADR) Exercises and SOPs (Standard Operating Procedures) for HADR. Capacity building in this area is also important as the region is prone to natural disasters.

Maritime connectivity is a multifaceted task that requires implementing strong policy initiatives. A pro-active strategy to strengthen India's maritime connectivity with its neighbours would not only promote India's merchandise trade but also generate opportunities for industrial development as well as unlock trade potential in Indo-Pacific region. Therefore, one of the key priorities of maritime cooperation in the Indo-Pacific should be to achieve a safe, sustainable, and efficient multi-modal transport system in the region.

In this context, following three broad measures may be considered:

- build a synergy with India's maritime plan (for example, Sagarmala) with that of immediate and extended neighbours, particularly where the markets matter;
- strengthen the multi-modal interface(s) between land and ocean transportation wherever possible. For example, ports are gateways and hubs and, hence, need to build adequate interface with land, rail, water, and pipelines; and
- utilise the resources optimally that lead to protect marine environment.

India has been taking steps to augment infrastructure and capacity at all major ports under the Sagarmala Project, particularly on the eastern sea board. Partnership with ports located in Myanmar, Thailand, Indonesia, Malaysia, Singapore, and Vietnam can make Indian ports important gateways to ASEAN countries, and vice versa. The ongoing Kaladan Multimodal Transit Transport project aims at providing connectivity between Indian ports on the eastern sea board and the Sittwe Port in Myanmar, which would promote economic and commercial links with Myanmar, and facilitate the transit of goods to and from North East India.

The expeditious conclusion of the ASEAN-India Maritime Transport Agreement (AIMTA) would strengthen maritime connectivity between India and ASEAN. This Agreement would help improve access to maritime services through greater transparency in maritime regulations, policies, and practices of trading partners; by facilitating the flow of commercial goods at sea and at ports; and paving the way for the establishment of joint ventures in the fields of maritime transportation, shipbuilding and repairs, maritime training, information technology (including the development of simulators), port facilities, and related maritime activities.

Enhancing regional connectivity and trade through direct short-sea shipping and shipping facilitation agreements would strengthen maritime connectivity between ASEAN and India. Therefore, maritime connectivity in the Indo-Pacific region would lead to bolster economic integration through higher trade and investment; the promotion of tourism; building seaports and shipping networks; signing the Mutual Recognition Agreement (MRA) in shipping and logistics services; cooperation for improving efficiency of ports joining ASEAN Ro-Ro and Cruise Network; etc. ASEAN and India may also decide the possibility of developing RoRo terminals, ports, and building connectivity between islands under the Sagarmala project. Low carbon shipping; regional fisheries agreements; ocean surveillance; information sharing; marine biotechnology; cyber security; and IT services are some of the other areas for cooperation.

Trade Facilitation Priority

The key priority of trade facilitation should be to achieve a safe, sustainable, and efficient trade and transport system in the region. Most of the Indo-Pacific countries are signatories to the WTO Trade Facilitation Agreement (TFA), besides numerous bilateral or regional agreements on trade facilitation. A regional trade facilitation arrangement may not be difficult to design and implement.

The following are some of the new trade facilitation priorities:

- Indo-Pacific countries shall aim for regulatory convergence in transportation standards;
- Indo-Pacific countries may agree to customs cooperation for sharing of information, generate inter-operatibility of customs single windows, dispute settlement, etc;
- Indo-Pacific countries may adopt a paperless trading system. The UN Paperless Trade Agreement offers good lessons. This will help countries to simplify trade procedures, support value chains, among others; and
- Training and capacity building should be the focus of the trade facilitation programme. Learning from each other's experiences can contribute to regional integration in an effective way.

To spearhead the connectivity programme, countries may consider setting up working groups and conduct joint studies to design a vision and an Indo-Pacific connectivity master plan. The ASEAN Secretariat in Jakarta, and the Economic Research Institute for ASEAN and East Asia (ERIA) in Jakarta may take the lead to complete the study.

The Completion of Projects Driving Connectivity

India has been implementing several connectivity projects in Southeast Asia. Physical connectivity in the present form comprises three important projects: (i) the India-Myanmar-Thailand Trilateral Highway; (ii) the Kaladan Multimodal Transit Transport Project; (iii) the Mekong-India Economic Corridor; (iv) development of ports in Oman (Duqm), Iran (Chabahar) and Mozambique (Beira); and harbour and anchoring facilities in Mauritius and Seychelles. The completion of these projects would certainly strengthen Indo-Pacific connectivity.

(i) The Trilateral Highway

The Trilateral Highway (TH) was first proposed at a Trilateral Ministerial meeting on transport linkages in Yangon in April 2002. This India-Myanmar-Thailand Trilateral Highway aims to connect India with the ASEAN region. The length of the Trilateral Highway is approximately 1,360 km. Under the Trilateral Highway project, India assumes the responsibility of building 78 kms of missing links, upgrading 58 kms of the existing roads, and improving further 132 kms of road in Myanmar. About 132 kms have been completed and handed over to Myanmar. India has also undertaken the task of repairing/ upgrading 69 bridges on the Tamu-Kalewa Friendship Road, and upgrading 120 kms of the Kalewa-Yargyi segment to highway standards.

Myanmar has completed the upgrading of the Yargyi to Monywa stretch of the highway. The alignment of the Trilateral Highway falls within Asian Highways 1 and 2. The agreed route of the TH (1,360 kms) is as follows: Moreh (India)-Tamu-Kalewa-Yargi-Monywa-Mandalay-NayPyiTaw-Yangon-Thaton-Hypaan-Kawkareik-Myawaddy-MaeSot (Thailand). Along this corridor, there are two border crossings (India-Myanmar, and Myanmar-Thailand); four customs check-points; three international time zones; three customs EDI systems; two different vehicle-driving standards; and three different motor vehicle laws. The challenge is to reach convergence in standards and procedures along the corridor. This project would help in establishing trilateral land connectivity between India, Myanmar, and Thailand. It is likely to be completed by 2020. It has also been decided to extend the Trilateral Highway to Lao PDR, Vietnam, and Cambodia to add greater momentum to the growing trade and investment linkages between the ASEAN and India.

(ii) The Kaladan Multi-Modal Transit Transport Project

Sittwe is the capital of the Rakhine State in Myanmar. The Ministry of External Affairs (MEA) entered into a Framework Agreement with the Myanmar Government in April 2008 to facilitate the implementation of the Kaladan Multi-modal Transit Transport Project. The Framework Agreement and two protocols (the Protocol on Transit Transport and the Protocol on Maintenance) were signed by India and Myanmar on 2 April 2008. The project has been jointly identified by India and Myanmar to create a multi-modal transportation of cargo from the eastern ports of India to Myanmar as well as to North East India through Myanmar. It connects the Sittwe Port in Myanmar to the India-Myanmar border, and is expected to contribute to the economic development of the North East Indian states by opening up the sea route for products. It envisages connectivity between Indian ports and the Sittwe port in Myanmar, and road and inland waterway links from Sittwe to India's northeastern region.

The Kaladan project aims to provide an alternate route for the transportation of goods to northeastern India through Myanmar. It has two major components: (i) the development of the port and Inland Water Transport (IWT) between Sittwe and Kaletwa in Myanmar along the Kaladan River, and (ii) building a highway (129 kms) from Kaletwa to the India-Myanmar border in Mizoram. It includes (i) the construction of an integrated Port and IWT terminal at Sittwe, including dredging; (ii) the development of a navigational channel along the river Kaladan from Sittwe to Paletwa (158 kms); (iii) the construction of an IWT Highway trans-shipment terminal at Paletwa; (iv) the construction of six IWT barges (each with a capacity of 300 tonnes) for the transportation of cargo between Sittwe and Paletwa; and (v) the building of a highway (109 kms) from Paletwa to the India-Myanmar border (Zorinpui) in Mizoram. The construction of the integrated port-IWT jetty at Sittwe is almost complete. In April 2013, construction work on the IWT terminal at Paletwa was started, which is likely to be completed in 2018-19.

The construction of the India-Mizoram border at Zorinpui to NH 54 (Lawngtlai) road on the Indian side in Mizoram is in progress under India's Ministry of Road Transport and Highways. It is termed the National Highway 502A (NH 502A). About 66 per cent of the new 99.83 kms NH 502A, starting from NH 54 at Lawngtlai to Zorinpui in Mizoram, has been done, and rest would be complete by 2019. However, the 109 kms road from Zorinpuion the India-Myanmar border to Paletwa in Myanmar is yet to be completed. Once completed, this corridor would provide a strategic link to North East India, thereby reducing the transportation load on the Siliguri Corridor in West Bengal state. In the absence of an alternate route, the development of this project would not only serve the economic, commercial, and strategic interests but would also contribute to the development of Myanmar, and its economic integration with India. Situated at the mouth of the Kaladan river, the port has been developed by India as a part of the Kaladan Multi-Modal Transit Transport Project, and has already been handed over to the Myanmar government. To attract investments in the Sittwe belt, the Myanmar government may consider developing an SEZ in the vicinity of the port.

(iii) The Mekong-India Economic Corridor (MIEC)

Another important cross-border connectivity project is the Mekong-India Economic Corridor (MIEC). The MIEC involves integrating the four Mekong countries: Myanmar, Thailand, Cambodia, and Vietnam with India. It connects Ho Chi Minh City (Vietnam) with Dawei (Myanmar) via Bangkok (Thailand) and Phnom Penh (Cambodia) and Chennai in India. The Dawei Port and SEZ is located in the Charkae village of Dawei district of the Tanintharyi Division in the Mon State of Myanmar. It is situated about 614.3 kms south of Yangon on the northern bank of the Dawei river. Proposed infrastructures in Dawei SEZ include the development of a deep sea port; of an industrial estate divided into six industrial zones; a residential and commercial zone; and an oil and gas pipeline. The project aims to become a major logistic hub in Southeast Asia. It involves the development of the port along with a cross-border road link from Dawei to Thailand, and a rail link from Dawei-Yangon-Mandalay-Muse. The industrial estate and related supporting facilities will serve as a regional manufacturing and trading hub.

The project will also serve as an alternative sea route to India, China, West Asia, Europe, and Africa. This will lessen dependence on the congested straits of Malacca, thereby reducing transportation time and costs. Its strategic location will provide direct access to the Andaman Sea and the Indian Ocean for cargo transportation. The industrial estate will strengthen economic cooperation, trade, and development among the Greater Mekong Sub-region (GMS) countries. Industrial parks aim to promote sustainable SEZ development involving local communities and business. They work to protect natural habitats, and implement the international standards for health and safety.

Major investment will be required for the development of a port at Dawei and SEZ. The Myanmar government has decided to develop the Dawei port and SEZ in a joint venture. The SEZ and its related project area has six major development goals, including infrastructure and construction; industry and business development; power; community development and relocation; rules and regulations; and finance. The Dawei port can accommodate up to 300,000 DWT vessels, with a design capacity for 250 million tonnes cargo throughput. It is equipped with terminals for handling containerised cargo, break bulk, dry bulk, liquid bulk, and LNG. It has modern port and vessel management systems to ensure safety, security, and efficiency. An integrated logistics hub, with an intermodal freight transport system is also available at the port. There is a shortcut link connecting Thailand road networks to Dawei (approx. 132 kms). A 4-lane Highway (8 lanes in the future) has been developed on the lines of the ASEAN Highway standard. The project has a large raw water reservoir, with 400 million cubic metre raw water storage capacity to ensure the all-year round supply of fresh water. A centralized water treatment plant operates it, with the maximum capacity of 1.05 million cubic metres per day.

When completed, the MIEC is expected to augment trade with India by reducing the travel distance between India and the MIEC countries, and removing supply side bottlenecks. The emphasis of the corridor is on expanding the manufacturing base and trade with the rest of the world, particularly with India. The corridor will enable the economies of ASEAN and India to integrate further, and collectively emerge as a globally competitive economic bloc. India may consider joining the MIEC as an official partner.

Conclusions

Regional cooperation in the Indo-Pacific with a focus on the maritime domain can be enhanced to benefit all nations economically, and through enhanced maritime security. A formal shape to the Indo-Pacific may also lead to the generation of new economic activities in the region. In the maritime sector, India's Security and Growth for All in the Region (SAGAR) could be a good beginning to strengthen maritime connectivity. In particular, India shall focus on improving maritime connectivity with IORA, ASEAN, and the EAS countries.

The Indo-Pacific countries must continuously engage in exploring newer and collective approaches to address multifaceted maritime security threats and challenges to enhance the safety and security of the maritime domain as well as shared prosperity. Enhanced cooperation at sea amongst the concerned stakeholders would help not only in dealing with maritime threats and challenges but also forge partnerships through the prism of maritime multilateralism. Countries have to promote technical cooperation; capacity building; the exchange of experience; and the sharing of knowledge and expertise through various international and national forums. Some soft connectivity projects, such as Project Mausam, shall also be taken up for implementation.

Greater maritime connectivity in the Indo-Pacific is an imperative to form greater markets and strengthen security. This would help not only to achieve the higher performance and efficiency of maritime services but also increase the growth of trade and investment in the Indo-Pacific region.

One way to achieve better mutual understanding is to broaden and increase dialogue. Dialogue is essential for understanding and reconciliation. To start with, the Indo-Pacific countries may consider hosting an annual high-level dialogue on maritime cooperation.

The Indo-Pacific would move only when the bigger economies contribute, economically or otherwise, for the cause of integration. Alejandro Foxly has commented:

> Bottom-up approaches, in which companies develop supply chains across borders, are more effective in facilitating regional integration than are top-down approaches imposed by governments.[9]

Regional trade in the Indo-Pacific can be the building block for global trade, provided bigger economies contribute to build the requisite infrastructure for the integration of the region.

Finally, the success of the Indo-Pacific would depend on how the connectivity agenda, particularly maritime connectivity, leads to reduced transportation costs. Otherwise, rising transportation costs would generate disincentives to the great plan of the Indo-Pacific.

NOTES

1. Read, for example, Das Basu, Sanchita and Masahiro, Kawai, *Trade Regionalism in the Asia-Pacific: Developments and Future Challenges*, ISEAS, Singapore, 2016.
2. Refer, for example, De, Prabir and Suthiphand Chirathivat, *Celebrating the Third Decade and Beyond: New Challenges to the ASEAN-India Economic Partnership*, Routledge, New Delhi, 2018.
3. The term Indo-Pacific was first introduced by Captain Gurpreet Khurana. See, Khurana, Gurpreet S., 'Security of Sea Lines: Prospects for India-Japan Cooperation', *Strategic Analysis*, Vol. 31, No. 1, 2007, pp. 139–153. Also see, http://www.maritimeindia.org/View%20Profile/636661962200993580.pdf
4. Appendix 1 presents the list of countries considered in this study.
5. See also, Government of India Press Release, at http://pib.nic.in/newsite/PrintRelease.aspx?relid=138911
6. Available at https://www.mea.gov.in/Speeches-Statements.htm?dtl/29943/Prime+Ministers+Keynote+Address+at+Shangri+La+Dialogue+June+01+2018
7. See also, the set of brilliant background documented by the National Maritime Foundation (NMF), New Delhi.
8. See, Delhi Declaration, available at http://pib.nic.in/newsite/PrintRelease.aspx?relid=175908
9. See, Foxley, Alejandro, *Regional Trade Blocs: The Way To The Future?* Carnegie Endowment for International Peace, Washington, D.C. 2010

Appendix 1

List of Indo-Pacific Countries

South East Asia: Brunei Darussalam, Cambodia, Lao PDR, Myanmar, Malaysia, Indonesia, Singapore, Thailand, Vietnam, Philippines

South Asia: India, Sri Lanka, Pakistan, Bangladesh, Maldives

Latin and North America: Colombia, Chile, Mexico, United States, Canada, Ecuador

North East Asia: China, Japan, South Korea, Russia

Pacific: Australia, New Zealand, Papua New Guinea, Fiji

South West Asia: Iran, Islamic Rep.

Africa: Kenya, Oman, Somalia, Yemen, Rep., Tanzania, Madagascar, Mozambique, South Africa, Mauritius, Seychelles

MARITIME CONNECTIVITY AND SECURITY IN THE INDO-PACIFIC

9

Opening Remarks

R.K. Dhowan

Honourable Minister Gamini Jayawickrama Perera, from Sri Lanka, Ambassador Lalit Mansingh, Chairman, Kalinga International Foundation (KIF), Excellencies, distinguished guests, eminent panellists, ladies and gentlemen.

It is indeed a distinct honour for me to be present here for PURBASA: East Meets East, a conference on synergising the North East and Eastern India with the Indo-Pacific. I would like to thank Ambassador Lalit Mansingh for inviting me to chair this session on maritime connectivity and the security issue in the Indo-Pacific.

I would like to thank the Kalinga International Foundation and Ambassador Lalit Mansingh for focussing our attention on India's maritime heritage which forms the foundation keel for India which is once again turning towards the seas, and is destined to emerge as a resurgent maritime nation in the 21st century.

India is essentially a maritime nation, and the Indian seaboard has been the vortex of intense maritime activity over centuries. The Indus Valley civilisation, which existed in the western part of the country, dates back to 3300 BC. Even today in India we have a day dock at Lothal in Gujarat which dates back to 2200 BC. It is from these small ports that ancient mariners sailed off to distant lands in Mesopotamia, ancient Egypt, and the East Coast of Africa.

On the East Coast of India, not far from where we are seated today, we had the seafaring kingdom of Kalinga, and the seafarers sailed to distant lands in the East over waters which we call the Indo-Pacific today. In fact, the Bay of Bengal was also called the Kalinga Sea. Further south, we had the Kingdoms—the Cholas, the Pandyas, and Cheras—who sailed off to distant countries in South East Asia. Even today, we can see glimpses of India's rich cultural heritage in these countries.

Today, India is a vibrant maritime nation, with a natural outflow towards the seas. The country sits astride busy sea lines of communication which transit across the Indian ocean, over which nearly 120,000 ships transit every year, carrying 66 per cent of the world's oil, 50 per cent of the world container traffic, and 33 per cent of the world's cargo traffic. Nearly one billion tonnes of oil transits through the Indian Ocean every year, and these oil arteries and trade routes lead further East to ASEAN and countries like Japan, South Korea, and China. Nearly five trillion US Dollars worth of commercial shipping and energy suppliers transit through the South China Sea every year.

The Seas are no longer a benign medium, and globalisation has resulted in the vulnerability of the oceans. The Indo-Pacific region has emerged as the world's economic and strategic centre of gravity in the maritime domain. It is the largest trading region in the world, and home to nearly 60 per cent of the world's population.

The threats and challenges on the waters of the Indo-Pacific Region, range from asymmetric threats like piracy and maritime terrorism to arms trafficking, drug smuggling, human trafficking, and poaching.

The instabilities and turbulence in some parts of the Indo-Pacific Region have the potential to spill over into the maritime domain, and the situation can best be described as fragile. Consequently, over 120 warships from over 20 navies are always present in the Indian Ocean to safeguard their maritime interests. The issues in the South China Sea range from territorial claims and the claims of sovereignty to freedom of navigation and the control of resources.

India has advocated adherence to international law and the maintenance and promotion of peace and stability, maritime security and safety, freedom of navigation, and overflight in the region.

The waters of the Indo-Pacific Region have emerged as global economic highways, and the interests of the countries in the region are linked to the unfettered flow of oil and trade.

Another unique feature of the Indian Ocean is that 80 per cent of the oil and trade that emanates in the Indian Ocean Region is extra regional in nature. This implies that if there is any impediment to the free flow of oil or trade, it would have a detrimental impact not just on the economies of the region but on the global economy as well. Safety, security, and stability on the waters of the Indo-Pacific Region is of paramount importance, and it is the collective responsibility of the navies to ensure the security of the 'global commons'. As part of India's Act East Policy, networking between the Indian Navy and the other navies of the region and, therefore, maritime partnerships between India and the countries of the Indo-Pacific Region need to be strengthened in the coming years.

10

Maritime Security and Connectivity in the Indo-Pacific Oceans: Need for a Rule Based Maritime Order

Jayanath Colombage

Introduction: The Indian Ocean and the Bay of Bengal

The Indian Ocean, together with the Pacific Ocean, is dominating international seaborne trade in the 21st century, which has now been named as 'Asian Century'. Asia is in the middle of a historic transformation. As per an Asian Development Bank Report, if Asia could continue its recent trajectory, by 2050, its per capita income could rise six-fold in Purchasing Power Parity (PPP) to reach current European levels.[1] As per the same report, Asia would regain the dominant economic position it held some 300 years ago, before the industrial revolution. The Indian Ocean will play a critical role in this economic transformation. According to United Nations Conference on Trade and Development (UNCTAD), around 80 percent of global trade by volume and 70 percent of global trade by value are carried out by sea and handled by ports worldwide (Padmaja, 2018).[2] Shipping is the most cost-effective mode of transportation for most goods. There are more than 60000 ships engaged in ocean trade. Hence, shipping and maritime trade is indispensable to the world. There is a growing interdependence between activities on sea and wealth created on land (Padmaja, 2018).

The Indian Ocean now accounts for 70 per cent oil, 50 per cent containers, and 35 per cent bulk cargo of the world. This ocean is also called the 'Energy super highway of the world'. As the countries develop, their energy requirements also grow, and these now become net-importers of energy. The Persian Gulf, a marginal sea of the Indian Ocean, is the world's main oil producing region. Many developed and developing countries are deeply concerned about 'energy security' in the Indian Ocean. Hence, it can be concluded that the Indian Ocean is the world's economic live-wire.

As more and more countries develop to become middle income countries in South Asia and BIMSTEC regions, they will need to produce and trade more. The unprecedented rise of the economic power of China and the rapid growth of India are two key factors impacting the Indian Ocean as their spheres of influence coincide.

The Western Indian Ocean and the Bay of Bengal

The Western Indian Ocean is considered a volatile region. The Middle East, though rich in hydrocarbons, continues to experience conflict and crisis. The Arab-Israel and Palestine-Israel conflicts have not been resolved. The nuclear program in Iran, and the Sunni-Shia fault lines continue to make the region unstable. The ungoverned states of Somalia and Yemen located on either side of Bab El Mandeb—one of the most important choke points—give rise to instability in the western Indian Ocean. The Syrian conflict has seen the large scale destruction of properties and human lives, and the unprecedented level of destruction is still continuing. Daesh is losing ground; but their ideology and radicalization remain relevant. The two nuclear rivals, India and Pakistan, are adding to the instability of this region.

On the other hand, the Bay of Bengal that connects the Indian Ocean with the Western Pacific Ocean is a relatively peaceful ocean region, with no maritime boundary disputes. Bangladesh, India, Myanmar, and Sri Lanka are located in a vital linkage covering the entire Bay of Bengal region. Sri Lanka and India have the unique advantage of belonging to the Western Indian Ocean as well as the Bay of Bengal. Maritime commerce has been a cornerstone of the history of Bay of Bengal countries that are members of the BIMSTEC as well. People of these three countries have been seafarers and travellers since ancient times. They have also welcomed foreigners to trade, learn, and explore. These countries have been well-connected across the Bay of Bengal long before the arrival of the colonial powers. They have traded in spices, elephants, jute products, timber, etc., and there was plenty of raw materials available for building and repairing wooden hulled sailing ships. Very early on, there were diplomatic relations across the seas, and the coastal regions flourished with maritime trade.

The task now is how to reconnect the countries in the Bay of Bengal, and how to link it with the Western Indian Ocean. Another important factor is that the Bay of Bengal is not immune from what is happening in Western Pacific. The confluence of the Bay of Bengal and Western Pacific Ocean can be seen as one large ocean space, and hence mutual influence is inevitable.

The Indian Ocean and Geo-Strategic Competition

The Indian Ocean has now become the focus of attention not only for the resident emerging powers such as India, but also for the non-resident powers such as China, Japan, South Korea, and ASEAN. China has become the second largest economy in the world in terms of GDP and India is in the seventh position. The International Monetary Fund predicts that China will be the number one economy, and India will rise to the number three position by 2040. This augers well for the entire Indo-Pacific region. However, strategic competition and mistrust are hampering the economic progress of the region.

India in the Indo-Pacific

India is in the geographical centre of the Indian Ocean, and through its Andaman Nicobar Islands, has a direct link to the western Pacific Ocean. India has a coast line of 7,500 kms, covering 13 states and union territories. Addressing the Indo-Pacific Regional Dialogue, 2018 edition in New Delhi, the Indian Minister for Defence, Nirmala Sitharaman[3] indicated that India is not a mere tactical player but a global influence and a player. She stressed that India has many global advantages such as democracy, human resources, digital technologies, and a global value chain. When the world is moving from being uni-polar to multi-polar, India aspires to be a global leader commensurate with her capacities and capabilities.

India's economy largely depends on the freedom of oceans, which is a global common. The Minister for Defence asserted that this freedom of navigation and oceans can never be unilaterally taken away by any other power. India firmly believes in a rule based maritime order to pursue its mercantile maritime interests. Although India has the biggest Navy and Coastguard in the region, it is unable to be the net security provider. The costs associated with providing security are huge and, hence, burden sharing is needed. India has come up with some new initiatives, such as SAGAR, which aims at Security and Growth for all in the region; Sagarmala, a national program aimed at accelerating economic development by a port led development initiative harnessing India's ports along the coast line; river networks; and hinterland connectivity. There is also the policy of Act East, targeting the enhancement of economic and political relations with countries such as Japan and ASEAN. India and Japan have introduced another maritime initiative—the Asia Africa Growth Corridor (AAGC)—to link Asia with Africa by using Japanese technology, funding, as well as Indian influence in the East African Region.

China in the Indo-Pacific

China is the second largest economy in the world, and has the newest fleet of warships. Since around 2009, the China's People's Liberation Army Navy (PLAN) was compelled to be physically present in the Indian Ocean in order to protect their merchant ships from Somali pirates. Since then, there has been a constant Chinese presence in this region. China has invested heavily in port related infrastructure projects in countries along its Belt and Road Initiative (BRI).[4] As the People's Republic of China (PRC) expands its global economic and security interests, a region of growing importance to Beijing will be the Indian Ocean area. Not only must a significant portion of China's oil imports transit this region, but one of China's enduring friends (Pakistan) and one of its long time rivals (India) border this region. China has indicated its ambition to be a major power with a modernised military. However, China has asserted, time and again, that it does not have hegemonic or expansionist intentions. However, the USA, India, and Japan do not believe this assertion, and cite China's unilateral behaviour in the South China Sea and East China Sea as a threat to the freedom of maritime commerce in the Indo-Pacific Ocean region. Further, Chinese infrastructure and loan diplomacy are referred to as China's attempting to strategically strangulate India.

The USA Rebalancing of the Indo-Pacific

The recently promulgated National Defence Strategy (NDS) and National Security Strategy (NSS) by USA have clearly identified that its focus is rebalancing its attention to the Indo-Pacific. These strategies have also identified China as a common adversary for the USA and India and, therefore, both seek to enhance further defence and security cooperation between their two countries. The USA is also keen to move ahead with 'Quad'—Australia, India, Japan, and the USA. There is the possibility for a 'Quad Plus' involving the UK and France also. The USA wishes to maintain pre-eminence in all contested and interlinked global commons such as the maritime domain, enhance its deterrence posture, and reverse the growing perception of America's decline. The USA hopes to convey a strong deterrent message to political adversaries, and reassure allies and partners that the US capabilities have not been lost.

Japan and Free and Open Indo-Pacific

Japan is heavily dependent on the energy security of the Indo-Pacific oceans. Japan has even changed its Constitution to enable its maritime forces to play a more active role in the defence of its energy supplies and maritime trade. Prime Minister Abe announced the "Free and Open Indo-Pacific Strategy" in 2017, with the aim of 'developing an environment for International peace, stability and prosperity and sharing universal values and also to enhance 'connectivity' between Asia and Africa to promote stability across the regions'.[5] Japan is concerned about Chinese behaviour in the western Pacific, especially in the East China Sea, and wishes to partner with India since India's Act East policy matches Japanese strategy.

Maritime Security and a Regional Maritime Architecture

Due to the mistrust and strategic competition in the IOR, the region has become heavily militarised, and will continue to be so. As per the Sri Lanka Navy, from 2009 to 2018, 402 warships—including offensive platforms such as aircraft carriers and submarines have visited the port of Colombo for operational, logistic, formal, and recreation visits. This large number of warships belonged to 27 nations. Being the closest neighbour, India sent the highest number of warships, closely followed by Japan. Chinese warships are the next in the list; but at a much lower number. Although this is not a scientific derivative of the military presence in the Indian Ocean, it gives an idea about the players and their presence in the Indian Ocean. It is not only state rivalry which is of concern in this ocean space. There are a large number of non-state actors also present, and waiting to operate in the IOR. These can be terrorists, extremists, smugglers of humans, narcotics, and weapons as well as Illegal, Unreported, and Unregulated Fisheries as well. In this situation of heavy militarisation, mistrust, and strategic competition, the question is: how does one maintain a rule based maritime order and the freedom of navigation and overfly in the Indian Ocean?

Can one large, security architecture be created in the Indian and Pacific Oceans? Building a multi-polar, open, and inclusive security order across the Indo-Pacific will be difficult due to many factors. These include the objectives of the Great Powers; mutual suspicion; and the inequality and vastness of the ocean. But this should be the desired goal: that is, to proceed from a zero sum to positive sum, resulting in a win-win situation. In order to achieve this condition, there is a need to eliminate a trust deficiency with confidence building measures. As such, collaborative solutions across national boundaries, regions, and sectors are needed as there also exist other issues such as Environmental, Energy, Terrorism/Radicalisation, and Cyber Security concerns. Therefore, it is necessary to combine the security sector in establishing a regional solution. In this endeavour, it is necessary to link up ASEAN and IORA.

Conclusion: Sri Lanka and a New 'Indian Ocean Order'

It can be concluded that the Indo-Pacific oceans, whilst playing a critical role at this juncture, have also seen renewed strategic competition. This has resulted in the increasing militarisation and nuclearisation of the region. There is an urgent need to address this growing mistrust and militarisation of the region. The need of the hour is to have a more energetic and vibrant Indian Ocean, with respect for International Law and enhanced connectivity. The coordination of all states is necessary for more practical collaborative efforts in maintaining the sanctity of the ocean space. The IOR needs to look more closely at the ASEAN, and enhance connectivity and collaboration with the ten-member countries of ASEAN.

Sri Lanka is geographically located in the centre of the Indian Ocean—in the midst of one of the busiest international shipping routes. Its proximity to India also brings it under the maritime and air security umbrella of India. The Chinese presence in Sri Lanka at present is phenomenal. This has led to strategic concerns in India and in the minds of other major players. The port of Colombo is the best trans-shipment port in the Indian Ocean. All twenty main line operators call at this port. The Port handled 6 million Twenty Equivalent Units (TEU) in 2017. This is the only port in the region in which mega container ships can berth. Incidentally, nearly 70 per cent of trans-shipment containers handled in this port go to and come from India. Then, there is also the unexplored natural and protected harbour of Trincomalee with an un-dredged depth of 25 meters. Theoretically, even the biggest ships in the world today can berth in this harbour. With an unused oil tank farm, Trincomalee can also be the energy hub for the region. It can also be the hub port for the Bay of Bengal, and countries such as Bangladesh, India, Myanmar and Nepal can benefit from this port to enhance their trade. Furthermore, the development of the Hambanthota port is on the way. This port is the nearest to the main East-West shipping route across the Indian Ocean.

The Indian Ocean Zone of Peace, proposed by the former Prime Minister of Sri Lanka, Sirimavo Bandaranaike in 1971, was adopted by the United Nations General Assembly, with 61 members in favour and none against, with 55 absentees. The proposal called the Great Powers to halt the further escalation and expansion of their military presence, and to move all military bases out of the Indian Ocean. It also called for unimpeded freedom to all ships and aircraft, whether military or commercial, based on International law. Unfortunately, by the close of the 20th century, all efforts in this regard came to a close. This could be considered a missed opportunity as, nearly 47 years later, we aspire to a similar condition in the Indian Ocean. In February 2017, the Prime Minister of Sri Lanka proposed that it is the 'ideal solution for all parties is to agree on a Code of Conduct for military vessels in the Indian Ocean with an effective and realistic mechanism for dispute resolution'. At the Indian Ocean Conference (IOC) held in Colombo in September 2017, the Prime Minister reiterated the call for a 'New Indian Ocean Order.'

The External Affairs Minister of India, Sushma Swaraj, made a statement at the Indian Ocean Conference in Colombo declaring that 'it is important to develop a security architecture that strengthens the culture of cooperation and collective action'.[6] The foremost objective of a Code of conduct has seen support from USA, Japan, and China, and India has not positively commented on this subject. Meanwhile, the Indian Ocean Rim Association (IORA) is also discussing security based issues in the 'Jakarta Accord' of March 2017, which is accompanied with an action plan.

It is important to note that, at a meeting of the Council of Ministers in Durban, South Africa, Sri Lanka was chosen as the lead coordinator for IORA's working group on Maritime Safety and Security. This is based on Sri Lanka's growing self-awareness of its strategic location in the Indian Ocean, as well as its vulnerability in the context of Great Power competition. With a view to sustaining the discussion of a new regional security architecture, a Code of Conduct (COC) is needed. The recently established Centre for the Law of the Sea (at the Pathfinder Foundation) has launched a draft of a COC for IORA to address 'Illicit Criminal Activity by Non-State Actors' in the Indian Ocean. However, this is not a legally binding document, and prescribes rules to be observed in organising cooperation in the pursuit of a common set of objectives.

NOTES

1. Asian Development Bank, *Asia 2050 (2011: Realizing the Asian Century*, Manila, 2011, at https://www.adb.org/sites/default/files/publication/28608/asia2050-executive-summary.pdf, accessed 3 March 2018.
2. Padmaja, G., 'IMOs View on Shipping and India's Sagarmala: Examining the Convergences', in P. Chauhan and G. Khurana (eds.), *Maritime Perspectives 2017*, National Maritime Foundation, New Delhi, 2018.
3. Seetharaman, N., Address to the Indo-Pacific Regional Dialogue, 2018 Edition, New Delhi, 27–28 February 2018.
4. Bhatt, P., 'India can be a "Census Builder" in its Neighbourhood before Moving ahead with its Role as a "Net-Security Provider"', *The Hindu*, 30 January 2018, at http://www.thehindu.com/opinion/op-ed/a-pivot-in-asia/article22567706.ece, accessed 4 March 2018.
5. 'Priority Policy for Development Cooperation for FY 2017', Ministry of Foreign Affairs (MOFA) Japan, 2017, at http://www.mofa.go.jp/files/000259285.pdf, accessed 4 March 2018.
6. Address by External Affairs Minister, Sushma Swaraj to the Second Indian Ocean Conference, on 1/8/2017 in Colombo, Sri Lanka.

11

Security Challenges of Maritime Connectivity in the Indo-Pacific Region

P.K. Singh

Connectivity is an old game which empires and great nations have played since times immemorial. The rivers, seas and land routes have been used for trade, exploration, colonization, blockades etc. The first recorded sea battle occurred about 1210 BC and the first naval blockade in 458 BC and the first combined land and sea blockade occurs during the Peloponnesian War in 457 BC between Sparta and Athens forcing Athens to surrender to Sparta. The first naval blockade in the Western-Pacific region occurred in 1894-95 when Imperial Japan blockaded the Qing Empire during the First Sino-Japanese War.

Use of naval forces is not something new for the Indo-Pacific Region. The Sui and Tang Dynasties of China were involved in several naval affairs with medieval Korea. In 668 AD, the Tang Dynasty supported by Japanese Naval Forces aided the Korean Kingdom of Silla and defeated the other Korean Kingdom of Baekje. Later in 1274-1281 AD the Yuan Emperor Kublai Khan twice unsuccessfully attempted to invade Japan with large naval fleets.

Similarly, the Chola Dynasty of medieval India was a dominant sea power in the Indian Ocean and sent naval expeditions to SE Asia.

It is China's turn to play this strategic game now through its Belt and Road Initiative (BRI) also called OBOR. Strategically speaking, the BRI is a well conceived grand design for geopolitical dominance in which its foreign, security and economic interests are closely inter-twined. It has a facade of a soft power project which tries to hide the hard power military component, complete with its bases and other facilities.

Far from integrating the Region BRI, is polarizing Asia with its growing military footprint.

I will now turn towards security issues of today. The Indo-Pacific Region is the most dynamic region of the Century and for the 21st Century to be truly an Asian Century, all countries of the region have to work together to make it happen.

India's Look East, Act East Policy is the fulcrum of our efforts towards globalization and is an important aspect of our strategic autonomy. It builds on our historic, cultural, economic and security relationship with countries of the region, but it may not be enough to match China's present day economic, political, diplomatic and military capabilities.

China is asserting itself more strongly in the region. The intersection of increasing Indian presence including its Naval presence in the Indo-Pacific region and the corresponding increasing presence of China in the Indian Ocean coupled with its BRI has a great bearing on the unfolding geo-strategic scenario.

In an article written in April 2017, Ambassador Shivshankar Menon, the former NSA, had stated that and I quote, "The Maritime order in the Indian Ocean is calm but fragile due to the lack of an overarching security architecture and a diverse range of traditional and non-traditional security threats facing the region."

If BRI was a benign project to help countries develop their infrastructure and economy, why is there a worry about instability and insecurity in the Region? Reading the comments of some world leaders would highlight the concerns, e.g.:

(i) PM Modi has articulated that the primary responsibility for Indian Ocean security remains with those who live in the region. He also warns that "regional connectivity cannot undermine sovereignty of nations."

(ii) President Macron stated, "These roads cannot be those of a new hegemony, which would transform those that they cross into vassals."

An analysis of China's 2015 White Paper on its Military Strategy clearly shows the path China will follow specially along the routes of the BRI. This paper projects an expeditionary strategic posture and gives a roadmap for attaining Naval and Air Power superiority which will be used for defending its overseas interests. The paper also talks about "preparing for maritime military struggle."

Reading between the lines it becomes clear that China realises that sea power capabilities will be instrumental for pursuing its global great power ambitions —its growing military power and acquisition and constructions of ports extending from the SCS to Djibouti needs to be viewed in this context. A word about China's acquisition of ports may interest you. As we are aware China is busy buying up ports. Nearly two thirds of the World's 50 major ports are either owned by China or have received investments. A quick check will reveal that China has acquired Pakistan's Gwadar Port for 40 years, Sri Lanka's Hambantota for 99 years, Greece's Piraeus port for 35 years, Djibouti for 10 years, 20 per cent of Cambodia's total coastline for 99 years, Maldivian island of Feydhoo Findhu for 50 years and is putting pressure on Myanmar to raise China's stake from 50% to 80% in the Kyaukpyu Port and to lease it for 99 years to overcome its debt problems.

China's frequent forays in the Indian Ocean also need to be viewed in the context of the 2015 White Paper and are aimed at gaining experience in naval operations far away from their home base. It must also be remembered that China's maritime escort missions have seen over half of PLA Navy's guided missile destroyers, frigates and helicopters carrying out tactical manoeuvres in the Indian Ocean. The presence of Chinese submarines including its nuclear submarines, the fiber optic network being laid out to control the flow of information and the mapping of the Northern Indian Ocean sea bed to monitor maritime traffic etc. also needs to be factored in.

We need to carefully monitor the implications of growing Chinese Naval presence in our neighbourhood. China's CPEC with Gwadar Port and the Kunming-Kyaukpyu railway, pipeline and port are two critical projects which give China direct access to the Indian Ocean through the Arabian Sea and the Bay of Bengal. Chinese naval presence here will definitely lead to maritime destabilization of the region.

With growing Chinese military presence, specially its naval presence in the Indo-Pacific Region, and its ports in Sri Lanka, Pakistan, Maldives, Oman and Myanmar etc., it is only a matter of time when we will see the same type of contest in the Indian Ocean that we now see in the East China Sea and the South China Sea.

In response to this increasing uncertainty caused by China's increasing assertive and aggressive behaviour, states in the Indo-Pacific region have undertaken naval build up concentrating not just on defensive but increasingly on offensive capabilities too.

In conclusion I would like to say President Xi's "China Dream and BRI" form inseparable parts of China's grand strategy that will play out over the long term. It must be remembered that trade and connectivity by themselves cannot reduce political and security risks.

The security competition that is taking place in the Region is largely in the maritime context and future regional crisis will occur and be decided in the maritime domain, though for India the crisis could occur simultaneously in the maritime and continental domain. The security challenges will grow overtime. We will have to forge long term strategic partnerships, the QUAD may just be the beginning.

I have flagged the emerging security challenges in the Indo-Pacific so that we can have an informed debate to ensure that the Indo-Pacific remains peaceful and stable and unimpeded trade and commerce continues over the SLOCs.

12

India-ASEAN Maritime Security Cooperation

Aruna Gopinath

India and ASEAN remain committed to enhance their practical cooperation in their shared maritime domain. As India and ASEAN share 25 years of relations, India is pursuing an Act East policy of developing ties with the ASEAN countries. India shares the ASEAN vision for rule based societies and the values of peace. In order to implement the ASEAN-India Partnership for Peace, Progress, and Shared Prosperity (2016–2020), both ASEAN and India hope to:

1. Promote maritime security and safety, freedom of navigation and overflight, unimpeded commerce, the exercise of self-restraint, the non-use of force or the threat to use force, and the resolution of disputes by peaceful means, in accordance with universally recognised principles of international law, including the 1982 United Nations Convention on the Law of the Sea (UNCLOS) and the relevant standards and recommended practices by the International Civil Aviation Organisation (ICAO).
2. Promote maritime cooperation, including maritime security, counter piracy, and search and rescue cooperation through appropriate ASEAN mechanisms and ASEAN-led fora, such as the ASEAN-India framework, EAS, ARF, ADMM-Plus, ASEAN Maritime Forum and its Expanded ASEAN Maritime Forum and where appropriate, promote technical cooperation, capacity building, exchange of experience, and sharing of knowledge and expertise.
3. Encourage cooperation in preventing and combating transnational

crimes such as terrorism and the financing of terrorism, arms smuggling, and sea piracy.

As China and India continue their strong economic growth, maritime trade through regional SLOC's—particularly the Straits of Malacca and Singapore—is expected to increase correspondingly. Major economic states and the littoral states of Southeast Asia all have stakes in ensuring the safe passage of shipping through the region. Any disruption in shipping through such passage can have disastrous consequences. The other maritime security concerns are more effective maritime law enforcement and the maintenance of maritime order. The challenges are part constabulary, part economic, and part human welfare. This necessitates an examination of maritime security issues and current economic cooperation in ASEAN with an analysis of challenges and prospects of maritime security in ASEAN and India.

13

Maritime Security in India's Perception of the Indo-Pacific Concept

Vo Xuan Vinh

The Indo-Pacific concept is an evolving strategic mechanism encompassing the Pacific and Indian Oceans. The 'two ocean navy' concept was initiated by Australia in the late 1980s and, several decades later, the idea of 'the two seas of Indian and Pacific Oceans' for a 'a new broader Asia' was charted by Japanese Prime Minister, Shinzo Abe, in 2007. Prime Minister Abe continued his idea of the two seas by drawing an Asia's Democratic Security Diamond comprising Australia, India, Japan, and the US state of Hawaii. However, the concept of the Indo-Pacific seems only to have been brought to life when US President, Donald Trump, shared the USA's 'vision for a free and open Indo-Pacific' in his remarks at the APEC CEO Summit in Vietnam in November 2017. And then, the Australia-India-Japan-USA Consultations on the Indo-Pacific took place for the first time in the Philippines in the same month. Japan deployed a Free and Open Indo-Pacific Strategy in April 2017 as a part of its Priority Policy for Development Cooperation FY 2017. The USA announced a Briefing on the Indo-Pacific Strategy in April 2018. Australia released its 2017 Foreign Policy White Paper in November 2017, comprising, among others, a chapter on 'A Stable and Prosperous Indo-Pacific'.

As the founder of the concept, India has been supporting and pursuing it to serve its national security and development. Maritime security has become an important pillar of India's perception of the Indo-Pacific concept. This presentation will examine the history of the Indo-Pacific concept, and India's perception of the concept as the background within which to understand the role of maritime security in its calculations about the idea.

A Brief History of Indo-Pacific Concept

Australia should have been regarded as the first country to initiate the idea of the Indo-Pacific when the Royal Australian Navy was decided to be established as a two ocean Navy.[1] However, the trans-ocean strategy seems to be revived two decades later by Japanese Prime Minister, Shinzo Abe, when he proposed an idea of 'the two seas of Indian and Pacific Oceans' for a 'a new broader Asia' in his speech at the Parliament of the Republic of India in 22 August 2007. By quoting the title of a book, *Confluence of the Two Seas*, authored by the Mughal prince Dara Shikoh in 1655, Prime Minister Abe emphasised the ambitions of India in a 'broader Asia', and the preparedness of both India and Japan in working together to 'carry out the pursuit of freedom and prosperity in the region'.[2] Prime Minister Abe affirmed India and Japan's 'vital interests in the security of sea lanes' which are 'are the shipping routes that are the most critical for the world economy'. Interestingly, the Japanese Prime Minister also identified the key stakeholders of the idea—Japan and India, 'incorporating with the United States of America and Australia'.

After Prime Minister Abe's proposal, in 2008, the Australian Prime Minister Kevin Rudd initiated an idea envisaging an Asia-Pacific Community in 2020 as 'a regional institution which spans the entire Asia-Pacific region—including the USA, Japan, China, India, Indonesia, and the other states of the region.'[3] According to Rudd, the community is 'a regional institution which is able to engage in the full spectrum of dialogue, cooperation and action on economic and political matters and future challenges related to security'.[4] Although Rudd's proposal was not named the 'Indo-Pacific', the presence of India in the community indicated that the proposed Asia-Pacific community went beyond the mere geography of the Asia-Pacific, like the East Asia Summit (EAS).

By deploying the balance and then pivot strategy to Asia, whose 'dramatic economic growth has increased its connection to America's future prosperity',[5] the USA began paying more attention to the Indo-Pacific region. In her remarks delivered in Honolulu, Hawaii (October 2010), Secretary of State Hillary Rodham Clinton stated:

> In Southeast Asia and the Pacific, we are shifting our presence to reflect these principles. For example, we have increased our naval presence in Singapore. We are engaging more with the Philippines and Thailand to enhance their capacity to counter terrorists and respond to

> humanitarian disasters. We have created new parameters for military cooperation with New Zealand, and we continue to modernize our defence ties with Australia to respond to a more complex maritime environment. And we are expanding our work with the Indian navy in the Pacific, because we understand how important the Indo-Pacific basin is to global trade and commerce.[6]

In her remarks one year later, Clinton reaffirmed the US commitment to expanding its strategy from the Asia-Pacific to the Indo-Pacific by emphasising that their

> treaty alliances with Japan, South Korea, Australia, the Philippines, and Thailand are the fulcrum for [their] strategic turn to the Asia-Pacific ... We are also expanding our alliance with Australia from a Pacific partnership to an Indo-Pacific one, and indeed a global partnership.[7]

In US perception, Australia and India play very important roles in its pivot to Asia:

> Australia's gateway to the vibrant trade and energy routes that connect the Indian Ocean to the Pacific, the oil, the natural gas, the iron ore produced here that flows through those trade routes to the entire world. It is no surprise that foreign investment is soaring, including more than $100 billion from the United States, because increasingly, these waters are at the heart of the global economy and a key focus of America's expanding engagement in the region, what we sometimes call our pivot to Asia' ... 'We've made it a strategic priority to support India's Look East policy and to encourage Delhi to play a larger role in Asian institutions and affairs. And it's exciting to see the developments as the world's largest democracy and a dynamic emerging economy begin to contribute more broadly to the region.[8]

Inspired and encouraged by the US commitments to Asia, Australia, and Japan, they also began to focus more on the concept of the Indo-Pacific. In his remarks to the Australian Strategic Policy Institute in August 2012, the Australian Minister of Defence, Stephen Smith, clarified his country's shift towards the Indo-Pacific because the USA believes that the Indo-Pacific will become 'the world's strategic centre of gravity'. He felt that it will be charted by (i) the rise of China, of India, and of the ASEAN economies combined; (ii) the major and enduring economic strengths of Japan and South Korea; (iii) the great individual potential of Indonesia and its importance to Australia; and (iv) greater

US military, economic and political engagement in the region through its re-balance strategy.[9] The Secretary of the Department of Foreign Affairs and Trade of Australia, Peter Varghese, then identified that 'a new Indo-Pacific strategic arc is beginning to emerge, extending from India through Southeast Asia to Northeast Asia, including the sea lines of communication on which the region depends'.[10]

Japan, for its part, has strongly responded with the idea of Asia's Democratic Security Diamond.[11] It was initiated by Prime Minister Abe in November 2012, right before the election which he won. Prime Minister Abe's idea came from his concern over the all too possible tragic scene of the South China Sea become 'Lake Beijing', and China's efforts to establish its jurisdiction in the waters surrounding the Senkaku/Daoyu Islands. He pointed out that

> if Japan were to yield, the South China Sea would become even more fortified. Freedom of navigation, vital for trading countries such as Japan and South Korea, would be seriously hindered. The naval assets of the United States, in addition to those of Japan, would find it difficult to enter the entire area, though the majority of the two China seas is international water.

Facing the challenges caused by China, Prime Minister Abe suggested that 'the Indian and Japanese governments ... join together to shoulder more responsibility as guardians of navigational freedom across the Pacific and Indian oceans', because 'peace, stability, and freedom of navigation in the Pacific Ocean are inseparable from peace, stability, and freedom of navigation in the Indian Ocean'. Under Prime Minister Abe, Japan has also made more efforts to realise the idea on a larger scope. In his address at the Opening Session of the Sixth Tokyo International Conference on African Development in Kenya in August 2016, Prime Minister Abe stated that:

> Japan bears the responsibility of fostering the confluence of the Pacific and Indian Oceans and of Asia and Africa into a place that values freedom, the rule of law, and the market economy, free from force or coercion, and making it prosperous.[12]

When President Donald Trump, in his remarks at APEC CEO Summit in Danang, Vietnam (10 November 2017), shared his 'vision for a free and open Indo-Pacific',[13] some thought that the concept was Trump's legacy;[14] but, in fact, Japan was the first country to chart the strategy. In April 2017, the Land of Rising Sun announced the Priority Policy for Development Cooperation –

FY 2017, including three key areas. In order to develop 'an environment for international peace, stability, and prosperity, and [the] sharing [of] universal values,'[15] Japan charted out the Free and Open Indo-Pacific Strategy which focused on three groups of activities to be implemented: (i) counterterrorism, capacity building of law enforcement authorities, and countermeasures against violent extremism; (ii) humanitarian assistance including assistance for refugees, the stabilisation of society, peace building, the removal of landmines; and (iii) strengthening the rule of law through support for capacity building to ensure maritime safety and the establishing of legal systems, and reinforcing the capacity of both law enforcement authorities and their government officials.[16]

After Trump's remarks at APEC CEO Summit 2017, the US National Security Strategy 2017 (released December 2017) considered the Indo-Pacific as the first among seven strategic regions, including the Indo-Pacific, Europe, the Middle East, South and Central Asia, the Western Hemisphere, and Africa. The NSS 2017 outlined priority actions in political, economic, military, and security fields in the context of the Indo-Pacific region.[17] In one of the latest developments, the USA has made a clarification about its free and open Indo-Pacific strategy when Deputy Assistant Secretary, Bureau of East Asian and Pacific Affairs, Alex N. Wong, in his Briefing on the Indo-Pacific Strategy (2 April 2018) explained that a free Indo-Pacific has two levels. On the international plane, the nations in the region are 'free from coercion'.[18] At the national level, the societies of countries in the region are 'free in terms of good governance, in terms of fundamental rights, in terms of transparency, and anti-corruption'. According to Wong, an open Indo-Pacific 'means open sea lines of communication and open airways', 'more open logistics-infrastructure', 'more open investment', and 'more open trade'.

The strategic changes in the region have encouraged Australia to chart its foreign policy in which the concept of the Indo-Pacific emerges as playing an important role. In the 2017 Australian Foreign Policy White Paper (released November 2017), Australia officially defines 'the 'Indo-Pacific' as the region ranging from the eastern Indian Ocean to the Pacific Ocean connected by Southeast Asia, including India, North Asia, and the United States'.[19] It set(s) out a 'vision for a neighbourhood in which adherence to rules delivers lasting peace, where the rights of all states are respected, and where open markets facilitate the free flow of trade, capital, and ideas'.[20]

India's Perception of the Concept of the Indo-Pacific

From the second half of the first decade of 21st century, Indian academic circles began to discuss the concept of the Indo-Pacific. The concept was formally introduced and explained in an academic paper[21] for the first time, by Captain Gurpreet S. Khurana in January 2007.[22] Vice Admiral A.G. Thapliyal even commented that the 'spirit of the term Indo-Pacific' was picked up by Japan's Prime Minister Abe, as reflected in his speech to the Indian Parliament in August 2007.[23] The concept of the Indo-Pacific has gained increasing prevalence in geopolitical and strategic discourse since 2011 among Indian policy-makers, analysts, and academics.[24]

However, India officially launched this concept after MEA's Secretary (East) Sanjay Singh used the term in an address titled 'Geopolitics of the Indo-Pacific Region: Asian Perspectives' at the Asian Relations Conference IV in March, 2013. India's approach to, and the deployment of the concept have been clarified in documents such as Ensuring Secure Seas: Indian's Maritime Security Strategy 2015; Joint Statement on India and Japan Vision 2025: Special Strategic and Global Partnership Working Together for Peace and Prosperity of the Indo-Pacific Region and the World (12 December 2015); India-Australia Joint Statement during the State visit of Prime Minister of Australia to India (10 April 2017); Joint Statement by United States and India: Prosperity Through Partnership (27 June 2017); Opening Statement by Indian Prime Minister at 15th ASEAN-India Summit (14 November 2017); and the answers of the Indian Minister of External Affairs to Rajya Sabha question No. 525 on Indo-US-Japan Maritime Security (02 December 2015); question No.653 on Meeting with Officials on the Sidelines of the ASEAN (21 December 2017), and question No.1930 on The Security Partnership with USA, Japan and Australia (4 January 2018), etc.

In general, India's perception of the concept of the Indo-Pacific concept could be described as follows. Firstly, India supports and pursues the concept of the Indo-Pacific because 'peace, stability and development in the Indo-Pacific region is indispensable to [its] national security and prosperity',[25] and 'a stable, secure and prosperous Indo-Pacific region is crucial for [India's] own progress and prosperity'.[26] Importantly, 'the Indo-Pacific comes at a time of significant progress in India's 'Look East' Policy', and is 'a logical corollary to India's Look East Policy, and an extension of the region of interest to also include within its ambit the Western Pacific'.[27] The new phase of India's Look East Policy—the

Act East Policy—is 'the cornerstone of [India's] engagement in the Indo-Pacific region'.[28]

Secondly, although the Indo-Pacific is an inclusive concept, India—like the USA and Japan—are also considered key stakeholders of the concept, along with Australia. The mechanisms of the Indo-Pacific concept are now dialogues and consultations, such as the India-Japan-the USA, and *India-Australia-Japan Trilateral Dialogues. Recently*, the Australia-India-Japan-US Consultations on the Indo-Pacific were held for the first time in the Philippines, on the sidelines of ASEAN Summit in November 2017. Besides, India continues to appreciate the importance of regional forums, such as the ASEAN Regional Forum (ARF), the ASEAN Defence Ministers Meeting Plus (ADMM+), the Expanded ASEAN Maritime Forum (EAMF),[29] and the East Asia Summit (EAS); seeing all of them as 'the premier leaders-led forum[s] to discuss regional peace and security agenda' with ASEAN at its core.[30]

Thirdly, in order to realise the Indo-Pacific as a peaceful, open, equitable, stable and rule-based order, the viewpoints of India and its partners as stated in the Joint Statement on India and Japan Vision 2025: Special Strategic and Global Partnership Working Together for Peace and Prosperity of the Indo-Pacific Region and the World (12 December 2015), in the India-Australia Joint Statement during the State visit of Prime Minister of Australia to India (10 April 2017); in the Joint Statement of the United States and India: Prosperity Through Partnership (27 June 2017), are: (i) upholding the principles of sovereignty and territorial integrity; (ii) resolving maritime disputes by peaceful means, in accordance with international law, including UNCLOS; iii) sharing a commitment to democratic values, the rule of law, international peace and security, and shared prosperity; and (iv) respecting the freedom of navigation, overflight, and commerce throughout the region.

Fourthly, although India's approach to the region since the second phase of its Look East Policy (2002) is comprehensive, its emphasis is on 'economic and security cooperation'.[31] In the frameworks of bilateral, trilateral, and quadrilateral cooperation between India and its three main partners in the Indo-Pacific, India's defence and security cooperation is reflected in the utilisation of Malabar Exercises, the '2+2 Dialogue', the Defence Policy Dialogue, the Military-to-Military Talks, Coast Guard to Coast Guard cooperation, and Air Force-to-Air Force staff Talks[32] which address security challenges in the two oceans. These challenges are partly decided by the 'critical importance of the sea lanes of communications in the South China Sea for regional energy security, trade, and commerce which underpin the continued peace and prosperity of the Indo-Pacific'.[33] Thus, cooperation in the maritime domain has become one of the key focus areas between not only India and the USA, Australia, and Japan but also India and the ASEAN in the Indo-Pacific region.[34] In the field of economics, 'a free, open, prosperous and inclusive Indo-Pacific region'[35] is the shared viewpoint of India, the USA, Japan, and Australia.

Fifthly, the support and coordination between the USA, Japan, and Australia can be seen as an important impetus for India to get involved in the strategy. After India and the USA established a global partnership[36] in July 2005 under the Bush administration, the USA 'wanted India not only to Look East but also Engage East[37] during President Obama's visit to India in November 2010. Under the Trump administration, the USA has welcomed 'India's emergence as a leading global power and a stronger strategic and defence partner'.[38] The USA has supported 'India's growing relationships throughout the region'[39] of the Indo-Pacific [author added] as well as supported the latter's 'leadership role in Indian Ocean security and throughout the broader region'.[40] Japan encouraged India to engage in the Pacific when Prime Minister Abe chose India as the nation to deliver his speech on 'the Confluence of the Two Seas' in August 2007. Again, in his idea of Asia's Democratic Security Diamond announced in 2012, he also included India as one of the four members of the quad. In its Free and Open Indo-Pacific Strategy (released in April 2017), 'Japan will strengthen strategic collaboration with India, which has a historical relationship with East Africa, as well as the USA and Australia'.[41]

Australia, for its part, has affirmed that its 'alliance with the United States is central to Australia's approach to the Indo-Pacific'[42] on the one hand, and considers India, along with Japan, Indonesia, and Republic of Korea, as central to the agenda on the other.[43] Importantly, Australia-India-Japan-USA Consultations on the Indo-Pacific commenced, for the first time, on 12 November 2017 in the Philippines, where four countries 'discussed measures to ensure a free and open international order based on the rule of law in the Indo-Pacific'.[44] This could be seen as the best example of India's formal participation in the initiative.

Sixthly, although India has shared interests and strategy with the USA, Japan, and Australia, the approach of this country seems to be very cautious.

In practice, India enlarged the scope of its Look East Policy to the Western Pacific and, in 2013 this country, for the first time, publicly announced its point of view on the concept of the Indo-Pacific. However, till 2015, the term Indo-Pacific appeared for the first time in the Joint Statement on India and Japan Vision 2025: Special Strategic and Global Partnership Working Together for Peace and Prosperity of the Indo-Pacific Region and the World (released 12 December 2015). Bilateral documents between India and Australia, and India and the USA used this term from the second half of 2017 onwards. Although India has been considering ASEAN as the centre of its Look East/Act East Policy, the Opening Statement by Indian Prime Minister at 15th ASEAN-India Summit (14 November 2017) was the first Indian document in the framework of the ASEAN-India summit meetings to officially use the term Indo-Pacific.[45]

Maritime Security in India's Perception of the Indo-Pacific

The term Indo-Pacific also reflects the oceanic-ness of the concept. Therefore, maritime issues in general and maritime security in particular have become key pillars in the concept of the Indo-Pacific. This is clear from examining documents which have been charted out India's own vision in its bilateral relationships with Australia, Japan, and the USA respectively, as also in its approach to the framework of India-ASEAN cooperation.

The presentation titled, 'Geopolitics of the Indo-Pacific Region: Asian Perspectives',[46] delivered by Secretary (East) at the Asian Relations Conference IV in 2013, is the first official document introducing the term Indo-Pacific. In it, maritime security accounts for a priority area of India's cooperation and engagement in the context of the Indian Ocean and the Pacific Ocean. Maritime safety and security is the first of the six priority areas of policy towards the IOR-ARC mechanism. In a wider Indo-Pacific, maritime security continues to dominate India's vision towards the region. In the speech of Secretary Sanjay Singh, India was stated to be 'actively engaged in the process of constructive dialogue on security issues'; and of supporting 'ongoing initiatives in building inclusive security architecture', such as the ASEAN Regional Forum (ARF), the ASEAN Defence Ministers Meeting Plus (ADMM+), and the expanded ASEAN Maritime Forum. The Indian Navy is coordinating with the Navies in the region in the fields of maritime security, such as anti-piracy and disaster management exercises, as well as conducting multi-national maritime exercises focusing on other maritime security issues, including gun running, anti-narcotics, and humanitarian issues.

Maritime security has been the centre of India's bilateral relations with Australia, Japan, and the USA, respectively. India and Japan highlighted 'the need to leverage their excellent bilateral relations to promote trilateral dialogues and cooperation with major partners in the region' to 'seek closer cooperation in such areas as humanitarian assistance and disaster relief, regional connectivity as well as maritime security' in order to 'evolve an open, inclusive, stable and transparent economic, political and security architecture in the Indo-Pacific region'.[47] India and Australia 'underscored the importance of respecting the maritime legal order based on the 1982 United Nations Convention on the Law of the Sea (UNCLOS)', and 'common interests in ensuring maritime security and the safety of sea lines of communication', 'recognised the importance of the freedom of navigation and overflight, unimpeded lawful commerce, as well as resolving maritime disputes by peaceful means, in accordance with international law, including UNCLOS'.[48] India and the USA have committed to 'expand[ing] their maritime security cooperation', 'announced their intention to build on the implementation of their "White Shipping" data sharing arrangement, which enhances collaboration on maritime domain awareness'. The two sides also attached 'importance to the upcoming MALABAR naval exercise' and 'determined to expand their engagements on shared maritime objectives and to explore new exercises'.[49]

In the framework of the trilateral Indo-US-Japan maritime security cooperation, three countries 'agreed to work together to maintain maritime security through greater collaboration, considering the growing convergence of their respective interests in the Indo-Pacific region'.[50] India has 'engaged with Australia, Japan, and the USA in a plurilateral consultation on issues of common interest in the Indo-Pacific region' through 'exploring practical steps to enhance cooperation on issues of common interest, including in the areas of maritime security, proliferation, and counterterrorism' in 'its engagements with Australia, Japan, and the USA under various plurilateral platforms'.[51] At the first Australia-India-Japan-USA Consultations on the Indo-Pacific, held in the Philippines in 12 November 2017, India and its partners ensured freedom of navigation and maritime security, among others, in the Indo-Pacific region.[52]

Maritime security has been an important pillar in India's relations with ASEAN to which India's Act East Policy is shaped around, and its centrality in the regional security architecture of the Indo-Pacific region[53] in the context of Act East Policy as the cornerstone of India's engagement in the Indo-Pacific region.[54] In the first remarks delivered by an Indian leader in the framework of India-ASEAN formal meetings, Prime Minister Narendra Modi mentioned the term Indo-Pacific. He underlined the importance of maritime links established thousands of years ago between India and ASEAN countries, committed to working closely to further strengthen them, and assured ASEAN of India's steady support towards achieving a rules-based regional security architecture that best attests to the region's interests and its peaceful development.[55]

Conclusion

To date, India seems to be the only country among four key founders of the Indo-Pacific concept which has not released a strategy for the initiative. Japan was the first country to introduce the Free and Open Indo-Pacific Strategy in April 2017 as a part of Priority Policy for Development Cooperation FY 2017 (as examined above). The USA announced a Briefing on the Indo-Pacific Strategy by Deputy Assistant Secretary, Bureau of East Asian and Pacific Affairs, Alex N. Wong, on 2 April 2018. By charting in Chapter three: 'A Stable and Prosperous Indo-Pacific' in its 2017 Foreign Policy White Paper (released in November 2017), it is fair to say that Australia has built an Indo-Pacific strategy of its own. However, as the first country officially using the term Indo-Pacific (by Secretary East Sanjay Singh, March 2013), India has followed this idea from the beginning, but cautiously due to the general view that the USA has been leading the idea.

As being called by its name, maritime issues, especially maritime security, has become an important pillar of the Indo-Pacific concept. India, for its part, sees national security and prosperity indispensible to peace, stability, and development in the Indo-Pacific region. Thus, maritime security accounts for a significant position in its relations with important partners such as the founders of the Indo-Pacific concept as well as ASEAN with its centrality in the regional security architecture.

NOTES

1. *The Defence of Australia 1987*, Department of Defence, Canberra: Australian Government Publishing Service, 1987, p. viii.

2. 'Confluence of the Two Seas', Speech by Prime Minister Shinzo Abe, Prime Minister of Japan, in the Parliament of the Republic of India, 22 August 2007, at http://www.mofa.go.jp/region/asia-paci/pmv0708/speech-2.html
3. Kevin Rudd, 'It's time to build an Asia Pacific Community', Address to the Asia Society, Austral Asia Centre, Sydney, 4 June 2008, at https://pmtranscripts.pmc.gov.au/release/transcript-15947
4. Ibid.
5. 'National Security Strategy', The White House, Washington, May 2010, p. 43.
6. 'America's Engagement in the Asia-Pacific', Remarks by Hillary Rodham Clinton, Secretary of State, Kahala Hotel, Honolulu, HI, 28 October 2010, at http://www.state.gov/secretary/rm/2010/10/150141.htm
7. Hillary Rodham Clinton, 'America's Pacific Century', *Foreign Policy* Magazine, 11 October 2011, at http://www.state.gov/secretary/rm/2011/10/175215.htm
8. Hillary Rodham Clinton, Remarks at the Launch of Perth US-Asia Centre, Perth, Australia, 13 November 2012, at https://2009-2017.state.gov/secretary/20092013clinton/rm/2012/11/200455.htm
9. 'Australia's Changing Strategic Circumstances', Minister for Defence, Address to the Australian Strategic Policy Institute (ASPI), 1 August 2012, at http://www.minister.defence.gov.au/2012/08/01/minister-for-defence-to-the-australian-strategic-policy-institute-aspi-australias-changing-strategic-circumstances/
10. 'Australia and Asia', Speech of Mr Peter Varghese, Secretary of the Department of Foreign Affairs and Trade of Australia, at Asia Society Luncheon, 29 April 2013, at http://dfat.gov.au/news/speeches/Pages/asia-society-luncheon-australia-and-asia.aspx
11. Shinzo Abe, 'Asia's Democratic Security Diamond', Project Syndicate, 27 December 2012, at http://www.project-syndicate.org/commentary/a-strategic-alliance-for-japan-and-india-by-shinzo-abe
12. 'Address by Prime Minister Shinzo Abe at the Opening Session of the Sixth Tokyo International Conference on African Development (TICAD VI)', Nairobi, Kenya, 27 August 2016, at http://www.mofa.go.jp/afr/af2/page4e_000496.html
13. Remarks by President Trump at the APEC CEO Summit, Da Nang, Vietnam, issued on 10 November 2017, at https://www.whitehouse.gov/briefings-statements/remarks-president-trump-apec-ceo-summit-da-nang-vietnam/
14. Nirmal Ghosh, 'Free and open Indo-Pacific: a Trump '"legacy"', *The Straits Times*, 11 January 2018, at http://www.straitstimes.com/world/united-states/free-and-open-indo-pacific-a-trump-legacy
15. International Cooperation Bureau (MOFA, Japan), 'Priority Policy for Development Cooperation FY 2017', April 2017, p. 3, at http://www.mofa.go.jp/files/000259285.pdf
16. International Cooperation Bureau (MOFA, Japan), 'Priority Policy for Development Cooperation FY 2017', April 2017, p. 4, at http://www.mofa.go.jp/files/000259285.pdf
17. National Security Strategy of the United States of America, The White House, Washington DC, December 2017, pp. 46–47.
18. Alex N. Wong, 'Briefing on the Indo-Pacific Strategy', Washington, DC, 2 April 2018, at https://www.state.gov/r/pa/prs/ps/2018/04/280134.htm, accessed 4 April 2018.
19. The 2017 Foreign Policy White Paper, Australian Government, Canberra: CanPrint Communications Pty Ltd, p. 1.
20. Ibid., p. 4.
21. Gurpreet S. Khurana, 'Security of Sea Lines: Prospects for India-Japan Cooperation', *Strategic Analysis*, Vol. 31 (1), January 2007, pp.139–153
22. Gurpreet S. Khurana, The 'Indo-Pacific Concept: Restrospect and Prospect', *CIMSEC*, November 14, 2017, at http://cimsec.org/indo-pacific-concept-retrospect-prospect/34710

23. A.G. Thaplival, 'Strategic & Geostrategic Context', in Sharad Tewari, Roshan Khanijo (eds.), *The Indo-Pacific Region: Security Dynamics and Challenges*, New Delhi: Vij Books India Pvt. Ltd, 2016.
24. See also, Shyam Saran, 'Mapping the Indo-Pacific', in *The Indian Express*, 29 October 2011; Rukhmani Gupta, 'India puts the Indo in "Indo-Pacific"', *Asia Times*, 2 December 2011; D. Gnanagurunathan, 'India and the idea of the 'Indo-Pacific', East Asia Forum, 20 October 2012; D. Gnanagurunathan, 'India-Australia in the Indo-Pacific: A blossoming partnership', Viewpoint, Indian Council of World Affairs, 21 December 2012; Priya Chacko, 'India and the Indo-Pacific: An emerging regional vision', IPGRC Policy Brief, Adelaide: November, 2012; 'Indo-Pacific is the new geopolitical reality', Institute for Defence Studies and Analyses, Press Release, 1 November 2012.
25. 'Special Strategic and Global Partnership Working Together for Peace and Prosperity of the Indo-Pacific Region and the World', Joint Statement by India and Japan, Vision 2025, 12 December 2015, at http://www.mea.gov.in/bilateral-documents.htm?dtl/26176/joint+statement+on+india+and+japan+vision+2025+special+strategic+and+global+partnership+working+together+ for+ peace+ and+prosperity+ of+the+ indopacific+region+ and+the +worlddecember +12+2015
26. 'Geopolitics of the Indo-Pacific Region: Asian Perspectives', Valedictory Address by Secretary (East) at the Asian Relations Conference IV, 22 March 2013, at http://www.mea.gov.in/bilateral-documents.htm?dtl/21464/Valedictory+Address+by+Secretary+ East+ at+ the+Asian+Relations+Conference+IV+Geopolitics+of+the+IndoPacific+Region+Asian+Perspectives
27. Ibid.
28. India-Australia-Japan-U.S. Consultations on Indo-Pacific, 12 November 2017, at http://mea.gov.in/press-releases.htm?dtl/29110/IndiaAustraliaJapanUS_Consultations_on_Indo-Pacific_November_12_2017
29. 'Geopolitics of the Indo-Pacific Region: Asian Perspectives', n. 26.
30. 'Special Strategic and Global Partnership Working Together for Peace and Prosperity of the Indo-Pacific Region and the World', n. 25.
31. 'Ensuring Secure Seas: Indian's Maritime Security Strategy', Indian Navy, New Delhi, 10 October 2015, p. 23.
32. 'Special Strategic and Global Partnership Working Together for Peace and Prosperity of the Indo-Pacific Region and the World', n. 25
33. 'Joint Statement on India and Japan Vision 2025, 12 December 2015, at http://www.mea.gov.in/bilateral-documents.htm?dtl/26176/joint+statement+on+india+ and+ japan+vision+2025+special+strategic+and+global+partnership+working+together+for+peace+and+prosperity+of +the+indopacific+region+ and+the+worlddecember+12+2015
34. Opening remarks by the Prime Minister Narendra Modi at the Plenary Session of the India-ASEAN Commemorative Summit, New Delhi, 25 January 2018, at http://www.mea.gov.in/Speeches-Statements.htm?dtl/29390/Opening_remarks_by_the_PM_at_the_ Plenary_Session_of_the_INDIA_ASEAN_Commemorative_Summit_January_25_2018
35. India-Australia-Japan-USA Consultations on Indo-Pacific, 12 November 2017, at http://mea.gov.in/press-releases.htm?dtl/29110/IndiaAustraliaJapanUS _Consultations_on_IndoPacific_November_12_2017
36. Joint Statement, India-USA, 18 July 2005, at http://www.mea.gov.in/Speeches-Statements.htm?dtl/2617/Joint_Statement_IndiaUS
37. Remarks by President Mr. Barack Obama to Members of both Houses of the Indian Parliament in the Central Hall, 8 November 2010, at http://www.mea.gov.in/Speeches-Statements.htm?dtl/823/Remarks_by_President_Mr_Barack_ Obama_to_ Members_ of_both_Houses_of_Parliament_in_the_Central_Hall
38. National Security Strategy of the United States of America, The White House, Washington DC, December 2017, p. 46.

39. Ibid., p. 47.
40. Ibid., p. 50.
41. 'Priority Policy for Development Cooperation FY 2017', International Cooperation Bureau (MOFA, Japan), April 2017, p. 9, at http://www.mofa.go.jp/files/000259285.pdf
42. The 2017 Foreign Policy White Paper, Australian Government, Canberra: CanPrint Communications Pty Ltd, p. 4.
43. Ibid.
44. Australia-India-Japan-U.S. Consultations on the Indo-Pacific, November 12, 2017, http://www.mofa.go.jp/press/release/press4e_001789.html
45. Opening Statement by Prime Minister at 15th ASEAN-India Summit, Manila, 14 November 2017, at http://www.mea.gov.in/Speeches-Statements.htm?dtl/29113/Opening_Statement_by_ Prime_Minister_at_15th_ASEANIndia_Summit_Manila_November_14_2017
46. 'Geopolitics of the Indo-Pacific Region: Asian Perspectives', n. 26.
47. 'Special Strategic and Global Partnership Working Together for Peace and Prosperity of the Indo-Pacific Region and the World', n. 25
48. India-Australia Joint Statement during the State visit of Prime Minister of Australia to India, 10 April 2017, at http://www.mea.gov.in/bilateral-documents.htm?dtl/28367/indiaaustralia+joint+statement+during+the+state+visit+of+prime+minister+of+australia+to+india
49. 'Prosperity Through Partnership', Joint Statement-USA and India, 27 June 2017, at http://www.mea.gov.in/bilateral-documents.htm?dtl/28560/joint+statement++united+states+and+india+prosperity+through+partnership
50. 'Indo-US-Japan Maritime Security', Lok Sabha Unstarred Question No. 525, 2 December 2015, at http://www.mea.gov.in/lok-sabha.htm?dtl/26087/q+no525+indousjapan + maritime+security
51. 'Security Partnership with USA, Japan and Australia', Rajya Sabha Unstarred Question No.1930, 4 January 2018, at http://www.mea.gov.in/rajya-sabha.htm?dtl/29322/question+no1930+security+partnership+with+usa+japan+and+australia
52. Australia-India-Japan-USA Consultations on the Indo-Pacific, 12 November 2017, at http://www.mofa.go.jp/press/release/press4e_001789.html
53. Opening Statement by Indian Prime Minister at 15th ASEAN-India Summit, Manila, November 14, 2017, at http://www.mea.gov.in/Speeches-Statements.htm?dtl/29113/Opening_Statement_by_Prime_Minister_at_15th_ASEANIndia_Summit_Manila_November_14_2017
54. India-Australia-Japan-USA Consultations on Indo-Pacific, 12 November 2017, at http://mea.gov.in/press-releases.htm?dtl/29110/IndiaAustraliaJapanUS_Consultations_on_IndoPacific_November_12_2017
55. Opening Statement by Indian Prime Minister at 15th ASEAN-India Summit, Manila, 14 November 2017, at http://www.mea.gov.in/Speeches-Statements.htm?dtl/29113/Opening_Statement_by_Prime_Minister_at_15th_ASEANIndia_Summit_Manila_November_14_2017

14

Regional Maritime Security and the Roles of Myanmar Navy

Naing Swe Oo

The Myanmar Navy has close contacts with the regional countries to protect terrorism, piracy and armed robbery, drug trafficking, human trafficking, gun running, illegal fishing, the proliferation of weapons of mass destruction, and natural disasters in the Myanmar sea area and contiguous zones. Myanmar cooperates with ASEAN countries as well as international organisations for maritime security. Human trafficking, sea robbery, and piracy are most common threats for regional maritime security. To enhance maritime security in the Bay of Bengal and the Andaman Sea, the Myanmar Navy has conducted Navy to Navy Staff Talks with the Bangladesh Navy once and with the Indian Navy four times. As a result of the talks, the Indian Navy and the Myanmar Navy could conduct four CORPATs since 2013. The Myanmar Navy also participated in the MILAN Multilateral Naval Exercises hosted by the Indian Navy.

Introduction

The changing maritime security scenario in the post-Cold War era is reflected in the transformation of naval doctrines, strategies, and force structures evident in several Indian Ocean navies. There is an increasing focus on combating the common non-traditional threats of the region through naval cooperation. However, maritime safety and security becomes a multi-faceted issue in the realm of non-traditional threats. The Indian Ocean represents an increasingly significant avenue for global trade and, consequently, an arena for global security.

Rising prosperity in Asia, growing dependence on natural resource flows linking producers and consumers across the Middle East, Africa, and Asia, and globalised supply chains and distribution networks are knitting the region ever more closely together by sea. At the same time, emerging problems ranging from piracy and territorial disputes in the regional seas to global environmental pressures on coastal and marine resources pose significant governance challenges for maritime policymakers around the Indian Ocean region (IOR).

Concepts of Maritime Security

The term 'maritime security' can conjure up different meanings to different people and organisations, depending upon their organisational interests, or even political or ideological biases. The US maritime strategy views 'maritime security' in the following terms, consistent with the ideas and the counter terrorism focus of the US National Strategy for Maritime Security:

> The creation and maintenance of security at sea is essential to mitigating threats short of war, including piracy, terrorism, weapons proliferation, drug trafficking, and other illicit activities. Countering these irregular and transnational threats protects our homeland, enhances global stability, and secures freedom of navigation for the benefit of all nations.

Alternative Perspectives on Maritime Security

There are some alternative perspectives on maritime security. These perspectives are arbitrary and nonexclusive. They are interrelated and overlap and, to a certain degree, represent different aspects of the same problem: the effective management of the oceans, and good order upon them. The practical policy and operational responses by states to their maritime security needs usually incorporate aspects of more than one of these approaches. The five perspectives are:

- The security of the sea itself;
- Ocean governance;
- Maritime border protection;
- Military activities at sea; and
- Security regulation of the maritime transportation system

What are the Maritime Security Challenges?

Figure 1: Elements of Maritime Security

Traditional Maritime Security	Non-Traditional Maritime Security	Maritime Safety
Government owned or Military Vessels	Piracy and Armed Robbery against Ships	Safety of Navigation
Threat to/Use of Force	Maritime Terrorism	Design, Construction, Manning, Equipment
War	Trafficking of Drugs	Rules of the Road
	Human Trafficking and Smuggling of Migrants	
	Illegal Trade of Arms	
	IUU Fishing	
	Others	

Source: Zhen Sun, Research Fellow, Centre for International Law, National University of Singapore.

Myanmar as a Bay of Bengal Country

Measured from the mouth of the Naaf River (on the border with Bangladesh) to Kawthaung, the border crossing from Thailand, the Myanmar coastline has a total length of 2,228 kilometers. The Rakhine coastline measures 713 kilometers, the Ayeyarwaddy Delta coastline 437 kilometers, and the Tanintharyi coastline 1,078 kilometers. Myanmar's waters also comprise 852 islands of various sizes. These are distributed in the Bay of Bengal, mostly off the Rakhine coast, south of the Ayeyarwaddy Delta, and form the Myeik archipelago off the Tanintharyi coast. In addition, Myanmar also has sovereignty over the Coco islands that geographically form part of the Andaman and Nicobar Islands archipelago.

India and Myanmar have signed 11 agreements in a range of sectors, including one on maritime security cooperation, to further strengthen their multifaceted partnership during the Indian Prime Minister Narendra Modi's visit to Myanmar last year. The two sides signed an agreement for sharing white shipping information to improve data sharing on non-classified merchant navy ships or cargo ships.

Myanmar is promising to become more active with regard to bilateral and multilateral naval cooperation. For some years, it had participated in the biannual MILAN (Meeting of the Littorals of Bay of Bengal, Andaman, and

Nicobar) exchanges and exercises; but in 2013, Myanmar's navy also embarked on a port call to the Indian mainland, involving a frigate and a corvette for bilateral exercises and patrolling in the southern Bay of Bengal. Malaysia has invited Myanmar to become an observer of the Malacca Strait Patrols (MSP) initiative to combat piracy. This initiative was formed in 2006; it comprises the Malacca Strait Sea Patrol, Eyes in the Sky, and the MSP Intelligence Exchange Group. Thus, over the longer term, Myanmar's navy stands to become more integrated in collaborative efforts to address wider maritime security challenges.

Non-Traditional Maritime Security Issues

Myanmar is also concerned about some non-traditional security challenges in its maritime environment. One relates to the apparent rapid depletion of fish stocks, which is linked to a combination of overfishing and illegal fishing. In this regard, the activities of Thai fishing companies, who already by the late 1980s were keen on acquiring licenses from the (State Peace and Development Council), SPDC-run Myanmar—following the significant exhaustion of Thai marine resources, have been under particular scrutiny. Hundreds of foreign owned offshore fishing vessels seem to have compounded the issue of overfishing in Myanmar's EEZ. Thai companies were also allowed to fish in Myanmar territorial waters for relatively little compensation. Under the nominally civilian government, Myanmar has discontinued some agreements over fishing rights for Thai boats. Myanmar's fishermen have also received a boost by virtue of efforts by the current Thai military government to clean up that country's fishery industry. Other factors have also been contributing to greater earnings, including the global decrease in fuel costs, and the depreciation of the Myanmar currency, the kyat. As a consequence of these factors, the value of fisheries exports has reportedly risen from US $ 40 million in 2003 to US $ 144 million in 2014.

The protection of Myanmar's delineated maritime space is, thus, now more important than ever. Incidents of piracy and armed robbery have, at times, been a source of serious concern for some Southeast Asian governments. In recent years, such incidents have affected numerous vessels in the Bay of Bengal. Although most reported crimes refer to petty theft and robbery, mostly when ships are at anchor off Bangladeshi ports, some incidents have also occurred around Myanmar, often involving Singapore-flagged tugboats. Three such incidents occurred in the Bay of Bengal in 2010, one in 2011, and two in 2014. In the Andaman Sea, the last reported incident happened in 2010, involving a robbery on a Singapore flagged LPG-tanker. In marked contrast to Bangladesh, very few reported robberies have taken place with ships at anchor. Though numbers are relatively low, dealing effectively with piracy and armed robbery is a concern for Myanmar's authorities.

Myanmar cooperates with ASEAN countries as well as international organisations for maritime security. The ninth ASEAN Navy Chiefs' Meeting was held in Nay Pyi Taw on 19–22 August, 2015. The main theme of the meeting was 'Fostering ASEAN Naval Team Work in Regional Maritime Security'. The meeting passed firm resolutions on the ANCM Road Map, HADR SOP, and ASEAN Multilateral Naval Exercise to support the ASEAN Political and Security Community in making the theme 'ASEAN Integration 2015' a great success.

The Myanmar Navy has established a Maritime Rescue Coordination Centre (Ayeyarwady MRCC) at the Ayeyarwady Regional Naval Command. Also signed and ratified is the Regional Cooperation Agreement on Combating Piracy and Armed Robbery Against Ships in Asia (ReCAAP), established in Singapore. A focal point was also established in the Ministry of Home Affairs. An officer of the Myanmar Navy was attached to the Information Fusion Centre (IFC) situated at the Command and Control Centre (C2 Centre) in the Singapore Navy in February 2014 as an International Liaison Officer (ILO). Myanmar regularly sends representatives to attend workshop and meetings on maritime security. As a part of the National Search and Rescue Committee, the Myanmar Navy participates in the Maritime Rescue Coordination Centre (MRCC).

After the construction of Sittwe and Kyaukphyu deep sea ports, there will be many ships calling at these ports. Due to the significant increase of maritime trade, the challenges and threats to maritime security will become more complex and increase. The Myanmar Navy has a Direct Communication Link (DCL) and Hot Line with the neighbouring navies for maritime security. To conduct maritime security effectively and efficiently, the Myanmar Navy is enhancing cooperation in intelligence, information sharing, other maritime challenges and threats, including search and rescue.

To enhance maritime security in the Bay of Bengal and Andaman Sea, the Myanmar Navy has conducted Navy to Navy Staff Talks with the Bangladesh Navy for one time, with Indian Navy for four times. Moreover, the Myanmar

Navy has conducted Navy to Navy Talks with Royal Thai Navy four times and with Malaysian Navy twice. Regular talks between neighboring countries and regional countries could assist in the enhancement of maritime security. As the result of the Talks, the Indian Navy and the Myanmar Navy have conducted four Coordinated Patrols (CORPATs) since 2013. Moreover, the Myanmar Navy is arranging to be able to sign in the CORAT SOPs between the Bangladesh Navy and the Royal Thai Navy to conduct the CORPAT.

The Myanmar Navy has participated in MILAN exercises hosted by Indian Navy since 2006. MILAN is an effective platform for social, cultural, and professional interaction and the promotion of camaraderie, for maritime cooperation and inter-operability which is very useful during humanitarian missions. The 10th edition of MILAN 2018 exercise was held by the Andaman and Nicobar Command from March 6–13. It was the largest exercise since the beginning. 20 Ships from 11 countries participated in MILAN 2018. Myanmar sent an indigenously built Guided Missiles Frigate, the *UMS King Sin Phyu Sin* (F14) and Offshore patrol vessel *UMS Inlay* (54) to the exercise. After the exercise, Myanmar Naval vessels will conduct CORPAT with Indian Naval vessels.

Regional Situation: The Perspective of Myanmar

Human trafficking, sea robbery, and piracy are the most common threats for regional maritime security. However, maritime security is developing since the ASEAN and regional countries are cooperating. The ASEAN navies are coordinating with law enforcement agencies and ASEAN plus countries to enhance capacity building to implement ASEAN Political and Security Community of ASEAN Integration 2015.

The Myanmar government released a formal reaction to the award made by the Arbitral Tribunal relating to the South China Sea, on 13 July 2016. It mentioned that although Myanmar is not a claimant state, it attaches great importance to developments in the South China Sea. It supports all endeavours to promote a peaceful resolution of disputes through friendly consultations and negotiations in accordance with universally recognised principles of international law, including the 1982 UNCLOS. Myanmar has urged all parties to exercise restraint. Myanmar is going to coordinate with ASEAN countries and China to solve the disputes through international laws and negotiations by peaceful means.

Human Trafficking at Sea

Myanmar waters are adjacent to the Bay of Bengal and the Andaman Sea. Illegal migrants and human trafficking are the maritime threats encountered in geographically important Myanmar waters. Human trafficking affects every country of the world, either as countries of origin, transit, or destination. It is important to prevent the human trafficking; however, providing humanitarian assistance at sea is also needed.

Myanmar is not the original country of boat people; it is just a transit country. However, Myanmar is giving immediate assistance to illegal migrants at sea. The Myanmar Navy has searched and rescued 1047 victims of human trafficking from 2012 to 2015. Myanmar is now providing humanitarian assistance to boat people, and repatriating them to their original country. The Myanmar Navy is actively cooperating with the ASEAN navies in providing humanitarian assistance, and preventing the illegal migration at sea.

Conclusion

India's rising engagement with the East is a prominent feature of its expanding maritime character, inherited from its rich maritime culture. Myanmar cooperates with ASEAN countries as well as the international community and countries like India for maritime security. Sharing not only future prosperity but also regional security cooperation is important for ASEAN and India. The future of the security architecture in the Indo-Pacific region will be characterised by a mutual understanding of the circumstantial and structural roots of the gap between the expectations of regional players, the ASEAN community in particular, and India's capabilities.

REFERENCES

Christian Bueger, 'What is Maritime Security?' *Marine Policy*, Vol. 53, March 2015, pp. 159-164.

David Michel and Russell Sticklor, (eds.), *Indian Ocean Rising: Maritime Security and Policy Challenges*, Washington: Stimson, 2012

Maung Aung Myoe, 'Myanmar's Maritime Challenges and Priorities', in Joshua H. Ho and Sm Bateman (eds.) *Maritime Challenges and Priorities in Asia: Implications for Regional Security*, London: Routledge, 2012

Shishir Upadhyaya, 'Maritime security cooperation in the Indian Ocean Region: The role of the Indian Navy', *Australian Journal of Maritime and Ocean Affairs*, Vol. 6(4), 2014, pp 173–190

15

Maritime Connectivity & Security in the Indo-Pacific

Dhruva Jaishankar

Thank you for the kind invitation to address this august gathering in Bhubaneswar today, and my congratulations to Ambassador Lalit Mansingh and his colleagues at the Kalinga International Foundation for this wonderful new initiative.

There are perhaps few better places than Odisha to discuss India's growing role in world affairs. After all, this was the historical site of the Mauryan Emperor Ashoka's war against the Kalingas. It was after that conflict that Ashoka adopted his *dhamma*—his faith—grounded in Buddhism. Edicts to spread his philosophy were commissioned and displayed as far as today's Afghanistan and Nepal, and as far south as Karnataka, and they appeared in several languages, including Greek and Aramaic. Contrary to popular myth, these were not declarations of pacifism. Rather, Ashoka's edicts called for just and limited warfare; but they also elaborated upon norms regarding how to manage conflict. He made startling claims, not just about sending missionaries but about links across the Hellensitic world, as far as today's Greece and Libya. Indeed, Ashoka's efforts may represent the first recorded attempt in history at establishing a liberal international order. In many ways, India's recorded engagements with the world can be traced to this region.

Odisha is also proof that economics and security have always been deeply intertwined in Asia and the Indian Ocean region. European traders were initially drawn to India between the 15th and 18th centuries by cotton textile exports to finance the spice trade from Southeast Asia. The likes of Portugal and England established trading outposts—factories—along the east coast of India. The first English outpost was in Masulipatnam in Andhra Pradesh, but their presence expanded to include such places as Pipili and Hariharpur in today's Odisha, not very far from Bhubaneswar. The English and other Europeans tapped into existing networks established by Indian traders with Southeast Asia. The first East India Company vessel that arrived in Aceh found Bengali, Gujarati, and Malabari traders already present. Pre-existing trade networks extended across a sizeable Indo-Pacific region, from Formosa to Vietnam, from Siam to Sumatra, from Malacca to the Malabar, and from Gujarat to Hormuz.

Today, we are rediscovering these natural commercial, cultural, and political links, and the Indian Ocean has grown in relative importance. It is now a major conduit for sea borne international trade—which has seen a four-fold increase since 1970—between the largest centres of economic activity in the Pacific and on both sides of the Atlantic Ocean. Energy flows are particularly important, with about 40 per cent of world oil passing through strategic chokepoints in and out of the Indian Ocean. The Ocean is also a valuable source of natural resources, accounting for 15 per cent of the world's fishing and significant mineral resources. This region is also important in its own right, home to two billion people in some of the fastest growing parts of the world: Southeast and South Asia, East and South Africa, and West Asia.

However, there are also plenty of challenges, including natural and humanitarian disasters. Two of the most devastating natural disasters in recent decades were in the Indian Ocean: the 2004 Indian Ocean tsunami, which killed 228,000 people, and Cyclone Nargis in Myanmar which killed about 138,000. Humanitarian Assistance and Disaster Relief (HADR) operations have been required around the region, from Yemen to Sri Lanka, and the Maldives to Bangladesh. Piracy in the Indian Ocean has been among the many other threats, and led to about US $6 billion in annual losses to the shipping industry between 2010 and 2012. And, there are growing concerns about security competition increasing exponentially, with the greater activity of China's People's Liberation Army Navy (PLA-N) and its investment in potentially 'dual use' port infrastructure—infrastructure that can be used for both civilian and military purposes—in such places as Djibouti, Gwadar, Hambantota, Kyaukpyu, and the Maldives.

India has consequently started to pay greater attention to the Indian Ocean. In decades past, there were famously attempts at creating a zone of peace, while the 1980s saw a considerable amount of Indian interventionism and gunboat diplomacy in the region, including in Sri Lanka and the Maldives. But Indian efforts at regional leadership and engagement have received an added impetus over the past decade, in response to some of these new developments. The clearest articulation of India's Indian Ocean policy was, perhaps, made by Prime Minister Narendra Modi in a speech in Mauritius in 2015. Explicitly and implicitly, he outlined a number of objectives, including securing the Indian Ocean against both non-state actors and growing naval competition, improving HADR responses, ensuring the equitable harnessing of natural resources, and taking fuller advantage of the economic opportunities on offer.

Consequently, we have seen India assume a larger role as a security provider in the Indian Ocean region. These include, efforts at building capacity, improving interoperability, and exchanging information with a number of security partners, not least the USA, Japan, and Australia, but also several countries in Southeast and South Asia, the Gulf, and Africa. With the more capable navies of the region, India's cooperation on anti-submarine warfare (ASW) and maritime domain awareness (MDA) have increased in recent years. India has entered into or operationalised logistics agreements with the USA, France, and Singapore, giving its navy greater reach. It provides equipment and technical support to a number of armed forces, including coast guard vessels to Mauritius, aircraft to Seychelles, and assistance to Myanmar. It conducts joint patrols, and has navy-to-navy contacts with Indonesia and Thailand. India trains pilots of Sukhoi aircraft and Kilo-class submariners from Vietnam. It has bilateral MDA arrangements with Sri Lanka and the Maldives that have persisted despite political differences. And, it has entered into a host of white shipping arrangements, allowing India to better monitor military activity and illicit shipping.

The Indian Navy's operational tempo has also increased. This extends to disaster relief following cyclones in Sri Lanka, Bangladesh, and Myanmar, a water crisis in the Maldives, and civil conflict in Yemen. The Navy's presence in Southeast Asia and the Western Pacific has also grown: in 2017, an Indian vessel was east of the Malacca Strait for over half of the year. The MILAN naval exercise is an Indian-hosted multilateral effort to build confidence and cooperation in the region. For many years, India has been engaged in counter-piracy and counter-smuggling operations in the Gulf of Aden and the western

Indian Ocean. Year-round deployments in several zones are now a reality, and the acquisition of maritime surveillance aircraft has enhanced India's reconnaissance capabilities across the Indian Ocean while bringing down operational costs.

Of course, much more needs to be done. India's resources are still limited, and the naval budget in particular requires revisiting, given the relative importance of the maritime domain. Another area of urgent attention concerns maritime connectivity and infrastructure, including increased port capacity and restrictive cabotage policies. Despite recent growth, all of India's ports still move only about one-third the number of containers as Singapore. But, despite these limitations, which are being addressed, efforts are already underway for India to play a bigger role in the Indian and Pacific Oceans from a political, economic, and security perspective.

The history of Odisha has a cautionary tale for us. As long as the Indian Ocean remained an open and competitive space, India was relatively secure. To punish the Portuguese for piracy, the Mughals would simply retaliate by limiting their activity on land, thus benefiting their competitors: the French, English, Dutch, and Danes. But, as soon as England managed to establish an effective monopoly of maritime trade in the Indian Ocean following the Carnatic Wars with the French, it was able to translate its predominance to the control of the land. In just a few decades from the 1750s, British presence in India went from a few small garrisons to the direct governance and administrative control of Bengal, Bihar, and several other regions. If there is a lesson to be drawn from this history it is that India today cannot afford to be complacent about the growing maritime competition in the Indian Ocean. Recognising the importance of the Indo-Pacific by expanding strategic horizons, prioritising the maritime sphere, and playing a role in the balance of power is, therefore, necessary. This will require further investments in securing the Indian Ocean, improving connectivity and economic inter-linkages, and deepening security partnerships with a variety of actors who share similar concerns.

16

Closing Remarks

R.K. Dhowan

In recent years, under the leadership of the Honourable Prime Minister Narendra Modi, there have been a series of initiatives for development in the maritime domain, alongwith the quest to harness the Blue Economy. These initiatives, as well as the transition from the Look East to the Act East Policy, are pointers to indicate that India has once again turned towards the seas, and is destined to emerge as a resurgent maritime nation.

The Bay of Bengal is the largest bay in the World, with seven countries located on its rim. The Andaman and Nicobar Islands occupy a central position in the Bay. As a part of the Island Development Plan and the initiatives of the Act East Policy it is intended to enhance the port and tourism infrastructure in the Islands. This would serve to enhance seaborne connectivity between the ports in the Islands and the ASEAN, and promote cruise tourism.

The Government has launched the ambitious Sagarmala project which is a port led development initiative based on four pillars: port modernisation, connectivity, port led industrialisation, and coastal community development. The Development of Port infrastructure on the East coast of India and in the Andaman & Nicobar Islands would enhance seaborne connectivity, and open up coastal shipping routes between India and our littoral neighbours in the East, including ASEAN.

The Indo-Pacific has emerged as a contiguous maritime space, and we need to analyse the connectivity options such as the BRI, the North South Transport Corridor, the Asia Africa Growth Corridor, Project MAUSAM, the open oceans strategy, and the SAGAR concept as well as existing maritime structures such as the Indian Ocean Naval Symposium (IONS) and the Western Pacific Naval Symposium (WPNS) to examine areas of common concern and provide synergy to enhance maritime cooperation across the Indo-Pacific Region.

India and ASEAN are maritime neighbours who have extended their hands across the seas for maritime cooperation. In order to fully implement Prime Minister Modi's vision of SAGAR, which is security and growth for all in the region, we need to draw up a comprehensive roadmap for maritime security and cooperation with a whole of Government approach for the region. This would open up India's Act East Policy for maritime cooperation and harness the Blue Economy, which I would like to term as a partnership for prosperity in the maritime domain.

The seas around us are gaining new found importance as each day goes by, and there is no doubt that the current century is the century of the Seas. Networking among navies and maritime partnerships between countries of the region needs to be strengthened to the ensure peace, stability, and prosperity in the Indo-Pacific region.

REGIONAL CONNECTIVITY

17

Regional Connectivity and Integration

A.S. Lamba

The Geostrategic Convergence of Northeast

If India is to rise to its aspirations as well as the expectations of its neighbours as a credible regional security provider, the connectivity of the North East with the world will remain the primary and critical issue for action. This will require a comprehensive approach that addresses both the sensitive security environment with innumerable militant groups operating in the region, and the infrastructural connectivity that facilitates or restricts the operational movements of our own security forces even as they facilitate the insurgent groups.

Situated in a tough geopolitical neighbourhood, the greatest challenge for India even after seven decades of Independence is that of connectivity and security across more than three million square kilometres of its North Eastern region. By aligning India's Act East Policy with ASEAN members and beyond to East Asia, India needs to stabilise this geo-strategic space which stretches from Asia to the Indo Pacific region.

The turbulent political and security environment over several decades has led to movements of secession, and related threats to the territorial sovereignty and integrity of India as also other States in India's neighborhood. Militancy as well as the militarisation of the developing countries in the region have left it far behind in infrastructure, economic development, and industrialisation, despite decades of government programmes and schemes.

Regional connectivity as a concept has never emerged as a dominant narrative for India and its neighboring countries; neither has it been even prioritized seriously as a game changer with serious implications in the spheres of trade as well as regional integration. The lack of infrastructure, development, and trade linkages between India's own States or with regional countries have never progressed beyond being small scale, and man moved goods have remained minimal.

The Act East Policy

Briefly, India's Act East Policy enunciated by Prime Minister Narendra Modi at the East Asia Summit in Myanmar in November 2014, envisioned a major focus on the immediate and extended neighborhood in the Asia-Pacific region, drawing political, strategic and cultural dimensions alongside the setting up of institutional mechanisms for dialogue and cooperation.

With the overarching objective of the Act East Policy being to promote economic cooperation, cultural ties, as well as develop strategic relationships with countries in the Asia-Pacific region, this policy has warranted continuous engagement at the bilateral, regional, and multilateral levels that necessitates enhanced connectivity to the States of the North Eastern Region.

The high-level visits by India's President, Vice President, and Prime Minister to nine of the 10 ASEAN states, and the participation of ASEAN heads of State in India's Republic Day Parade this year (2018) has imparted greater vigor to India's ties with ASEAN. This policy has made engagement comprehensive, encompassing economic, security, strategic, political, counterterrorism, and defense collaboration that will witness a new dynamism.

New Initiatives for Connectivity

The connectivity strategy for the North-Eastern region is impelled by a vision of an Asian century and, within that, new and innovative dimensions as India and ASEAN get integrated closely for prosperity through an intricate network of rail, road, air, and maritime links.

India's major projects in this region include the Kaladan Multi-Modal Transit Transport Project between India and Myanmar which gives access to sea ports in Bangladesh to link the North East to South East Asian countries, and also to mainland India; the India-Myanmar-Thailand Trilateral Highway Project; and the Rhi-Tiddim Road Project as part of the increasing cooperation between North East India and the ASEAN region.

India has also helped Myanmar in completing 160 km of the Tamu-Kalewa-Kalemyo sector of the proposed Trilateral Highway that seeks to link India, Myanmar, and Thailand. By pursuing the Mekong-India Economic Corridor (MIEC) project, India seeks to get access to the CMLV countries: Cambodia, Myanmar, Laos, and Vietnam. The BCIM economic corridor highway will link Kolkata in India to Kunming in the Yunnan province of China.

Challenges

The perception of India in the 21st century as a regional power and player will swing upon India's strength to integrate the North East States within the country, and with its north eastern neighbours, particularly in the context of the challenges posed from a belligerent and assertive China that seeks to dominate the region

India's North East is in a tough geopolitical neighbourhood where major voids in road, rail, and waterways connectivity have, for several decades, failed connectivity and integration; in fact, this has blocked India's strategic and economic ambitions even as China has made this region its immediate neighbourhood. While it is true that the terrain, ridden by mountains, and hills, rivers, thick forestation, and undergrowth have been major factors complicating the building of infrastructure and connectivity, any justification on the part of agencies responsible for extreme delays and the inability to use funds effectively signals a major failure on the part of the Centre and State governments.

Bangladesh and Myanmar are the only two options for India, if India wishes to connect the East via the Indian Northeast Region (NER). However, both these countries suffer from several problems which makes it difficult for India to pave the way through these countries and connect to ASEAN and rest of Asia.

Terrorism is rising sharply in the region. It is being supported by major groups such as ISIS and Al Qaeda. This new and significant threat to development needs to be tackled not just by India but collectively by our partners in the immediate and extended neighbourhood as well.

The Way Forward

Regional connectivity can address both the security and economic challenges as this region is interdependent for its growth and the exploitation of its full potential.

Development in the North East has been closely impacted by the security situation in the region. While economic and infrastructural enhancement is imperative, security challenges will need to be addressed simultaneously as a part of the security policies of the individual countries as well as by a regional joint strategy agreed upon by these partners. Militant and terrorist groups in the region must be prevented by respective governments from making sanctuaries in their States with immunity so as not to raise security threats and challenges for any of the neighbours. Closer cooperation in combating terrorism, collaborating for peace and stability in the region, and the promotion of maritime security based on international norms and laws must be pursued.

A Coordination Forum for the Development of the North East is being set up to focus on strategic projects such as connectivity and road network development, electricity and disaster management, with representation from the northeastern states of Arunachal Pradesh, Assam, Manipur, Meghalaya, Mizoram, Nagaland, Sikkim, and Tripura. This must be given the required impetus to make it a reality. The Geostrategic Convergence of the Northeast has led to a profound realisation of the prosperity that this will bring to South Asia and Southeast Asia.

Regional connectivity is, therefore, critical to the comprehensive integration of this region. Events such as the Northeast Development summit, recently held at Imphal by India's President Ram Nath Kovind, reflects the priority being given to this need. President Kovind emphasised the continuum between South Asia and Southeast Asia, and that to explore the potential of the region has been at the heart of the Indian imagination. It is hoped that the summit will result in actionable decisions regarding the Northeast's development.

18

Challenges of Regional Connectivity: Focus on BIMSTEC

Rajiv Bhatia

Introduction

South Asia and Southeast Asia have been linked through a constant exchange of peoples, goods, ideas, philosophies, arts, and customs through millennia. In the contemporary period, the two regions existed in relative isolation until India's policy consciously turned eastwards in the early 1990s. From the Look East Policy through the launch of India's strategic partnership with ASEAN to the adoption of the Act East Policy, India—the largest South Asian country—has connected increasingly better with Southeast Asia.

Nevertheless, the two regions needed a common platform, a shared regional grouping. This was established in June 1997. Today, BIMSTEC is composed of five South Asian countries (India, Bangladesh, Sri Lanka, Nepal and Bhutan), and two Southeast Asian countries (Myanmar and Thailand). It aims to secure 'rapid economic development' and accelerate 'the economic growth and social progresses' of the sub-region.

The 20-year journey of BIMSTEC presents a mixed picture, raising some questions: where does it stand today? What has it achieved? And what do we need to do together to make it fulfil its mission more effectively?

BIMSTEC @ 20

The achievements of BIMSTEC have been modest: they include three Summits; 15 Ministerials; a few development projects relating to transport logistics and infrastructure; limited progress in energy cooperation, public health, and counter terrorism; the adoption of a Framework Agreement on FTA—but no FTA as yet.

The year October 2016–October 2017 showed a new promise: the BIMSTEC Retreat; Outreach Meeting with BRICS leaders (in the backdrop of a stalled SAARC); the Kathmandu Ministerial; a new Secretary General; and the holding of a major Disaster Management Exercise in Delhi. Between November 2017–March 2018, the Fourth summit was deferred; the BIMSTEC was impacted by political developments such as the Rohingya issue, the Nepal elections; and recent happenings in Sri Lanka, Myanmar and Thailand. The 'China shadow' was also relevant.

The BIMSTEC has remained underdeveloped due to a blend of reasons: ambivalence and deficit in political commitment; inadequate financial resources; the earlier absence of a Secretariat and now a weak Secretariat; attention and energy dispersed on too many sectors; and below par engagement of Business and People-to-People linkages.

What should be done?

- Institutional reform: Annual Summit; Annual Ministerial; strengthen Secretariat and give it a sizable budget; and invite three CLMV countries as Observers initially and as full members later.
- Policy reform:
  - Assign to BIMSTEC a special priority in the Indo-Pacific security and development architecture
  - Engage Japan more closely with the rejuvenation of BIMSTEC
  - Focus on building the 'Bay of Bengal Community'
- Sectoral Thrusts:
  - Conclude FTA and other trade promotion and expansion measures
  - Increase power trade and energy cooperation
  - Strengthen physical infrastructure linkages, and especially complete pending projects speedily
  - People-to-People linkages (culture, education, tourism, etc.)—expand the role of 'Third Space'
  - Enhance and innovate Business-to-Business communication, travel, links and cooperation

- Build BIMSTEC brand by expanding the arc of public awareness
- Concentrate on the role of India's North East as a central theatre for BIMSTEC

Conclusion

- Holding of the fourth summit ASAP is the principal priority now.
- Otherwise, rejuvenation will be still-born.
- The need of the hour is to transform a grouping of mere governments into a community of governments at different levels (ranging from federal to local), business, civil society, strategic community, and people at large.

19

Shared Values, Common Destiny—ASEAN-India Relations: A View from Malaysia*

Rizal Abdul Kadir

Introduction

When ASEAN and India celebrated 25 years of their Dialogue Relations on 25 January 2018, the cornerstone of the event was the Delhi Declaration. The theme of the Commemorative Summit, 'Shared Values, Common Destiny', inspired the vision of Prime Minister Shri Narendra Modi on the ASEAN-India partnership. In an article entitled 'ASEAN-India: Shared values, common destiny' carried by many news agencies, Prime Minister Modi wrote at length on the journey and aspirations of ASEAN-India relations.[1] As ASEAN marches towards its vision of ASEAN 2025, ASEAN envisions a Community where the Dialogue Partners have an integral role in 'Forging Ahead Together.'[2]

This paper offers an introductory overview of ASEAN-India relations. An attempt has also been made to identify some of the key issues in ASEAN-India relations. However, in-depth research into issues arising will require separate inquiry, and it is hoped that the discussion to follow will trigger debate and necessary further research. Accordingly, this paper is divided into three main parts: (i) the discussion which takes stock of ASEAN-India relations; (ii) an examination of the claims of asymmetries in the engagement; and (iii) a

* All weblinks accessible as of 14 March 2018. This paper has been prepared in conjunction with the PURBASA Conference in Bhubaneswar, India, 16–18 March 2018 by Dr Rizal Abdul Kadir, Deputy Director-General, Maritime Institute of Malaysia, and Adjunct Professor, National Defence University of Malaysia. All views expressed in this paper are entirely the author's own based on information in the public domain.

consideration of the critical success factors needed to strengthen ASEAN-India relations.

ASEAN-India Relations: Past and Present

It may be said that India substantiated its formal interest in ASEAN from its Look East Policy which was initiated by the government of India then led by Prime Minister Narashima Rao.[3] More generally, India's interest to its east may have started much earlier. Some observers consider that the eastward engagement of India actually evolved in four different waves over the centuries, with its Look East Policy of the 1990s constituting the fourth wave.[4]

Nevertheless, in the context of ASEAN-India relations, India's Look East policy evolved through sectoral dialogue.[5] In 1994, ASEAN and India established a Joint Sectoral Cooperation Committee to progress their dialogue relations.[6] During the first meeting of the Joint Sectoral Cooperation Committee in 1994, ASEAN-India agreed to strengthen cooperation in trade, investment, tourism, and science and technology.[7] In testimony of the seriousness to move forward ASEAN-India relations and cooperation in these areas, the same meeting adopted the Rules of Procedure and Terms of Reference of the ASEAN-India Joint Sectoral Cooperation Committee. The role of this committee was to facilitate ASEAN-India sectoral dialogue relations. The same first meeting of the Joint Sectoral Cooperation Committee in 1994 mentioned that activities would be funded by an ASEAN-India Fund. Notably, the meeting highlighted that the India's Technical and Economic Cooperation (ITEC) Programme would be the mechanism whereby India would work with ASEAN on specific projects, and where India would also provide training modules in specified areas of interest to ASEAN.[8]

By 1995, the pace of ASEAN-India relations intensified. India hosted the second meeting of the ASEAN-India Joint Sectoral Cooperation Committee in February 1995. A key take-away from this second meeting was the acknowledgement of the need for institutional mechanisms, with specific proposals identified in the Joint Press Release from the second meeting of the ASEAN-India Joint Sectoral Cooperation Committee.[9] To bolster relations, India announced at the second meeting a second contribution of approximately US$ 190,000.00 to support the intended activities in the agreed areas of cooperation, namely trade, investment, tourism, and science and technology.[10]

These developments paved the way for an upgradation of the ASEAN-India partnership.

By December 1995, ASEAN-India dialogue relations evolved from the initial level of sectoral dialogue partnership into a full dialogue partnership.[11] Effectively, this signalled a new beginning; it meant that ASEAN-India relations could go beyond trade, investment, tourism, and science and technology. ASEAN-India relations continued to flourish and, within a decade of the initial sectoral dialogue partnership, the first ASEAN-India Summit was held in 2002 in Phnom Penh, Cambodia.[12]

At the 13th ASEAN-India Summit held in Kuala Lumpur on 21 November 2015, India introduced its Act East Policy to ASEAN Leaders. ASEAN Leaders warmly welcomed this Act East Policy; noting that the policy could complement the community building efforts of ASEAN.[13] As a signal of the strategic importance placed by India on its relations with ASEAN, and a sign by India of a long-term commitment and an emphasis on connectivity with the Southeast Asian region, India announced at this 13th ASEAN Summit a Line of Credit of US$ 1 Billion for projects that supported physical and digital connectivity between India and ASEAN; India further committed INR 500 crore for a Project Development Fund to develop manufacturing hubs in Cambodia, Laos, Myanmar, and Vietnam.[14]

ASEAN Leaders encouraged India to work with ASEAN to realise the vision and goals outlined in the 136 page document entitled ASEAN 2025: Forging Ahead Together.[15] At a glance, with an emphasis on building an ASEAN Community, ASEAN 2025 is to be more action-oriented with strategic measures in place to realise the targets identified.[16] As a full dialogue partner of ASEAN, ASEAN partners are expected to have, and benefit from, India's integral role in building, strengthening, and sustaining an ASEAN Community.[17]

However, there is a broader issue underpinning the outlook of ASEAN-India relations. Some observers have described India as being ambivalent towards ASEAN during the early days of ASEAN.[18] Others feel that there is also a history of phases of discord and divergence in political understanding between India and ASEAN.[19] The question that, therefore, arises is: how then can ASEAN 2025 fit in with the Act East Policy of India? Before attempting to answer this question, it is relevant to understand why the outlook of India towards Southeast Asia, historically, has at best, been cautiously optimistic.

The initial apprehension of India towards ASEAN may have largely been linked to the existence and purpose of the now practically defunct entity known as the Southeast Asia Treaty Organisation, or SEATO. When SEATO was disbanded in 1977, observers noticed that initial misgivings by India towards ASEAN dissipated.[20] Quite significantly too, not all 10 Southeast Asian States of ASEAN were members of SEATO. However, a key driver in the shift in India's attitude towards ASEAN may be attributed to the disintegration of the former Soviet Union after which India needed new markets to develop its own economy.[21] If there is a lesson for ASEAN and other interested parties from the experience with SEATO, it may be this: organisations created exclusively, or even predominantly, for security interests may not only trigger suspicion but cause important parties to shy away at best, and at worst work against, the interests of such organisations.

Considering the historical outlook of India towards Southeast Asia in particular, the Look East Policy, and subsequently the Act East Policy of India, are two critical instruments employed by India to re-engage with States to its east. Undoubtedly, for India-ASEAN relations, the two instruments provide India with a fresh approach towards States in Southeast Asia. Critics might consider the Look East Policy and Act East Policy different only in nomenclature. Yet, the issue of continuity may not only be undeniable but prudent too. Indeed, perhaps because of the experience of India under its Look East Policy, some observers consider the Act East Policy has been able to go into areas well beyond what the Look East Policy achieved in over more than two decades.[22] An important new dimension in ASEAN-India relations is connectivity,[23] and its primacy in the Act East Policy.[24] On a broader plane, it is quite significant to note that the Act East Policy has enabled India to have multi-faced relations with ASEAN in not only economic and security interests, but also in culture and commerce as well as strategic and political considerations.[25]

The Future of ASEAN-India Relations

Returning to the question posed earlier: how can ASEAN 2025 possibly fit in with the Act East Policy of India? The shorter answer would be: ASEAN 2025 fits nicely into the Act East Policy—on paper at least. Indeed, in marking 25 years of ASEAN-India Dialogue Relations, the leaders of ASEAN and India made the relationship between ASEAN 2025 and the Act East Policy clear through the Delhi Declaration.[26] With the text of the Declaration prepared under the theme 'Shared Values, Common Destiny', its contents show a clear understanding and commitment from India on what is to be done to help realise ASEAN 2025.

However, implementing the Act East policy is not likely to be as straightforward. Take, for example, commitments in the Delhi Declaration concerning Political and Security Cooperation, particularly those concerning maritime safety and security, and freedom of navigation. This would relate primarily to the South China Sea, in the context of ASEAN interests. It will be interesting to see how India engages ASEAN on this subject. India will likely tread carefully on issues impacting the maritime domain in Southeast Asia, as is evidenced by clarification triggered by confusion concerning the purported US-India joint patrols in the South China Sea.[27] Not surprisingly, India would not want to provoke China on matters concerning the South China Sea because, despite a long-standing India-China border dispute, India would want to protect its substantial economic interests with China.[28] However, separate reports claim that the trade with ASEAN, as a whole, is larger.[29] India-China have a 'thousand year relationship'.[30] But, how 25 years of ASEAN-India Dialogue will shape India-China relations remains to be seen. One has to be mindful of the fact that India-China relations bear directly on ASEAN interests, notably those concerning the South China Sea.

Keeping in mind contemporary geopolitical realities in Southeast Asia, concrete steps are pivotal to enhancing ASEAN-India relations. Thus, it is significant that the Delhi Declaration reflected an agreement to 'continue to exert efforts and cooperate towards the full, effective and timely implementation' of the 2016–2020 Plan of Action[31]—an integral precursor for ASEAN-India relations towards ASEAN 2025. The 2016–2020 Plan of Action is the 3rd Plan of Action in ASEAN-India relations.[32] This current document in ASEAN-India relations maps out priorities and measures complementing the 3 Community Blueprints for ASEAN 2025.[33] India reports that, to-date, 70 of the 130 activities identified in the 3rd Plan of Action have been implemented.[34] The importance of the 3rd Plan of Action is underscored by ASEAN and India, having also finalised a list of priority areas for the period of 2016–2018.[35] Considering these contemporary developments in ASEAN-India relations, it is interesting to highlight views that it is ASEAN that is reaching out to India as a potential strategic counterweight to China.[36] In fact, however, China is also a strategic partner of ASEAN. More importantly, the aspirations of ASEAN for its relations with India and China are the same: to have a region that is stable, peaceful, and prosperous.[37] The difference however, lies not in the approach of ASEAN towards India or China; rather, it is in the pace of engagement between India-ASEAN and China-ASEAN relations.[38]

Asymmetries in ASEAN-India Relations

ASEAN 2025 is a vision with a roadmap that charts the path for ASEAN Community building until the year 2025.[39] The essence of ASEAN 2025 is for an inclusive Community that is politically cohesive, economically integrated, and socially responsible. The results of ASEAN 2025, therefore, are to benefit primarily the peoples of ASEAN, each Member State, and ASEAN as an entity. But, ASEAN is clear that it neither should, nor wants, to journey alone towards 2025. Because of this realisation, ASEAN 2025 sets out a role—expectations—for the partners of ASEAN.[40]

It is in this context that ASEAN-India relations now come under the microscope.

Even critics cannot deny the expanding ASEAN-India engagement. But the issue for present consideration is this: is there any truth in contentions that there continue to be asymmetries in the expanding engagement?[41] Observers note that ASEAN-India economic relations in particular have not flourished at the same pace as their political relations.[42] It is also said that there is a perception among ASEAN members that India has taken a protectionist stance; and that, in turn, the protectionist outlook limits the possibilities of the role India may play within the ASEAN region.[43] Looking at the 137th Report by the Parliamentary Standing Committee on Commerce in India on 'Trade with Association of South-East Asian Nations', it may be said that India is adopting a less than robust approach across a diverse range of sectors in its trade and economic relations with ASEAN.[44] It should also be noted that negotiations for the India-ASEAN Free Trade Agreement were protracted, and the signing of the agreement took place only after six years of negotiations,[45]—and this, in spite of the long history of relations between India and Southeast Asian States. Negotiations on the Free Trade Agreement started on a promising note. But in the process, it became clear that initial deadlines could not be met, and that an Early Harvest Programme (envisaged in the Framework Agreement for negotiations on the Free Trade Agreement) had to be dropped from the implementation schedule.[46]

Trade in goods between India and ASEAN, and the economic relations between ASEAN and India in general, warrants brief scrutiny. Reports state that from 1 January 2010 when the relevant agreement entered into force, India has continued to experience a deficit in its goods trade.[47] Another important economic initiative concerns the negotiations for an agreement on the Regional Comprehensive Economic Partnership. While India and ASEAN are deeply involved in the negotiations, reports suggest that India is likely to take a more cautionary rather than liberal approach in the negotiations.[48] Both, however, are clear that the Regional Comprehensive Economic Partnership is a vehicle for economic integration and inclusive development.[49]

Another area of concern is the contention of a glaring imbalance in terms of connectivity.[50] ASEAN sees the issue of connectivity through the lens of physical connectivity, institutional connectivity, and people-to-people linkages.[51] In this context, there is, for example, a disparity in the number of flights a week between Indian cities and States in ASEAN.[52] There are no direct flights from New Delhi to the capitals of Indonesia, the Philippines, and Vietnam.[53] Another aspect of connectivity concerns infrastructure projects. One significant infrastructure project at issue is the India-Myanmar-Thailand trilateral highway. The proposed trilateral highway is significant as, on completion, it will connect Northeast India with parts of Southeast Asia.[54] Uncertainty over its completion, however, hampers the potential of the trilateral highway serving as an important connectivity corridor into ASEAN. The deadline for completion has been shifted several times, with 2020 now being given as a tentative date from the original target of 2016.[55] The trilateral highway project is especially significant for ASEAN-India relations because, after the completion of the trilateral highway, the plan is to link the trilateral highway to other States in ASEAN, namely Cambodia, Lao PDR, and Vietnam.[56] Although the India-ASEAN Free Trade Agreement may facilitate greater links with Southeast Asia, observers have similar concerns. They consider that the agreement must first generate an economic equilibrium so as to facilitate realising the advantages from the potential connectivity offered by the Free Trade Agreement.[57]

Asymmetry in ASEAN-India relations is also said to exist in the security domain, particularly in the context of the maritime issues.[58] A key issue here is whether there should be an enhanced Indian maritime presence in the South

China Sea. Research suggests that while India seeks to uphold freedom of navigation in the South China Sea, the overall maritime aspirations of India are likely to see India and China working together, rather against, the interests of each other.[59] It is not entirely clear what this means in so far as the South China Sea region is concerned because, notably, China has openly objected to the presence of Indian Navy ships in the South China Sea.[60] At the same time, observers highlight that the Indian Navy maintains a heavy presence of battle-ready warships in the Arabian Sea (including many close to Maldives); with army amphibious forces available too. This signals a question of priority on the part of India of which ASEAN is well aware. Thus, the future scenario of maritime activity in the South China Sea will be interesting to observe, particularly since India has expressed a desire to enhance maritime cooperation with ASEAN and make it a strategic priority in ASEAN-India relations.[61] How India may engage ASEAN on maritime issues, and where, remains open to question and interesting to monitor. For, while India may leverage its quadrilateral cooperation for the interests of India in, for example, the South China Sea,[62] it is mindful not to upset its support for ASEAN centrality on matters concerning the ASEAN region.[63]

'Shared Values, Common Destiny': Critical Success Factors

The ideas under the Delhi Declaration are not merely lofty aspirations. Indeed, the 2016–2020 Plan of Action to Implement the ASEAN-India Partnership for Peace, Progress and Shared Prosperity will be instrumental in realising commitments made under the Delhi Declaration. As stated in the 2016–2020 Plan of Action, India and ASEAN have spelt out and set the course of joint actions, practical cooperation, and concrete projects and activities required. All this is intended to support the ASEAN Community building and integration process.

In the context of the above discussion, it is necessary to recall that observers have pointed out that the relationship between ASEAN and India has not always been close, particularly during the Cold War era.[64] In the present scheme of things, observers note that China has loomed large, particularly in contemporary ASEAN-India relations. In the context of ASEAN-India relations, it is open to question whether the growing interest from China in ASEAN is because of India's Look East Policy and Act East Policy, even as both policies may instead be described as a response to the growing influence of China in the Indo-Pacific region.[65] Nevertheless, it is interesting to highlight that observers believe that ASEAN-India relations, in particular through engagement and cooperation, may well define the geo-political landscape of the Indo-Pacific region.[66]

Therefore, it would appear that there are critical success factors for ASEAN-India relations to flourish through the 'Shared Values, Common Destiny' paradigm. A non-exhaustive list of critical success factors in equal order of priority may be as follows:

- Trust and confidence in ASEAN-India relations is important to 'fructify and sustain' the dynamics of their economic relationship.[67] The Look East Policy and the Act East Policy can, and should, also serve as instruments to instil and sustain political trust, in addition to facilitating economic linkages.
- ASEAN and India must prepare for structural change and uncertainty to ensure that ASEAN-India relations remain relevant and consequential. Structural change and uncertainty can be political, economic, or strategic in nature. It is, thus, significant to highlight two points from the ASEAN-India Plan of Action 2016–2020: that ASEAN and India will (i) further promote cooperation in addressing common and emerging challenges; (ii) enhance coordination in other international fora on issues of common concern to contribute to overall peace, stability and prosperity.[68]
- India should continue to leverage its successes on ASEAN platforms, such as the ASEAN Regional Forum, the ASEAN Post Ministerial Conference, and the ASEAN Defence Ministers Meeting-Plus.[69]
- The importance of connectivity on 'soft issues', like education, tourism, and cultural cooperation, should be accorded equal attention to connectivity on 'hard issues', like infrastructure through land, water, and air; because soft issues can serve as a confidence building measure for sustainable engagement on complex issues.
- The Look East Policy and the Act East Policy should serve to strengthen the profile of ASEAN, and thus ASEAN-India relations, rather than drive a wedge between members of ASEAN in view of similar interest by China in the Southeast Asian region.[70]
- If ASEAN connectivity is defined in a very broad sense to encompass not merely road, rail, and air links but also cooperation in

telecommunications, information, and energy,[71] India should leverage its expertise in these areas.

- ASEAN-India economic relations envisaged under their Plan of Action 2016–2020 should develop key sectors of mutual interest for trade and development. This requires India to study the trade architecture in ASEAN, be competitive, and target sectors that would drive the 'Make in India' initiative to seamlessly integrate into the ASEAN value chain.[72]
- ASEAN-India relations, in the context of 'Shared Values, Common Destiny', should have the kind of spontaneity and dynamism observers consider is found in ASEAN-China relations.[73] This would also be consistent with the notion of an inclusive ASEAN Community where ASEAN and its Dialogue Partners move in the same direction, and at the same pace for shared prosperity, peace, and stability in the region.
- The idea of 'Shared Values, Common Destiny' should instil a sense of urgency in decisions and actions, to enable ASEAN and India to reach the Common Destiny at the soonest available opportunity.[74]
- As India and ASEAN have committed to 'Shared Values, Common Destiny', India would do well, through its Act East Policy, to dispel longstanding views on its protectionist tendencies which observers note have been manifested in the protracted negotiations for a Regional Comprehensive Economic Partnership.[75]

Conclusion

The Delhi Declaration, guided by the vision towards ASEAN 2025, has the right spices to add zest into ASEAN-India relations. The notion of 'Shared Values, Common Destiny' through India's Look East Policy and the Act East Policy of India are critical building blocks—confidence building measures—to show that India is moving away from the effects of the Cold War era where tensions and suspicions dominated ASEAN-India relations.[76] Having long focused on what it can do at the global level, the litmus test for sustainably successful—particularly economic—ASEAN-India relations may depend upon how effectively India can scale its worldview to a regional perspective.[77] In other words, it remains to be seen how India may still think globally but act regionally; and to do so in a manner that benefits ASEAN institutionally, while also symmetrically enhancing, among others, bilateral relations between India and individual members of ASEAN. The ability of India to translate its Act East Policy into an instrument for regionalism is significant; considering reports suggesting many Southeast Asians within influential circles contend that India has not acted sufficiently on its Act East Policy.[78] Indeed, observers argue more can be done in the economic and security sphere of ASEAN-India relations.[79] By India being less guarded on security issues in ASEAN forums,[80] and leveraging culture, commerce, and connectivity,[81] it may yet provide a conducive environment to unleash the full potential of 'Shared Values, Common Destiny' in ASEAN-India relations.

NOTES

1. The full text of the article by the Prime Minister Modi is available at http://pib.nic.in/newsite/PrintRelease.aspx?relid=175913
2. For brief insight into ASEAN 2025, see also, 'ASEAN 2025 at A Glance', available at http://asean.org/asean-2025-at-a-glance/. See especially, item 7 of 'ASEAN 2025 at A Glance'. For detailed information on ASEAN 2025 especially on the 3 Community Blueprints, see further at http://asean.org/storage/2015/11/67.-December-2015-ASEAN-2025-Forging-Ahead-Together-2nd-Reprint.pdf
3. See Harsh V. Pant, Avantika Deb, 'India-ASEAN partnership at 25', ORF Issue Brief, July 2017, Introduction available at http://www.orfonline.org/research/india-asean-partnership-at-25/ (hereafter 'Pant & Deb').
4. The fourth wave opened an era of dialogue and cooperation with the 'East' on strategic issues focusing on regional and global security; see further, S.D. Muni, 'India's Look East Policy: The Strategic Dimension', ISAS Working Paper No.121, 1 February 2011 at https://www.files.ethz.ch/isn/126612/ISAS_Working_Paper_121-_Email-_India's_'look-east'_policy_the_strategic_dimension_01022011145800.pdf
5. See Overview Paper, 'ASEAN-India Dialogue Relations', January 2018, at http://asean.org/asean/external-relations/india/(hereafter 'ASEAN-India: Overview').
6. See, Joint Press Release, 'The First Meeting of the ASEAN-India Joint Sectoral Cooperation Committee', Bali, Indonesia, 7–8 January 1994, at www.asean.org (hereafter 'ASEAN-India JSC 1994').
7. Ibid.
8. Ibid., para. 13.
9. The proposals were in fact provided by representatives of the ASEAN-India Business Council who formed part of the delegation at the meeting. See Joint Press Release, 'The Second Meeting of the ASEAN-India Joint Sectoral Cooperation Committee', New Delhi and Panjim, India, 13–17 February 1995, para. 13, at www.asean.org (hereafter 'ASEAN-India JSC 1995').
10. Ibid., para. 10.
11. ASEAN-India: Overview, above n. 5.
12. Ibid.
13. See Chairman's Statement of the 13th ASEAN-India Summit, 21 November 2015, Kuala Lumpur, Malaysia, at http://asean.org/asean/external-relations/india/(hereafter '13th ASEAN Summit, Chairman's Statement').
14. Shristi Pukhrem, 'The Upward Trajectory in India-ASEAN Relations', Jan-Feb 2018, *India Foundation Journal*, at http://www.indiafoundation.in/the-upward-trajectory-in-india-asean-

relations/; note also the references in the article.

15. Ibid., para. 4; see also, 'ASEAN 2025: Forging Ahead Together', at http://asean.org/?static_post=asean-2025-forging-ahead-together
16. See 'ASEAN 2025 at A Glance', para.4, at http://asean.org/asean-2025-at-a-glance/
17. Ibid.
18. See, Pankaj K. Jha, 'India-ASEAN Relations: An Assessment', at http://www.kas.de/wf/doc/23557-1442-2-30.pdf (hereafter 'Pankaj'), p. 109.
19. Ibid., pp. 108, 110.
20. Ibid., p. 109.
21. Ibid., pp. 109, 110; see also, Ashok Sajjanhar, 'The India-ASEAN Partnership at 25', Institute for Defence Studies and Analyses, at https://idsa.in/idsacomments/india-asean-partnership-at-25_asajjanhar_040118 (hereafter 'Sajjanhar-India-ASEAN Partnership at 25').
22. See discussion in Ashok Sajjanhar, '2 Years On, Has Modi's Act East Policy Made a Difference for India?', *The Diplomat*, at https://thediplomat.com/2016/06/2-years-on-has-modis-act-east-policy-made-a-difference-for-india/ (hereafter 'Sajjanhar-2 Years On').
23. For further discussion on the issue of connectivity and its relevance in the context of ASEAN-India relations, see Sajjanhar, India-ASEAN Partnership at 25, above n. 21, under the section headed 'Challenges and Opportunities.'
24. See discussion in Sajjanhar, '2 Years On ...', above n. 22.
25. Ibid; See also, generally, Pant & Deb, above n. 3.
26. The full text of the Declaration issued last 25 January 2018, at http://asean.org/delhi-declaration-of-the-asean-india-commemorative-summit-to-mark-the-25th-anniversary-of-asean-india-dialogue-relations/
27. See Jeff Smith, Setting the Record Straight on US-India South China Sea Patrols, June 2016, The Diplomat, available via https://thediplomat.com/2016/06/setting-the-record-straight-on-us-india-south-china-sea-patrols/
28. Currently estimated to be worth about US$ 70 Billion; See further Michael Kugelman, India Acts East, 17 May 2016, The South Asia Channel, available via http://foreignpolicy.com/2016/05/17/india-acts-east/
29. See commentary by Danielle Rajendram, "India's new Asia-Pacific strategy: 'Act East'", at https://www.lowyinstitute.org/the-interpreter/indias-new-asia-pacific-strategy-act-east ; the full analysis by the same author at https://www.lowyinstitute.org/sites/default/files/indias-new-asia-pacific-strategy-modi-acts-east.pdf
30. 'A thousand-year relationship': Ambassador Nirupama Rao traces the ties between India and China; text of the 2015 Jawaharlal Nehru Memorial IFFCO Lecture given by India's former ambassador to China and the USA, at https://scroll.in/article/847935/a-thousand-year-relationship-ambassador-nirupama-rao-traces-the-ties-between-india-and-china
31. The full text of the 2016–2020 ASEAN-India Plan of Action is categorised as one among several Key Documents Guiding the Dialogue Relations, at http://asean.org/asean/external-relations/india/
32. Details of all three plans are available at http://asean.org/asean/external-relations/india/
33. The full text of the Political and Security Community Blueprint, Economic Community Blueprint, and Social-Cultural Community Blueprint are available at http://asean.org/
34. See also, 'Brief on ASEAN-India Relations', prepared by the Indian Mission to ASEAN, at http://www.indmissionasean.com/index.php/asean-india
35. Ibid.
36. See commentary by Danielle Rajendram, 'India's new Asia-Pacific strategy: 'Act East', at https://www.lowyinstitute.org/the-interpreter/indias-new-asia-pacific-strategy-act-east
37. Documents available at http://asean.org/asean/external-relations/china/, and http://asean.org/asean/external-relations/india/

38. It may also be worth noting that full dialogue partnership status was first accorded to India in December 1995, before the same status was accorded to China in July 1996; but, the strategic partnership status with China was arrived at in October 2003 while the same status with India came much later, in December 2012; and the first resident Ambassador of India to ASEAN took office in January 2015 while China appointed its first resident Ambassador to ASEAN in September 2012. See further, 'Brief on ASEAN-India Relations', prepared by the Indian Mission to ASEAN, at http://www.indmissionasean.com/index.php/asean-india and at http://asean.org/storage/2012/05/Overview-of-ASEAN-China-Relations-October-2017_For-Website.pdf
39. For a brief insight into ASEAN 2025, see also, 'ASEAN 2025 at A Glance', at http://asean.org/asean-2025-at-a-glance/; for detailed information on ASEAN 2025, especially on the 3 Community Blueprints, see further, http://asean.org/storage/2015/11/67.-December-2015-ASEAN-2025-Forging-Ahead-Together-2nd-Reprint.pdf
40. See, 'ASEAN 2025 at A Glance', item 7, at http://asean.org/asean-2025-at-a-glance/
41. See Shyam Saran, 'India-Asean ties: A cup half full?', *Hindustan Times*, 24 January 2018, at https://www.hindustantimes.com/analysis/india-asean-ties-a-cup-half-full/story-CetCGMx6nXmIPC8BHGwAJL.html (hereafter 'Saran')
42. Ibid.
43. 'Expert Gyan: India's Engagement with ASEAN and Asian Geopolitics', 25 Jan. 2018, Q & A discussion with experts by *The Wire*, as reported by Devirupa Mitra, at https://thewire.in/217684/india-asean-relations-asia-geopolitics/, see especially, interview with Suthiphand Chirathivat.
44. Report presented on 25 August 2017; see Press Release containing gist of recommendations by the Committee, at http://164.100.47.5/newcommittee/press_release/Press/Committee%20on%20Commerce/137th%20Press%20Release%20(English).pdf
45. Amita Batra, 'India-ASEAN FTA: A Critique', IPCS Issue Brief, No. 116, 2009, at https://www.files.ethz.ch/isn/106121/IB116-SEARP-BatraFTA.pdf (hereafter 'Batra').
46. Ibid.
47. Goods trade widened initially between the periods 2010–2016, before narrowing in the period 2016–2017. See also, Suhasini Haidar and Arun S., 'RCEP: India hardens stand ahead of summit with ASEAN', *The Hindu* 23 December 2017, at http://www.thehindu.com/business/rcep-progress-before-asean-india-summit-bleak/article22261467.ece (hereafter 'Haidar & Arun').
48. Ibid.
49. See, 'Joint Leaders' Statement on the Negotiations for the Regional Comprehensive Economic Partnership (RCEP)', at http://asean.org/storage/2017/11/RCEP-Summit_Leaders-Joint-Statement-FINAL1.pdf
50. See Saran, above n. 41.
51. Physical connectivity would include, for example, transport, ICT, and energy; while institutional connectivity would include, for example, trade, investment, and services liberalisation; while people-to-people linkages would include, for example, education, culture, and tourism. See further, 'Master Plan on ASEAN Connectivity 2025', at p. 8, at http://asean.org/storage/2016/09/Master-Plan-on-ASEAN-Connectivity-20251.pdf
52. See Saran, above n. 41.
53. See, 'Win-win lure of India-Asean air links', *The Straits Times,* 3 March 2018, at http://www.straitstimes.com/opinion/win-win-lure-of-india-asean-air-links-the-straits-times-says
54. See Dr. Rupakjyoti Borah, 'India-Myanmar-Thailand Trilateral Highway: A Promise to Transform the Region's Economic Landscape', 24 August 2017, Japan Forward, at https://japan-forward.com/india-myanmar-thailand-trilateral-highway-a-promise-to-transform-the-regions-economic-landscape/

55. See Ranjana Narayan, 'Connectivity Far Away Even as We Near 2018's India-Asean Summit', *The Quint*, 2017, at https://www.thequint.com/voices/opinion/trilateral-highway-project-incomplete-even-as-india-asean-summit-nears (hereafter 'Narayan').
56. Ibid.
57. The India-ASEAN Free Trade Agreement has been described as a potential vehicle to engage the Northeast region of India which shares borders and other potential complementarities with Southeast Asian countries; See also, Batra, above n. 45.
58. See Saran, above n. 41.
59. See Ulises Granados, 'India's Approaches to the South China Sea: Priorities and Balances', *Asia & The Pacific Policy Studies,* Vol. 5 (1), January 2018, pp. 122–137, at http://onlinelibrary.wiley.com/doi/10.1002/app5.223/full#app5223-sec-0003
60. See Dipanjan Roy Chaudhury, 'China objects to presence of Indian ships in South China Sea', *The Economic Times* [date?] May 2016, at https://economictimes.indiatimes.com/news/defence/china-objects-to-presence-of-indian-ships-in-south-china-sea/articleshow/52369749.cms
61. See, 'Asean-India agree to enhance maritime cooperation', The Staronline, January 2018, at https://www.thestar.com.my/news/nation/2018/01/25/asean-india-agree-to-enhance-maritime-cooperation/
62. See, Premesha Saha, 'The Quad in the Indo-Pacific: Why ASEAN remains cautious', February 2018, ORF Issue Brief, at http://www.orfonline.org/research/asean-quad/
63. See preamble to the Delhi Declaration issued 25 January 2018, at http://asean.org/delhi-declaration-of-the-asean-india-commemorative-summit-to-mark-the-25th-anniversary-of-asean-india-dialogue-relations/
64. During the Cold War era, India was generally not keen on involvement with regional organisations, compounded by the fact that the geopolitics of the Cold War era also saw India and ASEAN at opposing ends of ideological blocs. See also, Suyash Desai, 'Revisiting ASEAN-India Relations', 18 November 2017, *The Diplomat,* at https://thediplomat.com/2017/11/revisiting-asean-india-relations/ (hereafter 'Desai').
65. It is interesting to note that observers consider that what was once termed as the Asia-Pacific region is now being characterised as the Indo-Pacific region. The geopolitical and geostrategic implications of this characterisation become even more interesting with the revival of the Quadrilateral Security Dialogue, 12 November 2017. See further, 'The Indo Pacific: Defining a Region', November 2017, Stratfor, at https://worldview.stratfor.com/article/indo-pacific-defining-region
66. See Desai, above n. 64.
67. See Rahul Sen, Mukul G. Asher, Ramkishen S. Rajan, 'ASEAN-India Economic Relations: Current Status and Future Prospects', 2004, *Economic and Political Weekly*, pp.1–37, at p. 31, at https://www.researchgate.net/publication/229005649_ASEAN-India_Economic _ Relations_Current_Status_and_Future_Prospects
68. See introductory text of the 2016–2020 ASEAN-India Plan of Action, at http://asean.org/asean/external-relations/india/
69. For a discussion on the nature and account of successes by India with ASEAN through the stated platforms, see also, Desai, above n. 64.
70. See, Kavi Chongkittavorn, 'China's Effect on Asean-India ties', January 2018, *The Straits Times*, at http://www.straitstimes.com/opinion/chinas-effect-on-asean-india-ties (hereafter 'Kavi').
71. See interview with Singapore Prime Minister, Lee Hsien Loong, 'The more India engages with ASEAN, the more it can reap the benefits', in *The Hindu*, 25 December 2012, at http://www.thehindu.com/opinion/interview/the-more-india-engages-with-asean-the-more-it-can-reap-the-benefits/article4235898.ece

72. See also, Deeparghya Mukherjee, 'India-ASEAN Economic Linkages: Challenges and Way Forward', March 2016, IDEAS for India, at http://www.ideasforindia.in/article.aspx?article_id=1593
73. Kavi, above n. 70.
74. See also, Jonah Blank et al, 'Look East, Cross Black Waters', RAND, 2015, at https://www.rand.org/content/dam/rand/pubs/research_reports/RR1000/RR1021/RAND_RR1021.pdf
75. Kavi, above n. 70.
76. Desai, above n. 64.
77. See Editorial Notes, 'India is late in reaching out to ASEAN: *The Jakarta Post*, January 2018, at http://www.straitstimes.com/asia/se-asia/india-is-late-in-reaching-out-to-asean-the-jakarta-post
78. Bharath Gopalaswamy, 'India's Role and China's Roads in the Info-Pacific', February 2018, at https://thediplomat.com/2018/02/indias-role-and-chinas-roads-in-the-indo-pacific/
79. See F.P. Staff, '50 years of ASEAN: India's partnership with grouping leaves much to be desired in terms of economic, security cooperation', August 2017, at http://www.firstpost.com/india/50-years-of-asean-indias-partnership-with-grouping-leaves-much-to-be-desired-in-terms-of-economic-security-cooperation-3906771.html
80. Pankaj, above n,18, p.,123 *et seq.*
81. See 'Swaraj's 3-C formula for ties with ASEAN: culture, commerce, connectivity', Press Trust of India, January 2018, at http://www.business-standard.com/article/current-affairs/swaraj-s-3-c-formula-for-ties-with-asean-culture-commerce-connectivity-118010600452_1.html

20

Connectivity Corridors between Northeast India and Myanmar

*Sonu Trivedi**

Introduction

Security and stability in India's Northeast have been the guiding principle behind India's Myanmar policy which emerged out of its Look East policy in the early 1990s, and its Act East Policy in recent times. Amidst the strategic significance of the region, India aims to make its northeastern region as a pivot for its connectivity to the rest of Southeast Asia by bridging the missing link via Myanmar. This is the core argument of this essay; it is based on earlier field trips to study the connectivity corridors between India and Myanmar.

Although India has enjoyed competitive advantages until now—that is, well before Myanmar's reconciliation and bridge-building with the West and other regional powers such as the highly competitive Japan and big brother China—nevertheless certain critical concerns remain. One of the objectives of this essay is to focus on connectivity corridors, such as highways, railways, waterways, and their significance, in the sustainable development of the region. In this context, the essay focuses on the need to boost connectivity between the regions of Northeast India and Myanmar, and bridge the critical gaps in the missing connectivity links between the two countries.

* Sonu Trivedi is a Fellow at Nehru Memorial Museum and Library, New Delhi. An earlier version of this paper was presented at the National Conference on 'India's Act East Policy: Needs and Priorities of Northeast India and Myanmar' organised by the Centre for Northeast Studies and Policy Research, Jamia Millia Islamia, 12-13 March 2018.

It is believed that these corridors would be instrumental in connecting the borders and reducing asymmetries in the frontiers of both India and Myanmar. These corridors have been envisaged as development corridors, leading to better resource sharing amongst various communities on the border. This would lead to managing diversities and reducing centre-periphery contestations leading to the devolution of power and decentralised governance, and fulfilling the development aspirations of ethnic nationalities living in the border regions of the two countries. In this context, the following section covers the five major connectivity corridors between India and Myanmar. These have been explored to study their linkages with the development of the region, and their effects on the integration of the social groups living on the margins.

Connectivity Corridors between Northeast India and Myanmar

(1) The India-Myanmar-Thailand Trilateral Highway is a part of the Asian Highway Project connecting pre-existing roads between the three countries, and taking it further to *Vietnam*. At present, it is a 1400-km highway, linking the Indian border point in Moreh with Mae Sot in Thailand. The Joint Task Force on the Trilateral Highway had originally agreed to complete the work by 2016.[1] The new deadline for completion, however, has now been set at 2020.[2] In spite of the delay and procedural hurdles, it is a significant venture, as it would connect India, Myanmar and Thailand with the Asian Highway project—which seeks to link nations in Asia with Europe. It is supposed to give a boost to trade, business, health, education, and tourism ties among the three countries.[3]

A significant component of the Indian-Myanmar-Thailand Trilateral Highway is the 160 km Tamu-Kalay-Kalewa (TKK) road, also known as 'India-Myanmar Friendship Road' which was opened in 2001. Agreement has also been reached to 'repair and rebuild the bridges' as well as upgrade the 120-km Kalewa-Yargi segment of the road. Work on altogether 69 bridges in Tamu-Kyigone-Kalewa section has also started. Punj Lloyd and Varaha Infra Joint Venture has been authorised by the National Highways Authority of India for the construction of the road in the Kalewa-Yargi section of the proposed Trilateral Highway.[4] It is believed that, 'once this construction and upgradation are completed it would lead to seamless connectivity from Imphal (India) to Mandalay (Myanmar)'.[5]

Another component of the highway has been the India-Myanmar Bus Service which is expected to enhance cross-border trade, tourism, people-to-people contact, and the economic development of the areas on both sides of the border. An agreement is yet to be finalised for this cross-border bus service between India and Myanmar.[6] The trial run took place in December 2015. 'The project which was in a limbo for about two years got an impetus after the new government took over in India'.[7] With the signing of agreements during President U Htin Kyaw's visit, we have seen India repairing bridges and approach roads with a view to putting the trilateral highway project back on track.[8]

(2) The Kaladan Multi-Modal Transit Transport Project aims to provide an important access point for linking not only India's hitherto landlocked northeast but also a viable trade route from the countries of Southeast Asia such as Indonesia, Malaysia and Singapore. The project involves the development of the Sittwe seaport and the inland port at Paletwa in Chin state, thereby linking Sittwe and Paletwa via upstream river navigation. It also involves connecting Paletwa through the hilly terrains of Myanmar to Lawngtlai in Mizoram by the construction of a highway.[9] The project seeks to bridge the connectivity divide between India and Myanmar, which will lead to the development of trade between the two countries. It will also contribute to the economic development of Mizoram and other northeastern states, and is of strategic importance as it opens a new transport corridor between India and Myanmar. Aiming at connectivity, infrastructural development, job opportunities, and improving livelihood, it may be instrumental in development as well as reducing the sense of alienation prevailing amongst the most vulnerable social groups living in the sensitive region of Northeast India and Southwest Myanmar (the Rakhine State).

(3) Bangladesh-China-India-Myanmar – Economic Corridor (BCIM-EC) is a proposed connectivity corridor which has been subjected to bilateral political issues and suspicion among member countries. Questions are raised on the outcome of this initiative because of the Chinese intention of dominating the corridor, and making it a part of its larger 'Grand Strategy' of the One Belt One Road initiative. Although, the corridor aims to form a thriving economic belt with a focus on cross-border transport, energy, and telecommunication networks, transgressing the economic interests, the initiative also covers China's overarching geo-strategic intentions of controlling the smaller powers in the region, and using it as a tool to counter the USA's 'pivot to Asia' and the Trans-

Pacific Partnership (TPP). Given the mutual distrust between India and China over several bilateral issues at regional and international forums, the future of the BCIM Economic Corridor is going to be delayed in the times to come.[10]

(4) Stilwell Road connecting Arunachal Pradesh to Myanmar and extending further up to China, is a critical variable which needs to be taken into account. As for the rationale for its renovation and benefits to Myanmar, it has been proposed to reopen this road as the international highway linking India-Myanmar and China to other countries in the East. The historic significance of the road due to its Second World War legacy may also increase its importance as a major tourist destination in Asia. Besides boosting physical connectivity, it may also result in increased trade, commerce, and investment, giving leverage to the Northeastern region of India as a pivot to connectivity and integration with the larger Asia-Pacific. It is believed that the renovation and re-opening of the 'historic Stilwell Road' is also significant because it could 'act as a growth driver for the entire region', and make the Northeast region a gateway for India's trade along the corridor through Myanmar, and running into Kunming in China.[11]

(5) The Rhi-Tiddim Road is yet another 80 km road project which helps to connect the India-Myanmar-Thailand Trilateral Highway through the Zokhawthar-Rih border in Mizoram and Myanmar, respectively. It starts from Zokhawthar in Mizoram and Rhi in Myanmar, extending further up to Tiddim. The agreement for the construction and up-gradation of Rhi-Tiddim was signed in December 2012. A detailed project report is underway to develop it. This road component will link the northeastern state of Mizoram in India with the Chin State in Myanmar, and further enhance cross-border links and trade between the two countries.[12] The road will also provide travel links between Monywa, extending further up to Mandalay (see the official website of the Ministry of the Development of North Eastern Region).[13] However, for harnessing its full potential, it is important to upgrade the Tiddim-Kalay road so that it could provide a direct link from Mizoram to Mandalay.[14]

Border Trade Points

Having discussed the mega connectivity projects in the border region of the two countries, this section focuses on the border trade points where actual trade has been carried out for centuries. It has been a customary practice for a long time to carry on trade in traditional goods on head load. However, the border trade agreement signed between India and Myanmar in 1994 has given it a legal framework. It is believed that 'it serves as a life-belt to Myanmar's sinking economy'.[15]

> People living in the border regions have had economic and cultural links going back to several centuries. This interdependence of the peoples on the two sides of the boundaries has given rise to informal channels of trade in goods and services. This informal trade has provided sustenance to the economies of the region.[16]

This may be attributed to its high value owing to low transaction and transportation costs in the porous border. However, these local trade points have not been formally documented. In the absence of the lack of formal records, most of these exchanges are unofficial, and thereby have been continuing as informal arrangements.

The Land Customs Station (LCS) at Moreh was inaugurated in April 1995 on the Indian side of the border. Although border trade through Zokhawthar in Mizoram has been operational since January 2004, a new Land Customs Station started functioning in September 2007.[17] The Zowkhathar LC Son the Indian side was officially inaugurated in 2015. In an attempt to boost border trade and people-to-people connectivity, the official land route entry and exit points were opened between India and Myanmar by the Governments of both the countries on 8 August 2018. This land route visa facility has abolished the special 'land-route permit' required for entering the borders of two countries. The land and border point was simultaneously opened at Moreh-Tamu and also at Zowkhawthar-Rhi in the Manipur and Mizoram States of India, respectively. It is hoped that these will enhance trade, health and religious tourism, education facilities, and the socio-economic development of the border regions between the two countries.

Border *Haats*

Economic linkages and strong ethnic ties between the people living on the borders have helped in the furtherance of trade links through local trade points between the two countries. With the objective of further boosting cross-border trade, the setting up of border *haats* have been identified at various locations in the bordering states of Arunachal Pradesh, Nagaland, Manipur, and Mizoram. '*These* have been introduced to facilitate cross-border trade, curb informal channels of trade, and improve the livelihood patterns of people living adjacent to international borders'.[18] *Several locations have been suggested by local governments to the Ministry of External Affairs for* the *setting up of border haats. In this regard, an agreement has been signed between the two countries for setting up a border haat at Nampong in Arunachal Pradesh, and Pangsu in the Sagaing region of Myanmar.*[19] In order to facilitate border trade further, four border *haats* have been identified in Mizoram: Hnahlan, Vaphai, Zote, and Pangkhua; on the Myanmar side, they will be established in the Darkhai, Leilet, Fartlang, and Thau villages.[20] A formal agreement in this regard is yet to be executed.

Despite being separated through borders, the people on both sides of the border have remained united, and shared spaces as a result of these border *haats* which have been a unifying point for the people of the two countries.[21] Informal trade in the border regions of the Northeast through border *haats* helps boost local trade and increases people-to-people contact. Special mention may be made in this regard about the 'Pangsau Pass Winter Festival' being organised over the years at the Pangsau Pass in Arunachal Pradesh.[22] It not only promotes tourism and contributes to the local economy but is also a means of showcasing the cultural heritage, folk art, local customs and traditions, and glimpses of the vibrant cultural identity of the different tribes of the region. These are indications of the shared aspirations of the people of the region to open up to Myanmar and Southwest China.[23]

Critical Concerns in the Connectivity Corridors

The above mentioned connectivity corridors are envisaged to emerge as corridors for the sustainable development of the region, and to making 'Northeast India as the hub of India's Act East Policy and not just as a gateway to the East.'[24] The connectivity corridors are expected to emerge as development corridors facilitating trade and investment, and leading to peace and prosperity for the region. The possibilities of creating a development corridor with rural development projects like *haats* or local markets, with emphasis on agriculture, horticulture, handlooms, handicrafts, and processed food will add to the employment opportunities for the people living in these regions. The setting up of industrial corridors and economic activities in special economic zones may develop the region and transform the livelihood of the people. These could be instrumental in fulfilling the development aspirations of the people of the border regions by focusing on the border area development projects; capacity building and skill enhancement initiatives; medical and health tourism;

relief and rehabilitation during natural disasters; trade facilitation and investment in the border regions; infrastructural development; and focusing on peace and reconciliation in the region.

It is further believed that the sustainable development of the region and connecting the missing links between the people of the border regions of India and Myanmar will depend upon the successful implementation of the connectivity projects as well as the execution of the border trade agreements and other memorandums of understanding signed so far. However, certain critical concerns remain due to physical barriers; security and stability on the borders; procedural lapses; inadequate infrastructural facilities; the low intensity of the border trade; a poor service delivery system; ethnic conflict and sectarian violence. These have largely hindered strong ties in the border regions between the two countries, apparently sometimes making the shared frontiers, emerge as distant 'neighbours'.

One of the weakest links in India-Myanmar relations has been the porous border of Northeast India with Myanmar which has been a flourishing ground for drug trafficking, arms smuggling, illegal migration, and insurgency in the region. The cross-border trade of narcotics has been one of the main sources of income for most insurgent groups in Northeast India.[25] The illicit smuggling of arms and ammunition across Northeast India has added to the growing concern for peace and security in the region.[26] The porous borders have also been a cause of concern because of the continued presence of Indian 'rebel' groups in the Sagaing province of Myanmar.[27] In India, several rebel groups have been involved in ethnic and violent clashes, including illicit drug and arms trafficking. Many of these groups have taken shelter beyond the Indo-Myanmar border. These insurgents, together with the rebels in Myanmar, have created trouble for both the countries.[28]

Bilateral political and territorial issues as well as mutual suspicion have also been a major impediment to these connectivity projects. The Rohingya issue has been a critical challenge in the case of the India-Myanmar-Bangladesh borders. The unsolved border between India and China, and other bilateral political issues raised at regional and international forums have been a roadblock in the opening of Stilwell Road. The BCIM-Economic Corridor has also been set aside due to the existing distrust in India-China relations. Territorial and water sharing agreements have been pre-dominant in the case of India-Bangladesh relations. Besides, illegal migration has also been a critical area of concern between the two countries. Trans-border crimes, such as drug trafficking, arms trade, illegal migration and insurgency, have also added to the frustration and delay of these connectivity projects on both sides of the border.

To conclude, it can be said that, the development potential of India's northeastern states and western borders of Myanmar can only be realised through addressing the structural and systemic barriers in these infrastructural links and development corridors, which are supposed to be essential for the citizens residing in the border regions of both the countries. Identifying the common need for regional connectivity and building a development corridor has been the idea behind initiating various connectivity projects in this region. They are expected to boost trade and investment through the four states of northeast India that share borders with Myanmar. These would go a long way in connecting the missing links, and develop the border region as shared spaces between the two countries.

NOTES

1. V. S. Seshadri, 'Transforming Connectivity Corridors between India and Myanmar into Development Corridors', New Delhi: Research and Information System for Developing Countries, 2014.
2. Sudha Mahalingam, 'The Trouble with India's Projects in Myanmar', *The Diplomat*, 21 September 2016.
3. 'India-Myanmar-Trilateral Highway by 2019: Nitin Gadkari', Livemint, 23 January 2017.
4. 'NHAI Issues EPC Contract for Highway Project Linking India Myanmar Thailand', *Business Line*, 8 January 2018.
5. V.S. Seshadri, 2014, op. cit.
6. 'Cross Border Bus Service between India (Imphal) and Myanmar (Mandalay)', Press Information Bureau, Government of India, Ministry of Road Transport & Highways, 24 June 2014.
7. See, Moushumi Das Gupta, 'Soon a Bus Ride to Myanmar', *The Hindustan Times*, 24 June 2014.
8. Sudha Mahalingam, 2016, op. cit.
9. 'Implementation of the Kaladan Multi Modal Transit Transport Project in Myanmar at the Revised Cost Estimate of Rs 2904.04 Crore,' Press Information Bureau, Government of India, Cabinet, 14 October, 2015.
10. Ashok Sajjanhar, 'Understanding the BCIM Economic Corridor and India's Response', Observer Research Foundation, Issue Brief, No. 147, New Delhi: June 2016.
11. Jajati K. Patnaik, 'Should the Stilwell Road be Re-opened?' *Economic and Political Weekly*, Vol. 51 (15). April 9, 2016.
12. Prabir De and Jayanta Kumar Ray, *India-Myanmar Connectivity: Current Status and Future Prospects*, New Delhi: KW Publishers Pvt. Limited, 2013.
13. For more information, see official website of MDONER, 'Bilateral Projects with Myanmar & Indian Projects to Promote Connectivity & Trade with NER', Ministry for Development of Northeast Region, Government of India.
14. V.S. Seshadri, 2014, op. cit.

15. Konsam Ibo Singh, 'Indo-Myanmar Border Trade: Imperatives and Present Status', in Das, Gurudas and R.K. Purkayastha (eds.), *Border Trade: North-East India and Neighbouring Countries*, New Delhi: Akansha Publishing House, 2000.
16. Thiyam Bharat Singh, 'India's Border Trade with Its Neighbouring Countries with Special Reference to Myanmar', *Margin: The Journal of Applied Economic Research*, Vol. 1(4), pp. 359–382.
17. V.S. Seshadri, 2014, op. cit.
18. Ashish Nath, 'Border *Haats*', *Economic and Political Weekly*, Vol. 53, Issue No. 11, 17 March 2018.
19. 'Establishing Border *Haats* across the Border between India and Myanmar', Memorandum of Understanding between the Government of the Republic of India and the Government of the Republic of the Union of Myanmar, New Delhi: Ministry of Commerce & Industry, Government of India, 2012.
20. 'Four Border *Haats* on Mizoram-Myanmar Border soon', *Northeast Today*, 17 March 2017.
21. For more information, see, 'Zokhawthar: A deserted space between Act East Policy and formalisation of trade', *Northeast Now*, 12 December 2017, at https://nenow.in/neighbour/zokhawthar-deserted-space-act-east-policy-formalization-trade.html, accessed July 20, 2018.
22. 'Arunachal Festival Begins on High Note', *The Telegraph*, 21 January 2018.
23. See, 'Should the Stillwell Road between India-Myanmar-China Restored', The Wire, 2016, Online Edition, at https://thewire.in/external-affairs/india-myanmar-china-stilwell-road-restored, Accessed July 15, 2018.
24. This is based on Ram Madhav's Speech at Delhi Dialogue X, 19 July 2018.
25. To know more about the porous border, see, Namrata Goswami, 'Drugs and the Golden Triangle: Renewed Concerns for Northeast India', IDSA Comment, Online Edition, 2014 at http://www.idsa.in/idsacomments/DrugsandtheGoldenTriangle_ngoswami_100214.html Accessed July 10, 2018.
26. Gurmeet Kanwal, and Monika Chansoria, 'Small arms proliferation in South Asia', CLAWS, Issue Brief 18, May 2010, accessed 10 July 2018.
27. See for details, Subir Bhaumik, 'A Close Friendship that has Turned Sour', *The Telegraph*, 24 March 2015.
28. David Steinberg, 'Prospects for Democratisation in Myanmar: Impact on India', *Indian Defence Review*, Vol. 24(4), 2009.

21

A Fresh Look at Regional Connectivity between India's Northeast and Southeast Asia

Baladas Ghoshal

Connectivity is the means through which nations and regions develop closer and meaningful cooperation. Without connectivity relations between countries remain incomplete and meaningless. The Delhi Declaration after the recent commemorative summit between India and ASEAN reaffirms its "commitment to enhance physical and digital connectivity in line with the MPAC 2025 and the AIM 2020 by, among others, availing of the US$1 billion line of credit announced by India to promote physical infrastructure and digital connectivity." India-ASEAN engagement stands on two important legs – economic and strategic, besides the cultural one. Out of that, the economic leg happens to be its Achilles heel, and unless that can be improved, New Delhi will find it difficult to make any major impact on the region. The volume of ASEAN-China trade stood at $345 billion in 2015, the second largest after the $543-billion volume of intra-ASEAN trade. In 2017, it touched almost US$ 400 billion In contrast to that India's trade with ASEAN in 2017 stood at US$ 65 billion, six times less than that of China. The India-ASEAN FTA on goods and services went more in favour of the latter as it had a comparative advantage on the goods. India's strength lies in services and investments, but the ASEAN countries have not opened their markets to the movement of Indian experts to the region and other services related issues. As multinational firms undertook single production processes across multiple countries over the last few decades, China and ASEAN economies have become intertwined in a web of regional production networks, thus increasing their mutual dependence. In contrast again, India has not been able to connect itself with the value-chains in the region.

India's Connectivity Projects linking its Northeast with Southeast Asia

To give substance and meaning to India's Look East/Act East policy, New Delhi had to improve its connectivity with its extended neighbours and therefore currently is working with ASEAN on multiple connectivity projects, through land, water, and air. One of the flagship projects for land connectivity between ASEAN and India is the India-Myanmar-Thailand Trilateral Highway, that connects the three countries from Moreh in India to Mae Sot in Thailand to Bagan in Myanmar, was first proposed in 2002. India decided to further extend the Trilateral Highway to Cambodia and Vietnam at the Commemorative Summit between ASEAN and India in 2012. But somehow, the project did not progress, as was expected, mainly due to the lack of institutional and financial support from all three countries. Another project is the Kaladan Multi-Modal Transit Transport Project (KMMTTP) that aims to develop connectivity through land and water in order to seek an alternative route through Myanmar for the transportation of goods to the northeast region of India. The Kaladan project that began in 2008 was expected to ensure alternate connectivity to Mizoram through a mixture of sea, river and road transports from Sittwe Port at Kaladan river mouth in the Rakhine State of Myanmar. It will connect the eastern Indian seaport of Kolkata with Sittwe seaport in Rakhine State, Myanmar by sea. In Myanmar, it will then link Sittwe seaport to Paletwa, Chin State via the Kaladan river boat route, and then from Paletwa by road to Mizoram state in Northeast India. The project includes a waterway component of 158 km on Kaladan River from Sittwe to Paletwa in Myanmar and a road component of 109 km from Paletwa to Zorinpui along the India-Myanmar border in Mizoram. Last year, India completed the port project and handed it over to Myanmar. The inland river terminal at Paletwa upstream of Kaladan is nearing completion. At the Indian side, the extension of the Aizawal-Saiha National Highway by 90 km to the international border at Zorinpui is nearing completion too. It was one of the most challenging road projects taken up in many decades in this part of the country. But a 109-km road from Zorinpui to Paletwa is still missing. Over the last year, the project was tendered twice but unsuccessfully. And that is one and a half years after the Modi government revised the budget estimates by nearly six times, roped in State-owned Ircon Infrastructure and Services as the consultant and put a 2019 deadline for completion. Without the road link; the entire investment in Sittwe and the Paletwa terminal becomes useless.

There is an urgent need to ensure that no further delay takes place in the completion of the project. Or else, India's credibility will be eroded.

The other project, Mekong-India Económic Corridor (MIEC) that is supposed to link India with the Mekong countries (Cambodia, Laos, Myanmar and Vietnam or CLMV), also witnessed slow progress. South Asia's rail link with Southeast Asia linking New Delhi with Hanoi is still a dream. For the rail connectivity to materialize, it is essential for infrastructure in Northeast India to be upgraded, along with Myanmar and Thailand to ensure rail connectivity. Once the infrastructure in the Northeast India is improved, investments and other enabling factors will automatically follow giving boost to the economy of the region. Bangladesh should be made a stakeholder in the development of the region.

ASEAN-India Maritime Transportation Agreement

India and ASEAN are exploring the signing of an ASEAN-India Maritime Transport Cooperation Agreement, which will help to enhance cooperation and communication, eliminate barriers hindering maritime transport, and establish a regional maritime transport framework system. India, Myanmar, and Thailand Motor Vehicles Agreement (IMT MVA) needs to be finalized for free movement of cargo, passenger, and personal vehicles along the roads linking these three countries. Other projects, such as a railway link between New Delhi in India to Hanoi in Vietnam; the Mekong-India Economic Corridor (MIEC) connecting South and Southeast Asia; and Stilwell road and Dawei deep-sea port in Myanmar are under consideration. The MIEC involves the integration of four Mekong countries – Vietnam, Myanmar, Thailand, and Cambodia— along with India, connecting Ho Chi Minh City, Dawei, Bangkok, and Phnom Penh with Chennai. If the above corridor can be linked, it will especially reduce the transit distance between India and ASEAN countries. It is imperative that India consults with the other stakeholders to remove all the bottlenecks to bring the project to completion, otherwise, India's credibility to be an important player an important player in the Indo-Pacific will come into question. Air connectivity between Indian and ASEAN cities are also very poor lacking direct flights in most of the cases. India in the past has announced a Line of Credit of $1 billion to encourage such connectivity projects between India and ASEAN, and a Project Development Fund of 5 billion rupees ($78 million) with an aim to promote manufacturing hubs in the CLMV countries. What is needed is implementation of many of these programmes to bring results, particularly in the backdrop of China's massive Belt and Road Initiative (BRI) that involves infrastructure and connectivity projects linking China to Southeast Asia, Central Asia and even to Europe.

Proposed in September 2013, the BRI envisages a US$ 1.3 trillion Chinese-led investment program that aims to create a web of infrastructure, including roads, railways, telecommunications, energy pipelines, and ports, that will enhance economic interconnectivity and facilitate development across Eurasia, East Africa and more than 60 partner countries. The project has two primary components: the overland Silk Road Economic Belt (SREB), and the sea-based 21st-century Maritime Silk Road (MSR), together forming the "belt" and "road". A project of unprecedented geographical and financial scope, SREB's overland infrastructure network is projected to encompass the New Eurasia Land Bridge and five economic corridors: China-Mongolia-Russia; China Central Asia-West Asia; China-Pakistan; the China-Indochina peninsula; and Bangladesh-China-India-Myanmar, which New Delhi does not consider part of BRI. High-speed rail and hydrocarbon pipeline networks will link these corridors. The MSR is focused on developing key seaports that connect to land-based transportation routes.

BBIN (Bangladesh, Bhutan, India and Nepal)

The BBIN is another project that links India's immediate neighbours in South Asia to it and has great potential to promote not only connectivity but also economic development of the region. While the BBIN sought to impel the sub-region's latent socio-economic potential, harnessing disparate stages of development to augment each other, over years its objectives expanded to incorporate land and port connectivity. The formation worked toward economic synergy through arterial channels of trade and cross border initiatives. For instance, to link West Bengal and remote north eastern states through Bangladesh by rail, highway and maritime corridors, alongside north-south transport routes that span Nepal, Bhutan and Indian hill states to northern Bay of Bengal ports. These grids would then bridge extraneous regions throughout member states and beyond eastwards. With accession of Maldives and Sri Lanka to SASEC in March 2014, notions of quadripartite integration appeared subsumed or rendered dormant. The November 2014 Kathmandu summit saw endorsement of an accord on land transport by regional states, apart from one country's reservations causing it to fall through. The subsequent Summit Declaration reiterated sub regional steps as contributory to wider connectedness. A framework for co-operation was subsequently drawn, with the first quaternary Joint Working Group (JWG) meeting in January 2015.

The priority of "connectivity" further embodies seamless electrical grids, shared access to road, rail, air and port infrastructure, and ease of travel. To such ends, a sub-regional Motor Vehicle Agreement that garnered assent in Thimphu would allow buses and later private vehicles with BBIN permits to travel unobstructed by border hindrances. Although manifestly of economic intent, the diplomatic weight accorded to this structure as opposed to alternatives in a region considered least integrated was seen to connote purpose beyond interwoven commerce. The BBIN Motor Vehicles Agreement (MVA) was signed on 15 June 2015 at the BBIN transport ministers meeting in Thimpu, Bhutan. The agreement will permit the member states to ply their vehicles in each other's territory for transportation of cargo and passengers, including third country transport and personal vehicles. Each vehicle would require an electronic permit to enter another country's territory, and border security arrangement between nations' borders will also remain.[Cargo vehicles will be able to enter any of the four nations without the need for trans-shipment of goods from one country's truck to another's at the border. Under the system, cargo vehicles are tracked electronically, permits are issued online and sent electronically to all land ports. Vehicles are fitted with an electronic seal that alerts regulators every time the container door is opened.

The first cargo truck to take advantage of the motor vehicle agreement was flagged off from Kolkata on 1 November 2015. The truck travelled 640 km to reach Agartala via Dhaka. Prior to the signing of the BBIN Motor Vehicle Agreement, the truck would have had to travel 1550 km through the Indian Territory to reach Agartala. In August 2016, Bangladesh dispatched a truck carrying garments from Dhaka to New Delhi as part of a trial run of the agreement. The truck received an electronic permit to enter Indian Territory through an online web-based system. Instead of having to undergo customs clearance and formalities as it would prior to the agreement, the truck was fitted with an electronic seal with a GPS tracking device. The truck was then inspected for custom clearance at New Delhi, rather than at the border. The agreement will enter into force after it is ratified by all four member nations. The agreement has been ratified by Bangladesh, India and Nepal. Bhutan, which has not ratified, has requested for a cap to be fixed on the number of vehicles entering its territory. An existing bilateral agreement between Bhutan and India already permits seamless vehicle movement between the two countries. Therefore, Bhutan's decision to not ratify the BBIN MVA would only affect its trade with Nepal and Bangladesh. The Bhutanese government requested the other BBIN members to proceed with the agreement and also clarified that it would attempt to ratify the MVA after the country held general elections in 2018. India approved $1.08 Billion for construction and upgradation of 558 km long roads that join Bangladesh, Bhutan and Nepal. The project will receive 50% funding from Asian Development Bank. The project is scheduled to be completed by 2018.

It is estimated that this project will increase the regional trade by 60 per cent while that with rest of the world by 30 per cent. Investments in hard infrastructure such as roads, bridges and border facilities must also be scaled up, particularly in Bangladesh. The MVA has identified 30 transport connectivity projects into which US$ 8 billion will be channelled, and their implementation in priority sectors should be done expeditiously; in reality, however, BBIN countries are yet to connect with each other through a comprehensive trade facilitation and connectivity measure due to a number of logistical handicaps. One of the most severe barriers is that trade in the region involves a high number of procedures and documents in all three BBIN corridors, requires multiple and complex obligations and compliances to product standards, and countries have yet to align customs procedures and recognise each other's services. To meet global, regional and sub-regional obligations, BBIN countries need enhanced trade facilitation measures. In the face of slow movements in trade facilitation, rather than focusing on the trade and investment agreements, issues such as connectivity, water resources management and energy have received increased attention.

Ideational Connectivity

Connectivity need not have to be physical or digital only. It should also extend to connectivity of ideas. An area that gets less attention in the strategic discourse on India's Act East Policy but must receive greater focus now as India and Southeast have developed 'Comprehensive Strategic Partnership' and coming closer to each other. India and most Southeast Asian countries are multi-racial, multi-cultural and multi-religious societies and share common problems in building an inclusive society and preserving social harmony. Ideational cooperation and connectivity are most relevant in the case of Indonesia and India, which are not only multi-religious but also multi-cultural and face the challenge of integrating their diverse and plural societies from primordial loyalties to civic loyalties and creating a sense of citizenship within a democratic framework through state motto of 'Bhineka Tunggal Eka' and 'Unity in Diversity'. While both Indonesia and India had been successful in maintaining social harmony and cohesion and building political stability for many years after they achieved their independence through trials and tribulations, in recent years they are facing the rise of primordial loyalties and identity politics that are posing a major threat to such social cohesion and harmony. In the case of Indonesia, there has been a creeping Islamization of the society and polity of the country. The inroads of Arab Wahhabi and Salafi variant of Islam into Southeast Asia and elsewhere have led to a growing assertiveness on the part of the fundamentalists. As yet, such fundamentalist elements have not occupied the mainstream in Indonesia and are still fringe groups, the danger of their occupying a major space cannot be underestimated. In India, the rise of radical Islamic politics around the region of South and Southeast have led to the rise of a fringe Hindu extremist group who wants to imitate Islamic fundamentalists and trying to codify their religious practices when there is no such thing in Hinduism. As a result, both Indonesia and India are facing the ire of such fringe groups in their attempt to create a harmonious and cohesive society.

Even while Islamists are slowly gaining ground in Indonesia, there are attempts on the part of both the government and the civil society to stand against religious fundamentalists' attempt to create an exclusivist society by experimenting with a concept of what is known as Pancasila villages, named after the secular state ideology of Pancasila. In a paper on "Pancasila Village and the preservation of socio-religious harmony; Lessons from Balun of Lamongan and Banuroja of Gorontalo," in a seminar in Delhi, an Indonesian scholar has shown that realities forming social harmony in these two villages are closely related to religious sites like Mosque, Catholic Church, Hindu temple standing side by side for decades helping them to preserve social harmony by mainstreaming common values of inter-faith, tolerant and peaceful interactions, mutual cooperation and maintaining representative character of village officers. Bollywood films and Indian drama are not only extremely popular in Indonesia, but in recent years they are also becoming a focus of academic inquiry of young researchers in Indonesian universities in different parts of the country. From online search, one Indonesian scholar has found more than 100 theses from state and private universities that deals with themes and values of Bollywood films. Values such as plural cultures and soft power diplomacy as found in a popular Salman Khan film, *Bajrangi Bhaijan*, in which the protagonist rescues and brings to her parents a young Pakistani girl child who somehow crosses into the Indian territory and gets lost. Such studies are undertaken with the specific objective of conveying to readers and movie goers values of pluralism, multiculturism and social harmony. Findings in such academic studies, according to a researcher, "indicate that Indonesia should follow Bollywood path in promoting and preserving plural cultures of Incredible India and build mutual cultural cooperation with India." Indonesia has been playing a key role in demonstrating the virtues of tolerance and mutual respect in a diverse, multi-ethnic and multi-religious polity. To make India-Indonesia partnership specifically and India-Southeast Asia broadly, more meaningful, they must also cooperate in sharing ideas and experiences besides the 'high politics' of defence and security.

People-to-People Connectivity

Finally, a major weakness of India's Act East Policy is the poor people to people contact. While inter-governmental interactions between India and the ASEAN countries are quite dense, yet its business to business and people to people contacts are much to be desired. There are hardly any contacts between the academics, journalists and civil society groups between the two regions. Student exchange programme need to be upgraded. Academic cooperation can be enhanced through joint research, exchange of scholars and students. One of the major hurdles in the development of closer cooperation are the negative images sometimes each held for the other, resulting essentially from the lack of knowledge of each other. This can be corrected through development of study centres in each other's country. India needs to have a centre for Southeast Asian studies like the one in Singapore, which has built one of the best research institutions of the kind in the world. While we have Centres in Indian Universities which specialise on Southeast Asia, but their resources are abysmally poor. Apart from upgrading the resource base of India-ASEAN Centre in

Shillong through more financial allocation, GOI should set up a research Centre on Southeast Asia in New Delhi that can pursue not only in depth study on political, economic and strategic aspects of our engagement with Southeast Asia, but also on internal political developments, foreign and defence policies of the countries of ASEAN, and bring out policy, and issue briefs that can act as feedback and input for our policy-makers.

22

Regional Security Challenges and Connectivity: An Indian Perspective

Udai Bhanu Singh

The concept of the Indo Pacific (or the Indian Ocean-Pacific Ocean continuum) is changing the way trade, resources, energy lifelines that run across it, and security are viewed in the region. The resultant situation has thrown up new security challenges and opportunities. The regional states' response to the evolving strategic environment in the Indo-Pacific has manifested itself in individual strategies. From the Indian standpoint, the Indo-Pacific region is not a strategy or a club of limited members; it is an inclusive concept and it is not directed against any country. The six main elements of the Indo-Pacific are: a free, open and inclusive region, ASEAN centrality; rules-based order; equal access to the global commons (sea and air); rules based trade environment; and last but not the least connectivity based on respect for sovereignty and territorial integrity.[1]

Shift to the Indo-Pacific

The concept of 'Indo Pacific' which has often been used in preference to the term 'Asia Pacific', or even 'Indo Pacific Asia' "combines the Indian Ocean Region (IOR) and the Western Pacific Region (WP)—inclusive of the contiguous seas off East Asia and Southeast Asia—into a singular regional construct." The use of the term ' Indo Pacific' has gained increasing currency due to the increasing connectedness of the Indian Ocean and the Pacific Ocean. Whether this geographic entity is referred to as Indo-Pacific or Asia Pacific is not so important. It does not matter if the US Pacific Command or 'PACOM' was renamed the 'Indo-Pacific Command after more than 70 years—because at least for now it is a symbolic move. What matters is the role that the major powers decide to play in this region. According to Global Times, "for [PM] Modi the Indo-Pacific region is no more than a geographical construct" whereas for the US' Mattis it is a "geo-strategic" one.[2] Even so there still remains the fundamental difference (in terms of geopolitics and security environment, and economic and social development) between the Indian Ocean Region and the Western Pacific.

What are the Regional Security Challenges?

New strategic uncertainties have arisen in the Indo-Pacific due to unresolved territorial disputes, the rise of terrorism, non-traditional threats like piracy, transnational crime etc. Second, the existing structures have not succeeded in dealing with many current conflict situations like those arising from provocations by a nuclearising North Korea, and the South China Sea dispute. Third, the rise of new powers like a number of regional conflict situations have arisen which the existing structures There is little doubt that India and ASEAN share a number of cultural and historical ties, and many political and economic complimentarities. They share a number of other similarities in terms of supporting the rule of law, international norms and the respect for state sovereignty and multilateral cooperation besides several institutional similarities.

South China Sea Territorial Dispute

China's military and economic rise accompanied by the rise of nationalism. When China rejected the Permanent Court of Arbitration ruling of July 2016 which went against it in the Philippine-China dispute in the South China Sea, it was seen as a blow to the rule-based global order that is the basis for a stable maritime regime and freedom of navigation. Earlier China's unilateral declaration of an air defence identification zone (ADIZ) in 2013 over a contested part of the East China Sea, land reclamation in the South China Sea and the new fishing regulations in the Hainan province (2014) generated fears among countries of the region. Would it be feasible to coordinate India's Act East Policy with Russia's "Asian Pivot"? Could the Indian Navy coordinate the Indian Maritime Security Strategy with Russia's new Naval Doctrine (2017) so that we both understand each other's concerns and priorities in the region?

The U.S. maintains that it takes no position on competing sovereignty claims in the South China Sea, but encourages all countries to uphold international law, including the law of the sea as reflected in the Law of the Sea Convention, and to respect unimpeded lawful commerce, freedom of navigation and overflight, and peaceful dispute resolution.

As pointed out by the recent Chatham House study, while Malcolm Turnbul, Modi and Abe do not have common views on China, they agree that China must be managed. Neither India, nor indeed Japan or Australia would like to see the relationship with China as a zero sum game.

North Korea Nuclear Crisis

North Korea's acquisition of ballistic missile capabilities and nuclear weapons since 2006 was a source of serious destabilisation for the region and the world. North Korea stands apart as the only country to have tested nuclear weapons in this century. Also Kim Jong-Un has repeatedly said that denuclearisation is not an option. The US regards North Korea as its most immediate threat in the Indo-Asia-Pacific. Russia in its official document says: "Russia has always championed a non-nuclear status for the Korean Peninsula and will support its denuclearization in every possible way, believing that this objective can be attained through the six-party talks." While Russia considers the situation in the Korean Peninsula alarming due to Pyongyang's actions, it is also opposed to the US deployment ofTHAAD in South Korea which could trigger a missile race in the region.

How can connectivity help solve these challenges? As former Foreign Secretary rightly said, Connectivity is the new 'Great Game' which includes both physical and softer forms of connectivity.

Connectivity

Connectivity should not imply Economic or trade connectivity alone. More than one connectivity initiative exists and they should not be working at crosspurposes. Connectivity should create unity and be based on trust. "And for that, these initiatives must be based on respect for sovereignty and territorial inegrity consultation, good governance, transparency, viability and sustainability. They must empower nations, not place them under impossible debt burden. They must promote trade, not strategic competition. On these principles we are prepared to work with everyone..."[3]

The Indian Government has committed investments of nearly $13 billion in shipping, ports and allied sectors. Government plans to invest over $190 billion over the next ten years to develop 27 industrial clusters and to improve connectivity with ports through new rail and road projects. There are various infrastructure projects nearing completion in India's North East—the Trilateral Highway Project, the Kaladan Multimodal Project, the Trans Asian Railway Project and so on. (These have been dealt at length elsewhere in the book). Once completed these projects will transform the landscape.

The Indian Government has cleared an international air connectivity scheme which will connect Guwahati airport to seven countries (Singapore, Bangladesh, Bhutan, Nepal, Myanmar, Malaysia and Vietnam.)[4]

India and ASEAN are looking to an early conclusion of an Agreement on Maritime Transport and are exploring maritime cargo routes and coastal shipping between the two.

Transport and Communications (Connectivity) also finds a mention in the BIMSTEC Summit Declaration of August 2018. It calls on Member States for an early conclusion of BIMSTEC Coastal Shipping Agreement and the BIMSTEC Motor Vehicle Agreement and for early adoption of the BIMSTEC Master Plan on Transport Connectivity. The BIMSTEC Master Plan on Transport Connectivity would serve as a strategic document that guides actions and promotes synergy among various connectivity frameworks such as the ASEAN Master Plan on Connectivity 2025 (MPAC 2025), the Ayeyawady-Chao Phraya-Mekong Economic Cooperation Strategy (ACMECS). Given the fact that two-thirds of world's oil, one third of bulk cargo, and half of the world's container shipment flow through the Indian Ocean, the Indian Navy has an increasingly important role to play in years to come. The Mumbai terror attack of November 2008 remains a constant reminder of the threat from the sea route that terrorism continues to pose.

The maritime challenge affects India directly, as the bulk of its trade is via maritime routes and thus requires freedom of navigation and the security of sea lines of communication. Even though India is not a party to any of the disputes in the South China Sea, it has a significant stake in the stability of the region because any conflict would disrupt the flow of trade and supplies. India closely followed the reaction to the decision of the Permanent Court of Arbitration in the Philippines' arbitration case against China's nine-dash line claim. A verdict that re-establishes trust in international law and norms on maritime issues is the best outcome that India can hope to see in the case involving China and the Philippines. To resolve a maritime dispute between India and Bangladesh, in July 2014 the court awarded Bangladesh 19,467 square kilometers of sea area in the Bay of Bengal, and New Delhi readily accepted the decision.

To address challenges in the maritime domain, the Indian Navy has stepped up its activities in regional waters. The Indian Navy released its maritime security strategy Ensuring Secure Seas: Indian Maritime Security Strategy at the Naval Commanders' Conference in October 2015, which replaced and updated the 2007 strategy. India was a founding member of the Indian Ocean Rim Association. It also founded the Indian Ocean Naval Symposium in 2009, which provides a forum to discuss issues that have a bearing on maritime security in the Indian Ocean region. The symposium includes 35 countries as members and has become a dialogue partner of the Indian Ocean Rim Association. Moreover, the Indian Navy has adopted a proactive approach to maritime security by organizing the 2016 International Fleet Review (its second ever) and the MILAN ("confluence") exercises in the Bay of Bengal.

The Digital Connectivity and Cyber Security

As technological innovations happen by leaps and bounds, there is a danger of growing digital divide and possibility of new inequalities emerging in the Indo-Pacific. To achieve the objective of maximum governance and minimum government, Indian Government is using digital platforms—whether it is railways, land records, taxation, defence etc. But since most of the hardware is of foreign origin, the security of the information on the network is in constant doubt. New Delhi now prepares to implement new rules on storage of financial data, which would restrict cross-border data flows on the internet. It is set to create a regime equivalent to nation-state borders in cyberspace.[5] Many other countries of the Indo-Pacific are in a similar dilemma. Government alertness could prevent this lack of digital-access to sections of its populations.

As countries like India witness a burst of digital access (in the form of digital technologies for governance, commerce, entertainment, education, defence etc) it is important that: 'Alertness towards cyber security concerns should become a way of life'.[6]

The Blue Economy

A Blue Economy or the ocean economy refers to the sustainable use of oceans, seas and marine resources for sustainable development. It is defined with reference to "ocean-based economic activities, including fisheries and aquaculture, renewable ocean energy, seaports and shipping, offshore hydrocarbons and seabed minerals, marine biotechnology, research and development, and tourism".[7] There exists immense potential for ASEAN-India cooperation in the field of Blue Economy. Through the clever use of new technologies, "the issues of poverty, food insecurity, unemployment and ecological imbalance can be effectively tackled."[8]

India's PM Narendra Modi articulated the concept of SAGAR "Security and Growth for all in the Region" in March 2015—his vision for the Indian Ocean. These include, interalia "enhancing capacities to safeguard land and maritime territories & interests; deepening economic and security cooperation in the littoral; promoting collective action to deal with natural disasters and maritime threats like piracy, terrorism and emergent non-state actors; working towards sustainable regional development through enhanced collaboration; and, engaging with countries beyond our shores with the aim of building greater trust and promoting respect for maritime rules, norms and peaceful resolution of disputes". India has a coastline of 7500 kms, an Exclusive Economic Zone of 2.4 million square kilometres, with 90 per cent of our trade by volume, and almost all our oil imports moving over the sea.

Addressing the Indian Ocean Conference in August 2017, External Affairs Minister Sushma Swaraj said: "We are already engaging our neighbours in Blue Economy initiatives, particularly in the areas of marine bio-technology, exploration and sustainable exploitation of ocean mineral resources, sustainable fishing practices, and harnessing of ocean energy."[9] The Sagarmala initiative seeks to promote connectivity between the ports of the littoral states of the Indian Ocean.

A Blue Economy Conference was held in Bangladesh in 2017 with participation from BIMSTEC Member countries. Through the BIMSTEC Summit Declaration of August 2018 the Members note the "importance of Blue economy and agree to cooperate in this sector for the sustainable development in the region and decide to establish an inter-governmental Expert Group to develop an action plan on blue economy, keeping in mind the special needs… of the landlocked Member States".

Is 'Minilateralism' the Solution?

In a lecture, the High Commissioner of Australia to India, Harinder Sidhu warned against the danger of unilateral action which is driven by a narrow conception of national interests. She highlighted Indian and Australian commitment to multilateral diplomacy as signified in the combined support to the UN system and regional forums such as the East Asia Summit, the ARF and IORA. According to her, while they do encourage dialogue and help in norm creation, they lack agility and have failed to provide a coordinated response to the many complex challenges of today. India and Australia must expand their "toolkit" and participate more frequently in small groups. She said: "Small group diplomacy will matter more over time in the Indo-Pacific. Small groups, overlapping groups and minilatralism are important because engaging different countries in different combinations gives us new flexibility in our common aim of increasing prosperity and security in the Indo-Pacific region".

Since 2015 (June), when the first trilateral at the foreign secretary level between India, Australia, and Japan was held in New Delhi, there is a re-emergence of the Quad. The Quad Formation was really the dialogue among middle ranking officials of the four countries at Manila—not aimed at any other country and coincided with Prime Minister Modi's visit to the Philippines to attend the ASEAN meetings and the 12th East Asia Summit. The MEA statement on the quadrilateral noted:

> "The discussions focussed on cooperation based on their converging vision and values for promotion of peace, stability and prosperity in an increasingly inter-connected region that they share with each other and with other partners. They agreed that a free, open, prosperous and inclusive Indo-Pacific region serves the long-term interests of all countries in the region and of the world at large. The officials also exchanged views on addressing common challenges of terrorism and proliferation linkages impacting the region as well as on enhancing connectivity,"

It revived memories of the inaugural US-India-Japan Trilateral Ministerial dialogue in September 2015 that was held in New York and attended by foreign ministers from the three nations. It also reminded of the quad concept which was initiated by Japanese PM Abe in his first tenure as Prime Minister in 2007: it had failed after it failed to get the necessary impetus from Kevin Rudd and Manmohan Singh.

Increased U.S.-India cooperation and New Delhi's cooperative approach has served to reduce the distance between India and ASEAN and fostered India's commitment to playing a role in the emerging security architecture in the Asia-Pacific. At the summit level, relations with ASEAN have been growing since 2002. The ASEAN-India Free Trade Area, which went into effect in 2010, promises to increase trade between the two sides to $200 billion by 2022. In 2012 the ASEAN-India Vision Statement raised the partnership to the strategic level. India now has a dedicated mission to ASEAN (in Jakarta) and the ASEAN-India Centre (in New Delhi). Furthermore, Prime Minister Narendra Modi declared at the 12th India-ASEAN Summit in Naypyidaw in November 2014 that India's Look East policy had been upgraded to an Act East policy.

Why has the need for this mini lateral partnership among India, Japan and Australia arisen? Possibly some external factors could be at work, including the nudging from the US. There is little doubt that India, Japan, and Australia share a number of political fundamentals—all are functioning liberal democracies and share a number of other similarities in terms of supporting the rule of law, international norms and the respect for state sovereignty and multilateral cooperation besides several institutional similarities. The additional push factor could be the economic complementarities between the three.

Conclusion

From India's perspective, security is a prerequisite for internal cohesion, economic development, and consolidation. India's primary interest is to create an enabling external environment for the economic progress of the country. Unless there is regional security, economic development cannot be envisaged.

At the 2016 Shangri-La Dialogue, the then Defence Minister Manohar Parrikar had identified three key challenges to India's security: territorial disputes that could degenerate into military conflict, terrorism, and protection of the maritime domain. Emphasizing the third challenge, he went on to state that "by virtue of geographical location, the Indo-Pacific is the crossroads of [the] world's maritime traffic. Over half of the world's commercial shipping passes through these waterways." Any adventurism would disrupt the process of economic growth and development not only for India but for the broader region. Parrikar referred to the seas and oceans as "critical enablers of our prosperity."

NOTES

1. Prime Minister Modi Speech at the 17th Shangri La Dialogue http://www.mea.gov.in/outoging-visit-detail.htm?29943/Prime+Ministers+Keynote+Address+at+ Shangri+ La+ Dialogue+June+01+2018
2. China's voice echoes at Shangri-La Dialogue at http://www.globaltimes.cn/content/1106329.shtml
3. Prime Minister Modi Speech at the 17th Shangri La Dialogue http://www.mea.gov.in/outoging-visit-detail.htm?29943/Prime+Ministers+Keynote+Address+at+ Shangri+ La+ Dialogue+June+01+2018
4. Bikash Singh, 'Guwahati Airport to be Directly Connected to Seven Countires', *Economic Times*, at https://economictimes.indiatimes.com/industry/transportation/airlines-/-aviation/guwahati-airport-to-be-directly-connected-to-seven-countries/articleshow/66210876.cms Accessed 15 October 2018.
5. Takehiko Koyanagi, 'India's proposed personal data rules unnerve business', *Nikkei Asian Review* at https://asia.nikkei.com/Business/Business-Trends/India-s-proposed-personal-data-rules-unnerve-business, 12 October 2018. Accessed October 14, 2018.
6. Prime Minister Modi at the Global Conference on Cyber Space, 2017. Cited in the chapter on 'Cyber Security Challenges', in Arvind Gupta, How India Manages its National Security, Penguin Random HOuse India: New Delhi, 2018.
7. The concept was first explained in the book: Gunter Pauli, The Blue Economy: 10 years, 100 innovations, 100 million jobs
8. 2nd ASEAN-India Blue Economy Workshop Keynote Address by Secretary (East), July 18, 2018, at https://mea.gov.in/Speeches-Statements.htm?dtl/30097/2nd_ASEANIndia_ Blue_ Economy_Workshop_Keynote_Address_by_Secretary_East. Accessed 17 August 2018.
9. Address by External Affairs Minister at the 2nd Indian Ocean Conference (August 31, 2017), at MEA website, https://mea.gov.in/Speeches-Statements.htm?dtl/28907/Address+ by+ External+Affairs+Minister+at+the+2nd+Indian+Ocean+Conference+August+31+2017. Accessed 20 January 2018.

23

Reflections on Regional Connectivity: A View from Bangladesh

Mustafizur Rahman

I would like to take this opportunity to register my deep appreciation for the warm hospitality extended by Ambassador Lalit Mansingh and his colleagues at the KIF, and for being such gracious hosts.

I would like to present my ideas and share my reflections on the theme of this session from the particular vantage point of Bangladesh as it strategizes to move forward in the 21st century. For Bangladesh, the need to deepen and broaden economic cooperation with countries of Southern Asia has emerged, both as an opportunity and a necessity, for several reasons. As may be noted, Bangladesh has, in recent times, graduated in two important areas: in 2015 the country graduated from being a lower income country (LIC) to a lower middle income country (LMIC) according to World Bank criteria; the second was very recently (in March 2018) when the country graduated to becoming eligible for moving out of the least developed country (LDC) group as defined by the UN. It will graduate finally in 2024 after the next two triennial reviews.

The first entails Bangladesh becoming ineligible for the concessional credit window of the World Bank, and will have to go in for blended (concessional and non-concessional) finance. In the near term future, it will be eligible for exclusively non-concessional loans. The middle income graduation means higher costs of borrowing, with a consequent impact on the rate of return, debt burden, and debt-servicing liability. The second graduation will also have serious implications for Bangladesh's competitiveness since, as a graduated LDC (beyond the year 2024), Bangladesh's exports will lose preferential market access in a majority of export destinations. There will be other ramifications in the form of the loss of special and differential status in the WTO, and preferential treatment accorded by other multilateral organisations. The emerging global trading scenario, with looming uncertainties—such as Brexit and the possibility of resurgent protectionism on the part of key trading powers—also do not bode well for the increasingly globally integrated economy of Bangladesh.

As is well known, whilst many developing countries and LDCs are at present trading increasingly more with southern countries, and developing closer relationships with their respective regions and neighbours, South Asian countries, in contrast, have been lagging behind in comparison. For example, till now, Bangladesh's exports to the SAARC countries, particularly to India as also to countries in the ASEAN, have remained rather negligible. A significant part of the potential benefits of deeper South-South cooperation remains unrealised. This seriously undermines the growth potentials of Bangladesh and other South Asian countries.

There is a growing literature which testifies that, regional integration could play an important role in promoting the cause of progress of developing countries, and could help the integration of their economies with the global economy from a position of strength. Realising this window of opportunity is important for Bangladesh, and it should be ready and able to pursue proactive policies and take appropriate measures to take advantage of the potential opportunities in the context of South-South cooperation. Indeed, sustainable LDC graduation and a smooth middle income journey of Bangladesh will, to a large extent, hinge on this. It is from this perspective that the discussion at this conference is so relevant and important for all in Bangladesh.

Emerging Developments, New Opportunities

A number of new developments in the context of South-South cooperation are likely to play an important role in the development of Bangladesh and other regional economies. India has already signed bilateral free trade agreement (FTA) with the Association of Southeast Asian Nations (ASEAN). Both Bangladesh and India are members of the SAFTA and the BIMSTEC. The proposed BIMSTEC FTA is significant for Bangladesh because it will provide her with a foothold in the ASEAN market through preferential access to the markets of Thailand and Myanmar. Projects and procurements under the three lines of credit offered by India to Bangladesh—US $ 1.0 billion, US $ 2.0

billion, and US $ 5.0 billion respectively—are expected to address some of the major infrastructure deficits in Bangladesh, and will help establish the needed transport connectivity with India. India has also provided a US $ 200 million grant to Bangladesh to help build the Padma Bridge.

Indeed, seamless transport connectivity is the key to establishing the other connectivities—in trade, investment, logistics, and people-to-people contact. The ongoing and envisaged projects under the Indian LoCs will help Bangladesh in establishing linkages with other trans-Asian initiatives, such as the Asian Highway, the Trans-Asian Railways link, and the proposed BCIM (Bangladesh-China-India-Myanmar) Economic Corridor. The Indian LoCs will, thus, enable Bangladesh to get into the markets of the emerging Southern Asian growth zone. The BBIN-MVA (Bangladesh-Bhutan-India-Nepal Motor Vehicle Agreement) is also an important development in recent times, with high potentials. The implementation of the MVA will help to reduce transport and transaction costs in intra-regional trade, raise the competitiveness of exporters, and benefit producers and consumers in partner countries. Bangladesh and India have also signed coastal shipping agreements which would also benefit both the countries. A test run of container train from Kolkata to Bangladesh is envisaged in the near future, and establishing additional passenger rail routes between the two countries is also being contemplated.

Bangladesh has already provided India with connectivity facilities to move goods between western and eastern regions of India. On the other hand, India has allowed Nepal and Bhutan access to Chittagong, Mongla, and the (now under construction) Payra ports of Bangladesh, through the Indian territory. The needed infrastructure for the above mentioned road and rail linkages are being built with partial/full support of India (depending on the particular project). Plans are being made for the joint exploration of hydro-electricity resources in Nepal and Bhutan. Bangladesh is now importing about 750 MW of electricity from the Indian eastern grid (Palatana in Meghalaya and Bahrampur in West Bengal). The additional import of electricity is being negotiated, including about 1000 MW from the Assam-Bihar transmission line passing through Bangladesh.

Indian companies have set up joint ventures to produce coal-based power stations in southern Bangladesh. Bangladesh has offered two of the planned special economic zones (SEZs) exclusively to companies from India. All these are promising developments which could go a long way in helping Bangladesh to realise the potential opportunities of closer economic cooperation with India, and countries in the South Asian region. Closer cooperation with ASEAN member countries will also be possible by taking advantage of the various transport links being built at present (for example, the Kaladan multimodal corridor, among others). As a matter of fact, Bangladesh's potential as a gateway to the Bay of Bengal will critically hinge on establishing connectivity with its large hinterland. Seamless connectivity will play a crucial role in this respect.

Initiatives such as the transport linkages, free trade agreements, and measures to establish a sub-regional energy grid will, hopefully, help Bangladesh to build the needed supply-side capacities, attract foreign direct investment, and raise export competitiveness in regional and global markets.

Going Forward

While the opportunities of regional, and particularly sub-regional, cooperation are formidable, much more will need to be done to realise the potential. Although India has provided Bangladesh (and other LDCs in the SAARC) with duty-free, quota-free market access for almost all items (excepting 25 items that include arms, liquor, and narcotics), Bangladesh, till now, has not been able to take advantage of the preferential access in any significant manner. Exports to India are only worth about US $ 650 million as against India's total import of about US $ 450 billion in 2017. In this context, Bangladesh's ability to attract Indian investment and targeting the Indian market could play a crucial role in enhancing her export to the Indian market. Indeed, many of the non-tariff barriers to bilateral trade with India arise from infrastructure deficits, and the current unsatisfactory state of trade facilitation.

To realise the potential of transport connectivity as well as initiatives such as the BBIN-MVA, significant investment will have to be made to improve the state of trade facilitation. These include setting up of a single window, the introduction of paperless trade and electronic data exchange, and the establishment of interoperable customs systems. Border points should be crossing points and not choking and control points. Vehicular movement across regional countries, supported by appropriate motor vehicle agreements and standard operating protocols, should be the norm. Standard-setting institutions should be strengthened to cater to the needs of laboratory testing and standards certification. Many non-tariff barriers to trade originate from the lack of these facilities and arrangements.

There is also a need to design well-crafted sequencing of various investment projects. For example, the potential of the Ashuganj International River Port (AIRP) in Bangladesh, which was expected to play an important role in providing river-road connectivity between Kolkata port and eastern India (to Agartala in Tripura), remain largely unrealised because of the lack of needed infrastructure, landing facilities for ship, warehouse facilities for storage, and an underdeveloped road link between Ashuganj and Agartala. As a result, in the absence of the required facilities and logistical support, traders are continuing to use the chicken neck corridor for India's west-east-west cargo movement. There is a need to expedite measures which would enable business people and cargo handlers to reduce time and costs while using the AIRP if they are to move goods through Bangladesh territory. Mutual recognition agreements concerning standards need to be signed on a bilateral basis with India, and also on a pan-SAARC basis. Here, SARSO (South Asia Regional Standards Organisation which is headquartered in Dhaka), mandated to come up with common SAARC-wide standards, could play an important role in addressing NTBs that relate to standards. Necessary investments will have to be made to strengthen the capacity of SARSO. Irritants concerning Indian LoCs—such as the conditionalities imposed by the Exim Bank of India in the form of upfront payments, the mandatory procurement requirement of 85 per cent (this has now been brought down to 65 per cent in certain cases)—should be resolved through bilateral negotiations. Factors which constrain the deepening of collaboration between and among countries in Southern Asia should be resolved through speedy negotiations.

Conclusion

As it is, the majority of the South Asian countries have commenced their middle-income journey in the recent past. Many East Asian countries which had embarked upon this journey several years ago, have fallen into what is called the "middle income trap". In view of this, both the regions should have keen interest to translate their respective comparative advantages into competitive advantage through closer collaboration at the regional, cross-regional, and sub-regional levels. Towards this, production networks and value chains, both vertical and horizontal, will need to be established, based on relative advantages. Such initiatives could play an important role in enabling South Asian countries to graduate from being lower-middle income countries to upper middle income countries, and to also help East-Asian countries to graduate from being middle income to developed countries by coming out of the middle income trap. Thus, both the regions could gain importantly from closer pan-southern Asian cooperation.

It is from the above perspectives that the conference on *East meets East* is so critically important for the economies of both South and East Asia. KIF ought to be complimented for bringing key stakeholders together to examine the ways and means to advance this cause from which our economies and our people could potentially draw enormous benefit.

24

India's Connectivity with Southeast India: Opportunities and Challenges of Linking East to East

Shankari Sundararaman

Introduction

As the Asian growth story has begun to take more concrete shape over the past several years, there is a realisation within the region regarding some of the critical factors that will continue to shape and enhance this reality. Over several years, from the eighties onwards, the momentum of global economic growth has shown a steady and clear shift eastwards where, prior to colonialism, this region had vibrant historical linkages wherein trade, commerce, and cultural influence had traversed across both territorial and maritime spaces, accounting for the exchange of goods, the movement of people, and the transfusion of cultural linkages. The core theme of this paper presented at the PURBASA Conference seeks to explore its main premise: East meets East. Linking India's eastern region to its eastern neighbours is a critical component of both the Look East and Act East policies. This paper seeks to examine the core focus of this linking between India's east and eastern neighbours: the issues relating to connectivity.

Northeast as a Gateway

For several centuries, connecting to your neighbour and beyond was the core of human movement across continents. In ancient times, borders were less defined and human endeavour aspired to go beyond its immediate region to discover the world and existence beyond. In his book *Bound Together: How Traders, Preachers, Adventurers and Warriors Shaped Globalization* (2007), Professor Nayan

Chanda refers to four sections of human society that took the processes of globalisation forward: traders, preachers, adventurers and warriors.[1] Inherently tied to the processes of globalisation, these linkages are also critical inputs for creating connectivity across human populations, where exchanges of goods, ideas, and cultural interactions have led to very important shifts in regional integration. Looking at the ancient patterns of trade between India and Southeast Asia, the trade links that were established became the conduits for the spread of cultural ties across the region. And, interestingly today, while analyzing economic integration under the Look East/Act East policy, there is a view that culture, or lack of cultural understanding, especially with regards to knowledge on the business culture in these regions, acts as an impediment to closer trade relations.[2]

Understanding connectivity and cross regional linkages from a historical point of view becomes relevant, especially while trying to correlate the linkages between the past and present. Economic growth and development has been harnessing communications and connectivity almost from the beginning of the industrial revolution. Initially, the use of communication and connectivity was focused on the procurement of raw materials, leading to the spread of colonialism. Throughout the colonial period, the expansion of both communications and connectivity increased the uninterrupted flow of raw materials to various destinations in the West from where manufactured goods once again reverted to the markets in the colonies and elsewhere.

Since the issue of improved connectivity dates back to the beginnings of the industrial revolution, it is interesting to note that the work of R.M. Hartwell, *The Industrial Revolution and Economic Growth* (1971) states clearly that by 'the 1830's the British were producing nearly 3/4th of the mined coal in Europe, half of the cotton goods and iron, [and] most of the steam engines'.[3] It was only through enhanced communications that this expanded further eastwards to other parts of Europe and to the colonies. In this work, Hartwell quotes from Adam Smith: 'good roads, canals and navigable rivers, by diminishing the expense of carriage, put remote parts of the country nearly on level with those in the neighbourhood of town'.[4] In other words, he emphasised the importance of connectivity as the core of economic expansion—an issue that has been critical for several years.

However, the end of the World War II began to witness a shift. With the onset of decolonisation, there was a clear shift in the patterns of economic integration globally. Primarily in Europe, followed by Asia in the late seventies and early eighties, the increased pace of economic growth also led to the exploration of increased regional connectivity and linkages. Connectivity per se, is therefore not a new concept. But, as the need for larger markets for goods and produce increased, the potential to explore connectivity linkages across what were former sub-units of the Asian continent has ensured a geopolitical shift in how Asia is being redefined, both territorially and by the maritime expanses of the Indo-Pacific, once again, assuming critical significance. This brings the question of enhancing connectivity and communications to the forefront of regional integration since, without these, there would be limits on the size of markets, the higher cost structures for the movement of goods and, most significantly, and disparities between adjacent regions and neighbouring territories because of the lack of connectivity.

Since, historically, the growth of connectivity was a factor in the removal of disparities among adjacent regions, today connectivity projects are seen as a method of reducing regional disparities within states and the adjoining border areas between countries. In the inaugural address to the PURBASA Conference, it was pointed out that there was need to ensure that the East of India was brought on par with the rest of India, and that enhanced connectivity was a critical factor to making this happen.[5] This disparity within the country is one of the first reasons for enhancing connectivity. Its applicability to the Look East and Act East policy lies in the recognition that Northeast India is the land link to the critical regions of Southeast Asia and where connectivity will have the greatest impact. With the onset of the Look East policy, the reference to Myanmar's significance as the land link to Southeast Asia has often been reiterated on the grounds of the connectivity that linked this region earlier under the British. The British expansion of trade into the inland areas of China was based on the connectivity established through the overland route via Burma. This relevance of Myanmar as the land link to the rest of Southeast Asia continues to exist even today.

Similarly, Northeast India is as relevant as Myanmar. As such, these areas act as the junctures where connectivity projects meet. Even while the northeast is seen as a crucial link in the integration eastwards, it remains essential that the region must create its own stakeholders which will act as drivers of both the foreign and economic policy initiatives, by seeking advantages that accrue from greater connectivity to its eastern neighbours.[6] This ability to create stakeholders locally has two impacts: firstly, this approach will create a convergence within

India's domestic politics and its foreign policy. Linkages through the India's northeast furthers its development by creating a locally driven approach to foreign economic integration. As a result, the region not only benefits from economic activity and cross border linkages but acts as the core of India's ties with the east through a land route. Secondly, the ability to bridge this gap will be important because both the issues of political sensitivity and development in the northeast are inversely proportional to each other—the higher the political sensitivity, the lower the potential for development; and the lower the political sensitivity, the higher the potential for development. One of the primary advantages of building up local stakeholders would be to address the convergence of interests driven by the centre's approach which is a top down one, and state level interest which would be bottoms up. However, addressing these convergences is still difficult in the region, despite several initiatives such as the BCIM Corridor and the BCIM Forum for Regional Cooperation, have been started. Their ability to make an impact on the region has remained limited. Moreover the debates relating to the complex interaction between regional integration and security are still areas of concern and, while the region remains politically sensitive, this factor will play out its course.[7]

Imperatives to Push Connectivity

While the political factors that determine the importance of connectivity projects have been discussed above, this section looks at the imperatives that are pushing connectivity in the region. If there is any one single factor that accounts for the need to give focused attention to connectivity in the region—it is the sheer magnitude of Asia's economic growth over the past few decades. Leading economist Rajat Nag states that Asia accounts for over a quarter of the global GDP, with three of the five largest economies centred in Asia. He also states that this is expected to rise to nearly half by the year 2050.[8] This is a factor that is the most compelling in furthering connectivity between India and the region.

As the end of the Cold War gave way to the shifts in the Asian regional scenario, India too showed significant changes in its foreign and economic policies. One of the critical drivers in this context was India's liberalisation which necessitated the need to expand its economic linkages with Southeast Asia under the Look East Policy. From 2014, this has been rechristened as the Act East policy, with a growing emphasis on addressing the implementation of various agreements. India's emergence in the regional order is factoring in a changed regional and global environment where the emergence of multi-polarity and multi-plexity seem to coexist.[9] According to Amitav Acharya, the nature of multi-polarity in the current world order remains different from what was understood as multi-polarity in the pre-war European era which was dominated by a set of alliance systems.[10] In the current context, multi-polarity and multi-plexity co-exist not only among the great powers and states, but also in the integration at the level of 'institutional mechanisms, non-governmental organisations, multinational corporations, and transnational networks—which also include liberalisation choices and connectivity corridors'.[11] This present scenario, wherein both multi-polarity and multi-plexity are co-existing, is a factor that will be critical in driving India's continued engagement eastwards.

As a global transformation occurs, there is a growing diversity of actors and players to choose from in terms of furthering India's integration processes. Moreover, today's visible shifts are not purely dominated by the traditional notions of integration that were, in the past, determined only by military alliances. They are founded on issues of economic complementarities. It is in this context that one must view the relevance of connectivity to India's growing regional identity and its integration with its extended neighbourhood in the East. ASEAN as a region accounts for a critical percentage of trade with India where it currently stands at the tune of nearly US $ 72 billion for the year 2017.[12] This includes exports from India, which stand at US $ 31.07 billion, while imports are at US $ 40.63 billion.[13]

Adding to the strength of India-ASEAN economic dimension is that, as regional economic integration expands, three of the largest economies in the Indo-Pacific region are going to be critical—India, China, and Japan. Together, they account for a combined GDP of nearly US $ 20.8 trillion. This is a critical factor that pushes India's integration further. The completion of the RCEP negotiations in this regards will be significant. However, with India not receiving the benefit of expanding its services sector under the India-ASEAN FTA, the reservations to move ahead on the RCEP will be a factor to address (See Figure 1).

In order to expand this economic advantage across the entire region, connecting the East and Northeast of India to the regions beyond to tap the benefits of this Asian economic success remains an imperative. While the development of these regions is not solely dependent on connectivity, it remains a crucial condition for further development. Today, there is an added incentive

Figure 1: Top 10 World Biggest Economies for 2018-19

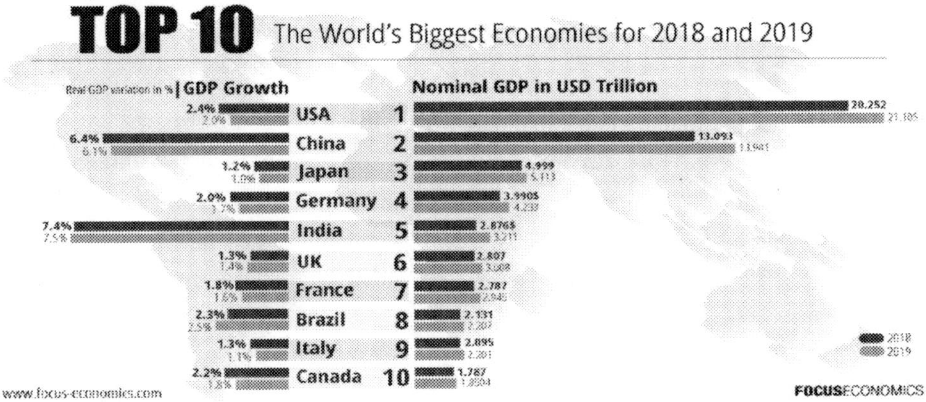

Source: https://www.focus-economics.com/sites/default/files/wysiwyg_images/focuseconomics_january_biggest_economies-01.jpg

for furthering connectivity, both within the state and across the borders to adjoining states, whereby the emphasis on developing economic corridors is pushing forwards the connectivity linkages across regions. Three factors are critical to the formation of these connectivity linkages that will allow for the furtherance of such corridors: first, it links the agents of economic activity to its various hubs and nodes, where there is an intensity of such pursuits.[14] Second, regional integration is enhanced by the formation of economic corridors which actually promote inclusive growth. Areas that remain on the periphery tend to stay cut off from the advantages that accrue from economic activities in more developed areas. As a result, connecting them through such corridors ensures the expansion of economic activities to areas that were earlier lagging behind. The assertion of continued focus on these regional initiatives critically expands the linkages both within and outside the region.[15] Third, by promoting the formation of economic corridors, there is an effort to link up contiguous regions together whereby investments in these regions will promote the acceleration of economic activity leading to greater development and linkages across border areas.[16] These three factors are clearly some of the imperatives under which the furtherance of connectivity projects must be examined for improving the economic integration of India's eastern regions with Southeast Asia.

Progress of India's Connectivity Projects

This section focuses on the progress of the connectivity projects proposed by

India.*[17] Some of the proposed connectivity projects that are critical in this regards are as follows:

- India-Myanmar-Thailand Trilateral Highway: This is a project that has been in the offing since 2002, and is currently slated to be completed in the end of 2019. This will link Moreh in Manipur, India to Mae Sot, in Thailand through Myanmar (See Figure 2). After sixteen years, a segment of this road was opened in August 2018, and was called the India Myanmar Friendship Highway (IMFH). The opening of the IMFH has also been advantaged by opening two areas for crossing into Myanmar through the land route – these are the Moreh-Tamu Crossing, linking Manipur in India to Sagaing in Myanmar. The other is the Zokhawthar-Rhikhawdar linking Mizoram to Chin state in Myanmar.[18] These three initiatives in recent times have been small incremental steps in the right direction to boost the connectivity initiatives across the land linkages.[19]

Figure 2: India-Myanmar-Thailand Trilateral Highway

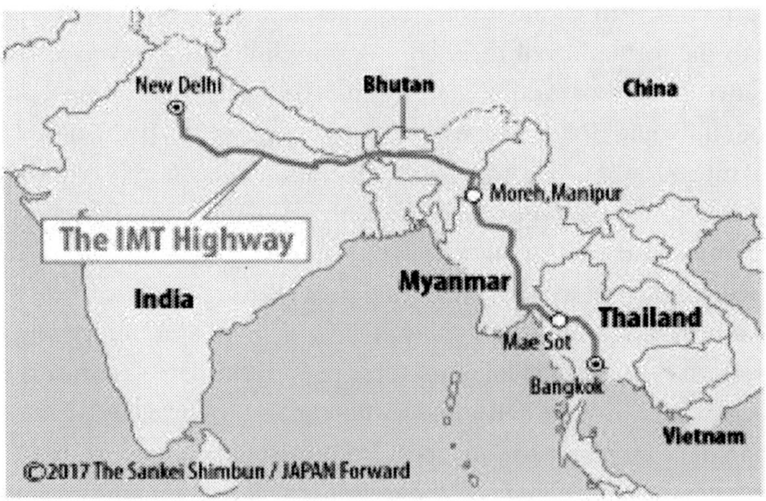

Source: https://japan-forward.com/india-myanmar-thailand-trilateral-highway-a-promise-to-transform-the-regions-economic-landscape.

- Stilwell Road or the Ledo Road: One of the most debated of the

* The methodology for this section showing the text and image on the connectivity project details has been inspired by the work of Dr. Rajat M. Nag. See Dr. Rajat M. Nag, 'Looking East: Security through Greater Cross Border Connectivity', in Namrata Goswami (ed.) *India's Approach to Asia: Strategy, Geopolitics and Responsibility*, New Delhi: Pentagon Press Publishers, 2016.

connectivity projects has been the Stilwell or the Ledo road (See Figure 3). Built during the Second World War, the road was a strategic link between British India and China during the war. Covering a distance of nearly 1800 km the road links Assam in India to Kunming in the Yunnan province of China, through Myanmar.[20] While India initially had concerns over security issues with the opening up of this road, there have been some indications that this may be positively considered with the significance of Myanmar to the Look East and Act East policies. The Indian side of this road is still far from usable and needs to be thoroughly reconstructed to ensure the movement of goods and people. The Chinese side of the road is operational which makes it possible to consider extending it.

Figure 3: Stilwell Road

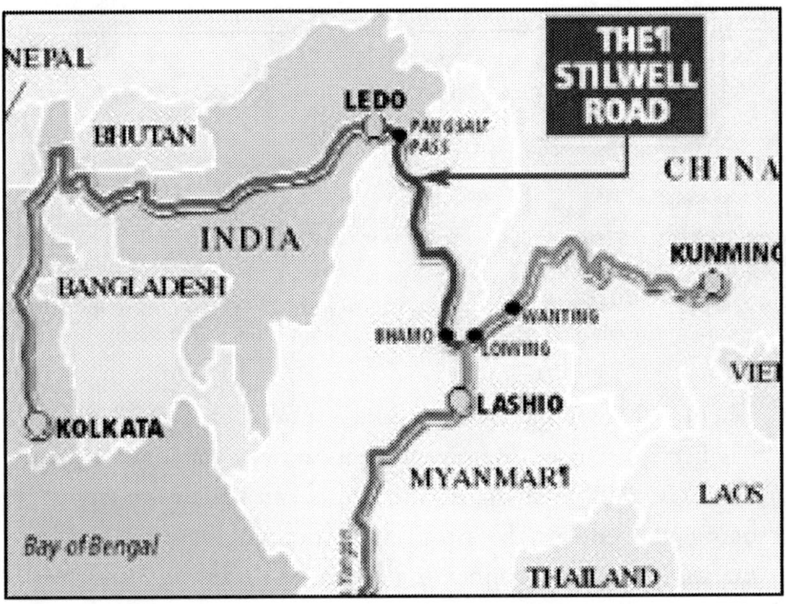

Source: *Indian Express*, 4 September 2007 URL http://archive.indianexpress.com/news/india-fasttracks-highway-shortcut-to-china-/214368/

- BCIM Corridor: One of the significant policy initiatives that linked and furthered the possibility of such economic corridors was the BCIM-EC (see Figure 4). As one the first initiatives that aimed to link an economic corridor at the sub-regional level, it was a critical meeting point for three sub-regions of Asia itself: that is, South Asia, Southeast

Asia, and China.[21] This has been a critical initiative, with a focus on developing the northeast of India. One of the other advantages of the BCIM corridor is that it will also act as a critical link to the furthering of the BIMSTEC processes which will be an expansion of the BCIM to include other countries of both South Asia and Southeast Asia into a sub-regional mechanism.

Figure 4: BCIM-EC

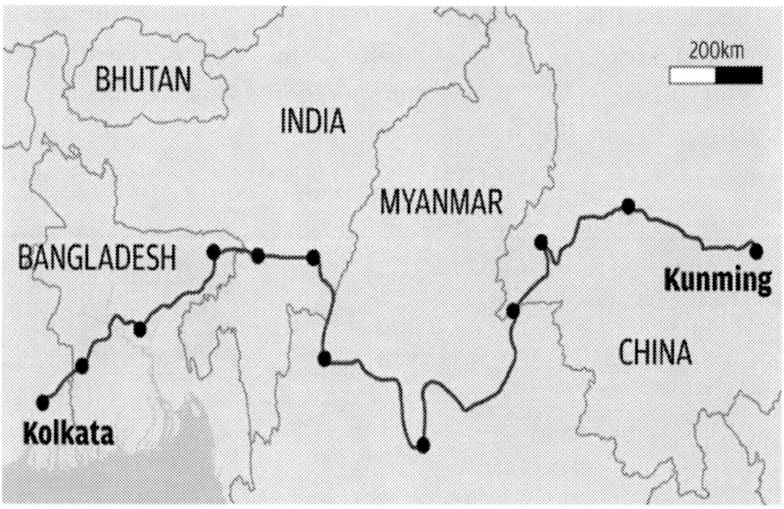

Source: *The Deccan Chronicle*, 25 November, 2014, at https://www.deccanchronicle.com/141125/nation-current-affairs/article/%E2%80%98bcim-economic-corridor-beneficial-north-eastern-regions

- Chennai Dawei Corridor: While connectivity across the land route has been discussed for several years now, a more recent initiative—which is credibly changing the manner in which the Bay of Bengal is being viewed—is the proposed Chennai Dawei Sea Link or the maritime corridor connecting Chennai in Tamil Nadu to Dawei in Myanmar (See Figure 5).[22] This is also a key initiative under the Master plan for ASEAN Connectivity where the sea link is an important investment by Thailand into the special economic zone in Myanmar centred around the port of Dawei. India's ability to link to this through the port of Chennai is still in its nascent stage, and may take several years to implement. However, with the growing recognition of the importance of the Bay of Bengal, this sea link can contribute significantly in linking the BIMSTEC countries to the proposed sea link and expanding the scope of the project, creating a very unique set of stakeholders for such a project. [23] It is further possible to link India to Thailand and to the Mekong Corridor connecting India to the entire region.

Figure 5: Chennai Dawei Sea Link

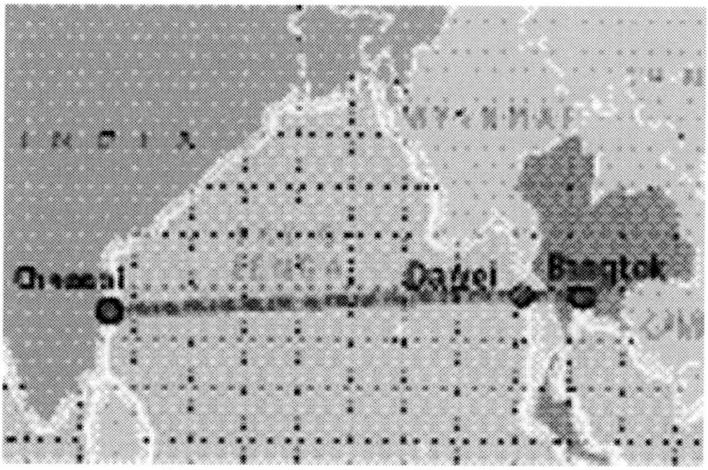

Source: *The Indian Express*, 26 January 2012, at http://archive.indianexpress.com/news/thai-pm-for-chennaidawei-corridor/904138/

- Kaladan Multimodal Transport Corridor: As a flagship of India's connectivity projects, the Kaladan Multimodal Transport Corridor links the port of Kolkata through the Sittwe port in Myanmar (See Figure 6). Using both the sea route and the river link, it uses the Kaladanriver to access interior Mizoram. The multimodal transport corridor will be a critical link in connecting Mizoram and Myanmar with Kolkata port, thereby reducing the dependence on the overland route through Bangladesh. One of the most challenging issues in the completion of this project has been the political volatility in the Rakhine province of Myanmar. India's current position in this regard is the completion of the final road link between Paletwa and Zorinpui in Mizoram which is a road stretching 109 km. There are still issues with the project that need to be completed; but this has, so far, been one of the most ambitious projects initiated by India and, despite the delays, the project will be a flagship of other connectivity projects for India.[24]

Figure 6: Kaladan Multimodal Transport Corridor

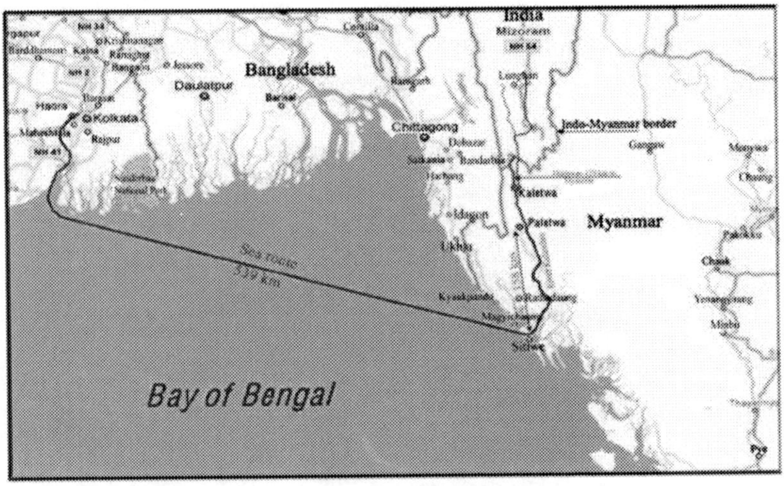

Source: The Master Builder, 10 June 2017, at https://www.masterbuilder.co.in/india-awards-fresh-road-contract-complete-kaladan-project-myanmar/

- BBIN: The BBIN is the Bangladesh, Bhutan, India and Nepal Motor Vehicle Agreement, which emerged from the 18th Summit of SAARC when the summit failed to move forward on a SAARC motor vehicles agreement, especially due to hurdles from Pakistan (See Figure 7). As a result a smaller and more tenable agreement was conceived among the four countries. However, this met further hurdles when the Bhutanese parliament failed to ratify the proposal. Bhutan's concerns over the movement of trucks from neighbouring countries, and the environmental hazards posed by this, has been a critical stumbling block in the efforts to operationalise this agreement. The current state of the initiative is that India will seek to move forward even in the absence of Bhutan.[25]

Challenges and Opportunities

Apart from the above connectivity projects, there are two other proposals that are in the pipeline. Under the India-ASEAN Comprehensive Framework Agreement, there is a proposal for a railway link between India and Vietnam. This will link India to the rest of its northeast, and from there to Southeast Asia through the land route. While this remains a very ambitious project, and is yet to take concrete shape, the proposal is one that has great potential in linking the regions together.[26] This is also supported by the overall linking

Figure 7: BBIN MVA

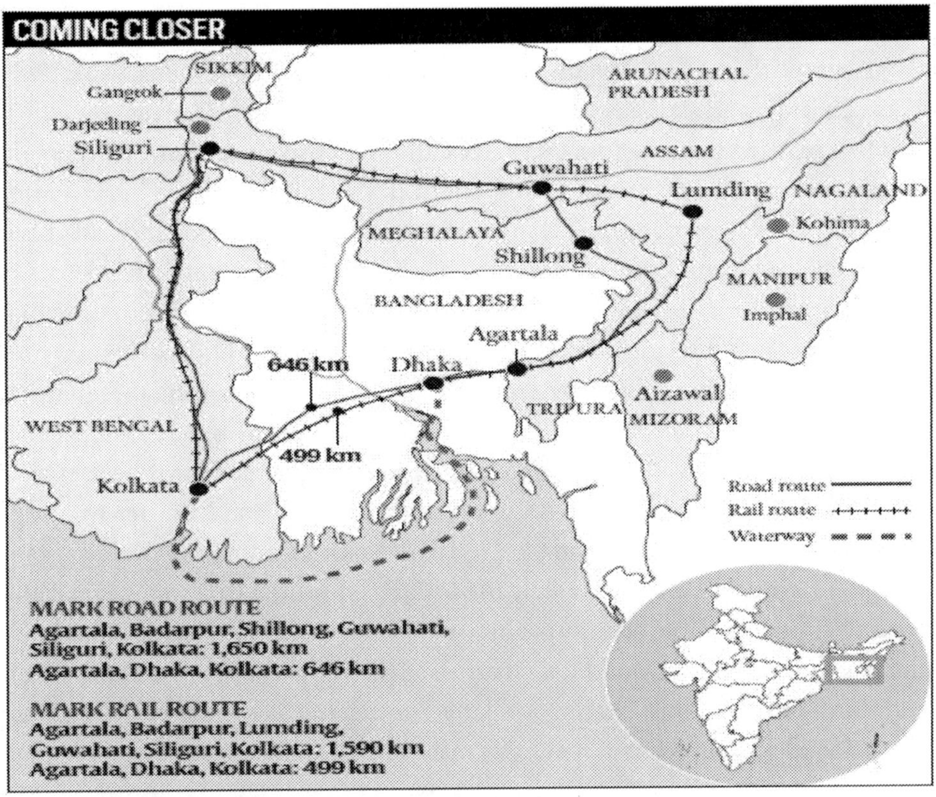

Source: *The Indian Express*, 25 November 2015, athttps://indianexpress.com/article/explained/through-bangla-a-development-shortcut-for-northeast/

between South Asia and Southeast Asia through the Indo-Pacific Economic Corridor. As for this, several challenges remain; the most significant is the cost of such a project which is enormous. According to an Asian Development Bank report, the cost of linking South Asia to Southeast Asia amounts to a total of US$ 73 billion—of which US $ 18 billion is for roads; US $ 34 billion for railway linkages; US$ 11 billion for ports; and US $ 10 billion towards energy trading.[27] However, the current allocation is to the tune of US $ 8 billion total. Of this, US $ 1 billion is for roads; US $ 5 billion for railway connectivity; and US $ 2 billion for ports.[28] The staggering cost of such a project linking South and Southeast Asia itself acts as a deterrent to furthering this project. While this can be addressed with a combination of both public and private funding options working in partnership with one another—the first imperative is to create stakeholders who would focus on these as a means of expanding their outreach and furthering the integration process.

An area that is still lagging behind is the issue of direct air connectivity between India and all the ASEAN countries. The Open Skies Agreement which was first referred to in the India ASEAN Comprehensive Economic Partnership Agreement is still not finalized, and continues to face hurdles. This is a huge challenge to overcome, especially given the delivery deficit which India has been responsible for. Many of the delays in the implementation of connectivity projects across the territorial extents linking South and Southeast Asia are due to structural impediments, such as the process of tendering a project. While these issues may delay the projects, the government must undoubtedly move beyond these hurdles to complete the connectivity projects in a time bound manner. Overcoming the challenges to implementing the Open Skies Agreement will be a critical step in also furthering the three C's as reiterated by Prime Minister Modi: of linking Culture, Commerce and Connectivity. With tourism being an important component of the Act East policy, the linking of tourist destinations as sister cities will be a credible step in promoting all the three C's. In this regard, the linking of cities in the Buddhist circuit will focus on Yangon, Bodhgaya, and Lumbini—the Buddhist circuit. Similarly, another option would be to link Siem Reap, Jogjakarta, and Thanjavur to form a similar tourism related circuit which will also brings about cultural linkages between three different countries. These approaches will automatically boost the tourism sector, act as a scheme for the promotion of the connectivity projects, and increase air connectivity.

One of the most important incentives in this regard is the furtherance of the community building process within ASEAN. The three pillars of the ASEAN community are clearly the focus of ASEAN among which the Socio-Cultural Community is being given serious emphasis. This initiative focuses on bringing together the ASEAN countries to look upon themselves as a single unit, which will actually consolidate the move towards building the other two pillars of the ASEAN community. In furthering its ties across these sectors, India too can make a credible contribution in furthering ASEAN's Socio-Cultural Community.[29]

Conclusion

As Asia's economic rise continues, the potential for closer economic integration drives forward the potential for greater connectivity too. The two are directly related to one another, necessitating a clear cut approach to how a country responds to the challenges of increasing connectivity while simultaneously safeguarding its political and economic space. It is impossible to further regional integration if that form of integration is detrimental to the national interest and sovereignty of a country. As such, one of the hurdles in opening up the road linkages across the wider region for India has been founded on certain security concerns which have hampered the processes of furthering connectivity projects. Often, most regional integration processes have begun from the prism of economic integration, which has also pushed forward connectivity leading to the lowering of political barriers.[30] However, this is easier said than done, especially in areas where there is greater political sensitivity, the progress of connectivity gets severely hampered.

Interestingly, in the maritime domain there is a growing awareness of the global commons as a critical asset to all mankind. This is, today, increasingly being seen as an area for the furtherance of global governance options. Similarly, this can be argued for the case of connectivity projects too: that is, there is need to view such projects as global public goods. It is an idea that is being increasingly argued to ensure that the balance between economic integration and security are founded upon a set of normative principles that will act as safeguards for connectivity projects. This measure will ensure that states are more comfortable with initiatives to protect connectivity projects through global governance mechanisms in order to address the conflicting interests between enhancing connectivity and safeguarding security.

NOTES

1. Nayan Chanda, *Bound Together: How Traders, Preachers, Adventurers and Warriors Shaped Globalization*, New Haven, Connecticut: Yale University Press, 2007.
2. V.S. Seshadri, 'Regional Comprehensive Economic Partnership Agreement: Need for Strategy, RIS-DP 209', RIS New Delhi, March 2017, pp. 29-32.
3. R.M. Hartwell, *The Industrial Revolution and Economic Growth*, Routledge Library Editions, New York: Routledge, 1971, pp. 157–160.
4. Adam Smith, *The Wealth of Nations*(ed.) by J. Thorold Rodgers, London: 1869, p. xxv, cited in Ibid.,
5. Inaugural Keynote Speech, by Honourable Dharmendra Pradhan, Minister for Petroleum, Government of India, at PURBASA Conference, Kalinga International Foundation, 16 March 2018, Bhubaneswar, Orissa.
6. Shankari Sundararaman, 'Indo-Pacific Economic Corridor: A Vision in Progress', in K. Yhome and Rajiv Ranjan Chaturvedy (eds.), *Emerging Trans-regional Corridors: South and Southeast Asia*, Global Policy-ORF Series (NUS, iSAS, Durhan University, Wiley Blackwell, 2017, ORF New Delhi), pp. 26–33.

7. Suba Chandran, 'The Indo-Pacific: India's Look East Policy 3.0', Institute for Peace and Conflict Studies, at http://www.ipcs.org/article/india/the-indo-pacific-india's-look-east-30-3843.html.
8. Rajat Nag, 'Looking East: Security Through Greater Cross Border Connectivity', in Namrata Goswami (ed.) *India's Approach to Asia: Strategy, Geopolitics and Responsibility*, New Delhi: Pentagon Press Publishers, 2016, pp. 143–182
9. For a detailed assessment of the distinctions between multipolarity and multiplexity and their impact on connectivity, see Amitav Acharya, 'Regionalism in the Evolving World Order: Power, Leadership and the Provision of Public Goods', in Antoni Estevadeordal and Louis. W. Goodman (eds.), *21st Century Cooperation: Regional Public Goods, Global Governance and Sustainable Development*, New York: Routledge, 2017, pp. 39–54.
10. Ibid.
11. Ibid.
12. Surojit Gupta, 'Indo-ASEAN trade Rises 10% to $ 72 bn in FY 17, but is long way off potential', The *Times of India*, 26 January 2018, at https://timesofindia.indiatimes.com/business/india-business/indo-asean-trade-rises-10-to-72bn-in-fy17-but-is-long-way-off-potential/articleshow/62657555.cms
13. Kritika Banerjee, 'Beyond Republic Day Show, ASEAN Can Help India Take on China in Southeast Asia', *India Today*, 24 January 2018, at https://www.indiatoday.in/india/story/beyond-republic-day-show-asean-can-help-india-take-on-china-in-southeast-asia-1153102-2018-01-24
14. Hans-Peter Brunner, 'What is Economic Corridors Development and What Can it Achieve in Asia's Sub-Regions', ADB Working Paper Series on Regional Economic Integration 117, 2013, 1, at http://www.adb.org/sites/default/files/piblication/100110/reiwp-117-economic-corridor-development-pdf
15. Kunal Sen, 'Global Production Networks and Economic Corridors: Can They be Drivers for South Asia's Growth and Regional Integration?' ADB South Asia Working Paper Series 33, 2014, 25, at http://www.adb.org/sites/default/files/publication/152708/south-asis-wp-033.pdf
16. Pradeep Srivastava, 'Regional Corridors Development in Regional Cooperation', ADB Economics Working Paper Series, 258, 2011, pp. 6–16.
17. Nirupama Subramanium, 'The Road to East: Connecting India, Myanmar and Thailand; gateway to ASEAN', *Indian Express*, 5 September 2018, at https://indianexpress.com/article/india/india-myanmar-friendship-highway-thailand-asean-5335551/
18. Rupakjyothi Borah, 'India-Myanmar-Thailand Trilateral Highway: A Promise to Transform the Region's Economic Landscape', *Japan Forward*, 24 August 2017, at https://japan-forward.com/india-myanmar-thailand-trilateral-highway-a-promise-to-transform-the-regions-economic-landscape/
19. 'Beijing Calls for Restoration of Stilwell Road Connecting India, China and Myanmar', *The Hindu*, 16 June 2016, at https://www.thehindu.com/news/international/Beijing-calls-for-restoration-of-Stillwell-Road-connecting-India-China-Myanmar/article14425879.ece
20. For a detailed account of the BCIM see K. Yhome, The BCIM Economic Corridor: Prospects and Challenges, in K. Yhome and Rajeev Ranjan Chaturvedi (eds.), Emerging Trans-regional Corridors: South and Southeast Asia, Global Policy-ORF Series (NUS, iSAS, Durhan University, Wiley Blackwell, 2017, ORF New Delhi), pp. 41-47.
21. C. Raja Mohan, 'Thai PM for Chennai-Dawei Corridor', The *Indian Express*, 26 January 2012, at http://archive.indianexpress.com/news/thai-pm-for-chennaidawei-corridor/904138/
22. Supalak Ganjanakhundee, 'High Potential Seen in Dawei-Chennai Link', *The Nation*, 3 August 2012, at http://www.nationmultimedia.com/business/High-potential-seen-in-Dawei-Chennai-link-30187571.html

23. 'India Awards Fresh Road Contract to Complete Kaladan Project in Myanmar', 10 July 2017, at https://www.masterbuilder.co.in/india-awards-fresh-road-contract-complete-kaladan-project-myanmar/
24. Elizabeth Roche, 'India to redraw BBIN Connectivity project as Bhutan Opts Out', LiveMint, 8 May 2017, at https://www.livemint.com/Politics/ol0E49p8V9WqXpJUXBqFPL/India-to-redraw-BBIN-connectivity-project-as-Bhutan-opts-out.html
25. Rajat Nag, n. 6, pp. 155–158.
26. 'Connecting South and Southeast Asia', Asian Development Bank, Asian Development Bank Institute, Japan: ADBI, 2015, pp. xx–xxi.
27. Ibid., For further details, see Shankari Sundararaman, 'Indo-Pacific Economic Corridor', in K. Yhome and Rajeev Ranjan Chaturvedi (eds.) *Emerging Trans-regional Corridors: South and Southeast Asia*, Global Policy-ORF Series, NUS, iSAS, Durhan University, ORF New Delhi, Wiley Blackwell, 2017, pp. 26–33.
28. Discussions with Ambassador Vongthep, ASEAN Deputy Secretary General for the ASEAN Socio-Cultural Community, 5 January 2018, 5th AINTT Conference, Jakarta, Indonesia.
29. Jayant Prasad, 'Connectivity and Infrastructure as a Regional Public Good', in Antoni Estevadeordal and Louis. W. Goodman (eds.), *21st Century Cooperation: Regional Public Goods, Global Governance and Sustainable Development*, New York: Routledge, 2017, pp. 137–157.

25

India and the Indo-Pacific: The Logic of Partnerships

Harsh V Pant

Speaking at the 2018 Shangri-La Dialogue in Singapore, Prime Minister Narendra Modi rightfully staked New Delhi's claim for a central role in the Indo-Pacific—a region stretching from the shores of Africa to those of America. Underlining the need for inclusive engagement and ensuring that the Indo-Pacific is not perceived as a "club of limited members," he argued that India's vision of the Indo-Pacific would not be directed against any country, and would be all about creating a rules-based and stable trade environment. Placing the Association of Southeast Asian Nations (ASEAN) at the heart of this vision, he suggested that there was a need for India and China to work together because an "Asia of rivalry" would hold back the entire region. Yet he also did some plain speaking when he raised some sensitive issues linked to Beijing that have caused concern across the Asia-Pacific region. Without naming China or referring to the disputes in the South China Sea or the Belt and Road Initiative (BRI), he called for a free and open region with a rules-based order without dependence on force.

This is a time of great turbulence in the global order with the US President Donald Trump intent on challenging its very foundations and the Chinese President Xi Jinping intent on building China as the nodal force on the global power matrix over the next two decades. India's response to this changing dynamic is, therefore, being very closely observed.

The Quad Takes Shape

In this context, an interesting development in the Indo-Pacific has been the re-emergence of the idea of a democratic "quad" focused on the United States, Japan, India, and Australia. A decade after it first appeared and was ignored by most states under Chinese pressure, it has now bounced back with a vigour few would have expected just a year ago. The reason is simple: there is growing nervousness in the regional power centres in the Indo-Pacific about China's emergence as a major global power (no one buys the peaceful rise of China argument anymore) and about the ability and willingness of the United States to manage this power transition effectively.

The current transition of power in the Indo-Pacific, underlined by America's relative decline and China's growing power, has significant implications for most of the Asian states. Though the uncertainty around the future of international politics, norms, and institutions does impinge upon all members of international society, Asian states find themselves at the forefront of this transition. For them the current transition of power is not only an ideological contest over the form and nature of the international political system but is inextricably linked to their own national security imperatives in a number of ways.

The rise of China and its increasingly assertive behaviour is unnerving key Asian states. These states lack internal capacity to balance China's growing economic and military strength on their own. Even when all these states have benefited enormously from China's economic rise and continue to do so, cumulatively they have also contributed to China's relative growth and its military capabilities. If until recently China's peaceful rise was a collective good for the Asian states, it has now turned into a collective military and security hazard. Regional economic growth is dependent on freedom of navigation in the Indo-Pacific—from the South China Sea to Straits of Malacca to the Indian Ocean. 25 percent of all traded goods pass through the Straits of Malacca. Asia has benefited from the post-Cold War security order underlined by U.S. primacy and now America's relative decline is leading to growing concerns over the future of this liberal order and Washington's capability and intention to defend the same.

And so soon after Shinzo Abe's landslide victory in the Japanese elections, his foreign minister, Taro Kono, said that Japan will propose a "top-level dialogue with the U.S., India, and Australia" to promote free trade and defence cooperation across the Indian Ocean—from South China Sea to Africa. The proposal is to countervail China's Belt and Road Initiative, which "would cement a sphere of influence for Beijing well beyond Asia." Abe had also articulated a need for such a new security architecture in 2012 when he had suggested "a strategy whereby Australia, India, Japan, and the U.S. state of Hawaii form a diamond to safeguard the maritime commons stretching from the Indian Ocean region to the western Pacific."

In 2007, Abe, in his earlier stint as prime minister, lobbied for Asia's democracies to come together. This was also actively supported by the United States. The initiative resulted in a five-nation naval exercise in the Bay of Bengal in September 2007—code-named Malabar 07-02. However, perceiving a possible ganging-up of Asia's democracies, China issued demarches to New Delhi and Canberra, causing this initiative to lose steam, since both Australia and New Delhi felt it unwise to provoke China.

But this time, unlike in the past, both India and Australia welcomed the move. India's Ministry of External Affairs suggested that India was open to working with countries "on issues that advance our interests and promote our viewpoint" and that New Delhi has "an open mind to cooperate with countries with convergence." Australia's then Foreign Minister Julie Bishop indicated her country is open to reviving the quadrilateral forum and since Australia has been having such engagements, it was "natural" to continue to have such discussions.

China's assertive foreign policies over the last decade have managed to pave the way for such a response whereby once diffident New Delhi and Canberra are now willing to openly accept the need for a security architecture, which privileges engagement with like minded democratic countries. So the Quad is back. It may still not work the way many would like it to. But the signals from the Indo-Pacific are that regional states are willing to work together to manage the externalities of China's rise and America's incompetence.

Closer Partnerships

India, Japan, and Australia are at the centre of this strategic flux in the Indo-Pacific.

The level of strategic convergence between Delhi and Tokyo can be gauged from the fact that in 2014, India invited the Japanese Navy to participate in the annual Malabar exercises with the U.S. Navy in the Pacific waters, reviving an earlier practice of joint India-U.S.-Japan trilateral exercises. This was a significant move considering the fact that India had earlier capitulated to China's reservations when the naval forces of India, U.S., Australia, Singapore, and Japan had conducted joint exercises in the Bay of Bengal in September 2007. After China made its displeasure clear, India refused to be a part of these exercises from 2008. With the coming of Modi government, Japan's participation in Malabar has been institutionalized. Both Japan and the United States have repeatedly expressed their desires to expand the scope of Malabar exercise. The vision document signed by Modi and Abe in September 2014 called out for the "regularization of bilateral maritime exercises as well as to Japan's continued participation in India." During the seventh round of the trilateral strategic dialogue between the three countries held in Honolulu in June 2015, India agreed to Tokyo's participation in the 2015 series of Malabar exercises.

India and Japan have an institutionalized trilateral strategic dialogue partnership with the United States. Initiated in 2011 maintaining a balance of power in the Asian-Pacific as well as maritime security in Indo-Pacific waters became an important element of this dialogue. A similar dialogue exists between the United States, Japan, and Australia. Under Modi, such security trilateralism in Asia has received not only new momentum and is being expanded to incorporate other regional powers: in June 2015, India, Australia, and Japan held their first ever high level dialogue in New Delhi. These trilateral initiatives have a serious potential to transform into a 'quad' of democracies in the Indo-Pacific region. The roots of this potential partnership were laid in late 2004 when navies from the U.S., India, Japan, and Australia collaborated in tsunami relief operations all across the Indian Ocean. Japan has been the most vocal supporter of such an initiative.

India and Australia are wary of China's assault on maritime security and freedom of navigation in the Indo-Pacific region. These common concerns have strengthened the need for greater maritime cooperation between the two nations and the two have started conducting joint naval combat exercises. During Modi's visit to Australia, a security framework agreement was signed by the two countries, further underscoring the importance of defence cooperation in the Indian Ocean region. India and Australia are leading powers in the Indian Ocean region. The two countries are also at the helm of Indian Ocean Regional Association (IORA), a formal grouping consisting of the Indian Ocean Littoral

States. Australia is also a permanent member of Indian Ocean Naval Symposium, which brings together the local navies of Indian Ocean region. The extent of their regional cooperation in Indian Ocean can also be ascertained by their annual trilateral dialogues with countries like Japan and Indonesia.

The ASEAN Connect

Addressing the 15th ASEAN-India Summit, Mr. Modi said India's relationship with ASEAN is a key pillar of its foreign policy. Referring to India's Act East Policy, he underlined that "its centrality in the regional security architecture of the Indo-Pacific region is evident." He focused on terrorism as well, suggesting, "It is time that we jointly address this challenge by intensifying cooperation in this crucial area." In a symbolic move, all 10 ASEAN heads of state were invited to be guests of honour for Republic Day function in 2018. Targeting China, Mr. Modi also assured ASEAN of "steady support towards achieving a rules-based regional security architecture that best attests to the region's interests and its peaceful development." The East Asia Summit, which includes India, China, Japan, South Korea, Australia, New Zealand, the U.S. and Russia apart from the 10 ASEAN member states, also gave Mr. Modi another opportunity to underline ASEAN's credentials: "ASEAN began in times of a great global divide, but today as it celebrates its golden jubilee, it shines as a beacon of hope; a symbol of peace and prosperity."

As China's profile grows, and the U.S. continues to be unsure of its security commitments, there is a new opportunity for India in the region. As the US has gone back to protectionism, China has actually managed to emerge as a beacon of open and free global trade order. This has resulted in the regional powers taking it upon themselves to shape the regional economic and security order. On the one hand, the Trans-Pacific Partnership (TPP) is being resurrected without the U.S., and on the other, the idea of an Indo-Pacific quadrilateral involving Japan, Australia, India and the U.S. is back. Unlike in the past, New Delhi is no longer diffident about engaging with other regional players if it helps to further Indian interests in maintaining a stable balance of power in the region.

The ASEAN members and India together consist one of the largest economic regions with a total population of about 1.8 billion. ASEAN is currently India's fourth largest trading partner, accounting for 10.2 per cent of India's total trade. India is ASEAN's seventh largest trading partner. India's service-oriented economy perfectly complements the manufacturing-based economies of ASEAN countries. There is, however, considerable scope for further growth. Formidable security challenges remain, and the two sides must think strategically to increase cooperation for a favourable balance of power that would ensure regional stability.

India needs to do a more convincing job as a beneficial strategic partner of ASEAN by boosting its domestic economic reforms agenda, enhancing connectivity within the region, and increasing its presence in regional institutions. The ASEAN nations should be clearer and more specific in their expectations from New Delhi and nudge India for a deeper, more broad-based engagement. There is much at stake for both sides.

The need of the hour is to push for greater engagement with such like-minded nations. Despite the hype about the possibility of India emerging as the guarantor of the liberal economic and security order in Asia, there are now new possibilities for reimagining New Delhi's regional and global role. Greater cooperation with like-minded countries in the region and beyond will give it greater space to emerge as a credible regional interlocutor at a time when Washington's policies remain far from clear and Beijing is challenging the foundations of the extant order.

ENERGY CO-OPERATION

26

Energy Cooperation: Summary Report on the Session Proceedings

The Chairperson, Ambassador (Ms.) Neelam Deo, initiated the session by saying that Energy is the engine of our economy which drives all our other industries. The Sources and Users of energy are often very diverse countries, companies and people. There is also a politics of energy cooperation, both at the international and national levels. At the individual level too, the politics of energy affects people directly, yet quite differently. The politics of sources means that resource rich countries act in a different way; indeed, they are often forced to do so because of their situation. A discussion on energy cooperation cannot be isolated from discussions on food, water, environment, and others as these are all interlinked issues. Energy is an umbrella term: the sources and types of energy are highly diversified, be it wave, waste, solar, wind, etc. This leads to different issues related to procurement, generation financing, distribution, and transmission. Governments often sabotage smooth operations by providing one group subsidies over the others within their political structures.

There are also demand and supply issues wherein demand is suppressed because state governments don't wish to buy electricity at the rate at which it is available; sometimes the cost is raised to finance subsidies for alternative sources. Chinese investments in the power sector have also raised certain new issues. In the BIMSTEC region, for example, it may not be necessary for India to invest as China has done the heavy lifting. Thus, cooperation on energy in the region can happen via aiding the financing of projects, the creation of pipelines and the sharing of LNG terminals with low income nations. There is also a need to encourage buyers to diversify the sources of their energy consumption in order to make consumption sustainable for the environment. Grid connectivity and buyer cartels are also important issues to focus on. With technological advancements, energy installations have become vulnerable to cyber threats, which need to be mitigated.

Mr. Prabhat Singh stated that we have now entered the 'Golden Age of Gas'. There is a need to look at the Asian region as a whole, which constitutes 50 per cent of the world's population. The sheer numbers in the region lead to demand creation for energy in different forms. Because of their monopoly over oil, the OPEC believes that they are obliging the world by keeping oil prices stable in order to maintain an economic balance. Even in the gas sector, there are deep pockets that have been in control. However the 'Golden age of Gas' has now begun because the fundamentals of producing oil and gas have changed. This means that the OPEC has not been able to control the prices—especially because of the Shale gas and oil revolution which was unviable until recent technological developments. Up until 2008, it was highly uneconomical to produce Shale, the recovery from which was only 15 per cent. Compare that to an oil well which is 30–32 per cent of gas, which is around 60 per cent. In the last five years, the volume of production has increased 2–4 times, more because of fracking, chicken leg, super fracking, and other such methods. The cost of drilling has also become much less, roughly 10 per cent of the cost—from US$ 80 a barrel to US$ 10 a barrel.

The world can be seen as energy 'haves' and 'have nots.' 1.3 billion people live without electricity, and 0.6 billion of them reside in Asia. The world is seeing a raised demand of 60 per cent while, on the other side, suppliers need markets and consumers, or else they will lose business and go bankrupt. The USA now has a surplus of Shale gas while Asia has an exceeding demand because of its sheer population. Now is the time for the Asian countries to find a mechanism for consumer cartelisation. If we don't act in time, the prices will rise, because the deep pockets are aiming to throttle the infrastructure in order to drive prices by sabotaging supply and increasing demand. The construction of Liquefaction terminals has been postponed for five years, which will drive prices further. The premium that Asian countries have to pay should be removed, and concessions and discounts be placed because Asian countries will need to buy in bulk. The politics of energy cooperation can be seen as a triad: between civil society, businesses, and governments. Civil society has initiated the process of reforms because they feel the pain, the business case is also emerging, and government sides now have to catch up by establishing a small steering committee and data analysis which can establish a detailed plan on how to go about issues related to LNG, like terminals, pipelines, etc. The reserve to gas ratio has also increased from 20 years to 300 years, making Shale gas practically a renewable. There are other renewables as well, like Solar; however, the technology is still developing while the technology for gas is proven, and already established.

Professor Govind Pokharel began his presentation by highlighting that energy needs infrastructure to travel. The increasing demands of the region need the effective utilisation of hydropower which is a renewable, with a hydro potential of 300 GWs. This regional potential can be trapped efficiently by improving transmission and synchronising our policies. Studies have shown that hydroelectricity isn't just about energy and electricity but is also related to many other issues, like floods, pollution, irrigation, and drinking water, etc. The region has a heavy dependence on thermal energy which has led to black carbon depositing on snow and pollution which adversely impact our sensitive environments, leading to the melting of snow and glaciers as well as flooding, especially in the Himalayan region.

The infrastructural and human costs of using fossil fuels and floods are immense; therefore, saving the Himalayas is of immense importance from an energy perspective. There needs to be a mix of sources to bridge the gaps between intermittent and readily usable energy. Variations in energy supply, load shedding, etc. can also be managed by using hydropower. In order to grow at the rate of 8 or 9 per cent—at which India, Bangladesh, etc. are growing and expected to grow—it will require even more energy, which a single source of energy may not be able to fulfil. Solar power which is being encouraged may not suffice; hydro power could help balance the regional grid and provide energy to the Sub-continent. The diversification of sources and the reliance on renewable energy can lead help in sustainable progress, and to provide electricity for the masses.

India is the hub for the energy networks of the region; it is also the centre of inter-connections between the smaller neighbouring states. Unilaterally developing power is not ideal; thus there is a need for policy synchronisation to address sub-regional concerns. Delivery deficiency can be solved by foreign investment as well as efficient regional integration and cooperation.

In the changing context, close cooperation is required among different actors to harness the potentials available in the sub-region. Considering the existing mismatch of capability and the comparative advantages of individual countries; the harnessing of natural resources, developing infrastructural connectivity, enhancing human resource capacity, and sharing the knowledge available in society can be augmented further by mobilising private and public-sector investments within the sub-region. An understanding of policy gaps, aligning policy instruments, and replicating successful models through economic cooperation will synergise initiatives that are targeted to realise the common destiny of the citizens—that is, bring prosperity for all.

The Chair opened the floor for discussions by raising two questions. Countries in need may not always have gas, but they do have access to solar energy. On the other hand, if they can utilise gas energy, then other related issues can be mitigated, like with desalination, water can be brought back into the cycle. Hydro energy may not have an adverse impact on the environment—like fossil fuels do—but it does have some impact. This is specially seen in the case of hydro power projects constructed in the upper stream of the Ganga or the Mekong rivers.

The following points emerged during the discussion.

- The reasons why Asian countries have to pay a premium on LNG were unravelled. Asia is a huge continent; the west and east of Asia are quite different. The Eastern countries were in dire need of energy to drive their economies, and so agreed to pay high premiums to derive the same. Now the situation has changed as the South and Southeast of Asia are the new sources of demand. The consumers can now change the nature of the industry which was primarily organised by, and for, the benefit sellers.
- It was observed that hybrid sources are used in most countries; however, compared to other sources, gas is still cheaper. The laws of economics would ensure that inefficient sources of energy are weeded out.
- Strict guidelines have been put in place to prevent and reduce the social and environmental costs related to hydro power.
- Energy mixing and energy banking can help to meet the different nature of demands that emerge because of seasonal changes in the Subcontinent.

CONNECTING WOMEN, YOUTH AND CIVIL SOCIETY

27

Northeast India: Connecting with Neighbours

Alana Golmei

Introduction

Northeast India, which is generally considered as remote and far-off from rest of the country due to its geographical location and poor connectivity, has lately emerged as a key attraction for rest of the country. One of the key attractions is attributed to its strategic location—sharing international borders with Bhutan, China, Bangladesh, Myanmar and Nepal and serving as the gateway to South-East Asia. Arunachal Pradesh shares borders with Bhutan, China and Myanmar; Assam with Bangladesh and Bhutan; Manipur with Myanmar; Meghalaya with Bangladesh; Mizoram with Bangladesh and Myanmar; Nagaland with Myanmar; Sikkim with Bhutan, China and Nepal; and Tripura shares its borders with Bangladesh.

The region is endowed with rich natural resources and has wide variety of attractions to promote tourism. However, the region is landlocked and lack of proper connectivity is always a drawback. Most of the Northeastern states have limited air and rail connectivity with major cities of India except Guwahati (Assam), which is the center or hub of the region. Good connectivity within the region itself will also enhance development and opportunities for the people.

Recently, a weekly express special train from Naharlagun of Arunachal Pradesh to Delhi was inaugurated by Minister of State for Home Affairs, Kiren Rijiju and Minister of State of Railways, Rajen Gohain. This was announced by Hon'ble PM Modi during his visit to Itanagar last year February. On 6 March 2018, the first plane landed at Pakyong airport in Sikkim which is a remarkable step. Subsequently, on 10 March 2018, SpiceJet flight from Kolkata becomes the first passenger plane to land in Sikkim. The region needs more of such time-bound development project to enhance its connectivity with rest of India.

Each state in the region has its own attractions, opportunities, and threats and therefore, meticulous and comprehensive prior assessment is inevitable for the successful implementation of any scheme or developmental programme.

Therefore it is important to equip and develop Northeast while the government is implementing its Act East Policy. In his *inaugural address, the President of India Shri Ram Nath Kovind at the North-East Development Summit in Imphal on 21 November, 2017, stressed on the potential of the region.* "The geographical location makes it the obvious gateway to India, linking the vast economies of the Indian subcontinent and of the ASEAN countries. This is the potential that needs to be tapped and this is the idea that must inspire the Summit. Central to the Government of India's approach to the development of the Northeast is an urgent and speedy enhancement of connectivity. This is a multi-modal programme, across land, water and air. It refers both to connectivity within India as well as to connectivity between India and its eastern and Southeast Asian neighbours."

People-to-People Ties

In order to strengthen people to people relations, it is important to connect with those who share common interest, experiences, political beliefs, religion and culture etc.

Myanmar and India have a strong historical and geographical link where Northeast shares a very close connection in terms of trade, political beliefs and culture. India and Myanmar share a 1,640 km border running between India's Northeast states of Arunachal Pradesh, Manipur, Mizoram, Nagaland and Myanmar's Chin state, Kachin state and Sagaing division.

According to Dr. Tint Swe, former MP, NLD, "for the eyes of 90 per cent of the Burmese population, the origin of Buddhism from India is not a small factor, and for them, the flourishing of Buddhism is even more important than the tourism industry in both countries. However the single airline between Calcutta and Yangon has dry seasons for 8 months per year. Although India is well-known for high level of education and information technology, only a small section of Burmese people can enjoy the taste of them and more students go to Southeast Asian Universities. The high profile border trade operating at Moreh-Tamu point is facing new challenges."

India's Moreh is no match for Maesot of Thailand. It should consider twice upon the implementation of the Trilateral Highway project and the rail link from Manipur to Vietnam via Myanmar.

Communities in India's border have strong historical and geographical link with ethnic groups on the other side of the border. For example, the Chin and Mizo people share similar historical, cultural and religious backgrounds, which opened doors for most of the Chin economic migrants, who crossed the India-Myanmar border for a better livelihood and future in India. Similarly in the Manipur border, Kuki-Chin family speaks the same language and practices the same culture and religion, which enables them to integrate well in the community. Nagaland is another border state with Myanmar connecting through Mon district.

With the Government of India implementing the Act East Policy, there is an opportunity for closer connection between peoples on both sides of the countries. Some of the important ongoing projects are the Kaladan Multi-Modal Transit Transport Project via Mizoram, construction of Rih-Tidim road and Rih-Falam road in Myanmar, maintenance of the Tamu-Kalaywa-Kalemyo Road connecting Moreh in Manipur to Myanmar, and the tri-lateral Highway between India-Myanmar and Thailand. The long awaited Bus service from Imphal (Manipur state) to Mandalay in Myanmar is yet to happen.

One of the key successes for India's Act East Policy lies in connectivity in terms of road and air. Developing infrastructural projects including transport facilities are crucial if India is to facilitate greater economic integration and people to people contact. Even if we have connectivity facilities without people-to-people relations it will be difficult for things to move.

Connecting Women, Youth and Civil Society

There are lots of avenues where the neighboring countries can share experiences. Cultural events, interaction at the University level and interaction with civil society groups, women's groups, etc need to be promoted.

Healthcare, education, sports, agriculture etc. are some of the important areas where Myanmar and Northeast India can connect. Handloom industry will be another successful area where womenfolk from the Northeast region and Myanmar can exchange. We have heard from both sides of the border areas, there is huge eagerness to do business and therefore many items need to be made legalized.

There are lots of similarities between Northeast India and Southeast Asian countries. One example is the scene of women in Northeast India dominating the market, which is similarly observed in Myanmar, Thailand, etc.

Some efforts have already been made to strengthen ties between people from Manipur and Myanmar. For example, during November 2017 Sangai festival in Imphal, Manipur, women football team from Mandalay came and played exhibition match with the women football team of the state as a part of the Sangai Tourism Festival.

According to news report, "The exhibition match between players of the two countries India and Myanmar is the first of its kind in the country and is being organised as a part of the Sangai Festival under the theme 'Connecting through Sports' to enhance better relationships between the two countries, particularly those living in Manipur and those at Mandalay."

In January 2018, Chief Minister N Biren Singh flagged off Manipur Women's team for the Women football exhibition match between Myanmar and India cum Business meet from Western Kangla Gate in Manipur. With the objective to promote relationship with Myanmar a team from Manipur visited Mandalay and Sagaing province where they hold women football matches and a business meet.

Equally important to bring about such ties will be for the leaders and law-makers of both India and its bordering countries to understand how the system works in the other country. In May 2013, Burma Centre Delhi facilitated meetings of 10 Burmese women delegation including 3 MPs with Indian organisations and Parliamentarians. The delegation interacted with different organisations, individuals, policy makers, etc., which helped them in understanding about various aspects such as Indian Legal Framework for Women Empowerment & Protection, Myanmar & Millennium Development Goals, Anti-trafficking law, etc.

Conclusion

As we talk of people to people relations, official relations also have an impact on them. Trade exchanges remain the main link between people separated by international boundaries. People on the Myanmar side of the border depend on India for goods such as food and household items. This is also mainly due to the poor transport infrastructure and distance within Myanmar, which makes it much easier for them to cross the border to buy goods from India. The exchanges between the people on two sides of the border have been there for many decades although some official policies have turned their links into illegal practices. The governments of India and Myanmar can improve and enhance this relation by providing good roads, banking and other facilities. The role of civil society is equally important in enhancing the relations and they can work towards synchronizing government policies with people's needs or requirements. The civil society groups can at the same time facilitate the improvement and better understanding of the exchange mechanism.

As Myanmar and India have strong historical and geographical links where the Northeast shares a very close connection in terms of trade, political beliefs and culture, it is important to have good connectivity.

28

The Role of Women: A Perspective from the Philippines

*Maria Teresita C. Daza**

Ambassador of the Philippines to India, HE (Ms) Maria Teresita C. Daza started her presentation by highlighting that at the heart of Act East Policy (AEP), and ASEAN's Economic Community (AEC) and connectivity initiatives is a strong development agenda. The AEP as an economic initiative among other objectives is envisaged to assist in the development of the North East (of India), while the AEC is expected to evolve as an integrated and cohesive region that would allow and encourage growth, progress and prosperity to all. Development can be defined in very strict economic terms: growth, modernisation, infrastructure development, increase trade and investment. But there is another construct of development—in ASEAN they have a construct of development that puts people at the heart of development; development that allows people's participation, empowerment to meet their basic needs and interests. ASEAN attempts to have more holistic inclusive people participatory type of development which is envisaged in ASEAN Socio-Cultural Community and inclusive sustainable capacity to achieve a better life for all of ASEAN.

In her presentation she shared two perspectives in terms of the role of women: the ASEAN Perspective and the Philippines' perspective.

From the ASEAN perspective, she wondered if ASEAN can move forward if women are left behind (50 per cent) of the population? ASEAN had celebrated 50 years of progress. It's women have seen wide ranging improvement in health,

* Based on the Rapporteur's report of the presentation by HE Amb.(Ms) Maria Teresita Daza, Ambassador of the Philippines to India.

education attainment, participation in government job and business but also required other measures that will propel them to move forward. Measure such as skills upgrading, enhanced education and government support. An educated woman with fewer and healthier children can better contribute to the society. To have a full benefit of the trade and economic integration, trade and non-trade policy need to avoid biases towards particular sex or gender. Other researches have shown that any company or organisation that increased its women participation or leadership in decision making have more percentage increases in its profit margins. Women continue to be overlooked as source of talent in propelling economic growth and prosperity across the region and other region as well.

Coming to the Philippine perspective she said that in the past women as a whole were relegated to the background in the Philippines. This was largely true in the past and is also largely true in the present. Women's voices have been muted in public discourse—whether it is on political issues or on economic issues or a whole range of issues that affect the well being of the public. Discussions were mostly made among men and in consultation with men as if the affairs of society did not concern women. We all know that this should not be so because our fate rests on the shoulders of both men and women. Fortunately we in the Philippines and the region are slowly moving towards a world where the contributions of women to decision making and nation making and community building are increasingly being recognised. We see steps big and small to empower women and bring their voices to the main stream. Philippine has much to share in terms of experience of empowering women and in harnessing their potential in nation building. The Philippines granted its women the right to suffrage in 1937—way ahead of our counterparts in Asia and the world at that time. Harmonizing the society in nation building. In 2014 the Philippines ranked ninth in the Global Gender Gap Index—the highest ranking country in Asia after Finland, Norway, Iceland the rest and since then has been at the top of the GGG index. There are about 25-30 per cent women representatives elected in our Legislative Assembly and Parliament. The Philippines has had two female Presidents (Corazon Aquino and Gloria Macapagal-Arroyo). Many women occupy important positions both in the public and private sector. Philippines also has a Commission for Women which was first established in 1975. The country also adopted the National Action Plan for Women, Peace and Security, the first in Asia, followed by Nepal.

Several factors explain why this country had some progress in putting women in the mainstream. First of all, the Philippines has historically been a matriarchal society with women playing important roles in planning and decision making—the respect accorded to women is quite high notwithstanding the fact the country is still male dominated. But the struggle for equal recognition and opportunities did not come on a silver platter—it was a product of hard work and a constant reminder to society that the world would only be half as good without them. Secondly, education has been a key enabler of our women to participate in the public sphere. On this point we are fortunate because we have no less than our national hero and a host of other personalities encouraging women to education in order for them to be empowered. It is with knowledge and learning that one can see in a clearer perspective and women realise their fullest potential to contribute their best to society. Yet women cannot fully succeed in this endeavour without the involvement of men. It is important that women make men realise the value of women in running the society. For instance, the enactment of the law in support of Gender Equality and Empowerment in the Philippines may be credited in large measure to men in Parliament and legislature as well as the push given by nongovernmental organisation. Equally there is the need to involve government in matters pertaining to women because in the end it is the government that will legislate and provide the necessary funding in support of programmes that lead to desired goals. In the Philippines we have several legislations in support of mainstreaming gender issues as well as empowering women. For instance we have the Law on Gender and Development (GAD) that has been a major factor in enabling women to work outside their home. The GAD legislation requires government entities to allocate 5 per cent of their budget for addressing the needs of working women such as providing day-care centre—so that women's children can stay near the workplace of the mother. This is not to say that the Philippines has achieved the goals for women. There are still gaps and concerns that need to be addressed such as sustaining the gains of the past decades to continuous support from succeeding governments and civil society. Civil society is instrumental in making things happen. They know the issues very well because they work at the grassroots. The challenge is how they can bring the change they want, knowing they have the power and capacity to do so within the realities of the environment they find themselves in. Ultimately the true empowerment of women starts with the home, where they are responsible for educating the next generation of men and children in general.

29

The Force of the Divine Femininity: Connecting Beliefs and Oral Traditions Across Southeast Asia and Beyond

Lopamudra Maitra Bajpai

Numerous divine feminine forces have been historically worshipped across the regions of India, neighbouring countries, Southeast Asia, and beyond. These include deities like, Mary, Durga, Kali, Kuan Yin, Sarasvati, Hecate, Tara, Hokmah, Shekinah, Sophia, Cybele, Brigit, amidst others, including natural and powerful forces which are Creator Beings and belong to lesser known folk cults. This belief unites the entire region and has been, historically, expressed through much of the folklore, oral traditions, monuments, statues, sculpture, and inscriptions. This presentation is an attempt to highlight this diversity through oral traditions, and to understand its strength and relevance in present times.

Goddess worship occupies an important segment of Indian socio-cultural phenomenon from very ancient times. The concept of a 'Mother' acts as a placating symbol for all fears on the one hand, and is also a source of hope, expectation, and anticipation for a better tomorrow, on the other. Through time, mother worship portrays the difficult existence of humankind, and the power of regeneration and procreation of 'the mother' has, over the years, been associated with the symbol of proliferation at a subsistence level. A dominant thought that underlines the belief even today remains the same, and the worship of the Divine Mother or the Divine Feminine Force/Energy still occupies an important part in our socio-cultural as well as our religious beliefs and philosophy. The idea of the Goddess is that of a divine and sacred female force with supernatural attributes. Across the region of India and Southeast Asia, there are many female divine powers which are worshipped. Through history, their mention can be found across oral traditions, folklore, and often in manuscripts, inscriptions, monuments, and sculptures.

This presentation attempts to highlight the manifold significance of the power of the Female Divine Force in India as well as in Southeast Asia in ancient times which are still considered prominent. These are forces that have been primarily associated with the powers of procreation, regeneration, and creation from ancient times. Often, feminine forces are considered to form an equal balance with the male force in the universe in local mythology. This essay focuses on the primary concept of the female divine force as procreation as expressed in the earliest available oral traditions and beliefs from mainstream thought processes in India, and various adjoining regions across Southeast Asia. While innumerable examples across the region constitute important parts of folk religion as well, this is an attempt to highlight a common thread between the most prominent thought processes across the region, with examples from the mainstream elements of various regions. This common conceptualisation connects the region, irrespective of religious and geographical boundaries.

The goddess is a primordial being who was believed in and worshipped by people for several thousands of years. The reason for the worship of this supreme female identity has been variously defined by scholars down the ages. She is often variously referred to as a source of all life, and many examples can be found in caves (Palaeolithic art), in excavated terracotta female figurines from several sites from around the world (from the Neolithic age which vary worldwide, but are found generally between 5000–10000 BCE), and in several manuscripts, monuments, structures as well as in numerous oral traditions and folklore. Thus, the notion arose of an omnipotent Mother whose worship symbolised ... a cultural continuity from the Palaeolithic era to modern times (Meskell, 1995).[1] In the course of history, she has often been referred to as a balancing force of nature, and partnered with the masculine forces of nature.

While it is not possible to trace exactly the very beginnings of the concept of worship of deities as a force, several ideologies provide assistance. The traces of several female figurines as well as the many oral traditions (later available in manuscripts and in inscriptions) associated with the worship of many mainstream deities provide help in the historiographical understanding of some of the ideas of worship. The several female figurines found in archaeological sites across the world (dating mostly from Neolithic times onwards) initially gave rise to the idea of commonly labelling any stylised female figurine Mother Goddess. However, this thought process gradually evolved as scholars grew increasingly aware about the many stylistic and technical differences amidst the assemblages. The primary notion of connoting the female figurine as Mother Goddess was linked to the worship of the fertility goddess, important in agricultural societies all over the world. And, there was a tendency to view the same through the ideologies behind the several mentions of female deities in oral traditions and scriptures of the Indian Subcontinent across the last 5000 years.

Another view highlights the fact that all Goddesses might not have necessarily been a part of, or the continuation of, a single Goddess cult, or been associated with maternity. However, this also does not mean that several of the figurines may not have any cultic significance. The need of the hour is to study the origins in their proper context in which they are found.

Connecting India and Southeast Asia through Oral Traditions of the Primordial Powers of Creation

Since time immemorial, the concept of the female divine force has been prominent across Europe and Africa. Much evidence has also been found in the remains of the 5000 year old Indus Valley civilisation. Here, goddess worship seemed to have occupied an important segment of the socio-cultural phenomenon. Though various speculations about deciphering the Indus script continue unabated, various examples of terracotta female figurines have made scholars make various assessments down the ages. These are the earliest examples from India and the adjoining regions; and, it would be completely radical to comment that the preceding cultures did not have some influence of this vast civilization,[2] or to mention that the existing population did not have a belief in worshipping the female divine force.

With reference to the proto-historic times of the Indus Valley civilisation, Stuart Piggot (in his book titled *Prehistoric India*, 1950) speaks of clay female figurines in the Kulli and Zhob cultures of southern Baluchistan—that is, contemporary sites of Harappa. The ones from the Kulli culture have been described as 'ornamented and decorated to resemble the everyday woman of the time', which could have been used in 'household shrines—something in similar lines with the several clay figures used as votive offerings in rural shrines across the nation' (pp. 105–106). The figurines of the Zhob culture are adorned with necklaces and decorations, and have a more or less 'terrifying' appearance; they seem to be the 'embodiment of mother goddess...a guardian of the dead...concerned with the corpses and seed-corn-buried beneath the earth' (Piggot, pp. 126–127).

These stylised female figurines offer ample evidence of the importance of the concepts of mother and child, birth, womb, plant, and thereby regeneration. The iron-age in India also witnesses numerous examples pertaining to terracotta (TC) female figurines, with exaggerated secondary sexual organs and pronounced breasts. The places where these have been found are Sangameœvara, Matrakuta, Māhūr, Māhūrjhari in Karnataka and Maharashtra in India as well as in the excavations of Inamgaon which have yielded a variety of goddesses in terracotta (TC), dated as early as 2nd century BC.

However, the oral traditions as we know them can be traced only to Vedic times, when change gradually emerged and the worship of the female force started to incorporate concepts of nature, with the all-encompassing ideologies of speech, dawn, earth, river, sun, and horizon, etc. Within the *Vedas*, both gods and goddesses are praised; the earliest *mandalas*[3] of the *Rigveda* have been estimated to have been composed sometime in 2nd millennium BCE. Usha (the Goddess of Dawn) is praised in twenty Hymns,[4] and one of them[5] declares Usha, the Goddess of Dawn as the one who must be worshipped first.

> The shining tints of the Dawn have spread like the waves of the waters,
> Beautifying the world, she renders all good roads easy to traverse,
> She who is replete with delight, excellence, and health,
> Divine Ushas, though art seen auspicious, thou shinest afar,
> thy bright rays spread over the sky, lovely and radiant with great splendour;
> Do thou Ushas bring me opulence, daughter of heaven;
> thou who art divine, who art lovely, who art to be worshipped at the first daily rite;
> At thy dawning, divine Ushas, birds fly from their resting places, men arise to work;
> Thou, divine Ushas, bring ample wealth to the mortal, the offerer of these prayers.
>
> —(abridged) *Rigveda*, VI.64

Besides Usha, there is also mention of Aditi (considered the mother of all

Gods), Usas (or the Dawn), Vāk (presiding deity over speech), etc. as is evident from the early Vedic *Samhitā* where there is mention of female divinities. However, they are mostly all subservient in nature (Banerjea 1966, pp. 113) to the male deities. There is no mention of *Śakti* as conceived in later times in early literature. It was much later that the idea of energy was transformed into that of a consort,[6] and the name of the significant deity Durga appears much later. The mention of goddess Ambika is seen in the *Satapatha* and *Taittiriya Upanishads.* In the *sutras* of *Boudhayana* and *Sankhayana*, the name 'Durga' appears for the first time. In the *Puranas*, the earliest reference of the Devi is in the *Devi Mahatmya* section of the *Markandeya Purana*, which specifies through a story the victory of Durga over the demon-king, *Mahishasura.* This mention is significant as she is soon seen to be included amidst the famous Hindu pantheon of the three gods: 'Brahma, Vishnu and Maheshwar'. According to oral traditions, it was from the forehead of Durgathat Kalisprang to defeat Durga's enemy, *Mahishashura.*

Thus, the initiation of the concept of *Shakti* and *Adi Shakti* started to manifest itself, giving the platform for the worship of Female divine forces. Kali was considered as primordial energy and the power of Time. She manifests herself in several forms, including Tara, Maya, and Prakrrti. The concept of the Kali also manifests herself as Devi, or Mother Nature (*Mula Prakriti*), giving birth to all, sustaining and nourishing all, and finally absorbing the same from which, once again, new life emanates.

Shaktaism also helped to further influence the concept of the divine feminine force across the region of Southeast Asia. Shaktaism is also closely associated with Samkhya and Tantra Hindu philosophy, and has influenced further the concept of creation. Shaktaism propagates the divine feminine force to be the creative-preservative-destructive energy that can free all from the demons of ego, ignorance, and desire, and is the main force behind the creation of all actions and existence. The cosmos is considered as male or *Purush* while the creator is considered as female or the *Devi.* Thus, the entire universe is balanced between these two forces of creation and destruction. This balancing act of bipolar forces, as well as the regenerative powers of Buddhism as well as Hinduism can also be seen to further influence many cultures across Southeast Asia. Slowly and steadily, the significance of the Devi, along with the ideology of Shaktaism, spread to other regions of Southeast Asia through the patronage of many kings—especially from the 3rd century onwards. The famous triad became 'Vishnu, Siva and Devi', and the significance of Brahma was reduced considerably.

Hindu as well as Buddhist influences had started to spread across the regions of South-east Asia from

> Burma in the north to Java and Annam (Vietnam) in the south and south-east. This is also further assisted by the discovery of Amaravati-style Buddha images belonging to 2nd or 3rd century AD across the islands of Sumatra, Java and Celebes and on the mainland in Siam (Thailand) and Annam (Vietnam).

Thus, the extended relation also helped to spread not only Hindu ideas and ideologies, but Buddhism as well across Southeast Asia. This is attested to by the many archaeological findings, including various beads and other artefacts as well as the influence of the gods and goddesses on the oral traditions of the region. Thus, Majumdar also adds that Indian mariners might have been quite familiar with the regions of Indo-China and the Malay Archipelago by the 2nd century BCE, and the trade relations between India and China can be traced to that time as well. There are several oral traditions of various female divinities from the region which also highlight the same.

Early examples of the worship of the female power of procreation in oral traditions of South-east Asia

Through time, as religious influences spread far and wide from the Indian Subcontinent, the forces of Hinduism, including Shaktaism and Buddhism, reached across Southeast Asia. This influenced many identities of folk as well as mainstream deities across the region. One such important example comes from the Khmer civilization that grew to unify most of Southeast Asia between the 8th–14th centuries. Various examples in architecture depict their respect towards women as reflected in *devata* goddess temples. The Khmer leaders implemented systems of government, religion, education, agriculture, and architecture which are still visible in modern life in Cambodia, Thailand, Laos, and Vietnam today. Exactly what roles women played in establishing these systems is still largely unknown; but new research indicates that women were politically, socially, spiritually, and economically empowered, and they were important contributors to shaping Khmer society.

Today, we still see Khmer temples filled with images of sacred women—termed *devata, apsara,* or Khmer goddesses—who embody the feminine forces of the universe. While women and goddesses appear as icons in many ancient and modern societies, the Khmers gave sanctified women dominance over their state temples more consistently and more visibly than any other group. As the architecture of Khmer highlights the various influences of Hindu deities, interestingly enough, many examples also highlight the influence of Buddhism. One such example is of the earliest goddesses of life: *Phra Mae Thorani.* Her mention is not only limited to Cambodia alone; several adjoining regions of Burma, Thailand and Laos also mention her. Buddhist mythology mentions her to be a young woman, wringing the cool waters of detachment out of her hair to drown *Mara,* the demon sent to tempt Lord Gautam Buddha as he sat meditating under the Bodhi Tree. She is depicted variously in several inscriptions and murals in the region. The popular oral tradition highlights her benevolence by stating,

> As the Bodhisattva sat meditating under the Bodhi Tree, Mara (the Evil One) wanted to stop him from attaining enlightenment. Accompanied by his warriors, wild animals and his daughters, he tried to drive the Bodhisattva from his throne. All the gods were terrified and ran away, leaving the Bodhisattva alone to face Mara's challenge. The Bodhisattva stretched down his right hand and touched the earth, summoning her to be his witness. The earth deity in the form of a beautiful woman rose up from underneath the throne, and affirmed the Bodhisattva's right to occupy the *vajriisana.* She twisted her long hair, and torrents of water collected there from the innumerable donative libations of the Buddha over the ages and created a flood. The flood washed away Mara and his army, and the Bodhisattva was freed to reach enlightenment.[7]

In the adjoining regions of China, the concept of *yin* and *yang* is the polarity that describes the order of the universe, held in balance by the interaction of principles of growth (*shen*) and the principles of waning (*gui*), with act (*yang*) usually preferred over receptiveness (*yin*). This is very similar to the Buddhist ideologies of regeneration as well as the Shakta ideology of the Devi which, along with the *Purush* or male identity, forms the balance in the universe. An important aspect of Chinese folk religion is Shenism, which describes the many ethnic religious traditions which have traditionally formed the basic belief structure of Chinese religion, and is translated in Sanskrit as 'Satya Dharma'. It also forms an important aspect since it has derived its gods from the Hindu pantheon—like Brahma, Ganesha, and Hanuman. Across Southeast Asia, this plays an important role in various countries as well, especially amidst the many Chinese populations settled in various regions, including among the Burmese Chinese, the Singaporean Chinese, the Malaysian Chinese, Thai Chinese, and Hoa. Shenism describes the worship of 'shen' or a spirit of awareness, consciousness, etc.

By the eleventh century (the Song period), these practices had been blended together with Indian philosophical ideas of retribution, karma, and rebirth, as well as Taoist teachings about the hierarchies of the gods, to form the popular religious system which has lasted in many ways, until the present day. With a great diversity, the expressions across all of Chinese folk religion have a common core that can be summarised as spiritual, cosmological, and moral. Tian or Heaven is the source of moral meaning, the utmost God, and the universe itself; the breath or substance of the universe is *jingzu* or the veneration of ancestors; *baoying* is moral reciprocity; and two traditional concepts of fate and meaning are *theming yun* which is personal destiny or burgeoning, and *yuan fen* or the 'fateful coincidence' of good and bad chances and potential relationships.

An important and ancient deity of the Chinese religion is *Xiwangmu/Xi Wang Mu/Xi Wangmu/Hsi Wang Mu*, or more commonly referred to as the Queen Mother. Related to the keeper of Tao, she is the giver of prosperity and righteousness and is an important goddess of modern Taoism. She has been referred to have been worshipped for four thousand years, with several mention of her across inscriptions. In ancient times she is often described as having a dangerous look—with tiger fangs, claws and tail. She is also referred to as the giver of immortality. Thus, she is seen to rule, and is a dominant factor to reckon with reference to creation.

One famous folktale about King Mu, a powerful warrior king, tells the story of how, after having conquered most of the region and freeing it from the Huns, he decided to move to the West and travelled through *Xiwangmu's* kingdom. Having welcomed him, and both being impressed by the ruling powers of each other, he decided to marry her, having bestowed upon her many national treasures. He also knew about the powers of bestowing immortality on men. However, before the union, there were messages of a rebellion amidst his conquered kingdoms. He decided to leave, although he was warned that if he left early, he would not become immortal. But, keeping to his duties, Mu left. He died old and unhappy many years later, and *Xiwangmu* remained in her paradise, heartbroken. This is often mentioned across Chinese poetry. *Xiwangmu* is quite unlike the forces of female divinity from later times which are shown as subtle and submissive. Several works of poetry mention her, and compare her with the behaviour of women throughout Chinese history.

An important deity and The Mother or the Nine Imperial Gods is *Tou Mu*. An interesting fact about the deity associates her with eternity as well as the Indian influences. It is said that she was the wife of King Chou Yu, by whom she had nine sons. Some Chinese think she is the Polar Star near the heavenly palaces of her sons. In Taoism, *Tou Mu* has also been called *T'ien Hou* or 'Queen of Heaven', and has been compared with *Kuan Yin*, the female form of *Avalokitesvara*, the bodhisattva of Amitabha Buddha. Like *Kuan Yin, T'ien Hou* is of Indian origin. In India, she was the Goddess of Dawn or *Marici* (Ray of Light). The Tibetans called her *Semding*, and every successive abbess was considered to be a reincarnation of *Marici*. A temple of *Tou Mu*, the mother of the Nine Imperial Gods, was built in the eighth month of 1881 in Singapore, and was followed by other temples.

Associated with the Shinto religion in Japan is *Amaterasu/Amaterasu-ōmikami*, or *Ōhirume-no-muchi-no-kami*, the goddess of the sun and the universe. The name *Amaterasu* is derived from *Amateruor* or 'shining in heaven'. She is seen to be very similar to the Korean solar goddess *Hae-nim*, particularly with regard to shamanistic worship, using the same symbols and practices. Together with her siblings, she is supposed to have created the universe according to oral traditions. Her brothers are *Susanoo* the god of storms and the sea; and *Tsukuyomi*, the god of the moon. It is said that *Amaterasu* painted the landscape with her siblings while she created ancient Japan, and the royal family is her direct descendant.

The identity of the goddess of procreation is also manifested through the many harvest deities—with many of them arising from folk religion, but having been influenced by the Hindu pantheon of goddesses, or Shaktaism and Buddhism in later years. An important example from the region of Thailand and Laos is *Phosop*. She is an ancient deity from Thailand, and is considered as the rice goddess of the Thai people. With time, though, her worship has reduced;

but she forms an important part of the structured mainstream religion of the region. She is also known as *Mae Khwan Khao* (Mother of Rice Prosperity). She is also worshipped in adjoining regions, including in Laos, and is known as *Nang Khosop*. An important tale in Laotian folklore about her is narrated below.

Following a thousand year famine, one day a young man caught a golden fish. The king of the fishes heard its cry of agony, and went to ask the man to free the golden fish in exchange for a treasure. The treasure was *Nang Khosop*, the maiden who was the soul of rice. She lived in the rice fields and had nourished humans for many centuries during which the Buddhist doctrine progressed. One day, an unrighteous king brought famine on the land by storing the rice that was due to the people in order to acquire gold, elephants, and luxury goods for himself. During the hard days of the famine, an old couple of slaves met a hermit in the forest. Seeing that they were famished, the hermit appealed to *Nang Khosop* to feed them. But the rice goddess was angry, and refused. Then the hermit, fearing for the future of the Buddhist Dharma, slaughtered *Nang Khosop*, and cut her into many little pieces. As a consequence, the fragments of the rice goddess became the different varieties of rice, such as black rice, white rice, hard rice *(khâochao)*, and glutinous rice. The old couple taught humans how to cultivate this new rice in small grains, and the Buddhist doctrine flourished. This is significant as the goddess relates both to Hinduism, being similar to the goddess Lakshmi or the Goddess of wealth and prosperity who is worshipped for abundance in agriculture. On the other hand, the deity also relates to the Buddhist ideologies of regeneration, rebirth, and benevolence.

In Vietnam, the female divine force of procreation is reflected in *Dao Mau*. She is depicted through the representation of nature—that is, earth, water, and mountains. The ritual also involves a trance-like state of a medium, and it was initially banned by the government as superstition. However, the order was revoked in 1987. The very act of spiritual association with the world of spirits and forefathers highlight the basic animistic aspects of the folk religion, along with the generative powers of Shaktaism and the regenerative powers of Buddhism. This act of spiritual possession also reflects the Tantric association of Sahaktaism and the importance of the ferocious reflections of the power of procreation.

In and around Philippines, the goddess *Lakapati* is a primeval force that embodies and reflects the idea of the world and the cosmos as a balance between opposite forces. This concept is quite central to Shaktaism. The deity is considered to embody both male and female properties. Possessing both powers of procreation within him/herself, she is also known as *Ikapati,* and is said to have bestowed agriculture to mankind. During early Spanish rule, *Lakapati* was depicted as the Holy Spirit, as the people continued to revere her despite Spanish threats. In Tagalog animism, the small un-husked rice grain was *Lakapati's* emblem. There is an interesting mythological story around *Lakapati.* After marrying Mapulon, who courted her/him tirelessly, a daughter, *Anagolay*, was born. This marriage was symbolic, and is considered important as it represents a mutual bond between two people, irrespective of gender. *Anagolay* is known to help mankind when they have lost something or someone.

A similar and ancient supreme divine female force of procreation in Indonesia (Java) is, or *Shridevi Nyai Pohaci Sanghyang Asri.* She is also found amidst the Sundanese and the Balinese people. She is also associated with the Hindu goddess of prosperity and wealth, Lakshmi, which is also suggested in the very name 'Devi' meaning Goddess in Sanskrit. This is often associated with the influence of Hinduism in the area as early as 1st century. She is also believed to control hunger, poverty, famine, and disease.

A famous folktale describes the vitality of *Dewi Sri* in a Sundanese manuscript titled *Wawacan Sulanjana* or The Tale of Sulanjana. Once upon a time in heaven, Batara Guru, who is associated with Shiva in ancient Javanese mythology, commanded all the gods and goddesses to contribute their power to build a new palace; anybody who disobeyed would lose their limbs (arms and legs). Hearing this, Antaboga (Ananta Boga), the Naga/serpent god, became anxious as he didn't have any limbs at all to do the work. Seeking advice from Batara Narada, the younger brother of Batara Guru, also proved futile. As Anta sat crying, three teardrops fell on the ground. Upon touching the ground, these turned into three eggs and, upon the advice of Batara Narada, Anta carried them in his mouth as gifts for Batara Guru to seek pardon for not being able to contribute to the work. On the way to Batara Guru's place, Anta was approached by an eagle who asked him a question. Since Anta had the eggs in his mouth, he could not answer, but was mistaken for being arrogant. He was attacked by the eagle and, in the process, two eggs fell and broke on earth. They became the twin boars, Kalabuat and Budug Basu.

Upon reaching the palace of Batara Guru, Anta was advised by Batara Guru to nest the eggs till they hatched. This gave birth to a very beautiful baby girl. He gave the baby girl to the Batara Guru and his wife. This girl grew up to be *Nyai Pohaci* (sometimes spelled 'Pwah Aci') *Sanghyang Asri*. Being an attractive woman, she was liked by many male gods, including her foster father, Batara Guru. This was a worrying situation, and all the gods decided to put *Nyi Pohaci* to death. She was poisoned to death, and her body buried somewhere on earth in a far and hidden place. Nevertheless, her innocence flourished even after her death through her grave, giving rise to different trees from different parts of her grave. All of these plants benefitted mankind forever. From her head grew the coconut, from her nose, lips, and ears grew various spices and vegetables, from her hair grew grass and various flowering plants, from her breasts grew various fruit plants, from her arms and hands grew teak and various wood trees, from her genitals grew *Kawung* (*Aren* or *Enau*: sugar palm), from her thighs grew various types of bamboo, from her legs grew various tuber plants, and finally from her belly button grew a very useful plant that is called *padi* (rice). In some versions, white rice grew from her right eye, while red rice grew from her left eye. All of the useful plants, essential for human needs and well-being, are considered to come from the remnant of *Dewi Sri's* body. From that time, the people of Java have venerated and revered her as the benevolent Goddess of Rice and fertility. In the ancient Sunda Kingdom, she was considered as the highest goddess, the most important deity for agricultural society. The story is once again associated, on the one hand, with the Shakta ideologies of the female balancing force of nature and, on the other hand, is also influenced by the Buddhist ideas of regeneration, rebirth, and selflessness.

Conclusion

The act of transmission of cultural elements help to disseminate certain ethnic attributes through space as well as time through a shared belief structure. This type of communication refers to major areas of human anxiety, all of which have been a part of human culture from the day of its emergence, and through attempts of coping with changing circumstances and environment as has been seen in previous examples. Fertility plays a very important part in folklore, quite like in the mainstream religions, which has been evident from previous explanations. It is also looked at as another source of resource retrieval process. Any society which does not have a section of able-bodied young adults is likely to starve and perish. Thus, identity, love, fertility, and nature form the four major corners of human concern which folklore attempts to communicate (Bhattacharya, D.K., 2005: pp. 6–7).

The identity of the female divine force in mainstream religion acts as a placating symbol for all fears on the one hand, and is also a source of hope, expectation, and anticipation for a better tomorrow, on the other. Even today, this belief remains the same, and mother worship still occupies an important part in our socio-cultural and religious beliefs and philosophy. This is true for ideologies associated with folk religions as well. The folk mind, at both the tribal and the peasant level always constructs the image of an ideal, which is articulated within a cultural mapping (Bhattacharya, D.K., 2005, pp. 3–7). The art of transmission of cultural elements helps to preserve certain ethnic traits through time. Folk religion too, has its own basis for survival, and also specific reasons pertaining to mother goddess worship as well. As the primeval power of regeneration and the divine force of procreation, she is regarded as an aspect of a Great Goddess as well as an individual goddess, possessing a specific or particular role within the pantheon. As a similar concept is also reflected through the ideologies of Shaktaism, the Great Goddess or the female deity is regarded as primary—even the powers of the male god are derived from her (Gottner-Abenderoth, 1987).

Though the concept of the Great Goddess is not identical in all cultures, but, as has been discussed above, she bears a common thread across many ancient cultures. Thus, the region of Southeast Asia is endowed with a continuous pattern of cross-cultural influences. While Hinduism (particularly Shaktaism) and Buddhism play a major role in influencing the many regions across the area, yet the intrinsic properties of each region renders unique each female divine force. The several influences of the Buddhist Jataka tales are reflected through the oral traditions of the region; they highlight significant aspects of rebirth, selflessness, and regeneration. On the other hand, the significant aspect of the representation of creation, and of the universe as a balance between the powers of two genders as well as various opposite forces are elements which closely resonate with the ideologies of Shaktaism. Nevertheless, it is the intricate ethos of each region which makes the identity complete, and reflective of the socio-cultural and religious philosophy of that region.

Mother worship is an important aspect of Hindu religious tradition and has played a significant role in shaping much of the socio-cultural as well as religious life of the region. Referring to the importance of the association of Mother Goddess with the mysticism of life, there remains hardly any distinction between the mainstream goddesses and the folk goddesses. However, some basic theological assumptions do differ. Often, the former is theologically considered to be various manifestations of an underlying feminine principle or an overarching great goddess, while the latter is often seen to exert her own single and unique importance as the village deity (*grāmadevatā),* or a deity of supreme importance in a village who is worshipped without being labelled as a consort. However, be it from a traditional and mainstream background, or a folk one, most Hindu goddesses display unique characteristics. As Kinsley points out in his *Hindu Goddesses: Visions of the Divine Feminine in the Hindu Religious Tradition*

> some [goddesses] have strong maternal natures, whereas others are completely devoid of maternal characteristics. Some have strong independent natures and are great warriors; others are domestic in nature and closely identified with male deities. Some Hindu goddess are associated with the wild untamed fringes of civilisation, others are the very embodiment of art and culture.

From being the protector Mother to the bestower of richness, a bountiful harvest, or a cure deity, all goddesses are the manifestation of the perpetuation of anxieties and agonies of everyday life. They are not only viewed in awe as a life-giving force, but their maternal powers are also associated with the basic principles of life: the urge to survive and to live. Every goddess is seen as a symbol of proliferation and reproduction.

NOTES

1. Meskell, L., 'Goddesses, Gimbutas and 'New Age' archaeology', *Antiquity*, 69,1995, pp. 74–86.
2. According to the late Professor H.D. Sankalia, the so-called mother goddess figurines of baked clay are found only in Sind and Baluchistan, and they are found in large numbers at Mohenjo-daro and Harappa. These regions were the centres of the mother goddess cult. This view, however, seems to be correct as far as the archaeological data is concerned. (Agrawala 1984, p. 16).
3. Mandala = 'Books'; the authorship of each *mandala* is traditionally ascribed to a particular *rishi*, or that *rishi*'s family.
4. Chapters VI.64; VI.65; VII.78; and X.172.
5. Hymn VI.64.5.

6. The goddess Aditi in the *Vedas*, however, seem to have special honour. She is mentioned in the *Rg-veda* as being the mother of many of the gods. She is mentioned about 80 times in the *Rg-veda*. Compared to Uas and Prthivi, her character seems somewhat ill defined and is virtually featureless physically. The most outstanding feature of Aditi, being a *Rg-vedic* goddess, is the fact that she is mentioned as a supreme power and not as a consort—a fact diminishes significantly in the Brahmanical setup in later times as is prominent in the *Mārkandeya-Purāna*. She has the absolute power of progeny being mentioned as the mother of Adityas, a group of seven or eight gods, including Mitra, Aryaman, Bhaga, Varuna, Daksa, and Amsa (2.27.). She is also said to be the mother of the great god Indra, the mother of kings (2.7), and the mother of the gods (1.113.19). She is the provider of wealth; she frees people from hindrances and acts as the guardian of *rta*—those ordinances or rhythms that delineate order from chaos (Wilkins, 1882:17; Kinsley, 1975:10).
7. Elizabeth Guthrie, 'A Study of the History and Cult of the Buddhist Earth Deity in Mainland Southeast Asia', thesis submitted in partial fulfilment of the requirements for the Degree of Ph.D in Religious Studies, University of Canterbury, Christchurch: New Zealand, 2004.

REFERENCES

Agrawala, P.K., *Goddesses in ancient India,* New Delhi: Abhinav Publications, 1984.

Basu, Gopendrakrishna; *Banglar Loukik Debota* (Bengali), Calcutta: Dey's Publishing, 1966.

Bhattacharya, B., *Buddhist Iconography*, Calcutta: Oxford University Press, 1924.

Bhattacharya, Ashutosh, *Bangla Mangal Kavyer Itihash* (Bengali), Calcutta: A Mukherjee & Co. Pvt. Ltd., 1970.

Bhattacharya, D.K., *Studying Folklore: The Indian Experience*, unpublished lecture, University of Delhi, 2005.

Bhattacharya, D.K., *The Development Dilemma In Tribal India*, unpublished lecture, presented as Special Lecture in the Session on Anthropology, Indian Science Congress, Hyderabad, 2006.

Bhattacharya, D.K., Chattopadhyay R.K., 'History in Folk Culture', in Special issue, Culture Studies, Selected Papers from the 6th Congress of the National Academy of Psychology (NAOP), India, *Trends in Social Science Research*, Vol. 4, No. 1, June 1970.

Bhattacharya, P., *Manasha: An Epic of Fringe Bengal*, Paper presented in the 'National Seminar on Epics in Indian Languages,' Karnataka Bhavan, New Delhi, 1995.

Bhattasali, N.K., *Iconography of the Buddhist and Brahmanical Sculptures in the Decca Museum*, Decca, 1929.

Crooke, W., *Popular Religion and Folk-lore of Northern India*, Vol. II, Westminster, London: Archibald Constable & Co, 1896.

Dandekar, Deepra., *Folk Turned Sanskritic: Manasha*, unpublished Dissertation, Certificate Course in Women's Studies, University of Pune, 2000–2001.

Dandekar, R.N., *Vedic Bibliography,* Vol. II, Government Oriental Series, Class B, No 11, Reprint Bhandarkar Oriental Research Institute (BORI), Pune: 1977.

Dasgupta, Shashibhusan, *Obscure Religious Cults*, Calcutta: Firma Klm Private Limited, 1946.

Datta, Ashok, 'Chalcolithic Culture in West Bengal: A Study on Settlement and Transition', in Ray, Amita & Mukherjee, Samir (eds.), *Historical Archaeology of India: A Dialogue between Archaeology and Historians*, New Delhi: Books & Books Publishers and Distributors, 1990.

Datta, Rajat, 'The Agrarian Economy and the Dynamics of Commercial Transaction', in Marshall, P.J. (ed.), *The 18th Century in Indian History: Evolution or Revolution*, New Delhi: Oxford University Press, 2003.

Eaton, Richard M., *The Rise of Islam and the Bengal Frontier, 1204–1760*, Delhi Oxford University Press (1997).

Edwards, Eric Edwards, 'The Cult of the Mother Goddess', 2013, at https://ericwedwards.

wordpress.com/2013/07/17/the-cult-of-the-mother-goddess/?blogsub=confirming#subscribe-blog.

Guthrie, Elizabeth, 'A Study of the History and Cult of the Buddhist Earth Deity in Mainland Southeast Asia', thesis submitted in partial fulfilment of the requirements for the Degree of Ph.D in Religious Studies, University of Canterbury, Christchurch: New Zealand, 2004.

Heide, Goettner-Abendroth, *Matriarchal Societies: Studies on Indigenous Cultures across the Globe*, Peter Lang: New York, 2012.

Jash, Pranabananda, 'A Note on the Cult of Sitala', in Indian History Congress, Proceedings of the 43rd session, Kurukshetra University, Kurukshetra, 1982, Department of History, University of Delhi, New Delhi, 1983.

Kaviraj, Sudipta, 'The Two Histories of Literary Culture in Bengal', in Pollock, Sheldon (ed.): *Literary Cultures in History: Reconstruction from South Asia*, New Delhi: Oxford University Press, 2003.

Kinsley, David: *Hindu Goddesses: Visions of the Divine Feminine in the Hindu Religious Tradition*, Berkeley: University of California Press, 1994.

Kosambi, D.D., *Myth and Reality, studies in the formation of Indian Culture*, Bombay: Sangam Books Limited, 1962.

Maity, P.K., *Historical Studies in the Cult of the Goddess Manasha: A Socio-cultural Study*, Calcutta: Punthi Pustak, 1986.

Maitra Bajpai, Lopamudra, 'Myths and Folktales in the Patachitra Art of Bengal: Tradition and Modernity', in *Chitrolekha International Magazine on Art and Design*, Vol. V, No. 1, Theme: 'Visual Culture in the Indian Subcontinent', 2015.

'Preliminary Ethnographic Findings: Discovery of a local *Purana Durgarchanakalpamanjari* – Surviving Tangible and Intangible Heritage', in *International Journal of Research in Sociology and Anthropology* (IJRSA), Vol. 1, Issue 1, June, 2015, pp. 1–9, at www.arcjournals.org

'Complimentary Disciplines and their Significance in India—Oral Traditions, Folklore and Archaeology', in *International Journal of English Language, Literature and Humanities*, Bhopal, 2014.

'Indian Folklore and the "Three Worlds of Experiences": A New Theory to Understand "Learning" from Folklore in Modern Audio-Visual Media for Children', in *Indian Journal of Comparative Literature and Translation Studies*, Vol. 1, No. 1, September, 2013, pp. 53–75.

'Stories of *Tuntuni* from Bengal: Connecting Oral Traditions with the Global Age Across a century', in 'Heritage and Us', English e-journal, Year 2, Issue 1, March/April 2013, p. 40.

'Popular culture connecting history and media anthropology through imaging communities', in 'Folklore and Folkloristics' (English e-journal), Vol. 4, No. 2, December 2011.

'Change and Continuity as Means to Perpetuate Cultural Anxiety: A Brief Study of Tusubrata Rites and the Worship of Goddess Manasa in Specific Districts of Lateritic West Bengal', in Panchanan Mohanty, Ramesh C. Mallick, Eswarappa Kasi (ed.), *Ethnographic Discourse of the Other: Conceptual and Methodological Issues*, UK: Cambridge Scholars Publishing, 2008.

Majumdar, Ashutosh, *Meyeder Brotokatha* (Bengali), Calcutta: B.C. Majumdar, Dev Sahitya Kutir Private Limited, 2002.

Majumdar, R.C. (ed.), *The History of Bengal*, Vol. I. Decca: University of Decca, 1943.

Majumdar, R.C., *Ancient Indian Colonization in Southeast Asia*, Baroda: M.S. University, 1953.

Manguin, Pierre-Yves, A. Mani, Geoff Wade, *Early interactions between South and South-east Asia—Reflections on Cross-cultural exchange*, Institute of South-east Asian Studies, Singapore, 2011

Menon, Ramesh, *Devi: The Devi Bhagavatam Retold*, New Delhi, Rupa Publications Pvt. Ltd., 2006.

Metcalf, Thomas R.: *The New Cambridge History of India: Ideologies of the Raj*, Cambridge University Press, London, 1994.

Nehru, Jawaharlal: *The Discovery of India*, New Delhi: The Signet Press, 1946.

Piggot, Stuart, *Prehistoric India*, London: Penguin Books, 1950.

Radhakrishnan, S., *Indian Philosophy*, Vol. II, New Delhi: Oxford University Press, 1923

Rizvi, S. A. A., 'Islam in Medieval India', in Basham, A.L., (ed.), *A Cultural History of India*, New Delhi: Oxford University Press, 1975

Sastri, Hirananda, *The Origin of the Cult of Tara*, Memoirs of the Archaeological Survey of India, No 20, Government of India, Calcutta: Central Publication Branch, 1925

Sen, Sukumar, *Bangla Sahityer Itihas*, Vol. I (Bengali), Calcutta: Eastern Publishers, 1940

Sengupta, Shankar, *Folklore and Folk Life in India: an Objective Study in Indian Perspective*, Calcutta: Indian Publications, 1975

Sharma, R.S., 'Material Milieu of Tantrism', in Sharma, R.S. (ed.), *Indian Society, Historical Probings*, New Delhi: People's Publishing House, 1974

Sircar, Jawhar, 'The Construction of the Hindu Identity in the Medieval Western Bengal: The Role of Popular Cults', Occasional Paper 8, Institute of Development Studies, Calcutta University, Alipore Campus, Reformatory Street, Calcutta, July 2005

Srivastava, M.C.P., *Mother Goddess in Indian Art, Archaeology, and Literature*, New Delhi: Agam Kala Prakashan, 1979

Stein, Burton, *A History of India*, New Delhi: Oxford University Press, 1998

Trompf, Garry, *In search of Origins: The beginnings of Religions in Western Theory and Archaeological Practice*, UK, New Dawn Press Inc., 2005

Websites

https://www.britannica.com/event/Neolithic-Period

TOURISM, CULTURE, BUDDHISM

30

India's Cultural Diplomacy in Southeast Asia

Paramjit S. Sahai

Introduction

I am honoured to participate at this conference and happy to be a part of this new initiative taken by Ambassador Lalit Mansingh to focus on East and Northeast India, and to make this region as the centre for our connectivity efforts in Southeast Asia. It is the recognition of this reality that made Prime Minister Modi state that Northeast India would be the fulcrum to India's 'Act East Policy'. Ambassador Mansingh has further expanded the horizon by including East India in this thrust, given the historical and cultural linkages that the Odisha State has with the countries in Southeast Asia. The decision of the Modi Government to set up a new Ministry for the Development of Northeastern Affairs and create a new 'States Division' in the Ministry of External Affairs augur well in this direction, as we give shape to various policies and programmes that provide for a greater role to the Indian States.

The focus of the conference, as spelt out in the 'Approach Paper' is on three major themes: Commerce, Connectivity and Culture. It is rightly so, as there was continuum between culture and commerce, when India connected with Southeast Asia in the past. In some cases, culture preceded commerce; while in other cases, it was the other way round. Seen from the perspective of my presentation at the conference, I would like to change the sequence in this order to make it, 'Culture, Connectivity and Commerce'. Why it is so, because it is 'Culture' that provides the connectivity and lays the foundation and Cultural Diplomacy thus becomes the 'Mother of All Diplomacies'. Connectivity is the buzz word, be it among peoples or nations; be it the Northeast or East with the rest of India and of India with Southeast Asia. Cultural Diplomacy is that discipline of diplomacy that helps in promoting this connectivity.

Understanding Cultural Diplomacy

'Culture' in Cultural Diplomacy has a broader construct. It is in line with our 'Sanskriti'; a process of refinement and a 'way of life', touching the entire gamut of human activity and achievements (Singh, BP). It is also in line with the holistic definition of culture as used by UNESCO. It reads: 'Culture comprises the whole complex of distinctive spiritual, material, intellectual and emotional features that characterize a society or social group. It includes not only the arts and letters, but also modes of life, the fundamental rights of the human beings, value systems, traditions and beliefs' (UNESCO Conference, Mexico, 1982). It is also in keeping with the terminology used in India's Cultural Agreements with other countries.

Understanding of different cultures is essential to build connectivity among people. India's then Foreign Minister, MC Chagla fully grasped culture's role as a unifying force, in promoting understanding among nations and thereby creating an everlasting intellectual bond among people. Karan Singh's view on Diplomacy as the 'Ganga-Yamuna-Saraswati Triveni' is relevant in understanding the placement of cultural diplomacy in the diplomatic hierarchy. The 'Ganga' represents the political component of diplomacy, while the 'Yamuna' represents economic diplomacy and the invisible 'Saraswati' represents 'Cultural Diplomacy' (Misra, Satish). It derives its strength from the invisible manner in which it impacts through promoting understanding among different peoples and nations.

Indian Approach to Cultural Diplomacy

Cultural Diplomacy comes natural for India, given its cultural diversity and pluralistic ethos. India's cultural diplomacy, therefore, gets sustenance from cultural diversity, which is at the core of the 'Idea of India'. King Ashoka was the earlier pioneer of cultural diplomacy, when he spread the 'message of peace' across the world in 300 BC. In the modern day context, Swami Vivekanand gave voice to this message of plurality on cultural understanding at the Conference of World Religions at Chicago in 1893, when he talked of 'acceptance' and not 'toleration' of other religions. It is a positive way of looking at all religions as equals, which is centred on 'One Truth' that could be achieved through diverse paths. Cultural Diplomacy, therefore, involves viewing others through the prism of 'positivity' and not 'negativity', as stated by a former Director General of the Indian Council for Cultural Relations (ICCR), Dr. Suresh Goel.

Seeds of India's modern day cultural diplomacy were planted by Nehru at the Asian Relations Conference (ARC) in April 1947, even prior to India's independence. The focus of ARC was on strengthening of cultural exchanges and ties between India and Asian countries. In 1950, India adopted a structured approach, with the setting up of the Indian Council for Cultural Relations (ICCR), at New Delhi. It was given a global mandate. ICCR's twin objectives are:

- To strengthen cultural relations and mutual understanding.
- To promote cultural linkages.

Connectivity with everyone becomes central in this globalised world. India has adopted the credo 'Harek friend jaroorihotahai' (Every friend is essential) at its 'Diplomacy Ke Mahakumhb', Live Telecast on Diplomacy, *CNBC Awaz,* 6 July, 2013. A former External Affairs Minister Salman Rashid viewed the role of cultural diplomacy in strengthening relationship, while a former President of ICCR saw it as enhancing India's image.

Pursuit of Cultural Diplomacy is a shared responsibility between the Ministry of External Affairs (MEA) and the Ministry of Culture (MoC)). MEA is the nodal Ministry for the formulation of policy on cultural diplomacy and its implementation thereof. MEA's principal instrumentality is the Indian Council for Cultural Relations (ICCR). The External Publicity and Public Diplomacy Division also makes its contribution in this direction, by supplementing the activities of ICCR. ICCR uses the vehicles of Cultural Centres (36 in 2016) and Chairs of Indian Studies (70 in 2016) to promote its activities.

MoC's Mandate includes 'Dissemination of Culture' and developing 'cultural relations between India and various countries'. Its primary responsibilities are to enter into Cultural Agreements and to conclude Cultural Exchange Programmes (CEPs) under thereof as well as to organise Festivals of India abroad. India had signed 130 Cultural Agreements as on 2016. It may, however, be noted that signing of Cultural Agreements or CEPs is not a pre requisite for the conduct of cultural diplomacy.

Contours of Indian Cultural Diplomacy in Southeast Asia

Southeast Asia is India's extended neighbourhood, an area, where historical and traditional links have intertwined through culture and commerce. Cultural links became hostage to differing perceptions on world issues in the 1970s and the 1980s.

India's Dialogue Partnership with ASEAN in 1995 spurred up cooperation. At that juncture, Singapore's Foreign Minister Jeyakumar, stated, 'As we focus on developing economic and political links', it is important that we continue to strengthen our cultural links, which could be achieved through developing 'tourism, cultural, educational and other institutional links' [Sarkar, Bidyut (ed.) 1968]. This was a clear recognition of the role of cultural diplomacy.

India's then External Affairs Minister Gujral put special focus on promoting academic linkages through the establishment of ASEAN-India Lecture Series and setting up of ASEAN – India Centres in India and ASEAN countries (Gujral, I K, 1998). At the Singapore Lecture in 1997, the then Prime Minister P.V. Narasimha Rao underscored the need of promoting people-to-people linkages, as he said that 'the more we know each other, the better we understand each other' (Singapore Lecture, 1994).

ASEAN-India Summit 2012 focusing on Cultural Connectivity

ASEAN-India Summit in 2012 gave a further push to such connectivity. Its Vision Statement set up the future agenda for cultural connectivity, with emphasis on 'socio-cultural cooperation' through 'greater people to people interaction', in practically all the fields and areas of human activity. This could take the following form:

- 'To enhance contacts between parliamentarians, media personnel, academics and Track II institutes such as the network of think tanks;
- To encourage the study, documentation and dissemination of knowledge about the institutional links between ASEAN and India;
- To intensify efforts to preserve, protect and restore symbols and structures representing civilizational bonds between ASEAN and India' (Vision Statement, 2012).

2012 thus marked a watershed in India's approach on cultural diplomacy towards Southeast Asian countries. It brought about a qualitative change in India's pursuit of cultural diplomacy, which is now being viewed as a two dimensional phenomenon. It is only through a process of acculturation that a two-way connectivity could be enhanced with one other.

At the practical level, the Celebrations resulted in undertaking activities that further enhanced this connectivity, linking tradition to modernity. Dr. Suresh Goel, the then Director General, ICCR listed out some of these, which are recapitulated in the succeeding paragraphs (Goel, Suresh).

ASEAN-India Artists Camp: Partners in Residency, Darjeeling, June 2012

It brought together 20 painters from ASEAN countries—(Singapore, Brunei, Cambodia, Indonesia, Laos, Malaysia, Myanmar, Thailand, and Vietnam – two from each country) and 20 Indian painters, resulting in promoting acculturation of ideas.

ASEAN-India Civilizational Dialogue, Patna, July 2012

This seminar focused on centuries' old civilizational links between India and Southeast Asian countries, which went back to centuries. ICCR organized this in collaboration with the Nalanda University.

Exhibition of Archival Material, Delhi, December 2012

The exhibition highlighted shared heritage through photographs and manuscripts, going back to the 19th century. It included a letter from Bahadur Shah Zafar, the last Moghul King and was organised in collaboration with the National Archives of India.

Gala Cultural Performance at the Rashtrapati Bhawan, December 20, 2012

The performance was a 'spectacular display of our shared culture', where cultural troupes from India and ASEAN countries participated, represented a picture of unity in diversity.

At the popular level, ***ASEAN-India Car Rally***, a remarkable journey of 8000 kilometers through eight countries, was completed in 22 days on 21 December, 2012. The Rally symbolized the 'Vision of an ASEAN-India Community, where people, goods, services and ideas travel freely between us' (PM, 2012). The Rally not only rekindled the 'ancient bonds of friendship between India and ASEAN', but also highlighted 'the natural strategic imperative for our relationship in contemporary times' (PM, 2012).

Recent Thrust in India's Cultural Diplomacy in Southeast Asia

Preservation of Heritage Sites

The 2012 ASEAN-India Summit Vision Statement also renewed India's commitment to the preservation of edifices of ancient cultural heritage in Southeast Asia. This would cover the preservation of heritage sites, such as Angkor Wat in Cambodia, Borobudur and Prambanan temples in Indonesia, Wat Phu in Laos, Bagan in Myanmar, Sukhothai Historical Park in Thailand and My Son in Vietnam. This cooperation is viewed as an important part of the new thrust of India's cultural diplomacy (Bhattacharyya, Sanjay).

Establishment of ASEAN-India Centre

The External Affairs Minister Salman Khurshid launched the ASEAN-India Centre at the Resources and Information Systems (RIS) New Delhi on June 21, 2013, fulfilling the dream of Foreign Minister M.C. Chagla and Prime Minister I.K. Gujral. The Centre added a new dimension to the relationship, signifying that "The ASEAN-India Partnership is not only of long standing but also of great current and future strategic relevance, oriented as it is to economic growth, development, capacity building and peace and security" (EAM, 2013).

Nalanda University: A Joint Cultural Diplomacy Project

The setting up of the Nalanda University added another new dimension to Indian cultural diplomacy, given the fact that this is a collaborative project, enjoying the support of the Southeast and East Asian countries. Support for the establishment of this University was formalised at the 4th East Asia Summit (EAS) in Thailand on 24-25 October 2009.

At the 5th East Asian Summit on 30 October 2010, Indian Prime Minister extended an invitation to EAS member states to participate in the project. The primary funding for the university would come from the Government of India (Misra, J.N.). Financial support for this project has been received from the Governments of China, Thailand, Laos, Australia, Japan and Singapore.

This University is located at Rajgir in Bihar and started functioning from the academic year 2013-14. The University would focus on Asia and its Unique Selling Point (USP) would be research. It would be a non-Metropolitan University, with a commitment, to become a Net Zero Energy Campus, which would be one of its kinds (Sabharwal, Gopa).

The University is to have 'a non-state, non-profit, secular and self-governing international character', with a continental focus, as it brings together 'the brightest and most dedicated students from all the countries in Asia'. Dr. Karan Singh, President, ICCR viewed this as 'an important tool in the on-going effort to create a 'Pan-Asian Identity', which is assuming greater significance in the context of today's geo-politics' (Singh, Dr. Karan, 2013).

Establishment of MGC Museum of Asian Traditional Textiles

It was inaugurated on April 7, 2014 at Siem Reap, Cambodia. It enjoys substantial support from India. The Museum aims to become a 'Live' Museum that symbolises not only 'cultural and institutional linkages between us but also of our commercial trade over centuries' (Anil Wadhwa, Secretary East, MEA).

International Yoga Day (IYD): India Heralding its Entry with Celebrations

The First International Yoga Day on June 21, 2015 was celebrated with great gusto with the enthusiastic support from the local community. The Yoga event in Yogyakarta was organised in the famous Prambanan Temple complex, which is a World Heritage site. On 21 June, 2015 Cambodia marked the International Day of Yoga in front of Angkor Wat Temple, Siem Reap, with the participation of over 1,000 Cambodians and foreigners.

During his visit to Malaysia in November 2015, Prime Minister Modi released a bilingual (English and Bahasa Malaysia) book on Yoga, titled "Yoga for Holistic Health" at Ramakrishna Mission Malaysia, where he also unveiled a 12 ft. Bronze Statue of Swami Vivekananda.

Cooperation at Sub-Regional Levels

At the sub-regional level, the Mekong Ganga Cooperation (MGC) Programme connects India with five ASEAN countries (Cambodia, Laos, Myanmar, Thailand and Vietnam). The aim of MGC is to renew civilizational links by connecting people inhabiting two major river banks, in the areas of education, tourism, culture, transport and communication.

Another sub-regional group, Bay of Bengal Initiative for Multi-Sectoral Technical and Economic Cooperation (BIMSTEC) connects five South Asian countries (India, Bangladesh, Bhutan, Nepal and Sri Lanka) with two Southeast Asian countries (Myanmar and Thailand). Its focus is also on connectivity and people-to-people contacts.

ASEAN-India Commemorative Summit, January 2018

India played host to ten Heads of State/Governments to mark the 25th Anniversary of ASEAN-India Dialogue Relations. It was an unusual gesture and unique effort to host 10 leaders and their spouses, as our distinguished guests at the Republic Day Parade on January 26, 2018. In its preamble, the Delhi Declaration of the ASEAN-India Commemorative Summit took note of 'the cross-cultural exchanges and civilizational linkages between Southeast Asia and India over several millennia as a strong foundation for cooperation between ASEAN and India in an increasingly inter-connected world'.

A separate section in the Declaration dealt with 'Socio-Cultural Cooperation', which covered various areas in which countries were cooperating or were ripe for future connectivity. These are as follows:

- To provide 'platforms for knowledge exchanges' among policy-makers, managers, and the academicians concerned with tangible and intangible cultural heritage.
- To intensify efforts 'to preserve, protect and restore cultural and historical symbols and structures which are of mutual interest in reflecting the ASEAN-India cultural and historical connection'. This would include India's proposal on mapping inscriptions along the Mekong River.
- To 'cement a stronger cultural link by promoting cultural tourism'.
- To 'further enhance people-to-people contacts', through programmes such as Delhi Dialogue, ASEAN-India Network of Think Tanks (AINTT), ASEAN-India Eminent Persons Lecture Series (AIEPLS), diplomats training courses.
- To promote exchange programmes for students, parliamentarians, farmers and media.

- To 'strengthen cooperation in education and youth sectors, in the form of setting up of English Language Training, Entrepreneurship Development and Vocational Training Centres.
- To explore the possibility of setting up an ASEAN-India network of universities, and encourage other University to University exchanges, including with ASEAN University Network.

During the Summit, India announced 1,000 PhD fellowships in the IITs for students from the ASEAN countries. Other announcements included setting up of a virtual network of universities, and pilot projects on digital infrastructure. The participating countries also agreed to celebrate 2019 as the year of tourism for ASEAN nations Further, an ASEAN-India Startup festival is planned to be held later this year (*The Hindu*, 2018). Twenty-seven newspapers in 10 languages in 10 ASEAN countries carried an op-ed by Prime Minister PM Modi, whose focus was that India-ASEAN relations were 'free from contests, claims' (*The Tribune*, 2018).

In conjunction with the Summit, a Ramayana Festival was organised by ICCR in Delhi and five other cities (Ahmedabad, Lucknow, Kolkata, Hyderabad and Ayodhya) during January 20-24, 2018. Troupes from ten ASEAN countries gave their performances. This cultural event was designed to demonstrate, through the epic, cultural and emotional bonds that exist among ASEAN countries and India. The suggestion for holding this Festival was reportedly mooted by 'the Cambodian Prime Minister Hun Sen at the ASEAN-India Summit in Manila last November (2017), as he held the epic as a potent symbol of integration of the Southeast Asian region with India' (ICH Courier).

Troupes performing 'Ramakien' in Thailand; 'PhaLakPha Lam' in Laos; 'Yama Zatddaw' in Myanmar; 'Kakawin Ramayana' in Indonesia and 'Hikayat Seri Rama' in Malaysia participated at the festival. They showcased "the similarities of mudra (hand gestures) in our dance forms" and cultural interpretations of Ramayana across the ASEAN countries and India (*The Indian Express*, 2018).

Ramayana stamps, specially-made Khadi jackets, and, of course, tableaux from the North-East States, and the ASEAN countries added to the Republic Day splendour. Ramayana symbolizes both, the celebration of diversity and connectivity between countries.

Present Day Relationship

What is the present level of play of relationship between India and Southeast Asian countries? We would look at certain standard parameters, such as Cultural Agreements, Cultural Centres, Chairs of India Studies, Educational Links, Festivals of India and Partnership in Human Resource Development.

India has Cultural Agreements with Indonesia, Philippines, Vietnam, Thailand, Malaysia, Cambodia and Myanmar and an MoU with Singapore. These provide the broad framework for cultural connectivity. At present Cultural Exchange Programmes (CEPs) also exist with Indonesia, Laos, Malaysia, Philippines, Singapore and Thailand.

Chairs of Indian Studies have been established in various universities in Cambodia, Malaysia, Indonesia, Singapore and Vietnam. These help in enhancing academic linkages. These Chairs are for Indian, Buddhist and Sanskrit Studies.

The first Cultural Centre in Southeast Asia was opened in Jakarta in 1988 and another in 2004 in Bali, Indonesia. Among the other Southeast Asian countries, India has cultural centres in Thailand (2009), Kuala Lumpur (2010), Myanmar (2010) and Hanoi (2017). These centres help in projecting traditional links with modern India.

Education is emerging as a Two-way Connectivity Channel. India is linked through educational ties with these countries. Countries in Southeast Asia are also becoming attractive centres for education for Indian students. Every year, nearly 2000 Indian students go for studies in Malaysia, while nearly 1500 Malaysian students enroll themselves in Indian colleges. There are more than 4000 Indian students studying medicine in the Philippines. A large number of Thai students are also studying on self-financing basis.

Ministry of Human Resource Development provides for secondment of eight professors every semester for the Asian Institute of Technology (AIT), Bangkok. India has an MoU on Higher Education with Malaysia, signed in 2010 and another one with Thailand on Cooperation in the field of Education that was signed in 2005.

A new development that is taking place is the direct involvement of cities and the states in India with Southeast Asian countries. Singapore has become the focus country for visits by Chief Ministers from the Indian States. A number of State Governments have established contacts with Singapore to develop concrete projects in infrastructure, skills development, governance, waste management and other areas. Singapore is developing master plan for Amravati, new capital of the Andhra State.

The years 2014-16 turned out to be significant for the organisation of Festivals of India in these countries, which added a splash of colour to the relationship. The Festival of India, 'Sahabat India' in Indonesia was organised from 26 January to 15 August, 2015. The First Festival of India in Malaysia was organised between March-June 2015, where 45 events were held for 100 days. "Buddha Mahotsava" and Ramayana Festival was organised in Phnom Penh and Siem Reap in February 2014. Festivals of India were organised in Thailand and Singapore during 2014.

Goodwill visits by Indian Naval Ships have become a regular feature that results in connectivity at the people to people level. INS Delhi made its Maiden Visit to Malaysia in 1999, when the author was the High Commissioner. Frequency of such visits has increased over the years. Similarly, holding of Annual 'Milan' (Get Together) of Navies from India and ASEAN Members since 1997 provides an opportunity to build camaraderie among naval officers.

Northeast India and Southeast Asia: Cultural Connectivity

We now move to the next stage, as we look at the present day scenario on cultural connectivity between Northeast India and Southeast Asian countries. Indian Council for Cultural Relations (ICCR) has set up its Regional Offices at Gawahati and Shillong to serve this region. There is a Regional Office at Bhubaneswar also, which shifted in 2015 from Cuttack. These Regional Offices are involved in undertaking three-pronged activities. These include, looking after foreign students; facilitating exchange of cultural troupes, both incoming and outgoing; and organising seminars and holding exhibitions.

Northeast India is well connected with Southeast Asia, in terms of exchange of cultural troupes, as seen from the available data for the five years (2010-14). It received cultural troupes from Malaysia in 2009-10; Myanmar in 2010-11; Bangladesh and Korea in 2011-12; Vietnam in 2012-13 and Bangladesh in 2013-14. Similarly, there was a regular flow of cultural troupes from this region to the Southeast Asian countries. The details are as follows:

- A ten-member 'Bihu' Dance Group to Cambodia in 2009-10;

- A 5-Member Rock Band Group to Myanmar in 2010-11;
- A 4-Member Group of Aborigines to Bhutan in 1011-12;
- A 9-Member AJI LHAMU Masked Dance Group to Kathmandu in 2011-12;
- A 15-Member Folk Dance Group to Thailand in 2012-13; and
- A 15-Member Bihu Dance group to Sri Lanka in 2012-13.

ICCR's Regional Offices have been involved in organising other activities. Some of these included holding of Exhibition of Contemporary Art Works of Bangladesh, titled 'Rhythms of Colours' in Guwahati. Artists from Bangladesh and Assam participated in this exhibition. An international seminar on 'From Land-locked to Land-linked North-East India in BIMSTEC' was organised on April 9-10, 2010. The seminar was inaugurated at the North Eastern Hill University (NEHU) Campus in Shillong; Shashi Tharoor, Minister of State for External Affairs delivered the Inaugural Address. North East Hill University (NEHU) at Shillong is emerging as a centre of learning for students from Bhutan, Bangladesh, Myanmar and Nepal.

Concluding Observations: Connecting Odisha and Kalinga International Foundation (KIF) with Southeast Asia

What is the final picture that emerges? Indian Cultural Diplomacy in Southeast Asia has been a success story. It is largely on account of the existence of pluralistic societies in all the countries and secondly recognition of the realty that it is mutually beneficial to all the sides. India is, however, still at a nascent stage in connecting Northeast India with Southeast Asian countries?

There is still lack of awareness of one another. While India story does attract, yet Southeast Asia does not make the grade in the Indian Media. It is absolutely essential to increase the respective profiles of Indian and the Southeast Asian countries. India-ASEAN Media and Student Exchanges are expected to bridge this information gap. These are still baby steps and need to be fostered to facilitate exchange in greater numbers.

In the ultimate analysis, the continued success of our Cultural Diplomacy would lie in it becoming a bridge builder through the preservation and strengthening of pluralistic societies in India and Southeast. India would like to achieve this by celebrating epical story of 'Ramayana' in all its diverse renditions which adds to understanding. We need to view 'Yoga', not as a form of religious manifestation, but as a spiritual experience for any secular minded person.

To do so, we need to adopt a multi-pronged approach, as we give shape to India's 'Act East' Policy. I am glad that I am on the same page with the Ministry of External Affairs, having first talked about this approach and used this terminology at an India-ASEAN Seminar. 'Act East Policy' has also to filter into 'Act Northeast Policy'. Prime Minister Modi's visits to this region give us a hope, as we focus on new initiatives.

To cap it all, East and Northeast India has to be perceived as an integral part of India, both in terms of identity and physical connectivity. 'Act East Policy' has to be dovetailed into 'Act Northeast Policy' and find strength through cultural conversations that turn into a bridge of understanding, by involving Sates in the 'Act East' Policy, which should become 'Deliver East' as it becomes more result-oriented and delivers on promises and commitments.

Here are some specific suggestions, which the State of Odisha and the Kalinga International Foundation (KIF) could consider, as they move forward in their journey, to connect 'East with East':

- To involve the States as partners in the formulation and implementation of Look East Policy. One Chief Minister should invariably be included as a part of Indian Delegations.
- To open up more 'Border Haats' to provide for easier facilities for commercial and cultural connectivity.
- The State of Odisha to consider entering into a MoU with ICCR, as a number of States have such arrangements.
- Odisha to consider setting up an ASEAN Corner in the newly established Biju Patnaik Museum, to display artefacts from ASEAN countries.
- To encourage Bhubaneswar to establish City-to-City relationship with Bali in Indonesia by reviving the spirit of the 'Bali Yatra'.
- A cultural organisation in Odisha could tie up with The Sutra Theatre of Ramli Ibrahim, to promote Odissi Dance.
- Universities in Odisha to be encouraged to establish linkage with the Nalanda University, as a way to inlet with Southeast and East Asian countries.
- KIF to consider holding an International Conference with Vietnam

on the Champa Civilization, in coordination with the Indian Consul General in Ho Chi Minh City.

- Kalinga International Foundation (KIF) to consider entering into MoUs with Think Tanks in Southeast Asia.
- Kalinga International Foundation (KIF) to consider joining India-ASEAN Network of Think Tanks. RIS, Delhi is the nodal agency at the Indian end.
- To hold an Artists' Residency in Odisha, on the lines of 'ASEAN-India Artists Camp: Partners in Residency', organised by ICCR in Darjeeling in June 2012. KIF could consider coordinating with Jatin Das.
- To strengthen the existing Regional Offices of ICCR, so that they are in a position to launch more activities. KIF to consider liaising with the Regional Office in Bhubaneswar.
- To consider holding the Delhi Dialogue on ASEAN, alternately at Delhi and in one of the States. KIF could take the initiative and moot this proposal for holding in Odisha.

Let us strive for achieving the above goals and thus fulfill the 2002 dream of the then External Affairs Minister, Jaswant Singh, who highlighted the importance of weaving Asia "through multi-modal instrumental links in a most wonderful tapestry of cooperation" (EAM 2002). Let Odisha and the Kalinga International Foundation become an integral part of this 'Tapestry of Multi-Dimensional Relationship'.

REFERENCES

Anil Wadhwa, Remarks by Secretary (East) at the Inaugural of the MGC Museum of Asian Traditional Textiles in Siem Reap, Cambodia, April 7, 2014.

Bhattacharya, Sanjay, Joint Secretary (South), Ministry of External Affairs, New Delhi. Interaction on April 30, 2015 in Delhi.

Chagla, Inaugural Address by M.C. Chagla, 1968, President of ICCR as quoted in Bidyut Sarkar, ed., *India and Southeast* Asia, Proceedings of a Seminar on India and Southeast Asia, ICCR.

Delhi Declaration, 2018, The ASEAN-India Commemorative Summit to Mark the 25th Anniversary of ASEAN-India Dialogue Relations, January 25.

EAM, 2002, Statement by Jaswant Singh, External Affairs Minister at the Plenary Session of Trilateral Meeting, Yangon, April 6.

EAM, 2013, External Minister's Speech at the launch of ASEAN-India Centre in New Delhi, June 21.

Ghoshal, Baladas (ed.), 1996, *India and Southeast Asia: Challenges and Opportunities*, IIC, New Delhi.

Goel, Suresh, former Director General, ICCR, New Delhi. Interaction on May 25, 2015 in Delhi.

Goel, 2013, 'Message from Dr. Suresh Goel, DG, ICCR and Special Secretary, MEA in Sharma,

Anjana (ed.), *Civilizational Dialogue, Asian Inter-connections and Cross-cultural Exchanges,* ICCR & Manohar.

Gujral, I K, 1998, *A Foreign Policy for India', External Publicity Division*, Ministry of External Affairs, New Delhi.

Inaugural Address by M.C. Chagla, 1968, President of ICCR as quoted in Bidyut Sarkar, ed., *India and Southeast* Asia, Proceedings of a Seminar on India and Southeast Asia, ICCR.

ICH Courier, http://ichcourier.ichcap.org/en/2018-ramayana-festival-cultural-heritage-shared-between-india-and-the-eastern-world/

MEA 2014-15, Annual Report of the Ministry of External Affairs, New Delhi.

MEA 2015-16, Annual Report of the Ministry of External Affairs, New Delhi.

Misra, Satish, 2006, 'Karan Singh, 'Cultural diplomacy needs a big thrust', *The Tribune*, November 24.

Misra, J N, Additional Secretary, Ministry of External Affairs, New Delhi. Interaction on July 27, 2015 in Delhi.

Mahathir, Mohamad, 1996, First ASEAN Lecture, New Delhi, December.

Nadim, Farrukh, 2013, 'Nalanda University deserves place in World Heritage Sites: Salman Khurshid, *The Tribune*, February, 13.

Nehru, 1950, Inaugural Address of Prime Minister Nehru in 1950 at the time of the inauguration of the Indian Council of Cultural Relations (ICCR), quoted in a *Pamphlet on ICCR*, New Delhi.

Sarkar, Bidyut, (ed.) 1968, 'India and Southeast Asia', Proceedings of a Seminar, ICCR, Delhi.

Sarkar, HB, 1985, *Cultural Relations between India and Southeast Asian Countries*, ICCR and Motilal Banarsidas, Delhi.

Singapore Lecture, 1994, Lecture by Prime Minister P V Narasimha Rao, 'India and the Asia Pacific: Forging a New Partnership', Institute of Southeast Asian Studies, Singapore.

Singh, B P, 1998, *India's Culture, The State, The Arts and Beyond*, Oxford University Press, Delhi.

Nathan, K.S. (ed.), 2000, *India and ASEAN: The Growing Partnership for the 21st Century*, IFDR.

PBD 2009, Inaugural Address of Prime Minister of India, Pravasi Bharatiya Divas (PBD), January, New Delhi.

PM, 2012, 'Remarks by Prime Minister, Dr. Manmohan Singh at Flag Down of the ASEAN-India Car Rally', 21 December, New Delhi.

President, 2000, Speech by President of India at a Banquet in Singapore, November 10.

Sabharwal, Gopa, Vice Chancellor, Nalanda University. Interaction on July 27, 2015 in Delhi.

Sahai, P S, 2009, 'India's Cultural Diplomacy in Southeast Asia', HCMC University, May 16-19.

Sahai, P S., 2002, 'Globalisation, Cultural Diplomacy and the Indian Ocean: An Indian Perspective', Paper presented at the Panjab University, Chandigarh, Nov.

Sharma, Anjana (ed.), 2013. *Civilizational Dialogue, Asian Inter-connections and Cross-cultural Exchanges*, ICCR & Manohar.

Singh, Dr. Karan, 2013, Foreword in Sharma, Anjana (ed.), *Civilizational Dialogue, Asian Inter-connections and Cross-cultural Exchanges*, ICCR & Manohar.

The Hindu, 2018, India should be pro-active: ASEAN', January 25.

The Indian Express, 2018, 'Ramayana festival, khadi jackets: Stage set for ASEAN at Republic Day', January 27.

The Tribune, 2018, 'PM Modi writes op-ed, says India, ASEAN relations 'free from contests, claims', January 27.

UNESCO, 1982, UNESCO Conference at Mexico.

Vision Statement, 2012, 'Vision Statement, ASEAN-India Commemorative Summit, December 20, New Delhi.

31

Maritime Connectivity and Beyond: Cultural Interface between Kalinga and Java

Benudhar Patra

This presentation attempts to trace out maritime contacts between Kalinga or ancient Odisha and Java, in historical perspective. Java is one of the important islands of the Indonesian archipelago. It is bound on the west by the Sunda strait and on the east by the Bali strait. India has had maritime contacts with Java since the beginning of the Christian era. Indian traders, and the beads originating from India were probably present in Java as early as 2000 years ago.[1] Kalinga, located on the east coast of India, had a close maritime connection with the island of Java (Javadvipa). From a relative study of the cultures of both Kalinga and Java, it is gleaned that, among the Indian people, the Kalingans were the first to reach Java and other Indonesian countries, and played a leading role in spreading Indian culture there. The credit for the colonization of Java, thus, has been given to the people of Kalinga. Regarding the colonization of Java by the Kalingans, R.K. Mookerji remarks,

> Perhaps the most interesting and conspicuous fact in connection with the Indian maritime activity towards the East is the Hindu colonization of Java, one of the most glorious achievements recorded in the entire history of the country. And yet, the first impulse to this colonizing activity and expansion of India had its origin in the obscure kingdom of Kalinga, whose early history nobody knows or cares to know. As far back as the 75th year of the Christian era [*c.*75 CE], a band of Hindu navigators sailed from Kalinga, and instead of plying within the usual limits of the Bay of Bengal, boldly ventured out into the open limitless expanse of the Indian Ocean and arrived at the island of Java. There

> the adventurous navigators planted a colony, built towns and cities, and developed a trade with the mother country which existed for several centuries.[2]

M.M. Ganguly[3] expresses the same thing, but in a different manner giving a slightly different date. He says, 'In the year 75 BC [BCE], an expedition from Kalinga formed a colony in Java'. M. Elphinstone has also narrated that,

> The histories of Java give a distinct account of a numerous body of Hindus from Cling [Calinga/Kalinga], who landed on this island, civilized the inhabitants, and who fixed the date of their arrival by establishing the era still subsisting, the first year of which fell in the seventy-fifth year before Christ.[4]

Besides, the fact that Kalinga had a large share in the colonization of Java and the adjacent islands is hinted at not only in the native chronicles of Java but is also accepted as truth by many eminent scholars. J. Crawfurd (CE 1820) is of the opinion that all Hindu influence in Java was from Kalinga.[5] The *Bombay Gazetteer* observed that 'the Hindu settlements of Sumatra was almost entirely from the east coast of India, and that Bengal, Orissa [Odisha], and Masulipatnam had a large share in colonizing both Java and Cambodia cannot be doubted.'[6]

Legends and local traditions of Java mention, 'twenty thousand families were sent to Java by the prince of Kling [Kalinga]. These people prospered and multiplied.'[7] The spirit of adventure and the will to establish colonial empires might have induced the brave Kalingans to take such step. It can be presumed that, owing to the growth of population, the people of Kalinga migrated to Java. The term *Kling* is evidently derived from Kalinga, and denoted the people of Kalinga. Further, it also indicates that the people of Kalinga took a leading part not only in establishing a political relationship with Java but also developing Java economically.[8] In the course of time, however, *Kling* became a generic term, and the Indians coming to Java, irrespective of their origin, were called *Kling* or the people from Kalinga. Even now, the Indian immigrants in the Malay Archipelago are called *Orang Kling* (people of Kalinga origin), which is a survival of the name Kalinga, by which the inhabitants of Odisha were once known.[9]

R.D. Banerji says that the 'term *Keling* or *Kiling* by which immigrants from the Indian continent are generally designated among the inhabitants of the Archipelago is clearly derived from Kalinga, the ancient name of the Telugu country, situated on the East coast of India between the rivers Mahanadi and Godavari'.[10] Further, he also remarks, 'It is universally admitted that *Keling* or *Kiling* is the term applied in the Malay Peninsula, and all parts of the Indian Archipelago, to denote a man from India, irrespective of the province from which he comes. It proves directly that the earliest Indians with whom the Indonesians became familiar were people from Kalinga.'[11]

The view of R.D. Banerji has been corroborated by J. Crawfurd, who believes 'Kalinga is the only country of India known to the Javanese by its proper name—the only country familiar to them—and the only one mentioned in their books. Hence, they designate India always by this name'.[12] Further, he also observes, 'It is to Kalinga that the Javanese universally ascribe the origin of their Hinduism.'[13] The *Klings* were ardent lovers of Shaivism. It is also believed that the people of Kalinga played a significant role in the evolution of Shaivism in Indonesia.[14] From this, it is believed that only the dominant and powerful groups of the emigrants must have been successful in naming the places according to their likes and dislikes, which must have been accepted by the rest of the emigrant community and indigenous population.

The Kalingan origin of the earliest colonists from India does not depend merely on the term now applied to Indians in the Indian Archipelago, but also on definite archaeological and historical evidences.[15] The results of excavations prove that both in 'Further India' and the 'Indian Archipelago', the earliest Indian colonists were Hindus: that is Brahmanical in faith.[16] And, the Hindus from Kalinga may be regarded on satisfactory grounds, to have taken a leading part in establishing Hindu culture in Java.[17] It has been corroborated by K. Sridharan, who outlines,

> Indeed, they [the Kalingans] were responsible for having initiated the adventurous spirit of emigrating to Java. It is known that Kalinga seafarers made a bold oceanic voyage and managed to land at Java as early as 75 A.D. [CE]. Having landed, they settled in the island, built up their contacts, and developed regular trade with the mainland of India. This marked the beginning of an era of Hindu civilization in this area of the Far East.[18]

In connection of Kalinga's relationship with Java, in the *Malay Annals* there is an interesting story regarding one Kalinga Vichitra, who descended from heaven to appear upon a mountain in Palembang, became the ruler of the country, and married Sendari (Sundari), and had two sons. Though lacking in historical authenticity, such legends suggest that the people of Kalinga origin first reached the Malay-Indonesia region.[19]

During the seventh to the ninth centuries CE, central Java was known as Ho-ling in Chinese sources, particularly in the annals of the Tang period (CE 618–906). The Chinese sources refer to the exchange of ambassadors between the two kingdoms during that period. The earliest recorded ambassador from Ho-ling to China was sent in *c.* 640 CE, and the last one in *c.* 818 CE.[20] Scholars generally believe that Ho-ling was the Chinese, or the old Javanese, equivalent of Kalinga.[21] This would suggest that central Java was so much dominated by the people of Kalinga that the region was named as Ho-ling or Kalinga.

R.C. Majumdar, analyzing the matter, goes one step ahead and suggests that Kalinga or Ho-ling was the name of one of the important kingdoms of Java itself.[22] In his work *Suvarnadvipa,* Majumdar has observed that,

> Ho-ling has been generally admitted to be a Chinese transcription of Kalinga. It would, thus, appear that the leading kingdom in Java was named after the well-known province of India, and this can easily lead to the inference that colonists from Kalinga dominated in that quarter. It is generally held that the name of Java was changed to Kalinga about this time, and that this was due to a fresh stream of immigration from Kalinga or the eastern part of India.[23]

H.B. Sarkar, however, deals the matter from a different angle. According to him, the name Ho-ling undoubtedly stands for Kalinga, a famous state of ancient India. As many geographical names of India have been found in several places in Indonesia in particular, and South-East Asia in general, the phenomenon may not appear surprising, but the circumstances naturally demand certain explanation. It is generally believed that the emergence of Ho-ling for Kalinga synchronised with waves of fresh immigrants from India, perhaps from the region of Kalinga. This does not signify that all these immigrants were Kalinga people, but it may serve as an indication that the ports of Kalinga served as points of embarkation for central Java.[24]

If this view is considered to be correct, then the influx must have been heavy, as it succeeded in establishing a new colony in central Java or re-christening an old state of that region under a new name. To corroborate this, the Buddhist text *Aryamanjusrimulakalpa* mentions that 'all islands in the

Kalinga Sea (*Kalingodresu*)'. This would indicate that the sea around Java in the past was known as 'Kalinga Sea', being frequented by the ships of Kalinga.[25]

Scholars are of the opinion that the Sailendras, who ruled over central Java and Sri Vijaya, were a branch of the Sailodbhava dynasty that ruled in Odisha in the seventh century CE. The rule of the Sailendra dynasty was an epoch making period in the history of Indonesia. The Sailendras introduced a new type of culture, which became a model for other South-East Asian countries. The new vigour of the *Mahayana* form of Buddhism, and its highly developed art produced such splendid monuments as the Candi Kalasan, and the Borobudur in Java may also be mainly attributed to their patronage. The introduction of a new kind of alphabet, which has been called the Pre-*Nagari* script, and the adoption of a new name, Kalinga[26] for Malaysia (at least by the foreigners) were two most important achievements of the Sailendras.

S.C. Chandra,[27] H.K. Mahatab[28] and B.S. Das[29] are of the opinion that the Sailendras of *Suvarnadvipa* are supposed to be the Sailodbhava emigrants of Kongoda (ancient Kongoda comprised parts of modern Ganjam, Nayagarh, Khordha, and Puri districts of modern Odisha). M.N. Das observes that,

> The Sailendras who played such a prominent role in South Eastern Asia were the members and descendants of a Kalinga royal family in the mainland of India and who, for some unknown reason, left their original home and sailed off towards the *Suvaranadvipa* where, with the help of the former Kalingan inhabitants of the islands, they could establish their sway and gradually spread their empire to all the islands of the Archipelago.[30]

Tracing the origin of the Sailendras of Java, V. Venkayya is inclined to connect them with some part of Odisha, apparently on account of the similarity of names like Sailodbhava *vamsha* and Sailendra *vamsha*.[31] This view is supported by R.D. Banerji, who boldly asserts that 'At some subsequent date the Sailas or the Sailodbavas migrated to the Malay Peninsula, where their inscriptions have been discovered'.[32] But, the argument of R.D. Banerji seems to be inadequate in establishing the relationship between the Sailodbhavas and Sailendras. In fact, no Sailodbhava record has been discovered in Malayasia. However, in his monumental work *Suvarnadvipa*, R.C. Majumdar, has put forth his arguments regarding the Kalinga origin of the Sailendras in a more acceptable manner. He says,

> we must lay stress on the fact that there are some reasons to believe that the Sailendras were new arrivals from India. This would explain the introduction of [the] *Nagari* alphabet in their inscriptions and of a new name, Kalinga, for Malaysia, as we know from the Chinese records. The portion of the western coast of Bay of Bengal, which was known as Kalinga in [the] old days, contained the famous port 'Paloura' which was, from very early times, the port of embarkation for the Far East. The same region was ruled over in the sixth and seventh centuries AD[CE] by the Ganga and Sailodbhava dynasties, and behind them, in the Vindhya region, we find another dynasty called the Sailas [the Sila dynasty of Nandapur of present Jaypur region of Odisha]. In the preamble of an inscription, this family is said to have descended from Ganga, the daughter of Himalaya (Sailendra), and the first king is referred to as *Sailavamsha-tilaka* (ornament of the *Saila* family). Thus, the Ganga, Sailodbhava, and Saila dynasties may all be the source of a name like Sailendra.[33]

However, this statement does not offer any definite conclusion. Majumdar, however, believes that the famous Sailendras of Java originally went there from Kalinga, and spread their power in the Far East through Lower Burma and the Malay Peninsula. This assumption of Majumdar appears to be based on reasonable grounds, though the conclusion is not yet free from debate.[34]

S.C. Chandra observes, 'It is likely that the Sailodbhavas being hard pressed between the Bhaumas [Bhaumakaras] of Utkala and Gangas of Kalinga migrated to Malayasia.'[35] But, S.C. Behera partially refuted this hypothesis of S.C. Chandra. Putting forth his argument, Behera says that there is no evidence to show that the Sailodbhavas were ever hard pressed by the Gangas who, on the other hand, seem to have backed the cause of the Sailodbhavas.[36] Further, he says, 'it was the pressure from the Bhaumas in the north rather than from the Eastern Gangas in the south which was responsible for the shifting of the homeland of the Sailodbhavas (p.192)'. Again, he also points out that the cradle land of the Sailodbhavas of Kongoda was mount Mahendra of the Eastern Ghats.[37] The meaning of the term 'Sailendra' is 'Lord of the mountains', and Sailodbhava means 'one born out of rock'.

It seems quite likely that the Sailodbhavas, being ousted by the Bhaumakaras, moved across the high seas, and contributed to the expansion of Indian culture under the new nomenclature of the Sailendras in *Suvarnadvipa*.[38] They might have taken advantage of the great port of Palur, and migrated to

Suvarnadvipa with their powerful navy. A large population of Kalinga had already migrated to Malaysia, which might have helped the Sailodbhavas against the local kings. From an inscription of Java, it is learnt that the first Sailendra king of Java was called Raja Bhujya Tungadeva. The titles of Tunga and Tungadeva still continue in Odisha among the descendants of a few royal houses who might have been distantly related to the Sailodbhavas as the Sailendras were.

Thus, the Sailodbhavas of Odisha in all historical probability, might have established the Sailendra Empire of Malayasia.[39] But the Sailodbhavas of Odisha were non-Buddhists, whereas the Sailendras of Java were ardent followers of Buddhism. However, this difference could be due to several reasons. H.K. Mahatab explains the matter in the following manner. According to him,

> It is likely that the prevalent religion in *Suvarnadvipa* was Buddhism and the Sailodbhavas might have been converted into it after their settlement there. It is also quite reasonable to suppose that the Sailendras belonged to the Ganga or Saila dynasty of Orissa [Odisha]. Whatever might be their origin, whether Ganga or Sailodbhava, it is beyond doubt that they were immigrants from Orissa [Odisha].[40]

This theory may be criticised by scholars on the ground that the Sailendras built monuments in other parts of India, and not in their motherland Orissa [Odisha]. It is sufficient to say that people were not parochial then as they are today. Secondly, in those days, Orissa [Odisha] was dominated by Brahmanism, which had already ousted Buddhism. In such a situation, it was not necessary for the Sailendras to erect Buddhist monuments in Orissa [Odisha]. Further, the recent excavations at Kedah, which brought to light a number of objects of the *Mahayana* sect (stone caskets with gems and gold objects of the Sailendra period)[41] indicate that the Sailendras who constructed a number of *Mahayana* Buddhist temples—including the Great Borobudur in Java—were greatly influenced by their contemporary Sailodbhavas of ancient Odisha (Kongoda region).

The Kalinga origin of the Sailendras has been corroborated by certain references found in Javanese inscriptions. In Verse 8 of the Kalasan inscription (*c.* 776 CE), the Sailendra King Panangkarana styles himself as *Aryasantati*, that is, the scion of the Arya race or Arya land. H.B. Sarkar draws our attention to an old Javanese charter dated to *c.* 840 CE. In the third and fourth line of this charter, there is the mention of *Kling Haryya*. The word *Kling* denoted

Kalinga, and *Haryya* stood for *Arya*. Thus *Kling Haryya* denoted *Kling* or *Kalinga Arya*.[42] The words *Kling-Aryya* was, once again, coined in an inscription of King Airlangga dated between *c.* 1019–1042 CE. Hence, it is possible that the Sailendras went there from some parts of Aryanised India, most plausibly from Kalinga.

There are palaeographical similarities found in some of the inscriptions of Odisha and Java. The fact is corroborated by the discovery of a ring (ornament) of *c.* 14th century CE at Lambang, in northern Borneo, bearing letters *a-ra-kta* in *Nagari* characters, resembling those of the twelfth and thirteenth centuries Odisha.[43] The *Nagari* alphabet used in the inscriptions of Java is very similar to the inscriptions of Odisha.[44] Some affinity is also there in the script of the Mulavarman's inscription (*c.*400 CE) and the Kalingan script.

Apart from epigraphic evidence, there are some resemblances between Kalinga and Java in the domain of art and architecture, although the local incorporation is more. Buddhism played a significant role in the relations between Odisha and Indonesia. It had a popular career in Odisha, and Odisha contributed a great deal to the pan-Asian zeal of Buddhism.[45] Comparative studies of the Buddhist sculptural art of Odisha with those of the Indonesian islands show several common elements and striking affinities. The Sailendras, who were ruling over central Java, were great patrons of *Mahayana* Buddhism. They constructed the magnificent Borobudur monument at Java for legitimizing their rule. S.C. Chandra observes,

> The Mahayana Buddhist art of the Sailendras of Java has strong affinities with the early medieval Orissan [Odishan] art. The Orissan [Odishan] Buddha figures of the Cuttack hill [Ratnagiri Buddhist monastery of modern Jajpur district] may have served as prototypes for the contemporary Javanese Buddhas of Borobudur.[46]

This observation of S.C. Chandra seems to be true. Indeed, there is close Odishan affinity in the art of the Buddhist temple at Borobudur. The Borobudur temple, which was built under the patronage of the Sailendra kings, is said to be a piece of architecture of the highest magnitude in the world.[47] The Buddha images of Borobudur possess striking resemblance with the Buddha images of Ratnagiri in Odisha. Excavations conducted at Buddhist sites in Ratnagiri, Udayagiri, Lalitagiri, and Langudi in Odisha have brought to light masterpieces of Buddhist art.

The Buddha heads from these centres and those from central Java share common traits of massive form, sensitive modelling, and spiritual expressions.[48] The Javanese Boddhisattvas from Candi Mendut (Mendut Temple) have their attributes placed on long lotuses in the style distinctive of the Lalitagiri figures of Odisha.[49] The *dhyani* Buddhas of Borobudur reminds us of the massive heads of the Buddha at Ratnagiri, one on the slope and another at the top of the hill.[50] The squatish Buddha and Bodhisattva images of Lalitagiri (now displayed in the site museum at Lalitagiri) depicting a squat face, thick lips, and an innate smile are like those of the images at Borobudur. The Buddha images of *bhumisparsa mudra* (the seated Buddha images in earth touching pose) with curly hair at Ratnagiri and Lalitagiri in the Jajpur district of Odisha, possess striking resemblance with the images of Borobudur.

Besides, mention should be made of the stone architectural fragments—recovered from Monastery No.I, and Monastery No.III of Lalitagiri—having similarities with that of the famous Buddhist complex at Borobudur. The stepped tiers of *Candi* Bima (*c.* eighth century CE) on the Dieng Plateau in the north-west of central Java resemble the *shikharas* of Odishan temples.[51] The *parsvadevata* depiction in the Shaivite temples in Java are like those depicted in several temples in Odisha.[52] The *kalamakara* ornament probably migrated to Java from Odisha as *makara* heads (*makara* is mythical crocodile-like creature) at the springing of the arch, and the *kirtimukha* (the *kirtimukha* motif shows the head of a lion-like creature with beads coming out from its mouth) at the crown, are fairly common decorative motifs in Odisha. An excellent example of this device is the *mangala-torana* in front of the Muktesvara temple at Bhubaneswar in Odisha. The holding of a Javanese *kris* (dagger or distinctly shaped knife blade of Indonesia) by the door-keeper of the Parasuramesvara temple at Bhubaneswar also amply testifies to the widespread interaction between the two regions. The close connection between the art of Java and that of ancient Kalinga may even prove the migration of Odishan artists to Java, along with the merchants and missionaries.[53]

F.D.K. Bosch, a Dutch scholar in Indonesian archaeology, has propounded a theory known as 'counter-current theory (*tegenstroomtheorie*)' in this connection.[54] This theory brings to light the role played by young Indonesians themselves in the dissemination of Hindu and Buddhist culture in Indonesia, particularly in Java. This theory holds that the young Indonesians went to India to study religion, and

> made selections of Indian cultural elements considered suitable for inclusion in their own cultural patterns, and subsequently developed as their own although with Hinduistic traits. This process of Indian-Indonesian cultural diffusion or acculturation went on gradually and took a long time, a generation or more.

However, if this is true, then it must have happened only in the later period. One thing we can say is that, with the passage of time, there was a blending of Indian cultural elements with Indonesian indigenous traditions. In spite of living imprints of Indian cultural influences on Java, it can be said that the latter has retained its own identity, and has not been completely influenced by the former. According to P. P. Mishra, 'The Javanese had developed before they came into contact with Indians, many aspects of Indonesian cultural life: *wayang* or puppet shadow theatre, *garmelan* orchestra, *batik* work in textiles, a monetary system, knowledge of navigation, and rice cultivation.'[55]

The maritime interaction between Kalinga and Java can be more authentically established on the basis of old Javanese and Sanskrit inscriptions. The oldest dated inscription of Java—that of Canggal in Kedu of King Sanjaya belonging to *c.* 732 CE,[56] refers to the original home of Hindu immigrants as *Kunjara Kunjadeṣa* which has been identified by many scholars as Kalinga. *Kunjara* means 'elephant', and *Kunjadesa* means 'forest'; hence *Kunjara Kunjadesa* means 'elephant forest'. In ancient times, Kalinga or Odisha was very famous for the rearing of the best quality of elephants. The *Periplus of the Erythraean Sea* refers to Kalinga as the place for the rearing of the best type/quality elephants called *bosare*. Another inscription in Java, dated to *c.* 856 CE, written partly in Sanskrit and partly in Javanese, refers to *Klings* (the people of Kalinga).[57] The Kuki Copper Plates (*c.* 840 CE) of Jaha (Java) speaks of potters and all sorts of servants of inner apartments hailing from *Kling* (Kalinga).[58] From this precise inscriptional data, we can assume that the people of Kalinga or ancient Odisha went to Java, and other places of Indonesia, for commerce and in pursuit of missionary activities, which gradually resulted in colonization. It is significant to note that, in the inscriptions, the *Kling* people are mentioned first in the list of people of Indian origin—probably because they constituted the most numerous group among all. Besides, their dominance in business and trade gave them a position of significance for which reason they were mentioned first.[59]

The Tugu Rock Inscription of Purnavarman (*c.* fifth century CE) found in western Java (now preserved in the museum at Jakarta) refers to the construction of a canal fifteen kilometres in length named Chandrabhaga.[60] It is well-known that Chandrabhaga is ariver in the Puri district of Odisha, and has great sanctity in religious literature. Taking a dip (holy bath) on some auspicious days or occasions in the river Chandrabhaga is considered a pious activity by the Hindus of Odisha. Hence, it is presumed that the Chandrabhaga canal of Java could have been named after the river Chandrabhaga of Puri district in Odisha, which existed very near the port of Khalkattapatna, on the bank of which once the famous *Surya* (sun) temple of Konarak was located.[61] This inscription[62] also refers to the construction of another canal named Gomati, which was evidently named after river Gomati (flowing near Lucknow in UP) of India.

Some scholars have attempted to identify Chandrabhaga of Java with the Chenab of Punjab. However, when a river named Chandrabhaga is flowing in Odisha, and the people of ancient Odisha are considered as pioneers in maritime activities and colonization, then the Chandrabhaga canal of Java cannot be identified with the Chenab river of Punjab as suggested by B.C. Chhabra.[63] The original passage of the inscription reads,

> The Chandrabhaga [canal], formerly dug by the great king of kings, Pinabahu, passing along the famous city, flowed into the sea. The beautiful Gomati [canal] with clear water, dug within 21 days—beginning from the 8th day of the dark fortnight of the month of *Phalguna* to the 13th day of the bright fortnight of the month of *Caitra*—in the 22nd year of the prosperous reign of the illustrious Purnavarman, glorious, virtuous and powerful as also most excellent among kings,—measuring in length 6122 *dhanus* [bows], cutting across the cantonment of the grandfather, the saintly king, and having caused a great gift of 1000 cows to the Brahmans, is [now] flowing forth.[64]

The Kalinga people (the *Klings*) also occupied an important position in East Java. They had maximum influence there. In East Java, a river was named as Kali Keling.[65] Several inscriptions of the Javanese King Airlangga (*c.* 1019–1042 CE) mentions the flow of foreigners of various countries, including the merchants of Kalinga, to his kingdom. The merchants went to East Java through the ports situated on the Brantas River. (The Brantas is the longest river in East Java. It drains an area of over 11,000 km from the southern slope of Mount Kawi-Kelud-Butak, Mount Wilis, and the northern slopes of Mount Liman-Limas, Mount Welirang, and Mount Anjasmoro. Its course is semi-circular or spiral in shape; it empties into the Java Sea). An inscription states that when the river burst its banks, the King built a dam. This caused great joy to the 'foreign merchants and captains of ships'.[66] The inscription also refers to foreign boats carrying goods from *dvipantara*.[67]

The inscriptions supplied a list of foreigners which includes Kling (Kalinga), Singhala (Ceylon), Dravida (Chola kingdom), Karnataka (in south India), Champa (Annam), Kmir (Kamboja or Khmer), Aryya (north India), Pandikira (probably a combination of Pandya and Kerala), Remen (Pegu), etc.[68] The foreign people used to come to Java for trade or other peaceful pursuits of life.[69] It is, therefore, believed that, during the reign of Airlangga (which is considered as the golden age in the history of Java), the contact of Java with foreign lands (including Kalinga) was prolific. In an East Javanese inscription (*c.* 1194 CE), mention is made of a *Jurn Kling*—that is, the headman or chief of the Kalinga people.[70] A charter from Jiju of the Surabaya region (the Majapahit kingdom) refers to King Girindravardhana as *Bhatare Kling* (that is, lord of *Kling*), while another inscription of *c.* 1447 CE describes his wife Kamala Varnnadevi as queen of Kalingapura.[71] During the twelfth century CE, Jayabhaya—who happens to be one of the most famous kings of Java—believed himself to be a distant descendant of Kalinga families sent to Java by some Kalinga prince in a remote past.[72]

Even today, in different customs and nomenclatures of Java, many typical Kalingan terms are available. As in Odisha, a green leaf called *sajana* (drumstick) is a popular food item in Java. The sweet rice cakes of Odisha, known as *pitha*, are also prepared in the island of Java. The religious system of Java has much similarity with that of Kalinga. The Javanese worshipped three principal Hindu divinities: Brahma as the Creator, Vishnu as the Protector, and Shiva as the Destroyer (of evils), together with their *shaktis* or divine spouses, and a host of minor gods and goddesses related to them. The worship of Ganesha, the son of Shiva and Parvati was very common in Java. The god Kartikeya, another son of Shiva considered the commander-in-chief (*senapati*) of the gods and goddesses, was also worshipped in Java. Shiva, the popular deity of the Hindu pantheon, was also worshipped in the form of *linga*. In Java, a goddess is worshipped as the deity of corn (Ni Pohaci Sangyang Sri) and yield, exactly in the same way as the Odias worship Shri Lakshmi or Mahalakshmi (the goddesses of wealth). P.P. Mishrahas remarked,

> In west Java, Goddess Laksmi is still worshipped as promoting fertility in rice fields. She is known as Ni Pohaci Sangyang Sri. At the time of

harvesting in Orissa [Odisha], paddy is worshipped and it is known as Laksmi *puja*. Puri was named as *Srikshetra* after advent of Laksmi (Sri); so [the] name Sri for Laksmi in Orissa [Odisha] and name Ni Pohaci Sangyang Sri of Java point towards cultural affinity.[73]

Like the women of Odisha, the Javanese women prepare a symbolic image of sand called *Astabhuja Durga* (eight-armed Durga). In the Kutei inscription of Mulavarman (*c.*400 CE), there is a reference to the illumination of *akashadvipa*. The lighting of lamps in the month of *kartika* (October-November) on the occasion of the *boita bandana utsava*—which marks the beginning of ancient sea voyages to South-East Asian countries—is an important ritual in Odisha. Besides, even in the realm of language, there are many words which are of similar pronunciation and meaning to both the regions.[74] Some of the Malay-Indonesian words have much similarity in pronunciation and meaning with that of the Odias. Good examples are: *nadi* = *nadi* (river), *pancainderiya* = *pancaindriya* (five senses), *sendi* = *sandhi* (joint of bones), *kapala* (forehead), *roma* (hair), *selesem* = *slesma* (cough), *cerna* = *jirna* (digestion), etc.[75] All these indicate that, in the ancient period, there was vibrant cultural interaction between Odisha and the Indonesian island of Java.

NOTES

1. P. Bellwood, 'South-East Asia before History', in N. Tarling (ed.), *The Cambridge History of South-East Asia*, Vol. I, Singapore: Cambridge University Press, 1992, p.133.
2. R. K. Mookerji, *Indian Shipping*, Allahabad: Kitab Mahal, 1962, p. 103, New Delhi, Munshiram Manoharlal Publishers Pvt. Ltd, 1999 (edition), p.148.
3. M.M. Ganguly, *Orissa and Her Remains*, Delhi: Gian Publishing House, 1986, p.18.
4. M. Elphinstone, *The History of India*, Vol. I, London: John Murray, 1841 (2nd edition), p.327.
5. R.K. Mookerji, *op.cit* (1962 ed.), p.104; (1999 ed.), p. 149.
6. *The Bombay Gazetteer*, Vol. I, Pt. I, p. 493; Quoted in R.K. Mookerji, op.cit., (1962 ed.), p.104; (1999 ed.), p. 150.
7. R.C. Majumdar, *Hindu Colonies in the Far East*, Calcutta: Firma KLM Pvt. Ltd., 1963 and 1991, p.21.
8. K.S. Behera, 'Maritime Trade in Ancient Orissa', in M.N. Das (ed.), *Sidelights on the History and Culture of Orissa*, Cuttack: Vidya Puri, 1977, p.119.
9. A.K. Coomaraswamy, *History of Indian and Indonesian Art*, New York: 1927; New Delhi: Munshiram Manoharlal Publishers Pvt. Ltd 1972, p. 157.
10. R.D. Banerji, *History of Orissa*, Vol. I, Varanasi, 1980, p.93; *History of Orissa: from the Earliest Times to the British Period*, Cuttack: New Age Publications 2006, p. 82.
11. Ibid. (1980 ed.), pp. 93–94; (2006 ed.), pp.82–83.
12. J. Crawfurd, *History of the Indian Archipelago*, Vol. II, Delhi: Low Price Publications 1993, p. 226.
13. Ibid., p.227.

14. A.K. Rath, 'Saivism in South-East Asia', *Journal of Andhra Historical Research Society*, Vol. XXVIII, Pt. 1 &2 (1962–63), p.32.
15. R.D. Banerji, op.cit., (1980 ed.), p.94; (2006 ed.), pp. 83–84.
16. Ibid., (1980 ed.), p.96; (2006 ed.), p. 85.
17. R.C. Majumdar, *Suvarnadvipa*, Vol. I, New Delhi: 1986, p. 96.
18. K. Sridharan, *A Maritime History of India*, New Delhi: 1982, p.36.
19. K.S. Behera, 'Ancient Orissa/Kalinga and Indonesia: The Maritime Contacts', *Utkal Historical Research Journal* (hereafter *UHRJ*), Vol. IV, (1993), pp. 125–126.
20. K.S. Behera, 'Trade and Patterns of Commerce in Orissa (CAD. 700-1200)', *UHRJ*, Vol. II (1991), p. 4.
21. O.W. Wolters, *Early Indonesian Commerce: A Study of the Origin of Srivijaya*, New York: 1967, p. 213.
22. R.C. Majumdar, *Suvarnadvipa*, Vol. I, p. 112.
23. Ibid.
24. H.B. Sarkar, 'The Cultural and Political Background of Indo-Javanese History', *Journal of Indian History*, Vol. XLIII, Pt. I (April, 1965), pp.104–105.
25. K.S. Behera, 'Ancient Orissa/Kalinga and Indonesia: The Maritime Contacts', op. cit., p. 127.
26. D.P. Singhal, *India and World Civilization*, Vol. II, Calcutta: Rupa & Co., 1972, p.142.
27. S.C. Chandra, 'Early Medieval Sculptures of Utkal (Orissa)', *Orissa Historical Research Journal* (hereafter *OHRJ*), Vol. III, No. 2 (September 1954) p. 76, f.n. 2.
28. Quoted by H.K. Mahatab, *History of Orissa*, Vol. I, Cuttack: Student's Store 1981, p. 182.
29. B.S. Das, *Studies in the Economic History of Orissa: From Ancient Times to 1833*, Calcutta: Firma KLM Pvt. Ltd., 1978, p. 44.
30. M.N. Das, *Glimpses of Kalinga History*, Calcutta: Century Publishers, 1949, p. 117.
31. *ASR* (1911–1912), p. 175; quoted in S.C. Behera, *Rise and Fall of the Sailodbhavas*, Calcutta: Punthi Pustak 1982, p. 192.
32. R.D. Banerji, op.cit. (1980 ed.), p. 131; (2006 ed.), p. 117.
33. R.C. Majumdar, *Suvarnadvipa*, Vol. I, pp. 225–226.
34. Ibid., p. 227.
35. S.C. Chandra, op.cit., p.76, f.n. 2.
36. S.C. Behera, op.cit., pp.101–102.
37. Ibid., p.196. S.C. Behera observes that 'The same nomenclature of two hills—one in Cambodia, the other in Kongoda [ancient Odisha]—suggests the influence of the Sailodbhavas in this region… The greatness of mount Mahendra seems to have been carried from Kongoda to Cambodia through the Sailendras of Java'.
38. Ibid., p. 197.
39. H.K. Mahatab, op.cit., p. 182.
40. Ibid.
41. K. Nag, 'India and the Archaeology of Malaysia and Indonesia', *Indian Historical Quarterly*, Vol. XVI (1985), pp. 478–480.
42. T.K. Biswas, 'Javanese Buddha Images: A Historic and Aesthetic Evaluation', *OHRJ*, Vol. XXXVIII, No. 1 to 4 (1993), p. 3.
43. D. Devahuti, 'India, Malay and Borneo: Two Millennia of Contacts and Cultural Synthesis', in L. Chandra (ed.), *India's Contribution to World's Thought and Culture*, Madras: Vivekananda Kendra Prakashan Trust 1970, p. 528.
44. K.S. Behera, 'Maritime Trade in Ancient Orissa', op. cit., p.119.
45. H.S. Patnaik, 'Some Aspects of Buddhism in Far East and South-East Asia', *UHRJ*, Vol. II (1991), p.64.
46. S.C. Chandra, op.cit., p.76.

47. H.K. Mahatab, op.cit., pp.179–180.
48. K.S. Behera, 'Maritime Contacts of Orissa: Literary and Archaeological Evidence', *UHRJ*, Vol. V (1994), p.67.
49. Ibid., pp.67–68.
50. D.P. Ghosh, 'Relation between the Buddha Images of Orissa and Java', *Modern Review*, Calcutta: November, 1938, p.503.
51. R. Grousset, *The Civilizations of the East: India*, Delhi: Munshiram Manoharlal Publishers Pvt. Ltd 1969, p.316.
52. H. Santiko, 'Technological Transfer in Temple Architecture from India to Java', *UHRJ*, Vol. V, 1994, p.38.
53. K.S. Behera, 'Maritime Trade in Ancient Orissa', op. cit., p.119.
54. Quoted by H. Santiko, op.cit., pp.27–28.
55. P. P. Mishra, *Cultural Rapprochement between India and South-East Asia*, New Delhi: National Book Organisation 2005, p.46.
56. H.B. Sarkar, *Corpus of the Inscriptions of Java: up to 928 A.D.*, Vol. I, Calcutta: Firma KLM Pvt. Ltd. 1971, No.XII.
57. Ibid., No. XIX, p.29.
58. Ibid., pp. 80, 86 and 97.
59. K.S. Behera, 'Trade and Patterns of Commerce in Orissa (CAD 700–1200)', p.5
60. H.B. Sarkar, *Corpus of the Inscriptions of Java* (up to 928 A.D.), Vol. I, pp. 6 & 11; B.C. Chhabra, *Expansion of Indo-Aryan Culture during Pallava Rule*, Delhi: Munshiram Manoharlal Publishers Pvt. Ltd. 1965, pp. 42, 96 & 97.
61. B.C. Chhabra, op.cit., pp.96–97.
62. Ibid., pp.42 & 97.
63. Ibid.
64. Ibid., pp. 96–97.
65. K.S. Behera, 'Ancient Orissa/Kalinga and Indonesia: The Maritime Contacts', op. cit., p.128.
66. Ibid., p.127.
67. Ibid.
68. R.C. Majumdar, *Suvarnadvipa*, Vol. I, p.271; R.C. Majumdar, *Hindu Colonies in the Far East*, p.49.
69. Ibid.
70. K.S. Behera, 'Trade and Patterns of Commerce in Orissa (CAD 700–1200)', p.6; H.B. Sarkar, (ed.) *Corpus of Inscriptions of Java*, Vol. II, Calcutta: Firma KLM Pvt. Ltd 1971, p.210.
71. Ibid.
72. K.Patra, *The Ports in Orissa: A Study of Maritime History*, Bhubaneswar: Panchashila 1988, p.6.
73. P.P. Mishra, *Cultural Rapprochement between India and South East Asia*, p.150.
74. B.K. Tripathy, 'Dakshina Purva Asiara Samaj O Sahityare Kalingara Prabhaba', in K.S. Behera (ed.) *Sagara O Sahitya* (Odia), Cuttack: Dasarathi Pustakalaya, 1993, pp. 62–63.
75. H.B. Sarkar, *Literary Heritage of South-East Asia*, Calcutta, Firma KLM Pvt. Ltd 1980, p.217; H.B. Sarkar, 'The Language and Literature of Ancient Indonesia and Malaysia', *Journal of Indian History*, Vol. XLIV, Pt.III, 1966, p.669.

32

Intangible Cultural Heritage: Connectivity Across Traditions of South and Southeast Asia

Lopamudra Maitra Bajpai

The first attempts at an academic understanding of the word 'culture' came to the forefront more than a century ago. The initial attempts were possible because of various studies and academic understandings across the different disciplines of sociology, anthropology, archaeology, psychology, ethnography, amidst others, trying to understand the various interfaces between different cultures as a result of demographic movements and interactions. This also includes various ethnographic short documentaries which were primarily sponsored through the efforts of different royalties, or the diligent efforts of individuals. An example is the first feature-documentary by Robert Flaherty in 1922, titled *Nanook of the North*. Through the very opening scenes, the documentary introduces an important section of a habitat—One of the least known places around the world—Canada's northern Quebec region. The story revolves around the main protagonist Nanook, his family, and their travels across the snow-capped landscape. Though it is considered the first feature-documentary, yet the various efforts involved of shooting, enacting, re-enacting, and rehearsing for this audio-visual representation led to many criticisms after its release about the film being referred to as a documentary. Nevertheless, this opened up a direction to portray the socio-cultural ethos of a region—its tangible as well as its intangible cultural heritage using the audio-visual medium—for example, the igloo of the Inuits, their kayak boats, clothes, and their food habits, methods of hunting and gathering, and their travels and migrations in search of better and safer place to live.

Thus, across a broad framework of understanding, culture can be understood through two aspects: the tangible and the intangible facets of life. Just as monuments, sculptures, structures, and architecture form part of the tangible aspect, the many folktales, dance forms, music, handicrafts, the patterns of clothes and the textile weaving processes, culinary feats, etc. form elements of the intangible part of a cultural heritage. While the tangible aspects are often studied, the intangible elements are often lost to oblivion but which, nevertheless, contribute to frame an individual and her/his identity to a large extent. Perhaps, the best visual depiction towards this understanding is to imagine a giant iceberg where only a small tip is visible on top of the water. This is only, perhaps, the top twenty per cent of the entire ice-berg, while about eighty per cent of the remaining part lies undisclosed to most eyes under the water. If the tip of the ice-berg can be compared to the most visible parts of our existence—we can say that it shows some of the most obvious aspects visible while interacting with another person. These include behaviour, eating habits, clothing, body and facial features, among others. However, under this obvious surface, remains hidden a large section away from observation which includes beliefs, values, customs, experiences, linguistic differences, exposure to specific rites, rituals, and festivals, etc. Though the latter remain concealed during most interactions, they form an important part of what makes each of us unique in our own way. These are the intangible aspects of our representation. These are the feature that goes to make every one of us different even though many may share the same language or geographical areas. These are also the aspects that go into answering the various questions, and in to understanding the 'why' behind the behaviour of other people and societies which are not similar to ours.

Intangible culture has mostly remained an unspoken subject. However, the last decade has witnessed a burgeoning of discussions of intangible culture amidst various academic platforms and discussions. Thus, today, it has become an important part of different discussions highlighting cultural connectivity, communication, and cross-cultural understanding. As small and scattered efforts continued across the world through several decades across the last century to highlight the different features of what is now being described as our Intangible Cultural Heritage, the acceptance of the same by UNESCO has helped garner enough global support to provide it with a wider platform of expression. This has also helped to bring the matter to the notice to respective governments as well as local cultural and social bodies as well as organisations for the better understanding of the different elements that comprise this Intangible Cultural Heritage as well as spread awareness about them. This has also helped to build up financial help to support its various causes.

Intangible Cultural Heritage and the UNESCO List from India

A part of a speech made by Amadou Hampâté Bâ at the 1960 conference of UNESCO highlighted an important aspect: '*En Afrique, quand un vieillardmeurt, c'estunebibliothèque qui brûle.*" In Africa, when an old man dies, it's a library burning. The quote attracts immediate attention for its widespread applicability across the globe. The words stand as silent sentinels to an immediate need—understanding our intangible heritage. The saying's applicability far supersedes mere geographical boundaries, and sees similar reverberations across almost all spheres of the world. Intangible culture also speaks of centuries of the sources of education in various cultures. The many poems, riddles, songs, dances, handicrafts, festivals, culinary feats, and others—all boast of a remarkable contribution to the significance of local history and culture.

Amidst the glorious mix of the elements of Intangible Cultural Heritage are important examples from the Indian sub-continent, within which oral traditions occupy a significant part of communication as well as a process of learning. The oral tradition across the Indian Sub-continent has held an important place of honour for thousands of years. Mention should be made here of the *Guru-Sishyaparampara* or the tradition of maintaining a teacher-student relationship. Based on respect and knowledge-sharing, this tradition primarily involved a disciplined process of learning for the holistic development of mind and soul. The *parampara* tradition was based on the concept of the oral tradition being the only method of learning, through the two primary tools of *shruti* or listening, and *smriti* or committing to memory. Thus, for several centuries, the many histories from the region—including the great epics of The *Ramayana* and The *Mahabharata* as well as the many tales of The *Jatakas*, The *Panchatantras* and also the several thousands of folk tales from India—were all committed to memory. Only very recently—mainly during colonial times—have most of them been published by printing presses. Thus, from history to the performing arts, handicrafts, the essence of weaving multifarious patterns of cloth, beliefs, rites, rituals, festivals and others, were all preserved in time across cultures through oral traditions. These have stood as sentinels of time, the reflections of history, and knowledge-banks for learning in the future.

At the 2001 UNESCO Convention, an important observation was provided a platform: the elements of Intangible Cultural Heritage (ICH). These were identified as 'the practices, representations, expressions, knowledge, skills as well as the instruments, objects, artefacts, and cultural spaces associated therewith—that communities, groups and, in some cases, individuals recognised as part of their cultural heritage'. The preservation of these oral traditions meant the active participation of various states and countries, communities, groups, and the relevant non-governmental organisations. Over the years, this has helped to create not only an international recognition on a global platform, but has also been a great incentive for safeguarding the ICH even at regional and local levels. It has also helped to create and encourage cultural entrepreneurship and jobs. Over the last decade, India has successfully featured on the ICH UNESCO list.

The UNESCO List of the Intangible Cultural Heritage of the Humanity of India

2017:	The Kumbh Mela
2016:	Yoga
2014:	The traditional craft of making brass and copper utensils among the Thatheras of Jandiala Guru, Punjab
2013:	The Sankirtana, ritual singing, drumming, and dancing of Manipur
2012:	Buddhist chanting and the recitation of sacred Buddhist texts in the trans-Himalayan region of Ladakh, Jammu and Kashmir, India
2010:	The Chhau Dance of West Bengal; the Kalbelia folk songs and dances of Rajasthan; and the Mudiyettu ritual theatre and dance-drama of Kerala.
2009:	Novruz, Nowrouz, Nooruz, Navruz, Nauroz, Nevruzalong with India-Azerbaijan, Iran Islamic Republic of, Kyrgyzstan, Pakistan, Turkey, Uzbekistan Ramman, religious festival and ritual theatre of the Garhwal Himalayas, India.
2008:	Kutiyattam or Sanskrit theatre; Ramlila or the traditional performance of the story of the *Ramayana*; and Traditional Vedic chanting

The intangible heritage elements from India which have found mention in the UNESCO list since 2008.

The Kumbh Mela 2017

The festival of the *Sacred Pitcher* is the largest peaceful congregation of pilgrims in the world. It comprises of ascetics, saints, aspirants—*kalpavasis* and visitors—without any barriers of caste, creed, or religion. It is held every four years by rotation at Allahabad, Haridwar, Ujjain, and Nasik, and witnesses the congregation of believers taking a dip or bathing in the waters of the Holy *Ganga*/Ganges to cleanse off mortal sins, and obtain relief from the cycle of birth and death. The event encapsulates specific knowledge about oral traditions and history as well as the science of astronomy, astrology, spirituality, ritualistic traditions, and social and cultural customs and practices.

Yoga 2016

A well-known practice today and the world over, the concept of *Yoga* cuts across all geographical, race, age, religious, political, and gender barriers. It is considered that its formation took place through the 196 *sutras* aphorisms of the *Yoga Sutra*, the Sanskrit text written by the ancient Indian scholar Patanjali, prior to 400 BCE. Having been translated across many languages all over the world, this is considered to be one of the principal foundations of classical *Yoga* philosophy. Indian *Yoga* ideals have also been influenced by the *Bhagavad Gita*; the *Yoga Vasistha* texts attributed to *Yajnavalkya* and *Hiranyagarbha*; and literature on *Hatha Yoga, Tantric Yoga* and *Pashupata Yoga.*

The traditional craft of making brass and copper utensils among the Thatheras of Jandiala Guru, Punjab 2014

Thatheras make utensils from metals brass, copper, and certain alloys by hand, which are exported to various temples and *Gurdwaras* all over the world. The manual labour-intensive manufacturing process involves working with very high heat from the very first stage of moulding the metal plates to the final stages of polishing with tamarind juice and sand.

Sankirtana: ritual singing drumming and dancing in Manipur 2013

These are ritualistic dance performances amidst the *Vaishnava* community of the Manipur plains of North-east India that narrate the mythological stories of *Krishna* and his deeds as a human on earth. The long performances involve rigorous training, and are considered sacrosanct, and are deeply moving.

The Recitation of Buddhist texts in the Ladakh region of Jammu and Kashmir 2012

This represents the sacred texts, spirit, philosophy, and teachings of Lord Buddha. The *Mahayana* and *Vajrayana* forms of Buddhism are practiced in Ladakh. There are four major sects: *Nyngma, Kagyud, Shakya* and *Geluk*. Several ritual chantings are performed on important days in the Buddhist and agrarian calendars, and the process followed includes the use of special bells, drums, cymbals, trumpets, special robes, and the maintaining of rhythm.

Dances and Ritual Theatre 2010

The *Chhau* dance of West Bengal is traditionally performed by men enacting episodes from the *Ramayana* and the *Mahabharata*, and is traditionally performed during the Spring festival or the Bengali traditional New Year in April 14/15. A masked dance, it incorporates folk dances, mock combat techniques, stylised gaits of animals and birds, and the movements of village housewives.

The *Kalbelia* folk songs and dances of Rajasthan are also known as the snake charmer's dance. They are performed traditionally by the women in flowing skirts, accompanied by musical instruments such as the '*phoongi*' awind instrument and '*khanjari*' or hand-held cymbals. The music has evolved to express their everyday life, the environment around them, and happiness in general.

Mudiyettu is the ritual theatre and dance drama of Kerala which celebrates the victory of Goddess *Kali* over the demon *Darika*, and seeks the blessings of the Goddess after the summer harvest is completed. It begins with the drawing of a massive image of Goddess *Kali* on the floor in *rangoli/kalam* or designs using coloured powder before the performance, and incorporates the sense of collective participation.

Navroz 2009

Navroz is celebrated in India along with other countries, like Azerbaijan, Iran, Kyrgyzstan, Pakistan, Turkey and Uzbekistan. The word *Nav* means New, and *Roz* means Day. It is a spring festival welcoming the new year. It marks the first day of the Spring equinox and the beginning of the traditional New Year, around March 21 every year. It is believed to have its roots in ancient Persia 550–330 BCE since the Achaemedians, and pays respect to nature.

The Ramman festival and ritual theatre of Garhwal in the Himalayas 2009

Ramman is also a Spring festival held annually in April in the Saloor Village of Uttarakhand in North India, honouring the *Bhumiya Devta.* It honours the productive powers of the earth through the performance of The *Ramayana* with masked dances. Local legends or '*Jagar*' are performed, which include the participation of the entire society.

Kutiyattam or Sanskrit theatre performed across India 2008

Considered the oldest surviving theatre performance, having its origin more than 2000 years ago, this synthesises Sanskrit and local traditions. The eye gestures or *netraabhinaya*, and hand gestures or *hast abhinaya* are very prominent, coupled with sophisticated breathing techniques and swift muscle movements of the face and body. Qualified actors undergo 10–15 years of rigorous training, and elaborate plays can last upto even 40 days. Each performance begins by lighting a lamp to signify the divine presence.

The Ramlila 2008

The *Ramlila* consists of the traditional performances held every year across India, telling the story of Lord Rama and Sita from The *Ramayana.* A ritualistic performance, it follows the final draft of the play *Ramcharitmanas* written in the 16th century by poet Tulsidas. The play is performed without any props or set design, and mostly in the open air. Over the years, *Ramlila* performances have been incorporated in various countries all over the world, including in various parts of South Asia such as Thailand and Cambodia.

The Tradition of Vedic Chanting across India 2008

This incorporates the expression of the powers of mind and memory through the preservation of the four Vedas: *Rg Veda* anthology of sacred hymns; *Sama Veda* speaks of various musical arrangements of hymns from the Rg Veda and other sources; *Yajur Veda* prayers and sacrificial formulae used for various rites and rituals; and *Atharva Veda* incantations, spells, well-being chants, the beginning of the use of plants for medicinal purposes. The method of learning has followed the sacrosanct power of *Smriti* memory and *Sruti* hearing for more than 3,500 yrs. Once there were over 1000 Vedic recitation branches; however, now only 13 survive in present day India, notably in Maharashtra West India, Kerala and Karnataka South India, and Orissa East India.[1]

Cultural Connectivity Through UNESCO's ICH List with South and South-east Asia

As the elements of the Intangible Cultural Heritage carry forth through generations, they also embody a wonderful, lucid representation of cross-cultural communication. Folktales, dance forms, textile patterns, culinary recipes, songs and lyrics, rhymes and poems are all carried through from one region into another. In the process, they recreate a separate and unique identity through absorption within the local culture, and form an eloquent dialogue between them. Such articulate representations of cultural dialogue exist across the Indian Sub-continent and South and Southeast Asia. They can be understood through a close study of the different associations and reflections of the elements from India across the neighbouring countries.

This presentation highlights some of the most important cross-cultural dialogues through the UNESCO list of the Intangible Cultural Heritage elements of India and their close associations, influences as well as reflections across South and Southeast Asia. Though this is not an exhaustive list, and there might be several other elements from local and regional folk cultures which are significant, the present study highlights some of the most important aspects of cross-cultural connections.

Water-worshipping ceremonies

These form an important aspect of the cross-cultural discussion across the regions of South and Southeast Asia. They include both fresh and salt-water representations. Nevertheless, the absence of a regional overview across the region has resulted in little knowledge about the various worshipping ceremonies pertaining to water worship and water-spirit archetypes. As the Kumbh Mela or the Festival of the Water Pitcher celebrates the life giving forces of water and rivers across India, several countries of South and Southeast Asia also celebrate this gift of water through various ceremonies. A water-worshipping ceremony is observed across many countries as part of traditional New Year celebrations. These variously coincide with the dates between the 12th to the 16th of April every year. The Lao people call it the Bunpimay Festival; in Thailand water-worshipping is an important part of the Songkran festival; in Cambodia, the festival of Chol Chnam Thmey is important; and in Burma, the Thingyan Festival has similar reflections. The festival is meant to bring coolness and prosperity to all things, and to purify human life. On these days, people often splash water on each other to bless with the luck, and pray for a happy new year.

The Bunpimay Festival Laos generally takes place between 13th to 15th April. Though it is celebrated throughout the country, it is mainly significant in Luang Phrabang and Vang Vieng. Travellers, tourists, and locals all take part to pay respects to Lord Buddha, bathe the Buddha statues with aromatic water, and listen to the preaching of the priests. Houses and temples, roads, trees, and gardens are all splashed with water for purification as well as to wish away the old, and welcome the new. Good luck threads as a gesture of purification are also tied around the wrists of near and dear ones.

The Songkran Water Festival of Thailand celebrates the traditional Thai New Year, and is held between 13th to 15th April. Along with the worship of Lord Buddha, both in temples and at home, special foods are prepared, and houses are cleaned. The Water Festival attracts tourists in hundreds, and elephants join the procession as well. Water being considered auspicious, people drench each other with water through balloons, water-guns, and buckets, and wish each other happiness and prosperity.

The Chol Chnam Thmay Water Festival of Cambodia is also celebrated from 13th to 15th April each year. Large numbers of visitors assemble at Siem Reap and Phnom Penh for the water festival, which is celebrated along with traditional food and *Apsara* Dance demonstrations.

The Thingyan Festival in Myanmar is a water festival whose origin lies in a legendary story relating to the Gods. According to oral traditions, in a prolonged argument concerning astrology, the deities Indra and Brahma finally reach a decision that whoever loses the argument will lose his head. Indra wins the argument finally, but faces a difficult situation as he knows that discarding Brahma's head, either in water or land, will be an extremely bad omen. Throwing the head in water would drain the seas, and throwing it on land would make the earth explode. Indra finally decides to hand over Brahma's head to the *Nat* Gods who protect the Burmese, and take turns to hold that head. Every New Year's Day is celebrated to transform the head from *Nat* to *Nat.* Meanwhile, the Burmese believe that, every year, the Gods are sent down on earth to take care of and protect human life. Thus, according to legend, this New Year festival in Myanmar comes from the meaning of wanting to keep peace for all things in the world, and pray for the blessing of the gods.

The Beneficial Reach of Yoga

Yoga and its beneficial effects are famous across the world. Throughout South and Southeast Asia, there are a variety of yoga centres, including resorts and retreats which offer various courses on yoga and its beneficial effects. These include *asana* knowledge and practice, *kirtan*, *bhajans* and chanting, *kriyas*, mindfulness, and much more. Noted tourist places for yoga training and learning are to be found, among others, across Thailand, Sri Lanka, Cambodia, and Bali Indonesia.

The Spread of Buddhism

In various ways, Buddhism managed to peacefully spread throughout much of Asia, carrying its message of love, compassion, and wisdom while fitting into the needs and dispositions of different people. The influence of Buddhism across the region dates back to several thousand years—from around 500 BCE. Buddhism spread with the popularity of the preaching of Lord Buddha and, later, under the benevolent efforts of Emperor Ashoka. This spread of Buddhism is also connected to the Silk Route which helped many merchants, pilgrims, and travellers from across South and South-eastern Asia. Thus,

> before the era of large-scale tourism, trade was one of the principal means by which people of different religions and cultures came into contact with each other and Buddhism spread across South East Asia and became a widely followed religion in many countries in the Middle Ages, due largely to the voyages of Buddhist traders across Central Asia. Buddhist monks travelled on trading ships too, in order to go on pilgrimage, thus carrying their religious practices far a field.[2]

With time, various thought processes also travelled through these routes, and helped the spread and communication of the various beliefs of Buddhism, including *Mahayana*, *Hinayana*, *Vajrayana*, *Tantric*, *Zen Buddhism*, and *Theravada*, among the many other interpretations across the region. The *Theravada* tradition spread from India to Sri Lanka and Burma/Myanmar in the 3rd century BCE. From there, it reached the rest of Southeast Asia Thailand, Cambodia, and Laos. Other *Hinayana* schools spread to modern-day Pakistan, Afghanistan, the eastern and coastal Iran, and Central Asia. From Central Asia, they spread into China in the 2nd century CE. These forms of *Hinayana* were later combined with aspects of *Mahayana* that came through this same route from India, with it eventually becoming the dominant form of Buddhism in China and most of Central Asia.

The Chinese form of *Mahayana* later spread to Korea, Japan, and Vietnam. The Tibetan *Mahayana* tradition started in the 7th century CE, inheriting the full historical development of Indian Buddhism. From Tibet, it spread throughout the Himalayan regions to Mongolia, Central Asia, and several regions of Russia Buryatia, Kalmykia, and Tuva. In addition, from the 2nd century CE, Indian forms of *Mahayana* Buddhism spread to Vietnam, Cambodia, Malaysia, Sumatra, and Java along the sea trade route from India to South China.[3]

Masked Dance Forms and the Story of the Ramayana

Masked dance forms across South and Southeast Asia vary in rhythm, lyrics, and repertoire. However, they are connected by one feature: they all echo various aspects of nature through their performances. Masked dance forms spread across Southeast Asia between the 2nd century BC and 8th century AD. Gradually, they mixed with the already existing regional dance forms of Sri Lanka, Myanmar, Cambodia, Java, Sumatra, and Bali. Thus, along with local legends, the story of the great Indian epics The *Ramayana* and The *Mahabharata* became popular.

The masked dance of Myanmar also traditionally exhibits an Indian influence. The Burmese version of the *Ramayana* is known as *Yama Zatdaw*, and is an important part of this performance. Within the same dance form, the names are Burmese transliterations of Sanskrit names. The region's connection with India can be traced to the time of the Pala dynasty of eastern India, which was partly contemporaneous with the classical Pagan period in Myanmar from the 11th to 13th centuries. Later, the influences of Thailand also became pronounced, and the Thai *khon*—a form of mask dance theatre—enacts the story of the *Ramayana*. This has equivalents in Burmese dance theatre; other dances are labelled *yodayar*, referring to Ayutthaya, the former capital of Thailand.

In Sri Lanka, the masked dance form is traditionally from the western and southwestern coastal areas of the country. The exact origin of the art does not have a definite timeframe, but it has been around as an important reflection through several centuries and across many generations. The masks can be classified as *Raksha*, *Kolam* and *Sanni*. All the three varieties are used for dancing and decorative purposes. The *Raksha* masks are often seen in processions and festivals. The *Kolam* masks are used in staging comic plays, depicting various stories from everyday village life, and enacting different characters from a village lifestyle. Each section, profession, and occupation is portrayed, including the King and Queen. The *Sanni* masks are associated with devil dancing ceremonies for the purpose of curing illness or disease. There are about twenty-four kinds of *Rakshas* known by different names, such as Naga Raksha, Gurulu Raksha, Maru Raksha, etc. Across all categories and traditionally, the masks can be divided as those depicting Gods, human beings, rakshaya, Yakka, animals, and a section of Composite masks. There are also interesting oral traditions associated with the reflections of these masks.[4]

In Bangladesh, masked dances are performed in the last days of the traditional new year of the agricultural month of *Chaitra*, and are reflected through the festival of Gambhira. Performers mostly depict the significant deities such as Shiva and Dharma Thakur. However, during this festival, many other deities are also depicted, as well as landlords, ministers and the common man. In north Bengal, there's a cloaked dance known as *Mukha Khel* for which villagers create their own masks, with wood, cloth, paper, etc. The masked dances of Bangladesh saw a new structure under Tantric Buddhism in the 9th century CE; these were very similar to the masked dances of Kathmandu in Nepal and other Tibetan Buddhist dances. By the 12th century CE, Buddhist masked dances were adapted in the region to give rise to the *Mahakali Pyayakhan*, the *Devi Pyayakhan*, and other similar dances. The performances to invoke the deity Kali are famous as *Kali Nachh* the Dance of Kali wearing a mask.

In Japan, the *Noh* performance is based on traditional tales of supernatural beings. The *Noh* uses masks, costumes, and different props as well as music. The highly trained actors use the masks to represent each character, such as old women, ghosts, children, etc. The *Noh* are derived from the Sino-Japanese word for 'skill' or 'talent', and are being staged since the 14th century. It is also considered the oldest major theatre art which is still regularly performed today. The *Noh* masks help as an extension of facial expressions, and stimulate the imagination of the audience. Emotions are also conveyed through controlled body movements.

In Korea, the *Talchum* or *t'alch'um* are performed while wearing masks, with portrayals of man, animal, as well as supernatural beings. They mainly originated in Korean villages as part of shamanic rituals which included cleansing houses and villages from bad omen, offering protection, and seeking blessings for a good harvest. They are mainly associated with the dances of the Hwanghae Province in present day North Korea. Dances from the Seoul or the Gyeonggi Province region are known as *Sandaenoli*, whereas the dances from the southern coast are known as *Yayu* which means field play or *Obangsinjang*, signifying the dance of the five gods. However, the *Talchum* is nowadays accepted as a general term for a masked dance drama. The dance drama reflects the sentiments of the locals and their socio-cultural as well as religious anxieties, including adultery, cheating and betrayal, class problems, financial difficulties, etc.

In Tibet, masked dances form an important part of the culture, and are associated with Buddhism. Associated with some sects of Tibetan Buddhism and their festivals, the *Cham Dance* is famous in Tibet. It is a lively dance, and is accompanied by music played by monks using traditional instruments. These dances also offer moral instructions on compassion for all spectators as an important lesson. The *Cham Dances* also hold a sacrosanct position as they are considered a form of meditation and an offering to God.

In Bhutan, the *Drametse Nga Cham* was declared a masterpiece of the Oral and Intangible Cultural Heritage of Humanity on the third proclamation in Paris on 25 November 2005. Mask dances are performed annually in Bhutan in all important Dzongs, temples, and in monasteries, and they usually last for three to five days. The occasion is known as *Tshechu* as they normally taken place on the 10th day of the month, and are an occasion for the village people to gather round and partake in the festival. The dancers are only men, and it is widely believed that the dancers will be purified of their sins if they perform the *Chhams.*

In Cambodia, masked dances are popular across both male and female performances. The *Lakhon Khol* is a masked dance with male dancers, while the *Lakhon Pol Srey* is a masked dance with female dancers. Both types combine classical theatre, and are performed with the accompaniment of the pin peat orchestra. Both forms are performed along with narrators who explain the story to the audiences. The *Lakhon Khol* uses a separate group of narrators, while in the *Lakhon Pol Srey*, the dancers take turns narrating, as others continue to dance. Often the narration is done by lifting up the mask, and speaking to the audience directly.

In Nepal, the *Lâkhey* dance is performed with a mask, and represents a demon in Nepalese folklore. He is depicted with a ferocious face, protruding fangs, and the mane of red or black hair. This art form is an important part of the Newar culture of the Kathmandu Valley, and other Newar settlements in Nepal. *Lakhes* are referred to as demons who lived in the forests, and later became protectors of the town people. The performers usually perform in town and city squares during festivals.

Thailand has an important display of the local story of the *Ramayana* through their masked dance forms. This story is referred as the *Ramakien*, and the genre of dance drama based on this is called *Khon*. This is traditionally performed only at the royal court by men in masks, accompanied by narrators and a traditional piphat ensemble. There is also a variation with female performers, and is called the *khonphuying*. However, various changes have taken place in recent years in the *Khon*, and often female characters are played by female performers instead of males. The *Khon* story has many characters, and one of the most famous characters in the story are the monkey warriors, Hanuman and Phra Ram. The ogre and the monkey characters wear masks, and the human characters do not.

Across China, Vietnam, Japan, Korea, and Tibet, the Lion dance is famous. Operated by only two dancers, representing a large lion, it is supposed to bring good luck and fortune. This dance is primarily performed during the Chinese New Year festivals, other festivals and also marriages. In Vietnam, the lion dance is very popular, and familiar to most groups of people—especially the Kinh people. The Lion Dance in Vietnam is performed during the Tet Festival.

In Indonesia, the Topeng is a dramatic form of dance drama. The performers wear ornate costumes. The narratives are generally associated with local lore; however, many Buddhist Jataka stories are also performed as well as the epics the *Ramayana* and the *Mahabharata*. The most famous story, however, is derived from the locally developed Javanese Panji cycles based upon the tales and romance of Prince Panji and Princess Chandra Kirana, set in the 12th century Kadiri kingdom.

Malaysia also has important masked dances that speak of the story of the *Ramayana* and are known as *Hikayat Seri Rama*. This is the Malay literary adaptation of the *Ramayana* in the form of a *hikayat*.[5] Though the main story remains the same, specific aspects are developed as accretions to, or as extensions of the epic. These changes include the upgradation of minor characters to major ones as well as developing new characters. Thus, for example, the role as well as the display of courage of Lakshmana is increased. Another masked dance form in Malaysia is the one performed by the Mah Meri people. They perform one of the oldest dance forms with masks in Malaysia, and re-enact the everyday life of people. This is performed by a group of female performers and two male performers in tree-bark dress and palm-leaf skirts, respectively. The females invite the male performers—who represent the spirits of the ancestors—to join in the celebrations. The performance is accompanied by various traditional instruments.

As is evident, the great Indian the *Ramayana* connects across South and Southeast Asia. Other examples also include the Jain version of the epic, which has Rama and Lakshmana as followers of non-violence, who commit the crime of killing Ravana, but finally renounce their kingdom after killing him. A Buddhist version of the *Ramayna* is the *Dasharatha Jataka*. This narrates the story of Rama being sent to forest. The *Ramman* festival from India also portrays the story of the epic.

Celebrations of Nature and Harvest through many Art Forms across the Region

The celebration of Novruz, Nowrouz, Nooruz, Navruz, Nauroz, Nevruz in India, Azerbaijan, the Islamic Republic of Iran, Kyrgyzstan, Pakistan, Turkey, Uzbekistan forms an important part of the celebration of spring. This is a time that welcomes the regenerative powers of Mother Earth, the New Year as well as seeks blessings for a better tomorrow and a bountiful harvest for the next year. Similar in manner to Novruz, there are many other festivals across the region of South and Southeast Asia which celebrate spring and Mother Earth.

Many of these festivals have their origin in the folk culture of the respective countries, but were later influenced by the various Hindu as well as Buddhist Gods and Goddesses from across the Indian sub-continent. Thus, at present, several of these festivals echo rites, rituals, and celebrations which bear close resemblance to the celebrations not only of *Novruz* of India, but also of the many traditional New Year festivities from all across India. These include the various traditional new year celebrations from across India—In Eastern India, *Bohag Bihu* in Assam, *Poila Baisakh* in West Bengal, *Pana Sankranti* in Odisha, *Sangken* in Arunachal Pradesh and parts of Assam; in Western India, they include the *Gudi Padwa*in Maharashtra; in Southern India, *Vishu* in Kerala, *Ugadi* in and around Andhra Pradesh and Telengana regions, *Puthandu* in Tamilnadu and Puducherry, in India as well as Sri Lanka; in Northern India, the *Maithili New Year* in the Mithila region, *Vaisakhi* across various parts of northern India.

There are also the *Pahela Baisakh* in Bangladesh; the *Avurudu* and *Puthandu—Tamil New Year* in Sri Lanka; the *Bisket Jatra* in Bhaktapur; the *Dhapasi* and *Tokha* in Nepal as well as the *Maithili New Year* in the Mithila region of Nepal; the *Songkran* in Thailand; the *Thingyan* in Burma; the *Choul Chnam Thmey* in the Khmer language in Cambodia; the *Pi Mai* or less commonly referred to as *Songkran* in Lao; *The Water-Sprinkling Festival* of the Dai ethnic minority in Southern Yunnan, China.

Most of these celebrations are held between March and April, and the majority of them are held between 13–15 April. These are agrarian festivals, and they celebrate the winter harvest as also seek blessings—through many rites and rituals—from the gods and goddesses and also forefathers, for a bountiful harvest in the coming year. The entire region of South and Southeast Asia is connected through this agricultural calendar. The many auspicious rites and festivals mark an age-old connectivity across the region.

As many of these festivals celebrate spring, several of the rites and rituals exhibit influences of various mainstream religions as well, including Buddhism and Hinduism. The Water Sprinkling Festival of the Dai ethnic community in China portrays the important predominance of *Theravada* Buddhism. The Laotian Goddess *Phra Mae Thorani* is portrayed in folklore as well as Laotian Wat paintings: she is seen placing herself between the demons and Gautama Buddha. *Nang Khosop* in Laos, the rice goddess, is also part of the local rural culture. There are different versions of the Laotian origin myth regarding rice, and they show the influence of Buddhism. In Vietnam as well, the influence of Buddhism is prominent as the rice goddess *Phi Na* is believed to have originated in the skull, the mouth, and the teeth of *Nang Khosop* from the Laotian myth.

In various other instances, there is a strong reflection of the influence of Shaktaism across the region of South and Southeast Asia. The deity Phosop is a Siamese or Thai rice goddess, and is also known as *Mae Khwan Khao* Mother of Rice Prosperity. She is an ancient deity and is worshipped for a better harvest. The present iconography of the deity reflects a strong association with the image of *Devi Lakshmi* from Hinduism. The Goddess *Lakapati* from the Philippines is considered a deity of the crops, agriculture, and fertility. She is also considered a transgender, and exhibits the two genders as a union of nature.

This is also very close to the Hindu concept and iconography of the *Ardhanarishwar* or Half male and half female, in which God Shiva is often portrayed along with this consort—Goddess Parvati—as the union of two aspects of nature. The depiction of *Dewi Sri/Shridevi* in Central Java art also portrays a strong association with the Hindu deity Lakshmi. She is also worshipped across Indonesia, Java, Sudan, and Bali, and shrines of *Dewi Shri* amidst local rice fields are a common feature in these places.

Preserving ICH and Cultural Entrepreneurship: Some Examples from India

Cultural connectivity through the elements of India's intangible cultural heritage forms an important part of the region of South and Southeast Asia. However, many of these elements are fast losing their significance, and often get relegated to oblivion. The lack of financial opportunities also often leads present generations leaving out or omitting certain aspects of family traditions. Nevertheless, there are many examples from recent times which highlight the preservation and conservation of elements of India's intangible cultural heritage. This also helps to create a financially stable platform for the present generation, and thus creates cultural entrepreneurship.

As the preservation of intangible heritage silently burgeons ahead the world over, maintaining its tradition of travelling orally from generation to generation, cultural entrepreneurship has inspired a new beacon of light for the preservation of our intangible heritage, and its tradition of continuing as part of a 'living heritage' the world over. Beginning with a small journey, the road has travelled a long way down the path of history. Today, it is using mass media and mass communication as well, and which have become effective tools for reaching out and 'speaking' to the masses on a large scale. From the simplest form of mass media and communication—that is, the 'print' media—it has moved to the 'New Media', which is now the most effective platform that cuts across socio-cultural boundaries across the globe. Indeed, a culture's intangible heritage has been effectively woven into the various channels of communication.

Channelling aspects of ICH for the market in terms of demand and supply has often been criticised by academics as it often leads to diverting from the main pattern of the intangible heritage concerned. However, time and again, such sustainable acts of cultural entrepreneurship have been proven to have established effective models to show how an intangible heritage can survive over a period of time, and also spread its message across a wide space of geographical boundaries.

As various books in the print media started showing the way initially around the world, the tradition followed a similar path in India. The arduous and diligent efforts of various British army officers helped to gather folktales from various parts of India, and put them in to print. Books about India's heritage began to be published nearly 150 years ago. Some of these books are still in the market, and are also available as PDFs for free downloading over the Internet, or as re-prints by famous and leading publishing houses of the country who specialise in printing books in the English medium. Thus, what started with the print medium, gradually took forward strides, cutting across geographical boundaries and travelling across decades to the modern global world, when socio-cultural entrepreneurship took an important position in chalking out a way of expression for the various intangible aspects of Indian culture. Today, the UNESCO website lists a series of intangible cultural aspects from India which is listed to be recognised on a global platform and is, thus, open for further analysis, observation, and understanding by people from across various cultures and different countries.

The very first list of UNESCO in relation to the preservation of India's intangible heritage followed the 2001 UNESCO Convention of "inscrib[ing] those cultural practices and expressions of intangible heritage on the Convention's Lists."[6] These should be considered for preservation and conservation around the globe. This 'List of Intangible Cultural Heritage in Need of Urgent Safeguarding' is composed of

> intangible heritage elements that concerned communities and States Parties consider require urgent measures to keep them alive. Inscriptions on this List help to mobilize international cooperation and assistance for stakeholders to undertake appropriate safeguarding measures. During the period from 2009 to 2013, the Committee inscribed **35 elements** on this List. The Register of Best Safeguarding Practices contains programs, projects and activities that best reflect the principles and the objectives of the Convention. During the period from 2009 to 2013, the Committee selected **11 programmes, projects and activities** for this Register. The Representative List of the Intangible Cultural Heritage of Humanity is made up of those intangible heritage elements that help demonstrate the diversity of this heritage and raise awareness about its importance. In 2008 the Committee incorporated 90 elements

formerly[7] proclaimed Masterpieces into the Representative List. During the period from 2009 to 2013, it has also inscribed **192 new elements** on this List.

The UNESCO website reveals various nominations, their photos and videos, together with the Committee's decisions and evidence of community consent by a simple click of the curser on the names of the various elements listed. For India, the section, which began in 2009 with three simple elements, has grown with time. With international bodies marking a special place of recognition on the global map, various regional bodies from across the country were not far left behind. Different initiatives across various disciplines of mass media and communication have helped to frame specific elements of intangible heritage in proper perspective. There are many examples from across the nation: for example, the efforts of the Children's Film Society of India through its animation movie series *Krish, Trish and Baltiboy* which first aired on the popular Cartoon Network in 2010. It utilises various folk art-works from different corners of India, and creates stories woven around folktales from those specific regions. The entire set of drawings of the respective stories is drawn following the pattern of the folk art of, for example, of *Madhubani* painting from Bihar, *Patachitra* painting from West Bengal and Odisha, and folk painting from Rajasthan, Punjab, as well as Kerala folk art, etc. This renders an assimilation of two forms of expression: the visual as well as the audio-visual. Thus, the stories have reached the farthest corners of the globe—much beyond the peripheries of the small village where the art or the stories originated.

Another important example is the Kala Raksha Trust, Gujarat founded 1993. It works with Gujarati appliqué artists who have been evicted from their original villages both in India and Pakistan. These artists have been trained to re-draw their designs to depict the stories of their life through appliqué. In the process, the art centring around abstract designs, were given a concrete shape and frozen in time. The trust, along with Nina Sabnani from National Institute of Design, Ahmedabad, Gujarat, created a book titled *Tanko Bole Chhe*, or *The Stitches Speak* for children as well as a short animation movie on this book. Both tell the story of the people and their journey from Pakistan to India, till the formation of Kala Raksha. The latter not only helps the artists to survive but has also trained them to be more productive, and learn the finer aspects of creative design. The Trust ropes in several artists, graphic designers, and artists from time to time. The artefacts of creation are also sold across the state as well as outside, including the books that tell their story.

A similar effort was started by the print publishing house—Tara Books in 1994 in Chennai—with a collection of dedicated writers, designers, and artists who "survive for a union of fine form with rich content", offering their readers "unusual and rare voices in art and literature".[8] What Tara Books attempted was on lines similar to CFSI: to create works of literature based on specific folk arts. The artists who were roped in were original folk artists who explained to the production department the method of drawing for the mass production of the various books. Thus, today, Tara Books boasts a good range of books drawn in the expert strokes of well known Indian folk art—such as, *Madhubani, Warli, Patachitra* from Orissa and West Bengal, etc.

The popular publishing house Amar Chitra Katha made a genuine attempt, in 2008, to merge folktales with visuals. Thus, the *Karadi Tales* were created in audio as well as audio-visual formats. Many of the stories were drawn in the style of different folk arts from India. These stories, which are adapted from popular folktales taken from oral traditions across India, were given life by the voices of well-known personalities from the world of Hindi movies, for example, Naseruddin Shah and Saeed Jaffery. Thus, the set of DVDs along with the audio CD's are still popular amongst children across the nation.

Following the trend of keeping oral traditions alive amidst the young ones in society, several cartoon channels started, with shows based on popular characters from Indian mythology, for example, *Chhota Bheem, Krishna and Balaram* of Green Gold Animations, *Luv and Kush: Sons of Rama* of Amar Chitra Katha Pvt. Ltd., etc. All of these production houses have managed to make a special name for themselves ever since their first major hit, the animation movie *Hanuman* in 2005. This success inspired many more for years to come and provided many job opportunities in graphic and animation design studios across the nation in which Pune occupies a special place.

Geeta Ramanujan of Kathalaya—an independent organisation with its head office in Bangalore—India focuses on the very ethos of storytelling, and has spread stories from Indian mythology and Indian folktales across socio-economic classes and geographical boundaries through her school as well as her small courses. The latter often include teachers as well as young children who "simply want to listen to stories." With her recently opened branch in Mumbai 2014,

Kathalayais striding ahead in spreading the words of the original storytellers—who are almost obsolete in present times—from the few remaining *ghats* of Banaras to the classrooms across the world. This is an example of the art of storytelling utilising various folktales from around the globe which has been lately recognised, and included within the 'teaching plans' of different schools across the globe. India is no exception in this direction. This not only helps to spread the stories and keep them 'alive' through changing times, but also helps carry forward specific cultural messages and symbolism through generations, and so kept alive through thousands of years around the globe.

Last, but not the least, various governmental bodies do their bit to promote different local festivals, beliefs, rites, and rituals around the year in India. However, often such acts on part of the government has led to the scorn of critics as they feel such acts promote 'wrong beliefs' or mis-utilise the trust of the common man to meet narrow vested interests, often prompted by political zeal. Nevertheless, as various folk arts and incorporated folktales from different regions are created in animation for internet, or a DVD, or a graphic novel, or a novel/book, each time it is the concerned voice of cultural entrepreneurship speaking out, and expressing pride in our intangible heritage.

Conclusion

As the preservation and conservation models of various governmental and private organisations make a myriad attempts at bridging the disciplines of marketing, advertising, the performing arts, the visual medium, and the print media, there are various aspects which are highlighted in the process. Through these attempts, the very basic ethos of history connects across a large section of time. Thus, the *patachitras* of West Bengal are frozen in time to convey an important message across generations; in a similar manner, Vedic chants from across the Indian subcontinent are popularised by UNESCO by being listed in its 'preservation list'. Moreover, as the *Chhau* folk dance from the Purulia district of West Bengal found a place of mention in the 2010 UNESCO list, it was further popularised through the Hindi blockbuster movie *Barfi* 2012.[9] The movie highlighted the dance form through several popular songs as well as sequences. This led the dance form finding a way into several television advertisements as well as other Hindi movies in India in the following years.

As the various performing artists as well as painters create wonders for most parts of the urban world, the attempts at sustainable cultural entrepreneurship help in bridging the basic differences between mainstream and folk culture. In the end, such conservation attempts to place all expressions of intangible heritage on a single and common platform. In the process of such entrepreneurial efforts, sometimes the artists benefit;[10] at other times it is the art-form which remains in the limelight.[11] Nevertheless, in both the cases, it is the significant aspect of intangible heritage which is also preserved and reinvented. Thus, as the creators engage artists to create new designs, and utilise old platforms to express innovatively through new methods, the same level of expression of both urban and folk culture is created, and, to a certain extent, helps in connecting both in a folk-urban continuum.

Though various critics scorn the differences each change of medium creates with each element of intangible heritage, it is to be borne in mind that the very essence and the basic characteristics of 'culture' are not constant. New stories are moulded, packaged, and reproduced in new formats, alongside whole new genres of storytelling, all of which compliment the global reach of each regional folktale and its essence. Thus, the scorn of critics regarding the validity of such 'survival' and 'preservation' must be seen in this perspective.

Thus, the several animated television shows as well as movies which are based on mythological characters are made either in Hindi or English, and translated into other languages of India, including Tamil, Telugu, Marathi, and Bengali; through all these an important socio-cultural reflection is created. It helps to create employment opportunities for the many people involved in the each project, and also creates awareness for the art form.

With various dynamic methods of storytelling continuing to enthral people across the globe through popular culture, sustainable acts of cultural entrepreneurship will keep finding new platforms of expression. As cultures across different countries around the world reinvent themselves through trade and financial contacts that transforms rural and urban scenarios into different new chapters across the nation, it is the quintessential element of our intangible heritage which renders that specific ethnic touch to maintain the primary and ethnic importance of each culture. It is thus that people learn to live within the global family as the world becomes one within the broader paradigms of expression—*Vasudhaiva Kutumbakam.*

NOTES

1. UNESCO list of Intangible Cultural Heritage elements, from Indian Cultural Centre ICC, Colombo Newsletter, February, 2018
2. UNESCO website, at https://en.unesco.org/silkroad/knowledge-bank/expansion-buddhism-south-east-asia
3. https://studybuddhism.com/en/tibetan-buddhism/about-buddhism/the-world-of-buddhism/spread-of-buddhism-in-asia
4. From Maitra Bajpai, *Wooden Dolls of Sri Lanka: from Ancient to Modern Times*, Newsin. Asia, 23 March 2018
5. Hikayat is an Arabic word that translates as "stories". This is a form of Malay literature that tells the adventures of national heroes of the Malayan kingdoms, or royal chronicles.
6. http://www.unesco.org/culture/ich/index.php?lg=en&pg=00011
7. http://www.tarabooks.com/about/
8. http://en.wikipedia.org/wiki/Barfi!
9. A good example is the planning and utilisation of the procedure that went behind the creation of the Kala Raksha Trust in Gujarat which, in turn, created *Tanko Bole Chhe* or *The Stitches Speak*, and introduced it across both the print as well as audio-visual mediums; for example, the availability of the video on popular social networking sites as well as the audio-visual medium over the Internet. Also see, http://www.youtube.com/watch?v=7sBG8J2s-H8.
10. See, the attempts of Tara Books' section 'Through Visual Arts for all Ages', for example, *Tsunami, Sita's Ramayana, Circle of Life,* etc. See also, Children's Films Society of India's *Krish Trish and Baltiboy* which deserves special mention here. Though the artists were involved initially in both these spheres, the main workload was distributed in the production stage to majorly, the production, and conceptualization teams of respective departments. This also results in several displays of the same product, for which the artists are not paid repeatedly; neither does any royalty follow from these procedures. The artists are provided a one-time payment, and they are usually contacted on a need basis during the entire procedure of work.

REFERENCES

Agrawala, P.K., *Goddesses in Ancient India*, New Delhi: Abhinav Publications, 1984.

Basu, Gopendrakrishna, *Banglar Loukik Debota* Bengali, Calcutta: Dey's Publishing, 1966.

Bhattacharya, B., *Buddhist Iconography*, Calcutta: Oxford University Press, 1924.

Bhattacharya, Ashutosh, *Bangla Mangal Kavyer Itihash* (Bengali), Calcutta: A. Mukherjee & Co. Pvt. Ltd, 1970.

Bhattacharya, D.K., *Studying folklore: The Indian Experience*, unpublished lecture, University of Delhi, 2005.

Bhattacharya, D.K., *The Development Dilemma in Tribal India*, unpublished lecture, presented as Special Lecture in the Session on Anthropology, Indian Science Congress, Hyderabad, 2006.

Bhattacharya, D.K., Chattopadhyay, R.K., 'History in Folk Culture' in *Trends in Social Science Research*, Vol. 4, No. 1, June 1970, 'Special issue: culture studies', selected papers from the 6th Congress of the National Academy of Psychology NAOP, India.

Bhattasali, N.K., *Iconography of the Buddhist and Brahmanical Sculptures in the Dacca Museum,* Dacca: Bangladesh National Museum 1929.

Crooke, W., *Popular Religion and Folk-lore of Northern India*, Vol. II, Westminster: Archibald Constable & Co, London 1896.

Dandekar, R.N., *Vedic Bibliography*, Vol. II. Government Oriental Series, Class B, No, 11, Pune: Reprint Bhandarkar Oriental Research institute BORI, 1977.

Datta, Rajat, 'The Agrarian Economy and the Dynamics of Commercial Transactions', in Marshall, P.J. (ed.), *The 18th Century in Indian History: Evolution or Revolution*, New Delhi: Oxford University press, 2003.

Eric Edwards, 'The Cult of the Mother Goddess', 2013, at https://ericwedwards.wordpress.com/2013/07/17/the-cult-of-the-mother-goddess/?blogsub=confirming#subscribe-blog

Heide Goettner-Abendroth, *Matriarchal Societies: Studies on Indigenous Cultures across the Globe*, New York: Peter Lang, 2012.

Kinsley, David: *Hindu Goddesses—Visions of the Divine Feminine in the Hindu Religious Tradition*. University of California Press, Berkeley 1994.

Kosambi, D.D., *Myth and Reality: Studies in the Formation of Indian Culture*, Bombay: Sangam Books Limited, 1962.

Maitra Bajpai, Lopamudra, 2015 'Myths and Folktales in the Patachitra Art of Bengal: Tradition and Modernity', in 'Visual Culture in the Indian Subcontinent. India', *Chitrolekha International Magazine on Art and Design*, Vol. V, No. 1, 2015.

'Preliminary ethnographic findings: Discovery of a local Purana-Durgarchanakalpamanjari. Surviving tangible and intangible heritage', in *International Journal of Research in Sociology and Anthropology* IJRSA Volume 1, Issue 1, June 2015, pp. 1–9, at www.arcjournals.org

'Complimentary Disciplines and their Significance in India: Oral Traditions, Folklore and Archaeology', in *International Journal of English Language, Literature and Humanities*, Bhopal: India, 2014.

'Indian Folklore and the "Three Worlds of Experiences': A New Theory to Understand 'Learning', from 'Folklore in Modern Audio-Visual Media for Children', in *Indian Journal of Comparative Literature and Translation Studies*, Vol. 1, No. 1, September 2013, pp. 53–75.

'Stories of Tuntuni from Bengal: Connecting Oral Traditions with The Global Age Across a Century', in Heritage and Us English e-journal, Year 2, Issue 1, March/April 2013, p. 40.

'*Popular culture connecting history and media anthropology through imaging communities*', in Folklore and Folkloristics English e-journal, Vol. 4, No. 2, December 2011.

'Change and Continuity as Means to Perpetuate Cultural Anxiety: A Brief Study of Tusubrata Rites and the Worship of Goddess Manasa in Specific Districts of Lateritic West Bengal', in Panchanan Mohanty, Ramesh C. Mallick, Eswarappa Kasi (eds.) *Ethnographic Discourse of the Other: Conceptual and Methodological Issues*. UK: Cambridge Scholars Publishing, 2008.

Majumdar, Ashutosh: *Meyeder Brotokatha* (Bengali), Calcutta: B.C. Majumdar, Dev Sahitya Kutir Pvt. Ltd., 2002.

Majumdar, R.C. (ed.), *The History of Bengal*, Vol. I., Decca: University of Decca, 1943.

Majumdar, R.C., *Ancient Indian Colonization in Southeast Asia*, Baroda, M.S. University: 1953.

Manguin, Pierre-Yves, A. Mani, Geoff Wade, *Early Interactions between South and Southeast Asia: Reflections on Cross-cultural exchange*, Institute of South-east Asian Studies, Singapore, 2011.

Menon, Ramesh, *Devi: The Devi Bhagavatam Retold*, New Delhi: Rupa Publications Pvt. Ltd., 2006.

Metcalf, Thomas R., *The New Cambridge History of India: Ideologies of the Raj*, London: Cambridge University Press, 1994.

Nehru, Jawaharlal: *The Discovery of India*, New Delhi: The Signet Press, 1946.

Piggot, Stuart: *Prehistoric India*, London: Penguin Books, 1950.

Radhakrishnan, S.: *Indian Philosophy*, Vol. II, New Delhi: Oxford University Press, 1923.

Rizvi S. A. A., 'Islam In Medieval India', in Basham, A.L. (ed.), *A Cultural History of India*. New Delhi: Oxford University Press, 1975.

Sastri, Hirananda, 'The Origin of the Cult of Tara,' in *Memoirs of the Archaeological Survey of India*, No 20, Calcutta: Govt of India Central Publication Branch, 1925.

Sen, Sukumar: *Bangla Sahityer Itihas*, Vol. I Bnegali. Eastern Publishers, Calcutta 1940.

Sengupta, Shankar: *Folklore and folk life in India—an objective study in Indian perspective.* Indian Publications, Calcutta 1975.

Sharma, R.S., 'Material Milieu of Tantrism', in Sharma R.S. (ed.), *Indian Society: Historical Probings*, New Delhi: People's Publishing House, 1974.

Stein, Burton: *A History of India*, New Delhi: Oxford University Press, 1998.

Trompf, Garry, *In search of Origins: The Beginnings of Religions in Western Theory and Archaeological Practice*, UK: New Dawn Press Inc., 2005.

33

Odisha and Bali: The Cultural Connection

Jatin Das

The sun rises from the East and the first rays fall on the Konark Sun temple, hence the name. The tropics create their own heat and humidity. The perspiration and the brown tan shine like bronze and oiled black hair. This seeps into the varied lush, fragrant vegetation of palm, mangoes, banana, litchi, jasmine, mogra, champa, roses and so on. The East has a lot of passion, fragrance and erotica. This is visible in the dwelling units, day to day rituals, music, dance and paintings—full of poetry.

All festivals are connected to cultivation and seasonal transformation, and are celebrated in full spirit in the entire Eastern region. Odisha now was Orissa during the British period and in the ancient times, Kalinga and Utkala. Cultural traditions existed for a few thousand years in Odisha and the neighboring countries extending to Indonesia—the people have no idea of its linkage even though it is very evident in the many tangible and intangible artifacts, festivals and rituals. The *Pattachitra* of Odisha has great similarity to the paintings in Bali, as is the Applique work in both the regions. For many celebrations men and women decorate themselves with flowers in the ears and garlands around necks. The body language of people and their shining sun-bathed, bare bodied figures have many similarities. The gait of women carrying fruits and flowers on their heads is another such visual visible in both Bali and traditional Odisha. Balinese dance and *Abhinaya* are similar to Odishi dance with its *lalitya*. Their *ikat* and Odisha *ikat* have great similarity. There are many words that are similar too, like *Bhoomiputra*. This similarity runs in the intricate filigree as well.

Agung Rai of ARMA Museum in Ubud (Bali, Indonesia), an aristocrat and a dear friend of mine offers chicken to the deity when he is stressed. I have been to Bali many times, once at an artist residency in Ubud. I did a series of paintings there starting with oils but because of the humid climate, the paints did not dry and I couldn't continue. I picked up dozens of acid-free handmade paper and did a watercolour series. It was one of my greatest experiences as an artist. There was a wonderful energy in the large workspace with lush green plants and trees all around. And above all, the toilets were outside open to the sky—very traditional yet very modern! The food was heavenly. I personally believe that any country that has tasty food can produce good music, paintings and dance.

When I saw the Ramayana being enacted in Bali I was totally amazed with the beautiful costumes and depictions. In Bali, every house has a beautifully designed temple in their courtyard and chicken, cows and goats roam free. In spite of extensive tourism in Bali, it has retained its ancient culture but in Odisha we have lost it. I have visited China, Japan, Indonesia, Burma, Malaysia and Thailand. There is an undercurrent of an Eastern ethos and when you lift up the thread there is a similar resonance, in the manner in which the left hand touches the right to offer anything with respect and affection. In many cultural activities in these countries, I have felt at home. Eventually, fish and rice is the common link!

Love can be felt in the bent head Namaste whether in a bank, an office or wherever it maybe. They take as long as it takes to respectfully and gently greet. Here in Odisha and there in Indonesia, we have lived many centuries at the same time.

BILATERALS: INDIA'S MOST FAVOURED NATIONS

34

India and Sri Lanka: Shared Heritage

*V. Suryanarayan**

All aspects of Sri Lankan life—demography, religion, language, art, literature, and even dress and cuisine—have been profoundly influenced by India. In the course of a visit to Ceylon in 1927 to popularize khadi and prohibition, Mahatma Gandhi was so impressed by the all pervasive Indian influence that he referred to Ceylon as 'India's daughter state'.

The past weighs down heavily on the present; the facts of history have been unfortunately distorted to serve narrow political ends. The conviction among Sinhalese politicians that India constitutes a major security threat to the island is a classic example. In fact, the foreign policy makers of Sri Lanka were, and are, obsessed with the colossus in the north; India is looked upon, to quote Ivor Jennings, as a 'mountain, which might, at any time, send down destructive avalanches'. According to Sir John Kotelawala, former Prime Minister, 'The day Ceylon dispensed with Englishmen completely; the island would go under India'. He regarded the membership of the Commonwealth 'as the first insurance against any possibility of aggression from quarters closer home'.

More than anybody else, Jawaharlal Nehru was conscious of the twin facets of India-Sri Lanka relations. I would like to refer to it as love-hate relations. He frequently referred to the necessity to build bridges of understanding between the two countries on the basis of mutual trust and confidence. In the course of

* Dr. V. Suryanarayan is the Founding Director and Retired Senior Professor, Centre for South and Southeast Asian Studies, University of Madras. This essay is partly based on the author's earlier writings.

a visit to Ceylon in 1939 to study the problems of the Indian workers in Colombo, Nehru came face to face 'with the adamant and unresponsive attitude' of the Sinhalese leaders. Despite his frustration, Nehru took a long term view of India-Sri Lanka relations.

> Ceylon cannot forget that India and Ceylon are close, and that India, by her size, is like a giant. It is easy enough to create psychological barriers and ill will, but not easy to remove and control them. I cannot conceive of any hostile action on the part of India towards a country like Ceylon if it does not threaten her freedom.[1]

I cannot resist the temptation to quote another statement in the Lok Sabha made by Jawaharlal Nehru in 1954. To quote:

> We want an independent Ceylon and a friendly Ceylon, in many ways Ceylon is nearer to us than any other country—culturally, historically, linguistically and even in matters of religion. Why should we look with greedy eyes on Ceylon? We do not, but the fact remains there is fear, and because there is this fear, I would beg this house not to say at any time things which might add to that fear... We should treat and continue to deal with Ceylon in a friendly way, even though Ceylon's response might be unfriendly.

How do love-hate relations translate into actual practice? A few illustrations are given below from the post-independence era.

(1) Faced with the internal security threat posed by the Janatha Vimukti Peramuna (JVP) in April 1971, Prime Minister Sirimavo Bandaranaike asked for external assistance. The first country to respond spontaneously was India. The Indian Air Force planes flew from Bangalore to defend the Katunayake airport, and Indian naval ships provided security to the Colombo harbour. How did Colombo respond to these gestures of good will? Six months later, during the East Pakistani crisis, when India had banned over flights by Pakistani planes through Indian territory, Sri Lanka provided refuelling and transit facilities for Pakistani Air Force planes and soldiers on their way from West Pakistan to East Pakistan to carry on savage reprisals against East Pakistani civilians.

(2) During the 1970's, one of the major foreign policy initiatives of Sri Lanka was to get the Indian Ocean declared a Zone of Peace. With the support of non-aligned countries, especially India, Sri Lanka was able to muster a majority in the UN General Assembly to get the IOPZ

resolution passed. But with India's growing nuclear capability, Sri Lanka revised its stance, and began to support the Pakistani proposal for the declaration of South Asia as a nuclear weapons free zone. What is more, when India imploded the nuclear device in Pokhran in 1974, anti-India sentiments came out into the open. In addition to concerns about super power rivalry, Colombo began to express fears about India's capabilities. In November 1976, Sri Lankan diplomat Shirley Amarasinghe remarked:

We do not want any great power here. By the same token, we do not intend to drive out Satan by Beelzebub and allow some other powers within the group of littoral and hinterland states to take up the place of other super powers.

Shirley Amarasinghe was obviously referring to India.

(3) The induction of the Indian Peace Keeping Force (IPKF), on the invitation of President Jayewardene, under the provisions of the India-Sri Lanka Accord, enabled the Sri Lankan army to combat the JVP threat. What is instructive for India is the fact that the military marginalization of the LTTE, accomplished at the heavy cost of men and materials, did not earn for India the corresponding gratitude of the Sinhalese. On the contrary, it gave fillip to Sinhala-Buddhist chauvinism and provided justification for the argument that Sri Lanka would become the client state of its northern neighbour. What is more, it brought the two hitherto antagonistic entities, Prabhakaran and Premadasa, together. It is well known President Premadasa provided the Tigers with a substantial amount of finance and weapons. However, at the end, President Premadasa had to pay the wages of sin: he became a victim to the cult of the bomb and the bullet perfected by the Tigers. Ambassador Lakhan Mehrotra, who was Indian High Commissioner at that time, has written: 'All the shots were called by the LTTE and eventually his collusion with them proved his undoing. They won against him both in the battle of wits and in the killing on the ground'. The wheel turned full circle again. When the military crisis deepened during the Third Eelam War, after the fall of the Elephant Pass to the Tigers in April 2000, and the Tigers were ready to re-enter their former stronghold, not only the Sri Lankan Government, but also the hard line sections of the Sinhalese which had viewed any Indian role in the

island's affairs with bitter hostility, pleaded for Indian intervention.

(4) In his Memoirs, *My Days in Sri Lanka,* Ambassador Lakhan Mehrotra, Indian High Commissioner from April 1989 to June 1990, narrates the policy of brinkmanship practiced by President Premadasa. Sri Lanka was 'toying' with the idea of abrogating the India-Sri Lanka Accord by an Act of Parliament, recalling the Sri Lankan High Commissioner from New Delhi, thus leading to 'consequent rupture in diplomatic relations between the two countries. President Premadasa threatened B.G. Deshmukh, Principal Secretary to Prime Minister Rajiv Gandhi who was sent to Colombo as Special Envoy, that he would declare the IPKF as an 'occupying force' which would sully India's name. In a fit of anger Premadasa told Deshmukh that he would 'commit suicide if his request for the IPKF to cease its operations against the LTTE was not met before July 29'.

(5) When the tsunami struck Sri Lanka in December 2004, the Indian response was spontaneous. Though a victim of tsunami itself, the Government of India immediately mobilised its resources and extended timely help to its maritime neighbours. Sri Lanka, Maldives, Thailand, and Indonesia. India was the first country to send assistance to Sri Lanka—within hours—after the tsunami which claimed over 30,000 lives in the coastal districts spread across the northern, eastern, southern and southwestern parts of the island. Indian relief workers were involved in a range of operations, including emergency medical aid, the setting up of relief camps, clearing debris, restoring ports, and reconstructing damaged bridges. The magnificent role played by the Indian Navy constitutes one of the golden chapters in India's diplomatic history. It included the mapping of the sea bed of Colombo harbour, which was completed very effectively and swiftly.

It must be pointed out that the tsunami, which also brought havoc to Indonesia, had the effect of bringing together the Achenese rebels and the Indonesian Government, which paved the way for a settlement of the Achenese separatist problem. Hopes entertained by Indian observers that a similar denouement would take place in Sri Lanka did not materialize due to the intransigence of both sides—the Sri Lankan Government and the Tigers. As a result, Indian assistance extended to Sri Lanka did not reach the Tamils in the north and the east to the extent India would have liked.

We can choose our friends, but not our neighbours. What is more, in South Asia we cannot make a distinction between domestic developments and foreign policy. To illustrate, if there are Hindu-Muslim riots in India, the Muslims in neighbouring countries will naturally get agitated; if there is conversion of Hindus to Islam in Bangladesh and Pakistan, the Hindus in India will rise in anger; if the Tamils of Sri Lanka are discriminated against by the Sinhalese-dominated governments, the Tamils in Tami Nadu will express sympathy and solidarity with their brethren across the Palk Strait. Keeping this reality in mind, India has to evolve a neighbourhood policy. As the dominant power in the region, India also has to take responsibility for preventing genocide in neighbouring countries. In other words, in its foreign policy, New Delhi must uphold in letter and spirit the 'Responsibility to Protect (R2P)'.

NOTES

1. V. Suryanarayan, "India-Sri Lanka Equations: Geography as Opportunity", in David M. Malone, C. Raja Mohan, Srinath Raghavan (eds.), The Oxford Handbook of Indian Foreign Policy, Oxford: Oxford University Press, 2015.

35

Remarks by Indonesia's Ambassador to India

Sidharto R. Suryodipuro

Thank you, Kalinga International Foundation, for inviting me to speak before this conference and for providing the wonderful and generous hospitality. I would like to convey my thanks and appreciation in particular to Ambassador Lalit Mansingh, and my congratulations to him for his and the Kalinga International Foundation's success in holding this important conference.

For us Indonesians, the cultural event at the opening night on Friday was truly a symbol of the close historical ties between Odisha (and India) with Southeast Asia, and the highlight on Indonesia is appreciated.

Next year we will celebrate the 70th year of India-Indonesia full diplomatic relations. While we like to celebrate the adding of yearssas a sign of longevity, more importantly we celebrate the changes that have taken place in our countries, and in the relationship between the two countries. We are justifiably proud of our past strong relations, while realising that we want to learn from past mistakes and avoid *indifference*—an important point made by Ambassador Navrekha Sharma in her book (with Professor Baladas Ghoshal), *India's Relations with Indonesia.*

Our two countries have a roadmap to strengthen relations, which is the Report of the India-Indonesia Eminent Persons' Group of 2016. Ambassador Rajiv Bhatia was also a member of the EPG. The Report was submitted to Prime Minister Modi and President Joko Widodo at their meeting in December of 2016. I will not dwell on it, but I would like to share my thoughts of how the relationship is evolving and strengthening, along the broad outlines of the EPG Report.

In terms of government-to-government engagement, we may be experiencing one of the most intensive period in this seven-decade relationship. This has taken off since the 2016 Modi-Jokowi meeting; the past three months were particularly busy. The meetings that have taken place include those of the Ministers of Foreign Affairs, Security, Defence, Trade and, of course, the Modi-Jokowi meeting on 25 January. There were also the first Policy Planning Dialogue, and the revival of the second track dialogue. We will soon have a visit of the Chief of the Indonesian Armed Forces. A further engagement at the highest level will undoubtedly push relations further. This is timely, and I am personally very pleased, like many of us, to see all of these meetings taking place.

A few factors may explain this G-to-G reinvigoration. It makes perfect sense in today's uncertainties—including the rising tide of economic nationalism—that we create better synergies between the largest economies of South Asia with that of Southeast Asia.

As maritime neighbours, we want to benefit more from our relative proximity to have more direct air and maritime connectivity. Moreover, there are more flights from Indonesia than ever before—28 times per week, to be exact, wherein Garuda Indonesia, Batik Air, and Air Asia Indonesia are flying to Medan, Jakarta, and Denpasar and to Mumbai, Chennai, and Kolkata. We are still waiting for Indian carriers to fly to Indonesia. The Air Services Agreement of 2011 is also in need of updating. Direct maritime linkages still remain a wish to be realised—that is, other than coal barges and palm oil tankers serving India's needs.

We also want to strengthen international law, including UNCLOS, and regional rules and norms in the waters that we share, namely between Sumatera and the Bay of Bengal. Currently, our two governments are actively considering the determination of our EEZ boundaries. This will be in addition to the bilateral agreement on the continental shelf. We also want to create synergies between India's SAGAR and Indonesia's Global Maritime Fulcrum concepts. I hope new ideas and initiatives will be realised sooner rather than later.

In the face of rising and retreating of major countries, India and Indonesia want to become the anchor of regional stability and predictability. The big celebration—and the greater recognition in the world of the importance of the 25th anniversary of India-ASEAN and the attendance of all Southeast Asian leaders at India's Republic Day Parade (2018), therefore, make perfect sense.

Furthermore, Prime Minister Modi and President Jokowi share similar views on the Indo-Pacific. They believe that the architecture we build should be open, transparent, inclusive, rules-based, and aimed at common prosperity and security. The Government of Indonesia believes that India-Indonesia relations are a crucial building block of the architecture that we want to see. A fundamental question is, how do we address the security dilemma faced by all countries in, or involved in, our region?

Finally, we want to have greater bilateral cooperation in addressing the challenges arising from climate change and globalisation—including those of identity politics, radicalism, and extremism. We should also work together to strengthen democracy. India, for example, may consider giving further support to the Bali Democracy Forum that Indonesia holds every year.

While we welcome this crescendo in bilateral relations, we need to be mindful of the challenges this bilateral relation may be facing. We need to be mindful that, while each country needs to create jobs at home and protect workers and farmers, such efforts may inadvertently produce protectionism. For example, we in Indonesia are concerned at the rising import duties for Indonesian palm oil—from 7.5 per cent to 15 per cent to 30 per cent, to 44 per cent—all in a span of seven months. More worryingly, the last hike was exclusive for palm oil. To be clear, this is taking place even as Indonesia is undertaking efforts to open its market further for Indian products (pharmaceuticals, buffalo meat, rice, and dairy products). We should also be forward leaning and creative in finding ways to expand trade. Similarly, a question we need to answer is, if the RCEP does not move forward soon, then what would the alternative be for the region?

In a nutshell, I can assure you that Indonesia wants closer relations with India. It is crucial that we do not see India as a threat and vice-versa, and my government is actively and proactively seeking ways to build bilateral relations. We want more, not less, of India: more connectivity, more trade and investment and B-to-B, more two-way tourists and students, and more engagements for a stable and prosperous Indo-Pacific. This relationship is too important to be left on autopilot. Ballast is needed—or more 'stakeholders' and a 'bottom up approach', in the words of Professor Shankari this morning to avoid the *indifference* that Ambassador Sharma and Professor Ghoshal had warned against.

In my eight months in New Delhi, it appears that the KIF has become the tip of India's think tanks for the purpose of Looking and Acting East. It is doing so through practical work and using one of India's states—Odisha—as the geographical jumping board with Southeast Asia. I hope to be back in Bhubaneswar for the Bali Yatra Festival in November. I hope that we can build on the strong historical relationship between Odisha and Indonesia into concrete sectors that will help bring India and Indonesia closer.

36

Bangladesh-India Ties: The Triumph of Pragmatism

*Pinak Ranjan Chakravarty**

With a population of around 170 million, Bangladesh, is the 8th largest country in the world and is India's 3rd largest neighbour. With a GDP of US $ 250 billion, measured in PPP terms, Bangladesh is ranked 34th in global GDP rankings. In the last decade, Bangladesh has emerged as India's closest geo-strategic and geo-economic partner in South Asia. A positive transformation in bilateral ties has occurred, with political developments and discourses in India and Bangladesh changing under different governments. Pragmatic policy decisions and the successful conclusion of long-pending issues have aided this process. The two most important agreements which have given a fillip to the creation of a positive ambience are the Maritime Boundary Agreement and the Land Boundary Agreement.

Bangladesh and India share centuries old civilizational bonds. The shared history, cultural, and linguistic affinities as well as the longest land border connect the two countries in a unique way. Bangladesh's bloody War of Liberation in 1971 is the fountainhead of the memory of a shared struggle for independence. Bangladesh's internal developments in the post-1971 period, particularly the gruesome assassination of Sheikh Mujibur Rehman and most of his family, by disgruntled army personnel cut short the political career of the most towering leader of the freedom struggle. The military dictatorships of

* The author is a Distinguished Fellow at the Delhi-based Observer Research Foundation; he is a former Secretary in the Ministry of External Affairs, Government of India and was India's High Commissioner to Bangladesh from 2007–2009.

General Zia-ur-Rahman and General Muhammad Ershad that followed in Dhaka, led to the souring of the bilateral ties between India and Pakistan.

During the tenure of the military dictators, Bangladesh also turned its back on the secular principles of the Liberation War that were embedded in the 1972 Constitution. The Islamization of Bangladeshi society was encouraged under the military dictators who were trained in Pakistan. Their model of governance drew from their Pakistani experience and alliances with Islamist parties, including those who were accused of war crimes, collaboration with Pakistan to fund and arm Indian insurgent groups in the North-Eastern states. These were the primary reasons for India's suspicions, and the subsequent growth of mistrust between the two neighbours.

With the return of democracy in the early 1990s, hopes were raised for improvement in India-Bangladesh bilateral ties. The government formed by the Bangladesh Nationalist Party [BNP], under the leadership of Begum Khaleda Zia, widow of Gen Zia-ur-Rahman, continued with the anti-Indian bias in their policies. When Sheikh Hasina, the leader of the Awami League [AL], became Prime Minister in 1996 bilateral ties improved; but she was unable to shake off the tentacles of the intelligence agencies who continued their collaboration with Pakistan. A notable achievement during the first tenure of Sheikh Hasina was the signing of the Ganga Waters Treaty in 1996. This led to the lowering of anxieties in Bangladesh on the issue of sharing of water and Bangladesh's long campaign against the Farraka Barrage in West Bengal which diverted water from the Ganga into the Hooghly for flushing silt.

The return of Begum Khaleda Zia as Prime Minister, in 2001, reversed the trend in bilateral ties again. With the BNP in alliance with the Jamaat-e-Islami [JeI] forming the government, known war criminals became Ministers. The baleful influence of Tarique Rahman, the elder son of Begum Zia, led to a government defined by communal attacks on the Hindu minority, record levels of corruption, and continued collaboration with Pakistan to undermine India's security. This period also saw the growth of religious extremist organisations which mushroomed under the political patronage of sections of the ruling parties in government. Attacks on political opponents surged, and Sheikh Hasina narrowly escaped a grenade attack in 2004. Allegations of the involvement of the BNP and Jamaat members in the grenade attack surfaced, and fingers were pointed towards Tarique Rahman who virtually ran a parallel government. In

August 2005, over 500 bombs exploded almost simultaneously in 63 out of the 64 districts of Bangladesh. Militant organisations like the Jamaatul Mujahideen Bangladesh [JMB] and Harakatul Jihad al Islami Bangladesh [HUJI-B] claimed responsibility. Bilateral ties during this phase reached a nadir, when the BNP-led government was found complicit in the aborted supply of arms, arranged by Pakistan, to ULFA insurgents whose leaders enjoyed the hospitality of the government agencies in Bangladesh. Other insurgent groups were also permitted to open camps, and seek refuge in Bangladesh to carry on cross border attacks in India.

The interregnum from 2007–2008 saw the suspension of democracy and a caretaker government in Dhaka, under the close supervision of the Army which spearheaded a vigorous anti-corruption campaign, together with an unrealistic attempt to re-engineer politics. The Army's plan hinged on removing the two Begums from the political arena, the so-called 'minus two' formula. Concomitantly, the army tried very hard to create a political party led by well know economist and Nobel Laureate Muhammad Yunus, globally recognised as the father of micro-finance in Bangladesh. While these efforts failed, the army changed course and held elections, released the two Begums from detention, sent off Tarique Rahman into exile, and cleaned up the electoral list. The 2008 election were the most free and fair, and led to the thumping victory of the AL, catapulting Sheikh Hasina into the Prime Minister's chair.

With a renewed and massive mandate, Sheikh Hasina went about improving relations with India, and was re-elected in 2014 in an election which became controversial because the BNP boycotted the polling. This did not prevent Sheikh Hasina in implementing various electoral promises: setting up the war crimes tribunal which sent several war criminals to the gallows, amending the Constitution to remove the Caretaker government provision, and restoring secularism in the Constitution. Her tenure of a decade as Prime Minister has qualitatively changed the course of bilateral ties. The minority Hindu community felt reassured as Sheikh Hasina appointed and recruited Hindu officials, though stray attacks on the Hindu community and their temples have continued. Hindu leaders have often blamed members of the AL also for such attacks, at the root of which lies greed and the grabbing of property and land.

During Sheikh Hasina's tenure as Prime Minister, high level bilateral political engagement has intensified to building an irrevocable and irreversible consensus in upgrading ties across the complete spectrum of ties between Bangladesh and

India. India's 'neighbourhood policy' has focussed on Bangladesh which has emerged as a key interlocutor in India's Act East Policy, BIMSTEC, and BBIN. In Bangladesh, the last decade has also produced a growing domestic political consensus, overriding fractious politics and the India factor. Cooperation in security and intelligence matters and the denial of support to Indian insurgent groups, the handing over of insurgent leaders to India has progressively built trust and confidence between the two countries. In India too, an upswing in relations with Bangladesh has received bipartisan political support.

Improvement in bilateral ties has led to newer areas of cooperation, like Cyberspace. Bangladesh has provided cyber connectivity between the international gateway at Cox's Bazaar to Agartala for faster internet connectivity in India's north-eastern states. India has also become a partner in Bangladesh's nuclear power programme with the beginning of construction at the Roopur nuclear power plant.

Energy cooperation has reached a new high. India is poised to export around 800 MW of power to meet the energy deficit in Bangladesh. Over 3600 MW of power projects are under implementation by Indian companies to meet the growing demand for power as Bangladesh's economic performance tops 7 per cent growth in GDP. Though South Asia lags in intra-SAARC trade, bilateral trade has grown 17 per cent in the last 5 years. India is participating in the Padma multipurpose bridge and the Akhaura-Agartala rail link which will dramatically change connectivity within Bangladesh, and also add to the easier movement of goods and people between the two countries. Waterways are also being revived to ease the cost of trade.

India's exports have touched US $ 6.2 billion, and Bangladesh's exports have reached US $ 675 billion in 2016–17. The bulk of trade [50 per cent] flows via the Petrapole-Benapole land border, 36 Land Customs Stations, and 2 Integrated Check Posts [ICPs] spread over the 4,100 km long border. These land ports now function on a 24x7 basis, easing the congestion that has dogged cross border trade. The riverine route also provides connectivity for trade flows under the Protocol for the Inland Trade and Transit Agreement.

The adverse balance of trade has been an item of discussion, and an issue that has been addressed in discussions on bilateral trade. The asymmetry in the economies of India and Bangladesh is the major factor. To enable more Bangladeshi exports to flow into India, duty free entry was granted in 2011 under SAFTA. This has led to the increase in exports from Bangladesh from around US $ 350 million to the current level. Bangladeshi exports have plateaud because of demand constraints in India, and also because of limited items in the Bangladeshi export basket.

A special EEZ in Bangladesh for Indian manufacturing companies has been mooted and notified. When operational, it will encourage Indian companies to manufacture there and export to India. This is expected to mitigate the adverse trade balance. Another way to address this imbalance is the flow of Indian investment into Bangladesh. Indian investment in Bangladesh has reached US 4 3 billion, In 2017, 13 agreements worth around US $ 10 billion has been signed in the power and energy sectors.

Bangladesh is now the largest recipient of an Indian Line of Credit [LoC] and Grants, with commitments reaching US $ 8 billion. While the LoC mainly covers infrastructure and connectivity projects, grants flow into social sector development. Capacity building under the Indian ITEC programme is an important strand in bilateral ties and people-to-people interaction. Bangladeshis are the largest group of tourists into India. The visa regime has been liberalized, and over a million visas are issued to Bangladeshi citizens annually.

There are over 50 bilateral institutional mechanisms in place, covering security, trade and commerce, power and energy, transport connectivity, science and technology, defence, rivers, and maritime affairs. The Joint Consultative Committee [JCM], headed by the foreign Ministers of both countries, monitor the implementation of agreements and identify additional domains of cooperation. Establishing multi-modal connectivity between the two countries is a major objective that will lead to the easier transportation of goods and the movement of people.

While commercial and economic issues dominate the bilateral discourse, connectivity projects under implementation will facilitate trade and reduce cost of doing business. Transit trade will add to additional revenues for the Bangladeshi government. Defence and security issues will require greater cooperation with the rise of religious radicalism and terrorism. Bangladesh has taken strong and effective steps against those who have been inspired by ISIS, and indulged in terrorist strikes within the country. The Islamist organisations, though largely moderate, have been breeding grounds for religious radicals and extremist views. These forces will pose a considerable challenge for governance in Bangladesh in the future.

China's security and economic footprint has grown in South Asia, and managing this will remain a challenge for both countries. Bangladesh's overwhelming dependence on military hardware from China is a factor in bilateral ties. Professional cooperation between the security and defence forces of the two countries has increased. India has provided a US $ 500 million LoC for the procurement of defence related goods from India. This momentum must be maintained and intensified.

BIMSTEC and BBIN are two valuable platforms for cooperation that appear to be somewhat lagging behind other regional and sub-regional organisations. The broader Indo-Pacific region and the Bay of Bengal will remain the future domains for cooperation. With increased connectivity between Bangladesh and India, the whole eastern region of the Sub-continent will be able to connect to Myanmar and other ASEAN countries. No doubt, there will be setbacks, like the current Rohingya issue which has imposed a huge burden on Bangladesh. However, Myanmar and Bangladesh are cooperating to sort out this thorny problem with the help of regional partners.

Bangladesh and India head for general election in 2018 and 2019, respectively. Domestic issues in Bangladesh—like the quota in government jobs and the student agitation on controlling unruly and chaotic traffic in Dhaka—has the potential of undermining domestic stability. Bilaterally, the issue of illegal migration has already acquired a high profile in India with the publication of the draft National Register of Citizens [NRC] in Assam. Bilateral relations will have to be insulated from the collateral effect of the NRC. This would require the deft handling of bilateral ties. The sharing of river waters will remain a challenge in bilateral ties, but not an insurmountable one. Bangladesh-India relations have reached a stage of maturity, and with further integration of infrastructure, the upgrading of border trading stations, the Motor Vehicles Agreement, bilateral ties can be expected to grow stronger in the future.

37

Remarks by Myanmar's Ambassador to India

*Moe Kyaw Aung**

HE Mr Moe Kyaw Aung, Ambassador of Myanmar said that while bilateral trade has been growing—Indian export amounted to $1 billion and imports amounted to $1.67 bn. India is the sixth largest trade partner of Myanmar but the trading volume is much below potential.

Exports from Myanmar include agricultural products—Indian exports include sugar, pharmaceuticals, etc Border trade reached $87.89 mn—a fraction of the total trade volume of $743 mn. India is the tenth largest investor in Myanmar, with 26 companies investing. According to new investment laws, foreign companies are now allowed to invest 100 per cent. Both sides need to cooperate in the banking sector-to facilitate bilateral trade—Union Bank of India and State Bank of India have representative offices in Myanmar. Border trade takes place through Moreh-Tamu. Myanmar income is increasing—with increasing access to domestic and international products. Many Myanmar citizens come to India for medical treatment. Religious tourism for Buddhist pilgrims, education facilities for students, tourism, health care and film industry are new sectors which can have some investment.

Rice, pulses, beans, fruits and vegetables can be easily grown in Myanmar. Number of visitors to Myanmar are growing exponentially. This implies there are other areas for investment such as—hospitality, tourism, eco-tourism, cultural and community based tourism, infrastructure, and agriculture. Government of Myanmar prioritises better infrastructure along the border

---

* Based on the Rapporteur's report of the presentation by H.E. Amb. Moe Kyaw Aung, Ambassador of Myanmar to India.

utilising public and private partnerships. In terms of geographical location Myanmar stands as a bridge between South Asia and South East Asia—a centre for movement of goods and people to people contacts. Myanmar appreciates India's continued support in development cooperation and capacity building-and in particular, the trilateral highway—Kaladan Multimodal project—yet to take full advantage of their geographical proximity—to realise the potentialities—need to integrate the various projects planned so far-imo to understand what is demanded from increased connectivity in order to develop specific polices and projects—regional connectivity can help promote trade and economic integration of the region. Myanmar is creating a conducive environment for investments, trade and tourism—and it looks forward to expeditious cooperation in the future.

38

Japan's Role in the Development of India's Eastern States and Connectivity with ASEAN

*Deepa G. Wadhwa**

India's Act East Policy combines the deepening of ties with the ASEAN, East Asia, and beyond with the multipronged, accelerated development of the eastern periphery of India, from the states of the North East to the length of the eastern sea board, which are critical to connectivity and the success of the Policy.

Japan has emerged as the leading partner in India's efforts to this end by directing soft loans to projects to develop road, port and urban infrastructure, industrial nodes and corridors, skills training, and sustainable forestry and agriculture in Eastern India, as both countries seek synergies between India's Act East policy and Japan's Free and open Pacific strategy, which, inter alia, envision the strengthening of connectivity to build supply chains that link industrial networks to enhance the economic prosperity of the region.

India's former Ambassador to Japan said that the India-Japan relationship is marked by hyperbole, while Prime Minister Abe says the relationship with India is one with the greatest potential in the world. Prime Minister Modi has responded by saying that the future of the Asia-Pacific will be determined by India-Japan relations, and that this will impact on other regions of the world. There has been an exceptional growth in the relationship between the two countries since 2000. Today it is called a special strategic and global partnership. The reasons for closeness lie in the convergence of values, perspective and

---

* Based on the Rapporteur's report of the presentation by Ambassador Deepa G. Wadhwa during the Conference.

interests, and a commitment to democracy. Japan is the oldest democracy in Asia; India the largest. There is, today, bi-partisan political support to deepening the relationship; and a wide positive public perception on both sides with no historical baggage.

There were public gestures on both sides, particularly in the early phases of the relationship. There are many self-evident economic complementarities, including the convergence of views on regional and global challenges. There is a realisation that the two countries need to work together to achieve regional economic and strategic interests. We have also congruence on global issues such as UN Security Council reforms, counter terrorism, cyber terrorism etc. Both countries have established a multilayered architecture of dialogue at the apex, with annual Prime Ministerial meetings. Japan has this arrangement just with India—although India has such a dialogue with Japan and Russia. There are meetings of Foreign Ministers, the Defence Ministers, the Energy Ministers, the Finance Ministers also between the two countries. There is also a robust exchange of parliamentarians. Indeed, the interactions are not limited to the centre only—State ministers are to visit Japan to seek tie ups.

Economic complementarities are self evident: these include demography wherein Japan's decline in population contrasts with India's youth bulge; Japan has labour scarcity while India has an excess of it; India's human capital needs skills development while Japan has an abundance of human capital. India's large domestic market and rapid pace of urbanisation requires housing development and infrastructure, which provide the pull factor for Japanese businesses. India is a capital stretched country; but it is resource rich. India and Japan can combine to produce knowledge intensive capital goods. We have a success model in Maruti Suzuki cooperation.

Japan is the third largest investor in India in terms of FDI, with about 1,369 companies, growing 70–80 per year. Trade is falling. It is important that JICA is the large OD company in the world, and India is the largest recipient of aid from JICA. The development of the East, and JICA have strategic convergences.

The growing relationship between India and Japan focuses on building bilateral defence and security relations, and the desire to take on regional strategic and security responsibilities. In the bilateral field, there are agreements on the transfer of defence technology and equipment. Both countries participate in bilateral naval exercises, and Japan is a regular member of the Malabar Exercises. India has its AEP and Japan has its Free and Open Pacific Strategy. Both countries are seeking an alignment of the two. ASEAN plays an important role because India is trying to integrate its economic relationship with the supply chains and networks of ASEAN and to provide alternate options in the Asia Pacific.

If we look at the entire Indian Eastern seaboard, Japan already has a visible footprint. Japan's ODA has a high level of trust compared with other parties in our North East. Japan's ODA is a welcome partner. Japan's funding is towards India's priority areas: roadways, sustainable agriculture, forests, sports, energy supply, sustainable development. India's focus is on the extended east—from the north east to the south—all along the eastern sea board.

While the relationship between India and Japan has acquired momentum, it is still progressing. Our common wish list can be found in the Joint Statements already made. Japan has invested in important projects: the Bay of Bengal Industrial Growth Belt (at around the same time as China's Belt and Road Initiative or BRI). However, it was limited only to Bangladesh whereas India would want to extend it to whole of Bay of Bengal.

Thus, strategic convergences between India and Japan include

- building bilateral security and defence relations
- funding and ODA
- agreement on transfer of defence technology
- bilateral naval exercises
- India's Act East Policy complements Japan's and Free and Open Pacific Policy
- cooperation with ASEAN
- Japan is present in a large way in the east
- connectivity needed between India-Japan and ASEAN

39

Remarks by Sri Lanka's Ambassador to India

*Chitranganee Wagiswara**

Sri Lanka's unique location has attracted many travellers from many countries in the past. Sri Lanka's ancient history is interspersed with accounts of cultural connections. Buddhism is one of the most important linkages. With similar colonial background, India and Sri Lanka possess similar governmental systems and share a common language-English. Sri Lankan leaders joined the Indian freedom struggle and had fought together. India-Sri Lanka relations have fluctuated on the basis of political developments, changes in international scene, leadership etc. At the same time at present the relationship is excellent. After a 30-year conflict with the Liberation Tigers of Tamil Eelam (LTTE)—Sri Lanka was eventually successful in defeating them. India at various stages endeavoured to play a role and tried to find solutions to the issue—the role of the Indian Peace Keeping Force (IPKF)—had a great impact on the bilateral relationship.

The Tamil Nadu factor features significantly in Indo-Sri Lankan relations as 70 mn Tamil inhabitants-have close affinities-support from Tamil Nadu for their cause-which adversely affected the relations. The demise of Tamil Nadu Chief Minister Jayalalitha has also affected Sri Lanka significantly. Sensitivities of India and of Sri Lanka have to be taken into account—and we should not see each other as a threat. India is a large country, economically powerful and Sri Lanka is a small neighbour—the big neighbour should be generous. Take for instance the fisherman issue-Tamil Nadu fishermen crossing the international-maritime border line—affects Sri Lankan fishermen's livelihood.

---

* Based on the Rapporteur's report of the presentation by HE Amb. (Ms) Chitranganee Wagiswara, High Commissioner of Sri Lanka to India.

A task force was established to mitigate the issue. Many Sri Lankans who took exile are still living in Tamil Nadu—Sri Lanka welcomes them back. Conflict is over but challenges remain—to maintain and consolidate peace and security—after a 30 year war—focussing on reconciliation, focussing on economic growth and development. The new governments in power have created a good relationship—Indian Prime Minister Modi has visited twice in three years. The Sri Lanka leader has visited five times and the two countries have an FTA. It makes Sri Lanka a hub in the Ocean and Sri Lanka a stepping stone to India. 70 per cent of Indian transhipment goes through Sri Lanka which makes for tourism, connectivity, people to people contact.

China [has a role in Sri Lanka] with large scale investments and a close relationship from 1952 onwards. [It meets the] need to develop Sri Lankan economy; China provides the funds-which facilitate trade and connectivity.

40

India-Thailand Ties: Reinvigorating an Old Relationship

Pinak Ranjan Chakravarty

India and Thailand established diplomatic relations within months of India's independence. Thailand was among first the first few countries to open its diplomatic mission in Delhi. Centuries of interaction between the two countries led to both Hinduism and Buddhism spreading, leaving an indelible influence on Thailand. The Thai language has its roots in Sanskrit, Pali, and Khmer. Many streets and buildings in Thailand carry names derived from Sanskrit and Pali. Temples dedicated to Brahma, Vishnu, and Ganesh are ubiquitous, and the country hosts a thriving and well-integrated Indian origin community. The Kings of Thailand belonging to the Chakri dynasty; and the ruling monarchy, have traditionally adopted Rama as a title. Thus, the current King, Maha Vajiralongkorn Bodindradebayavarangkun, has taken the title Rama X. Though largely Buddhist in belief (93 per cent), the people of Thailand follow a syncretic mixture of Hindu and Buddhist beliefs and practices. Royal court rituals, for instance, are conducted by Hindu Brahmin priests.

Democracy in Thailand has had an uneasy and unpredictable history in Thailand, especially ever since the monarchy was forced into relinquishing its absolute powers in a bloodless revolution in 1932. Constitutional monarchy has not prevented a cabal of some members of the royal family, the Thai military, businesspersons, bureaucrats, and other segments of the Bangkok elite, from usurping power from time to time. There have been 19, major and minor coups in Thailand since 1932. The last one was in May 2014. Thailand's dysfunctional polity has hovered between a flawed democracy and a moderate autocracy in its political history. Military coups in Thailand are usually bloodless. Politicians and the people are not prone to violence even while opposing Army rule, though some sporadic and largely peaceful protests do take place. This has something to do with the Buddhist beliefs of the Thai people.

Despite this shared heritage, India and Thailand drifted apart in the years after India's independence. The Cold War found non-aligned India and Thailand, an American ally and founding member of SEATO, on opposite sides. Non-aligned India found no ideological or geo-strategic common ground with an aligned Thailand. Relations cooled further by a reportedly lukewarm response to a royal emissary who visited India to explore a State visit. The visit did not take place.

Since the beginning of this century, Thailand has seen two military coups. In 2006, the Thai Army ousted the then Prime Minister Thaksin Shinawatra, a billionaire telecommunication magnate whose entry into politics threatened the entrenched power of the cosy royalist coalition. In the run up to the May 2014 coup, the military first manipulated a guilty verdict by a pliant Constitutional Court, against then Prime Minister Yingluck Shinawatra [Thaksin's sister], the first female Prime Minister of Thailand. She was removed from office in a case which charged her for misusing her powers in a rice subsidy scheme. Her government had procured rice from farmers, paying around 50 per cent more than the market rate. Rice farmers in the north and east of Thailand are solid supporters of the Puea Thai Party which won a majority in the last election in 2011, leading to the formation of a government headed by Yingluck. Before she could be sentenced, she fled into exile like her brother, the former Prime Minister Thaksin Shinawatra.

Thailand's institutions, including the Constitutional Court, are packed with royalist sympathizers, and Yingluck's ouster has to be seen in the context of a broader struggle between the royalist elite in Bangkok and its supporters in southern Thailand, and the more populous North Eastern region of Thailand, home to the poorer peasantry and agricultural base that has made Thailand the world's second biggest rice exporter.

There has not been any significant external pressure on the military government to change course. Times have changed. The usual flag bearers of democracy and human rights, mainly governments and NGOs in the developed countries of the West, are far less vocal today. While the usual statements and noises have been made by the human rights lobbies since the military coup in Thailand, attempts to pressurise the Thai military government have been minimal and symbolic. A fundamental reason that has enabled the Thai military junta to shrug off any pressure is the changing geo-political and geo-economic scenario, engendered by the rise of China, a country that has always been ready to do business with Thailand, or any other country, regardless of the nature of government in power. The Thai military government has been playing its China card cleverly in its relations with the USA, and other major powers in Asia.

Under President Trump, the USA has toned down its criticism of the coup, and engaged with the military junta. The USA, which has a longstanding 'non-NATO Alliance' relationship going back to the early days of the Cold War, is trying to recover ground lost to China. The pro-Chinese Thai business elite and its supporters have helped China make deep ingress into the Thai economy. Over 9 million Chinese tourist arrivals in Thailand make them the largest group of tourists, comprising 25 per cent of all tourist arrivals, contributing over 28 per cent of tourist revenue. The need to counter China's influence is a motivating factor in American policy towards Thailand.

The end of the Cold War and the rise of the South East Asian economies led to India's Look East Policy. Under Prime Minister Modi, this policy has acquired a sharper edge as the Act East Policy. India too has taken a soft line on the Thai military junta, for the same reasons that have also underpinned India's relations with Myanmar. The tri-lateral highway project between India-Myanmar-Thailand is an important project which is expected to bring economic benefits to India's northeastern states. Thailand's economy, the second largest among ASEAN countries, and the eighth largest in Asia, has bounced back in the last three years. This has bolstered the military junta's claims to have provided stability, and facilitated economic growth. The Thai business elite and the middle class would rather have stability and economic growth than the rambunctious aspects of a democracy. India has growing trading and investment ties with Thailand, and remains mindful of Thailand's role in the regional grouping BIMSTEC and the Act East Policy.

With a GDP of US $455 billion, with per capita GDP of around US $ 5400, Thailand's exports contribute over 2/3rd to its GDP. India's trade with Thailand topped US $ 9 billion in 2014–15. Thailand and India are maritime neighbours, sharing a maritime boundary in the Andaman Sea in the Bay of Bengal. The two Navies collaborate regularly. Over a million Indian tourists visit Thailand annually, and India receives around 1.2 lakh Thai tourists, and over 10,000 students. India has also taken a pragmatic approach to the military government, and remained engaged, keeping in mind India's Act East policy, BIMSTEC, and connectivity projects. Despite the military coup, India has remained engaged with Thailand, and the leader of the military government Gen Prayuth Chan-ocha has visited India twice, in 2016 and 2018; Prime Minister Modi made a stopover visit in 2016 to pay respects to Thailand's much revered late King Bhumibol Adulyadej, the longest serving monarch in world till his demise.

The India-Thailand early harvest Free Trade Agreement (FTA) was signed in 2004, when Thaksin Shinawatra was Prime Minister. This agreement reduced tariffs on 82 tariff lines. Thailand rose to become India's 4th largest trading partner in ASEAN. While this FTA helped in raising trade, Thailand benefited disproportionately. This led to stalling of the comprehensive FTA, as India sought a more balanced agreement, with adequate benefits in the Services domain. Over 40 Indian companies have invested around US $ 2 billion, and around Thai 30 companies operate in India.

During the tenure of Prime Minister Yingluk Shinawatra, growing security cooperation has removed irritations associated with the Bangkok-based Mumbai underworld elements and some leaders of Naga insurgent groups. She was the Chief Guest for India's Republic Day celebrations in 2012. She visited India again for the India-ASEAN Commemorative Summit in December 2012. India-Thailand relations have been transformed qualitatively under administrations led by the two Shinawatras. A defence MoU facilitates cooperation in counter terrorism, joint naval patrolling as well as combating piracy and smuggling of contraband. Joint military exercises have become a regular feature of bilateral defence cooperation.

Looking East through the Kautilyan prism, Thailand is India's natural ally. The Trilateral Highway Project and the Dawei Industrial Corridor project, linking Thailand to the eastern seaboard of Myanmar, are strategically significant connectivity projects. Comprehensive Economic Partnership Agreements [CEPA] with Singapore, Japan, the Republic of Korea, and Malaysia have paved the way for closer economic partnership with East Asia. The FTA with ASEAN is in place, and the Services and Investment Agreements are under negotiations with ASEAN, Indonesia, and Thailand. Cooperation in the domain of Security and Defence has also expanded, particularly with Vietnam. For India, China's increasing footprint in the neighbourhood is a challenge for its foreign policy which has sought to adapt to this central phenomenon. India-Thailand ties are intricately embedded in the changing geo-strategic and geo-economic situation in Asia.

The author is a Distinguished Fellow at the Delhi-based Observer Research Foundation; he is a former Secretary in the Ministry of External Affairs, Government of India, and was India's Ambassador to Thailand from 2009–2011

VALEDICTORY SESSION

41

Special Address

Lalit Mansingh, Chairman, Kalinga International Foundation

His Excellency Dr. S.C. Jamir, Hon. Governor of Odisha; Hon. Gamini Jayawickrama Perera, Minister of Buddha Sasana, Sri Lanka; their Excellencies, the Heads of Diplomatic Missions; ladies and gentlemen.

I would like to recognise the distinguished presence in this audience of Dr Bhartruhari Mahtab, Hon. Member of Parliament and leader of the BJD. He has been a mentor and supporter of the Kalinga International Foundation from its inception. We are happy and grateful that he is here among us on this important occasion.

It is a privilege for me to welcome, on behalf of the Kalinga International Foundation, His Excellency Dr. S.C. Jamir, Hon. Governor of Odisha, as the Chief Guest for the Valedictory Function of 'PURBASA: East meets East'.

His Excellency the Governor has been a patron of the Kalinga International Foundation (KIF) even before it was created. It was he who inaugurated the Kalinga Lanka Dialogue in 2015 and the Kalinga Indonesia Dialogue in 2016. I recall discussing the idea of the KIF with him, and felt energised by his strong support and encouragement. As one of the tallest leaders of India, an elder statesman of the North Eastern region, and now the Governor of Odisha, he personifies to me the spirit of the KIF. We count on his continued blessings for our future activities.

Your Excellency, 'PURBASA: East meets East' was inaugurated just two days ago. It appears to me that in these two short days of intense dialogue, we have covered a long distance in bringing together our Eastern and North Eastern Regions with the Indo-Pacific neighbourhood of India.

The KIF's belief is that the North East and East represent a seamless, culturally connected, and viable economic region. This concept has received strong validation from the conference. The landlocked North East needs to have easy connectivity to the maritime infrastructure of the eastern region. The combined region faces common challenges of under development: it cries for better infrastructure, human resources development, and access to investments and exports from the Indo-Pacific region.

Over thirty experts from the Indo-Pacific region joined an equal number of outstanding panellists from India, and engaged in an intense, productive, and candid dialogue under PURBASA.

There are many take-aways from this conclave which we will compile and incorporate into the agenda for future meetings. Overall, it was strongly felt that the dialogue needs to be continued so that we can come up with suggestions and solutions which will help policy makers in making the Act East Policy more vibrant and effective. We, therefore, propose to resume the PURBASA dialogue, hopefully in the North East and in venues in the Indo-Pacific region.

My very special thanks go to Mr. Gamini Jayawickrama Perera, Hon. Minister for Buddha Sasana of Sri Lanka, for underlining the historical, cultural, and contemporary ties which bind Sri Lanka and Odisha together. I am also grateful to Professor Ajarn Sulak Sivaraksa, one of the most distinguished historians of the region, for conveying to us the vibrancy of the Buddhist heritage which India shares with the nations of South East Asia. And, to all of you, Excellencies, the Heads of missions, experts, and panellists, my deepest appreciation for sparing the time to contribute to this exciting dialogue.

42

Valedictory Message

Ajarn Sulak Sivaraksa

Excellencies, Distinguished Guests, Ladies and Gentlemen,

It is indeed a great privilege for me to take part in this wonderful gathering on the invitation of Kalinga International Foundation. As you are well aware, Kalinga was a significant place for Emperor Ashoka. Ashoka was the greatest emperor not only of Asia but also of the world. His vast empire extended from India to Pakistan and Afghanistan. However, his real greatness was not due to the extent of his empire, but to his transformation. And Kalinga was central to it. The battle of Kalinga was Ashoka's last battle. It proved to be a turning point. It was where he changed his heart fundamentally from being *Candaasokaraj* ('Ashoka the Fierce', the violent Ashoka) to becoming *Dhammasokaraj* ('Ashoka the Righteous', the nonviolent Ashoka). He became beloved of the gods, *Devanampiyatissa*.

I want to mention only one of Ashoka's great contributions. He sent *Dhammaduta* to Sri Lanka, Southeast Asia, and elsewhere. In other words, as a Buddhist, I feel indebted not only to the Buddha, but also to Ashoka. And being a good Buddhist is the most important part of life. As you know, the Buddha reminds us that success in life is not about having power, prestige and wealth. Rather, it is about having *Kalyanamitta*, or virtuous companions.

When Ananda tells the Buddha that *Kalyanamitta* is only half of the holy life, the latter responds: 'No! No! *Kalyanamitta* is the whole of holy life.' *Kalyanamitta* is the one who tells you what you don't want to hear—that is, the truths that make you uncomfortable, embarrassed, anxious, angry, and so on.

In general, we want to be praised. We don't want to hear negative things about ourselves—even if they are constructive or sincere criticisms. However, it is a mundane fact that we all have negative as well as positive features inside. Only a Kalyanmitta will make you aware of your negative features and acts. The Buddha says that Kalyanmitta is akin to the external voice of conscience, *Paratoghosa*. As such, a virtuous companion will help one to transform oneself into a better person.

Today, I will speak to you as a *Kalyanmitta*. Perhaps you may not like what you hear. But I am going to say it with sincerity. This meeting is held in India. I come from Southeast Asia. In most parts of Southeast Asia, we are indebted to India for introducing Buddhism, Brahmanism, and many other aspects of Indian culture. For example, Indonesia has the largest Muslim country in the world. Yet, as Abdurrahman Wahid, the former President of Indonesia told me, the country only became Islamic 500 years ago. Prior to that, Indonesia was Buddhist; and before that it was influenced by Brahmanism, The Borobudur is the greatest stupa in Indonesia.

If you go to Denpasar, Bali, you can see a big statue of Bhima. Both the *Mahabharata* and the *Ramayana* have great influence in Southeast Asia. Also you may not be aware that the former capital city of my country was called Ayodhaya. It was founded over 700 years ago. We moved the capital to Bangkok approximately 250 years ago. Yet, the official name is still Ayodhaya. Moreover, all our kings are Rama. The present King is Rama X. Some of you may know that the late Rama IX proposed an alternative economic philosophy rooted in Buddhism. As a footnote, the former king of Bhutan also proposed the concept of Gross National Happiness to challenge Gross National Product.

Perhaps today, more than ever, we have to look forward and move beyond the dominant ways of the world. We need to come up with viable alternatives, especially to capitalism. Appropriately, we have friends here who came from Burma. Some of you may know that the British government sent E.F. Schumacher to Burma over 70 years ago. Initially, Schumacher's task was to help develop Burma in the image of the UK. Fortunately, he turned the purpose of his mission upside down. He contended that it was Britain that had to develop like Burma. And he wrote his famous book on Buddhist economics, *Small is Beautiful.*

Right now in London, there is the New Economic Foundation, which aims to realise Buddhist economics in the world. Additionally, there is also the World Future Council (WFC). It is comprised of leading people from around the world. The WFC aims to be the voice of future generations, and promotes peace and sustainable development. Jakob von Uexkull launched the WFC in 2007. Roughly 50 years ago, he also started the so-called alternative Nobel Prize or Right Livelihood Award. As you know, Right Livelihood is part of the Buddha's Noble Eightfold Path. In a nutshell, all these—and many more—are coming from India, from Buddhism. In other words, we have plenty of intellectual, cultural, and spiritual resources to help build a new world, to help bring about a different future beyond the dominance of capitalism and the West.

So, back to Ashoka the Great again, in a fairly recent book, *To Uphold the World: A Call for a New Global Ethic from Ancient India*, Bruce Rich argues that in order to uphold the world, we must go back to Ashoka and Kautilya. People in the West may not be familiar with Kautilya. Kautilya wrote a famous book, the *Arthasastra*, which is still very important. Arguably, it is more important than Machiavelli's *The Prince*. Rich says that the whole world today is being controlled subconsciously by Kautilya on how to run things, to cheat, to compete, and so on. But, Rich continues, we need to go back to Ashoka, who provides us with clues about how to transform violence into nonviolence, and hatred into loving-kindness and compassion.

At present, we can also look to the Dalai Lama and the Tibetan people. They have been oppressed by the Chinese for over 60 years. The Dalai Lama and his people have come to live in India. Yet, he has consistently reminded us that, with love and understanding, not greed and violence, a new future is possible. We must not hate the Chinese. With love and compassion, we will be able to change the world. The Buddha said that if *Metta* prevails, the world will prevail.

In short, I am bringing the message from the Buddha and from Ashoka to this gathering. I hope that this meeting will be able to come up with concrete measures to uphold the world in the 21st century, based on Buddhist teachings of love and compassion.

Lastly, I must say that I am proud to be in India. Mother India is not perfect. She has many short comings. But Indians should be proud of their country's ongoing experiment with democracy. Democracy in India is still fragile and threatened by neoliberal capitalism, inequality, right-wing nationalism and populism, environmental devastation, and so on. However, the Indian people must not give up on democracy, and set a good example for all of us in South East Asia.

China wants to catch up with the West. China wants economic prosperity like Singapore. That small land is very rich, but hardly democratic. Also, the Chinese people have suffered so much under the dictatorship of the Communist regime. Globally, China may be able to compete with the USA, but it may not be able to set an example to people worldwide who are engaging in emancipatory struggles.

This is my last message to all of you.

43

Valedictory Address

Dr. S.C. Jamir, Hon'ble Governor of Odisha

I am delighted to be here amidst such an elite gathering for the valedictory session of the Conference 'PURBASA: East Meets East' being organised by the Kalinga International Foundation. I am happy to extend my greetings and good wishes to the international delegates, and those representing our Northeast states who have come here for this conference.

I understand that this is the second Conference organised by the Kalinga International Foundation; but it is the first one to be held in the state of Odisha. It is a proud moment that the land known for its long history of maritime activities of trade and commerce with South East Asia is taking centre stage to revive those golden days of economic prosperity and social and cultural integration.

I am happy that the conference supplements the Government's intention and efforts to enhance India's multifaceted engagement with ASEAN and the wider Asia Pacific through a series of events and activities. Very recently, having leaders from all 10 ASEAN countries as our esteemed guests at this year's (2018) Republic Day Parade in Delhi has given a great boost to our efforts. The country is very clear in its approach and commitment to build on the ASEAN-India Dialogue Partnership that recently celebrated its 25th anniversary.

I understand that the Conference, during these three days has deliberated on different aspects and opportunities to deepen the engagement between India and ASEAN to scale new heights, and script a defining partnership. My congratulations to all who have gathered here, and presented their valuable views and suggestions on how we can strengthen our civilizational links amidst the new challenges and opportunities of the 21st century. The Conference is of great interest to me too, and I have keenly followed it. Indeed, I would also be happy to see the final proceedings of the Conference.

It is said that the 21st century will be an Asian Century. It means Asia will drive growth and development in the 21st century, leading to increased prosperity. The region is criss-crossed with foreign direct investments, making it the most sophisticated, active, and dynamic end of the global supply chain. Being home to nearly half of humanity, Asia is closer to high levels of economic integration and becoming the world's number one economic hotspot. Also noteworthy is the constant rapidly growing intra-regional dynamics.

Various regional initiatives are important steps in this regard. ASEAN, a role model for regional cooperation, is appreciated for the stability it has brought to the region and its immediate neighbourhood. The region, comprising ASEAN and India together, represent a combined population of 1.85 billion, which is a quarter of the global population, and a GDP of over US $3.8 trillion, creating one of the largest economic spaces in the world. Further, India and countries of Southeast Asia enjoy close cultural and civilizational links which have lasted over the millenia. Evidence of this abounds in texts and folklore, architecture, literature, dance-forms, music, religion, and culture. Buddhism is also a major combining factor that spread to South East Asia from India through monks. You will be happy that Emperor Asoka, after embracing Buddhism following Kalinga War, sent Buddhist emissaries to South East Asia in the 3rd century B.C. With the passage of time, Buddhism took an indigenous form in all parts of South East Asia, and gradually underwent a process of the localisation of its tenets.

Our past has a common source; but, inevitably, our destinies are also linked. Our economic and diplomatic endeavours must draw from the same well-spring. India works closely with ASEAN to weave a mutually beneficial legacy which would be cherished by future generations. To sustain this focus, the promotion of socio-cultural ties through people-to-people contacts and exchange programmes hold immense importance.

Greater engagements and integration in the areas of regional trade agreements infrastructure, start-ups, and innovation as well as e-commerce and the digital economy and digital solutions are the key to strengthening the ASEAN-India partnership.

It is to be remembered that security is a prerequisite for internal cohesion, economic development, and consolidation. Our interest and effort should be to create an enabling external environment for regional security and peace.

Energy cooperation has become important and crucial in the face of exponential rates of energy consumption and the declining hydro-carbon reserves. Countries are seeking to secure multiple energy sources and identifying multiple sources of supply. India is looking to South East Asian countries and other sources in the Indo Pacific to overcome this challenge. I am happy that the Conference had a session on Energy Cooperation to address regional cooperation in both the conventional and non-conventional sectors.

The ocean based Blue Economy has great potential for economic growth, improved livelihoods, and jobs through the sustainable use of ocean resources, and deserves greater attention. The region comprising India and ASEAN countries presents tremendous trade potential. Besides significant trade and commerce in the fields of shipping, offshore oil and gas, fishing, undersea cables, and tourism, there are also other emerging industries—such as aquaculture marine biotechnology, ocean energy, and sea-bed mining—that have the potential to create jobs and spur worldwide economic growth. Countries in the region need not only to coordinate and manage the growing security challenges in the region but also realise the substantial economic potential presented by the Ocean.

The youth are the strength and asset to any country. They are our future generation; they must engage and bond in a more systematic way, and at a deeper level. To this end, in addition to organising the annual student exchange programmes, it is crucial to explore new means to encourage closer contacts among our youth, who hold the future of the ASEAN-India relationship.

Northeast India shares 98 per cent of its border with Bhutan, Bangladesh, China, and Myanmar, and should be seen more as a trade and commerce opportunity rather than a political one. For us, using the Northeast region to link up with ASEAN countries and their economies has many benefits. It could lead to better integration of this frontier region with the mainland and turn it into a strategic bridge, giving country access to the East on land as well as through sea for trade and human movement for a wide variety of economic and cultural activities. India's Act East Policy aims to enhance India's multi-faceted engagement with ASEAN and the wider Asia-Pacific; it seeks to deepen economic integration, politico-security cooperation, and socio-cultural dialogue with countries of the region for domestically better integrating India's Northeast with India as well as with South East Asia.

Today's Conference has provided a platform to build synergies between India and ASEAN member countries based on our civilizational links and commonalities, and to explore new areas of cooperation and collaboration while enhancing friendship. I am sure it would contribute to achieve peace and security through the promotion of the 3Cs: Commerce, Connectivity, and Culture. I further hope that the distinguished delegates would have their bag full with good memories of this beautiful state, and they would be looking forward to another such occasion to share their views on this topic of growing importance. Finally, I congratulate the Kalinga International Foundation on its laudable endeavour and wish it all success.

Jai Hind.

SUMMATION AND LOOKING FORWARD

44

The Purbasa Conference: A Critical Evaluation

Rajiv Bhatia

Introduction

Three months after its formal launch with an impressive inaugural conference in New Delhi on 13 December 2017, Kalinga International Foundation (KIF), an independent and non-partisan think tank, scored another notable success. Its first international conference—'**Purbasa: East Meets East: Synergizing the North-East and Eastern India with the Indo-Pacific**'—was held in Bhubaneswar, Odisha, from 16-18 March 2018. A critical appraisal of the conference is presented here for the information and benefit of KIF's multiple stakeholders and supporters, partially with the aim to develop further clarity with regard to its future programmes.

KIF is strongly committed to its vision: "Peace and prosperity in the region with the mission to build consensus on solutions for fulfilling these goals." The New Delhi conference strengthened the institution's resolve to initiate a series of meaningful dialogues, starting with a well-designed event in eastern India. Given the think tank's name, the choice of Bhubaneswar as the venue of the first international conference was a natural corollary.

The fact that the Purbasa Conference was the first major Track II event in India after the special India-ASEAN Commemorative Summit, hosted by Prime Minister Narendra Modi on 25 January 2018, was noticed. It certainly lent special importance to what a carefully choreographed convergence of politics, diplomacy, arts and scholarship could produce by way of specific ideas to deepen India's relationship with the East.

Purpose

The essential concept of the conference was delineated in the backdrop of changes in the Indo-Pacific region that faces many possibilities and challenges today. India's East and Northeast have enjoyed a civilizational connect with other countries, both overland and through the Indian Ocean and the Pacific Ocean, for centuries. India's Act East Policy has extended the nation's vision beyond ASEAN to the larger Indo-Pacific region which unifies the Indian Ocean Region (IOR) and the Western Pacific region into a singular construct. The conference's raison d'être was to discover answers to a seminal question: how should the relationship between India and countries of the region develop in this period of geopolitical flux in the wider Indo-Pacific?

The inaugural session was curated to stress the fundamental unity that links India's Northeast with eastern India as well as to stress the natural linkages between South Asia and East Asia stretching from Myanmar to Japan. Academic sessions were organised in such a manner that the Government's policy built around the troika of Cs—'Culture, Commerce and Connectivity'—could be showcased with a clear intent to bring out the notion that the implementation of sound programmes was as important as designing a sound policy.

Political Dimension

A total of 37 foreign experts and diplomats representing countries of the region and 34 experts from different areas of India formed part of a very sizable audience at the inaugural and valedictory sessions, held respectively on 16 and 18 March. The response from and engagement of Odisha's academics, intellectuals and media was both enthusiastic and substantial. Both sessions heard important messages from the political leadership.

Introducing the conference, KIF's Chairman, **Ambassador Lalit Mansingh**, projected its fundamental philosophy anchored in 'Purbasa' with its triple meanings—'the rise', 'the hope', 'the message' of the East. He noted that 16 countries were represented at the conference, all being from the "sun-rise states" of the Indo-Pacific. He referred to the Northeast and East India as a homogenous cultural and economic region of India that was playing a crucial role in India's Act East Policy.

In his keynote address, **Sri Dharmendra Pradhan**, India's Minister for Petroleum and Natural Gas, Skill Development and Entrepreneurship, spoke of the age-old linkages between Odisha and the East. "Our mythologies, languages, religions and architecture", he noted, "have seeped into each other in ways that have not yet been fully understood or explored." Referring to the current geopolitical climate and resultant uncertainty, he urged the region to stick together "as a group" and intensify "economic, cultural and trade imprints across our nations." Enhancing connectivity, the Minister emphasised, was critical to deepening India's diplomatic, economic and cultural ties with the Indo-Pacific countries. He also underlined the centrality of the Northeast in the formulation and implementation of India's Act East Policy.

In his remarks at the inaugural session as well as in subsequent sessions, Mr. **Gamini Jayawickrama Perera**, Sri Lanka's Minister of Buddha Sasna, Sustainable Development and Welfare, talked about the rich and old links between Sri Lanka and Odisha; the potentialities and opportunities concerning religious, cultural and socio-economic connections among the countries of South Asia, Southeast Asia and the Indo-Pacific; and the continuing impact of Buddhism on the entire region. Impressed by the Purbasa Conference, he offered to facilitate (and probably host) a follow-up conference in Sri Lanka. **Sri C.M. Patowari,** Assam's Minister for Industry and Commerce also spoke on the occasion. His presence embodied the natural link between the Northeast and eastern India.

As Odisha's Chief Minister was unable to participate in the conference due to his other pressing preoccupations, the state was represented by its head—**Dr S.C. Jamir,** Governor of Odisha. In a thoughtful and substantive statement at the valedictory session, he observed: "Our past has a common source—inevitably, our destiny too is linked." He hoped that the region's economic and diplomatic endeavours would "draw from the same well-spring." The importance of energy cooperation, the promising potential of the Blue Economy, and the need to engage the Youth was highlighted by the Governor. He expressed happiness that the conference supplemented the Government's intention and efforts to enhance India's multi-faceted engagement with ASEAN and the region beyond. He hailed the Purbasa Conference as "a platform to build synergies."

Expert View

The conference attracted a galaxy of experts—Ministers, MPs, serving and former ambassadors, former military leaders, academics, specialists from think tanks, business CEOs, and representatives of civil society—from India, other parts of South Asia, Southeast Asia, and Japan. They made interesting presentations, discussed issues among themselves in their respective panels, and engaged with an aware and well-informed audience composed of Odisha's elite.

Spread into **eight sessions**, the conference covered diverse aspects of India's relations with the region, namely (i) Economic Cooperation, (ii) Maritime Connectivity and Security in the Indo-Pacific, (iii)-(iv) Regional Connectivity (two sessions), (v) Connecting Women, Youth and Civil Society, (vi) Energy Cooperation, (vii) Tourism, Culture, Buddhism, and (viii) India's Bilateral Relations with Sri Lanka, Myanmar, Indonesia and ASEAN in general, and Japan. In the session entitled "Summation and Looking Ahead" just prior to the valedictory event, this author and an expert from IDSA presented their concise reports on the conference, with Ambassador Lalit Mansingh as the Chair. Deliberations lasting over 22 hours through the conference have produced sufficient material for a full-fledged book that KIF plans to publish in due course.

For the limited purpose of this report, one may be content by capturing and highlighting some of the more weighty and pertinent views, suggestions and recommendations. These are presented below, subject wise:

Economic Cooperation

- India's commercial and economic cooperation with the region has developed quite well, but in comparison to China, it is "insignificant and below par." Obstacles are there for everyone to see; the task is to prioritise and eliminate them.
- FTAs with ASEAN, South Korea and Japan have not helped India's exports much. Factors that hold back trade have been identified by experts; the challenge is now to address them, one by one. The "culture of business" is a central issue that needs to be understood and tackled.
- ASEAN should try to appreciate that in the current RCEP negotiations India can make only minimum concessions, at least till 2025, as the Indian industry needs time to face competition from China and others.
- For the Northeast to develop further and become a productive part of the larger region, two critical requirements are: peace and security should be ensured and; air connectivity should be enhanced within a short period of time.

- According to a former secretary in the Ministry of External Affairs, responsibility for the low level of economic cooperation rests on both sides – India and ASEAN, but a bigger slice thereof lies on Indian shoulders. It is now time to remove the deficiencies systematically if the nation is serious about seeing better results. "delivery deficit" was a widely shared perception.
- Implicitly on behalf of the East Asian region, a senior Japanese diplomat conceded that there was scope for them to improve their processes and master the art and culture of doing business in India. However, he underlined that many Japanese companies experienced "frustration" with Indian procedures and business environment.

Maritime Connectivity and Security

- On China's 'Belt and Road Initiative' (BRI), opinions in the panel were sharply polarized. The Indian view was that BRI was "not benign", and it posed a threat to India's security. The Sri Lankan view, articulated by a former Naval Chief, was that development-starved Sri Lanka could not manage without China's generous financial assistance (since no one else offered any major funding), and that Colombo "believed in China's affirmations that Beijing did not seek hegemony." Nevertheless, Sri Lanka would always be sensitive to India's security concerns. Hence, it favoured enhancing cooperation within the framework of IORA. Indian skepticism persisted.
- ASEAN panelists viewed India as "a counter to China" in the Indo-Pacific. They showed understanding for the need of the Quad, especially in view of China's aggressive actions in the South China Sea. But it was emphasised that the Quad should be "inclusive" i.e. it should consider forging cooperative arrangements with ASEAN countries that may be mutually acceptable.
- The Chair, a former Naval Chief of India, made a strong plea for all concerned to respond and follow UNCLOS. He stressed that India was in the midst of taking important maritime connectivity initiatives and it has extended its hand of friendship "to all neighbours."

Regional Connectivity

- Connectivity of various kinds—physical, infrastructural, institutional, P-to-P, and "ideational"—is of paramount importance. More and faster progress is needed in this domain than what the record shows so far.

- South Asian panelists (from Nepal and Bangladesh) emphasised their countries' specific grievances against India in order to argue that connectivity within South Asia should be accorded priority. Indian panelists specialising in Southeast Asian affairs largely set their sights on how to improve connectivity in Southeast Asia and beyond.
- Our neighbours' disappointment with the stalemate in SAARC came through sharply. Some support was voiced for current endeavours to make BIMSTEC and BBIN as truly effective institutions.

Other Themes

- On energy cooperation, CMD Petronet suggested that KIF should play a role in pushing for the proposed cooperation arrangements on gas linkages between India and Myanmar. Intervening from the floor, Chairman KIF accepted this suggestion and assured suitable follow-up.
- The 12-person panel on Tourism, Culture and Buddhism explored various segments of actual and potential cooperation, mainly between India and Southeast Asia.
- In the panel entitled "Bilaterals: India's Most Favoured Nations", experts presented their perspective on the present status and future prospects of India's ties with the select countries mentioned earlier.
- The Indonesian Ambassador pointed out that the present phase of G-to-G engagement was proving to be unusually hectic and productive. Indonesian airlines now ran 28 flights to India, but unfortunately no Indian carrier was going to Indonesia. He suggested that the EEZ boundary should be settled soon. On security issues, Indonesia did not see India as a threat; in fact it wanted more, not less, of India in ASEAN. Closer India-Indonesia relations would be useful for the stability of the Indo-Pacific. His two main concerns were: the sharp increase of import duties by India on Indonesian palm oil that would affect bilateral trade adversely; and in case of the failure of RCEP negotiations, alternatives should be considered.
- A former Indian Ambassador to Japan suggested that Japan should consider extending the Bay of Bengal Belt 'Initiative' to the whole of eastern India.
- The Myanmar Ambassador expressed appreciation for India's assistance to his country and observed that his government was trying to create a congenial environment for foreign investment and tourism in Myanmar.
- The Sri Lankan High Commissioner expressed the view that Sri Lanka did not see India as a threat, while suggesting that India should not see Sri

Lanka as a threat. There should be mutual respect for each other's sensitivities. China had "come a long way in Sri Lanka." It has been helping Sri Lanka to develop its economy through "funds." She underlined that Sri Lanka's national priorities were (1) peace and security consolidation, (2) ethnic reconciliation, and (3) socio-economic progress. India's support for these goals would be valuable.

Conclusion

In his final remarks, Chairman KIF expressed satisfaction that through the active participation of Odisha's intelligentsia and the coverage given by the provincial media (as well as social media), the message of Purbasa Conference has reached far and wide. He assured participants that Indian and foreign authorities would be suitably briefed and sensitised about the deliberations and their outcome.

He also indicated that KIF would focus on connecting with scholars, intellectuals and civil society in the North East before taking the themes of Purbasa to select capitals in Southeast Asia. KIF plans to explore the ways and means to promote political and economic cooperation, energy linkages, potential of the Blue Economy, and also support the establishment of 'the Bay of Bengal Community', anchored on BIMSTEC. The Sri Lankan offer of organising a follow-up conference would be taken up in due course.

Political leaders, panelists and participants have all commended KIF for hosting a highly successful conference. They noted that the logistics were excellent; the agenda was innovative and ambitious; the coverage of issues was extensive; and the quality of panel discussions was of a high order.

The highlight of the inaugural event was a dance programme showing Odisi, Manipuri and Balinese styles, which was choreographed by much-acclaimed Guru Aruna Mohanty. The conference was followed by a two-day excursion to Odisha's top tourist attractions, which was deeply appreciated by participants.

KIF is determined to pursue its mission in the future with a mix of renewed zeal, purposefulness and imagination.

About the Contributors

Senayangba Chubatoshi Jamir

Dr Senayangba Chubatoshi Jamir (born 17 October 1931) is an Indian politician and former Governor of Odisha. He had served as the Chief Minister of Nagaland, Governor of Maharashtra, Governor of Gujarat, and Governor of Goa before he became Governor of Odisha.

Gamini Jaywicrama Perera

H.E. Mr Gamini Jayawickrama Perera is Hon'ble Minister of Buddhasasana in Government of Sri Lanka.
He is:

Former Minister of Sustainable Development and Wildlife Former Cabinet Minister for Food Security
Former Minister of Regional Development
Former cabinet minister for irrigation and water management Chief Minister for Northern Western provincial council, 1987 District Minister for Kurunegala District, 1978
Member of Parliament, 1977
Member of the village council and involved in active politics, 1968
His other important positions are:
Member of the United National party Working committee Former chairman of the United National Party (2011-2012) Former General Secretary Asia Pacific parliamentary Environmental Authority
Former Kurunegala District Chairman (United National Party) Chair of the Asia Pacific forum on Sustainable Development 2016.

CM Patowary

Hon'ble Minister for Industry, Commerce, Transport, Parliamentary, Skill Development and Act East Policy Affairs, Government of Assam.

Dharmendra Pradhan

Hon'ble Minister for Petroleum, Natural Gas, Skill Development and Entrepreneurship, Government of India.

Sidharto Reza Suryodipuro

Ambassador Extraordinary and Plenipotentiary of the Republic of Indonesia to India.

Moe Kyaw Aung

Ambassador Extraordinary and Plenipotentiary of the Republic of the Union of Myanmar to India.

Maria Teresita C. Daza

Ambassador Extraordinary and Plenipotentiary of Republic of the Philippines to India.

Chitranganee Wagiswra

High Commissioner of Sri Lanka to India.

Chutintorn Gongsakdi

Ambassador of Thailand to India.

Ton Sinh Thanh

Ambassador Extraordinary and Plenipotentiary of the Socialist Republic of Vietnam to India.

Lalit Mansingh

Amb Lalit Mansingh has served as India's foreign secretary, ambassador to the United States and high commissioner to the United Kingdom. He has also been ambassador in the United Arab Emirates and high commissioner in Nigeria with concurrent accreditation to Benin, Chad and The Cameroons.

Ambassador Mansingh joined the Indian Foreign Service in 1963, securing the first position in the All India Civil Service Examination. After his initial posting in Geneva, he served as deputy chief of mission in the Indian Embassies in Kabul, Brussels, and Washington. At headquarters in Delhi, Ambassador Mansingh's assignments included: Joint Secretary in the Ministry of Finance, Director General of the Indian Council for Cultural Relations, Dean of the Foreign Service Institute and Secretary (West) in the Ministry of External Affairs.

Ambassador Mansingh is active in several international initiatives for conflict resolution, regional security and sustainable development. He is part of a number of Track II dialogues between India and its neighbours including Pakistan and Afghanistan. He is also a member of the Asia Pacific Leadership Network, Canberra. He is the founder Chairman of the Kalinga International Foundation (KIF).

Anup K. Mudgal

Ambassador Anup K. Mudgal, a member of the Indian Foreign Service (IFS) retired in May, 2016 as India's High Commissioner to Mauritius. As part of his diplomatic carrier spanning thirty two years, he served thrice at the Head Quarters of the Ministry of External Affairs handling relations with India's neighborhood; ASEAN region; Russian Federation and some countries of Central and Eastern Europe as well issues relating to Human Resource Development.

As part of his eight assignments abroad Amb. Mudgal served in different capacities at the Indian Missions in Mexico (including NAFTA matters), Peru, former Yugoslavia, Belgium (EU matters), Germany, Austria (work relating to: IAEA, UNIDO, UNODC, UNOOSA, UNCITRAL), and Mauritius (including IORA).

Post retirement, Amb Mudgal has been engaged in several voluntary assignments, the important ones being: Member, FICCI Task Force on Blue Economy; Member, Steering Committee on Blue Economy under PMEAC; Member, Core Team of Kalinga International Foundation; Chair, Diaspora Committee, ARSP; Joint Secretary, Association of Indian Diplomats; Guest lectures at various higher education and professional institutes.

Born in May, 1956, Amb Mudgal did most of his education in Delhi. He holds Masters' and M.Phil degrees in plant sciences from University of Delhi. He speaks Hindi, English and Spanish. Previously, he also briefly worked at the Department of Science and Technology, New Delhi and as a member of the Indian Forest Service.

Ajarn Sulak Sivarakasha

Ajarn Sulak Sivaraksa is director of the Santiprachad Hamma Institute, a project under the Sathirakoses Nagapradipa. The Institute has been working to promote rural development, social justice and human rights in Siam in the past two decades, and he has been working since the beginning as founder and director. It provides training on human rights for many activists and those in rural communities. He also has many published works in both Thai and English, most of which are related to the issues of culture, spirituality, religion, human rights and education. Throughout the past four decades, the organizations under the Foundation he founded have been having much ongoing collaboration with civil society organizations around the world, particularly in Europe and North America.

Ajarn Sulak Sivaraksa was awarded the Right Livelihood Award in 1995. He was chair of the Asian Cultural Forum on Development and has been a visiting professor at UC Berkeley, the University of Hawai and Cornell.

Alana Golmei

Dr. (Ms) Alana Golmei is the Director of Burma Centre Delhi which was founded in 2008 to work for restoration of peace, justice, democracy and human rights in Burma with a mission to strengthen relationships between the people of India and Burma for mutual understanding and solidarity.

She is the General Secretary of Northeast Support Centre & Helpline based in New Delhi which was launched in 2007 with the aim to prevent harassment, discrimination, molestation and abuses meted out to people from Northeast India living in Delhi and its NCR particularly women.

Dr. Alana Golmei holds a first class degree in her postgraduate in Political Science and has Ph.D. from the Department of Political Science, Manipur University. She also completed her Post Doctoral study under Northeast India Studies Program, School of Social Sciences, Jawaharlal Nehru University.

Alana Golmei was awarded the first annual awards "DCW Achievement Award" by Delhi Commission for Women on the occasion of International Women's Day, 8 March 2016 in recognition of her efforts towards spearheading the cause of women.

On 25 September 2014, Dr. Golmei was honored with the prestigious ALL Grassroots Women of the Decade Achievers Award by Assocham Ladies League for setting-up the Northeast Support Centre and 24/7 Helpline to prevent harassment, discrimination, and abuse faced by the people from Northeast India living in metros, particularly women

Anil Wadhwa

Ambassador Anil Wadhwa was born on 26 May, 1957 and was a member of the Indian Foreign Service from 1 July, 1979 to 31 May, 2017.

In his previous diplomatic assignments, he served as Third Secretary in the Commission of India, Hong Kong (Sep. 1981 to Sep. 1983);

Second Secretary/First Secretary in Embassy of India, Beijing (Nov. 1983 to Feb. 1987); Under Secretary/Deputy Secretary in Ministry of External Affairs, New Delhi (Feb. 1987-May 1989); UN Disarmament Fellow in Geneva (July-Nov. 1989); First Secretary (Disarmament) at the Permanent Mission of India in Geneva (Dec. 1989-Dec. 1992); Counsellor in Embassy of India, Beijing (Jan. 1993–Jul. 1993); Director/Joint Secretary on deputation to the Provisional Technical Secretariat and later the Technical Secretariat for the Organization for the Prohibition of Chemical Weapons (OPCW) in The Hague (July 1993-July 2000; Chief Adviser, Ministry of External Affairs (Earthquake Relief) in Gujarat State, (Dec. 2000 to Jan. 2001), Joint Secretary, Central and Eastern Europe, Ministry of External Affairs, New Delhi (Mar. 2001 to Feb. 2004). Ambassador Wadhwa served as the Indian Ambassador to Poland and Lithuania (March 2004 to August 2007), to the Sultanate of Oman (August 2007 to September 2011), to the Kingdom of Thailand (Nov 2011 to Jan 2014) and to the Republic of Italy and San Marino (March 2016 to May 2017). During this tenure, Ambassador Wadhwa has also served as a Permanent Representative of India to the Rome-based UN Agencies—FAO, IFAD and WFP. He was appointed President of the WFP Board on 22nd February, 2017.

Ambassador Wadhwa was Secretary (East) in the Ministry of External Affairs in New Delhi from 2014-2016 looking after South East Asia, Australia and Pacific, Gulf and West Asian regions, among other responsibilities. He was also the leader of the senior officials to all meetings of ASEAN, ASEM, ACD, Arab League, Mekong-Ganga Cooperation, ARF and East Asia Summit. During this period he coordinated the evacuation of Indian nationals from Iraq, Libya, and Yemen.

From 1989-2000, Ambassador Wadhwa attended meetings of the First Committee in UNDC in New York first as a Delegate of India and later as Representative of the OPCW where he worked as the Head of the Media and Public Affairs Branch and subsequently the Government Relations and Political Affairs Branch.

Aruna Gopinath

Prof. Dr. Aruna Gopinath was born in Kuala Lumpur. She graduated from the University of Malaya with a B.A. degree in 1974 and the M.A. degree in 1978. She was selected to pursue Philippine Studies for her doctorate at the University of the Philippines, Diliman as an ASEAN Scholar. She graduated as a President Scholar in 1984. Her areas of expertise are in Philippine politics, Southeast Asian politics, Gender studies, Minority problems, peace processes and conflict resolution. She has conducted fieldwork in the rebel areas of South Philippines. For dangerous work undertaken in the Philippines, she was honored by the International American Biographical Board as one of the Great Women Leaders of the 21st Century in 2005 and has an entry in the Encyclopedia of Women Leaders. In 2011 she was selected Woman of the Year for Malaysia by the same Board for her contributions in various fields. In 2012, she was given the award, Ambassador for Peace by the Secretary General of the United Nations, Ban Ki-moon at the Universal Peace Federation for her activities in South Philippines in the field of conflict resolution.

Prof. Dr. Gopinath taught at the Department of History, University of Malaya since 1974 and retired in 2007 after a service of 32 years. She was the Head of the Department of Politics and International Relations at HELP University from 2007-2009 but was invited by the National Defense University of Malaysia to be a Senior Fellow and Consultant at the Center of Defense and Strategic Studies in 2009. Since then, she has been a resource person in the field of Strategic Studies for Southeast Asia.

In 1991, she was a Visiting Fellow at Cornell University, Ithaca and taught at both the American University and George Washington University as a Fulbright Scholar. She was the recipient of the prestigious British Chevenning Award in 1997 and was a Visiting Professor at SOAS, University of London; LSE; University of Oxford; University of Cambridge; University of Hull; University of Warwicks, Coventry. As a recipient of the Visiting Professor from the Australian National University, she also was a guest professor at the University of Auckland, Wellington and Christ church in 1986/1987.

In 2002 she was awarded the Southeast Asian Visiting Professor's grant to teach at the University of Hanoi, Vietnam. She served as a Visiting Professor at the Center of South and Southeast Asian Studies, University of Madras in 2003 and the University of Cairo, Egypt in 2006. She has presented a total of 250 papers at international conferences. She has published extensively and has written 6 books, 250 articles and 4 monographs. Prof. Dr. Gopinath is a resource person and consultant on Southeast Asian affairs with the Gordon Business School, South Africa and also teaches at the Defense College, Ministry of Defense, Kuala Lumpur. She has trained officers both local and foreign in Strategic Studies. Three of the local officers have served in the peace process in Mindanao. She has been an adviser on the Moro problem to the Philippine Army, the Moro leaders and the American think-tanks. Since February 2009, she has been appointed by the CSIS, Washington to be a member of the Obama research tea m on terrorism in Southeast Asia.

Prof. Dr. Gopinath believes in rendering her services to organizations geared towards the upliftment of education in this country. She is currently the President of the All Malaysia Malayalee Association (AMMA) Foundation and Director and Chairman, Education and Loans Division. She is the President of SHE (Saluting Her Endeavor), working and helping the children of prisoners and juveniles at Kajang prison. She was the Chairman of GOPIO (Global Organization of People of Indian Origin) Education and Cultural Bureau and was partly responsible in setting up the Indian Cultural Center in Malaysia with her constant visits to Delhi and initiating for the setting up of the Center till it was approved by the Indian government headed by Dr. Manmohan Singh. She is also an honorary President of Lions International and Vice President of Carelove—an organization that deals with abused women.

She also sits in several international educational foundations in India, Philippines and Sri Lanka and is a member of the Consultative Education Council for Indians set up by the Honorable Prime Minister, Dato Sri Najib bin Tun Abdul Razak.

She is a trained Indian classical dancer in Baratha natyam and Mohini Attam and speaks 9 languages. For Prof. Dr. Gopinath, dance, music and theatre is her religion.

Arvinder Lamba

Lt Gen Arvinder Singh Lamba, from the elite Parachute Artillery Regiment, retired as Vice Chief of Army Staff after more than four decades of service to the nation.

As Vice Chief of the Army Staff, the officer was responsible for Army level monitoring of the External and Internal security environment, Planning and preparation to meet the threat perceptions at the National and regional levels, by synergizing Military Operations, Military Intelligence, Operational Logistics and Perspective Planning towards Force Transformation and Strategic Postulations for overall readiness of the Army.

The General officer has vast exposures to engagements in Defence cooperation and Military Diplomacy, Strategic Leadership, International Relations, and Conflict prevention.

A veteran of the 1971 war in Bangladesh, he has participated in every major operation ever since, served in important command and staff appointments across most borders and in Insurgencies within the country as also Sri Lanka. He has commanded a front line Division and Strike Corps on the western sector, and headed the Army Training Command before assuming charge as Vice Chief of Army Staff

The General officer is a Ph.D., M.Phil. and MSc in Strategic and Defence Studies, MA in International Affairs from Kings College London, has attended the prestigious RCDS Course in UK, and an MBA in International Marketing.

He is presently engaged with various strategic Forums for Strategic and Defence reviews/analysis, important high level Track II dialogues, and dialogues with Indian and International organisations/bodies in pursuit of India's Foreign Policy and Security perspectives.

Baladas Ghoshal

Prof Baladas Ghoshal currently Secretary General Society for Indian Ocean Studies; until recently ICCR Chair in Indian Studies at the Russian State University for the Humanities, Moscow, is also honorary Distinguished Fellow at the Institute of Peace and Conflict Studies and a Visiting Senior Fellow in Centre for Policy Research. From August 2016, he is also a Visiting Professor of Public Policy in Amity University, Noida. Professor Ghoshal is a former Professor of Southeast Asia and South-West Pacific Studies and Chairman of the Centre for South and Southeast Asian Studies at Jawaharlal Nehru University, New Delhi.

Between 2004 and 2007, he was a Visiting Professor of International Relations first at the International Christian University, Tokyo and then at Nagoya City University, taught at the University of Illinois at Urbana-Champaign (1990-91) National University of Malaysia (1998-1999), University of Malaya (2000) and the Universitity Utara Malaysia (2002-2003). He has held Senior Fulbright Fellowships at the Cornell and Rutgers Universities (1983-84); Fellow at the Institute of Southeast Asian Studies, Singapore (1985-86); Centre for Asian Studies, University of Hong Kong (Sept.-Oct. 2003), East West Centre (2010), Consultant to the United Nations Support Facility for Indonesian Recovery (November 2003-February 2004). Professor Ghoshal is a doyen in Southeast Asian Studies programme in India.

He has published extensively on Indonesian politics, ASEAN and regional security issues, reads, writes and speaks Malay and Bahasa Indonesia. Also published on Indian and Bangladesh politics and foreign policy. His most recent publications are a book on India-Indonesia Relations published by the Institute of South Asian

Studies, Singapore, and a monograph on China's Perception of India's Look East Policy, brought out by Institute for Defence Studies and Analyses, New Delhi. His latest publication was an edited volume "The Indo-Pacific Axis," 2018.

Benudhar Patra

Dr. Benudhar Patra, an Associate Professor is presently teaching in the P.G. Department of History, Post Graduate Government College, Sector-11, Chandigarh (UT). Graduated from Utkal University, Odisha, Dr. Patra passed his M.A. in History from the P.G. Department of History, Berhampur University, Odisha securing first position with first division in 1990. He did his M.Phil and Ph.D in history from the same University and passed the NET examination conducted by the UGC. His field of specialization is Ancient Indian History, Culture and Archaeology. He has been teaching history for the last 27 years.

After serving for some years as a lecturer in history at Gopalpur College, Gopalpur-on-Sea, Odisha, Dr. Patra was selected as a lecturer by the UPSC and joined the Education Department, Chandigarh Ad ministration.

He has to his credit more than 120 research papers which are published in various journals of national and international repute and in some edited books. He is a member of more than a dozen Academic Societies and Professional Organizations. He has attended more than 75 national and international seminars and conferences and delivered many invited lectures. He also successfully organized various seminars and workshops.

He has completed two Research Projects sponsored by UGC. Two students have been awarded their M.Phil and Ph.D degrees under his supervision while 06 are pursuing their research for their Ph.D. degree His publications include Studies in the Heritage, History and Archaeology of Orissa (Kolkata, 2008), Dalits in Historical Perspective in North-Western India (ed.) (Delhi 2010), Maritime Trade and Overseas Activities of Early India: Odishan Perspective (New Delhi, 2013), New Horizons in History and Culture (ed.) (Delhi, 2015) and Early Maritime Contacts of Odisha with Indonesia and Sri Lanka (Delhi 2017). Besides Maritime History, his other fields of research are urban history, agrarian history, gender history, state formation, art history, historiography and the Cult of Jagannath. Presently he is deeply involved in research on the maritime and urban history of early Odisha.

Deepa G Wadhwa

Ambassador Deepa Gopalan Wadhwa, IFS (Retd.) joined the Indian Foreign Service in 1979 and retired in December 2015. Served as Ambassador of India to: Japan 2012-2015; Qatar: 2009-2012; Sweden: 2005-2009. She was concurrently accredited as Ambassador to Latvia from Stockholm, and the Republic of the Marshall Islands from Tokyo.

Other significant assignments abroad have been: Geneva (1989-1992); Hong Kong and China (1981-1987), (1992-1994); The Netherlands (1994-1998).

Between postings abroad, also served in the Ministry of External Affairs, New Delhi as Desk Officer for Pakistan and Joint Secretary responsible for Indian relations with the United Nations and its agencies, including development related programmes of UNICEF, ILO, UNDP, WHO etc. in India.

Indian Council for Cultural Relations, Deputy Director General responsible for the projection of India's soft power through cultural diplomacy. International Labour Organization as head of the International Programme for the Elimination of Child Labour in India.

In the course of a career spanning over 36 years, handled a wideswathe of issues and subjects related to India's diplomatic practice and strategic policies, vis-a-vis, key countries such as Pakistan, China and Japan; participated in international conferences and negotiations related to climate change, sustainable development, disarmament and human rights; was instrumental in the active promotion of Indian economic interests in the areas of trade, technology, investments and energy security during postings in Europe, the GCC and Japan.

Other interests include reading, travelling and social work.

Dhruv Jaishankar

Mr Dhruva Jaishankar is Fellow in Foreign Policy Studies at Brookings India in New Delhi and the Brookings Institution in Washington DC. He is also a regular contributor to the Indian and international media on global affairs and security. Jaishankar was previously a Transatlantic Fellow and program officer with the German Marshall Fund (GMF) in Washington DC, a research assistant at Brookings, and a reporter for CNN-IBN television. He has also been a Visiting Fellow with the Rajaratnam School of International Studies, an IISS-SAIS Merrill Center Young Strategist, and a David Rockefeller Fellow with the Trilateral Commission. Jaishankar has a

B.A. in history and classics from Macalester College and an M.A. in security studies from Georgetown University.

Govind Pukharel

Over 20 years of professional experience in public policy, international development and academia, most recently as CEO of Reconstruction Authority (Ranked at Par with Cabinet Minister) and as Vice Chairman of the National Planning Commission (ranked at par with Minister of State), professor of industrial and mechanical engineering, and executive director of a large public institution for the promotion of renewable energy.

Expertise

Development policy, planning and strategy Energy, climate change, disaster management infrastructure, micro finance, rural development Science, technology and engineering

Experience and credentials

PhD in energy economics and policy; M.Sc. in Appropriate Rural Energy Technology and Extension Skills; and BE in Mechanical Engineering.

As Vice Chairman of the National Planning Commission, led the Government of Nepal's apex policy advisory body to guide annual and periodic development plans and programs, budgets, and sectoral policy reforms.

In the aftermath of the Great Nepal Earthquake of 2015, led a post earthquake recovery package and a rigorous Post-Disaster Needs Assessment (PDNA) and helped generate over US$4 billion in pledges from international development partners.

Served as Executive Director for two terms of the Alternative Energy Promotion Centre (AEPC), a national nodal agency for renewable energy and energy efficiency for about 5 years.

Authored or co-authored numerous research papers on sustainable energy, climate change, technical aspects of renewable energy technologies, and financing among others.

Served internationally as Manager of SNV Netherlands Development Organization across South and Southeast Asian locations.

Led numerous short-term assignments and projects, including the design and delivery of technical assistance to ministries, external development partners, civil society, public and private sector institutions.

Ran high-profile, technically-oriented international programs and projects (supported by EU, DFID, Ktw, ADB, World Bank, UNDP, Danida, Norad and others).

Highly versatile facilitator and hands-on mentor of teams in academia and civil society on social causes, public-private partnership and emergency response.

Adept at defining strategic direction that incorporates a rights based approach, community driven development, and good governance.

Mature and tactful in managing multi-task operations in complex and challenging conflict-ridden environments; skilled in effective communication, negotiation and decision-making with particular expertise in developing and maintaining relationships with high level political leadership, government officials and development partners.

Excellent knowledge of grassroots development activities and movements; widely networked nationally and internationally.

Harsh V Pant

Professor Harsh V Pant is Distinguished Fellow and Head of Strategic Studies at Observer Research Foundation, New Delhi. holds a joint appointment as Professor of International Relations in Defence Studies Department and the India Institute at King's College London. He is also a Non-Resident Fellow with the Wadhwani Chair in US-India Policy Studies at the Center for Strategic and International Studies, Washington, DC. He has been a Visiting Professor at the Indian Institute of Management, Bangalore; a Visiting Fellow at the Center for the Advanced Study of India, University of Pennsylvania; a Visiting Scholar at the Center for International Peace and Security Studies, McGill University; and an Emerging Leaders Fellow at the Australia-India Institute, University of Melbourne. His current research is focused on Asian security issues. His most recent books include The US Pivot and Indian Foreign Policy (Palgrave Macmillan), Hand book of Indian Defence Policy (Routledge), and The US-India Nuclear Pact Policy, Process and Great Power Politics (Oxford University Press). Pant is a columnist for the Diplomat and writes regularly for various media outlets including the Japan Times, the Wall Street Journal, the National (UAE), and the Indian Express.

Jatin Das

Mr Jatin Das is a Contemporary Indian artist.

Held more than 70 One Man Shows, participated in group exhibitions in India and Overseas.

Participated in Paris Biennale, 1971, Venice Biennale, 1978 and India Triennale, 1971, 1976 and 1978. Executed many murals and sculptures.

Padma Bhushan by the President of India, 2012.

Italian President Award, Star of Italian Solidarity, 2007. Conferred three D'Litt. (Honoris Causa)

Setup the JD Centre of Art in Bhubaneswar, Odisha, 1997.

One of the largest world class collection of Hand Fans (Pankha), will be donated to the proposed National Pankha Museum in Delhi.

Been a professor of art and a poet. Studied at Sir JJ School of Art, Bombay. Born in 1941, Mayurbhanj, Odisha.

Jayanath Colombage

Admiral (Dr.) Jayanath Colombage is a former chief of Sri Lanka navy who retired after an active service of 37 years as a four-star Admiral. He is a highly decorated officer for gallantry and distinguished service. He is a graduate of Defence Services Staff College in India and Royal College of Defence Studies, UK. He holds a PhD from General Sir John Kotelawala Defence University. He also holds M.Sc. on defence and strategic studies from Madras university and MA on International Studies from Kings college, London. He is a maritime security practitioner/specialist with wide experiences in countering maritime terrorism. He is a visiting lecturer at the University of Colombo, Defence Services Command and Staff College (Sri Lanka), Kotelawala Defence University, Bandran alike Center for International Studies and Bandaranaike International Diplomatic Training Institute. He was the former Chairman of Sri Lanka Shipping Corporation and an adviser to the President of Sri Lanka on maritime affairs. He is a Fellow of Nautical Institute, London U K. Admiral Colombage is currently the Director of the Centre for India-Lanka Initiatives of the Pathfinder Foundation. He is also a member of the Advisory council of the 'Institute of National Security Studies Sri Lanka'. He is a Guest Professor at Sichuan University in China.

Kenko Sone

Minister (Economic & Development), Embassy of Japan.

Le Van Toan

Prof Le Van Toan is Founder Director of Centre for Indian Studies, Ho Chi Minh Academy of Politics, Ha no He is Chairman of the Scientific Committee of the Centre for Indian Studies

Academic distinction: Doctor, Senior Lecturer

Major: Medieval Vietnamese literature, Chinese literature, Southeast Asian culture, Indian studies and Chinese studies.

Foreign language: Chinese (fluently in writing and speaking) Major publications: 117

Articles: more than 70 articles Books (author and co-author): 47 and others publications, such as: textbook, Academic paper in scientific conference.

Lopamudra Mitra Bajpai

Dr. Lopamudra Maitra Bajpai is a Visual Anthropologist with an experience of nearly two decades of research in Intangible Cultural Heritage, History and Popular Culture and ethnographic explorations of India, Sri Lanka and South Asia. She completed her undergraduate studies in History (Honours) from Presidency College, Kolkata with a first class and completed two M.A. degrees-from Deccan College Post-graduate and Research Institute, Pune in Ancient Indian History, Culture and Archaeology with a first class and the second one from Symbiosis International University (Deemed) in Media and Communication with a first class and honours. She completed her PhD from University of Calcutta Department of Archaeology and her topic for the same was "The continuity of folk art and religious tradition in fringe Bengal: An aid to understanding the ethnoarchaeology of the region"—with a focus on ethnoarchaeology, folk culture and communication of western part of rural Bengal. She is at present a Research Grant Fellow of India-Sri Lanka Foundation ofThe Indian High Commission in Sri Lanka. She is Former Culture Specialist (Research)—SAARC Cultural Centre, Colombo (Sri Lanka) .

She is also Former Assistant Professor—Symbiosis International University, Pune. She continues to be a Visiting Professor at various universities across India including—FLAME International University, MIT International University, University of Pune, West Bengal State University, Wigan and Leigh College,

International School of Business and Media (ISBM) and Sri Lanka—including—University of Kelaniya, University of Colombo and Eastern University.

She has been awarded with several national and international grants and awards, including—2016—Grant of IIAS (International Institute of Asian Studies)—Netherlands for international conference at Kathmandu to speak on India's Intangible Cultural Heritage, 2014—award of Official Nominee of Government of India to represent her research at the SAARC Cultural Centre conference, Colombo (Sri Lanka), 2006—ICHR (Indian Council of Historical Research) Junior Research Fellowship for PhD, 2003—Lokmanya Tilak Trophy and Pune Mayor's Trophy for 1st ranker at Symbiosis International University (Deemed), 2001—Symbiosis International University (Deemed) Merit Scholar Grant, 1999—UGC (University Grants Commission) award for M.A. She has several international publications (books and journals) on history, Intangible Cultural Heritage and Popular Culture to her credit. She has been writing about the same as a correspondent in several Indian & International English dailies/Magazines.

Mustafizur Rahman

Professor Mustafizu r Rahman is an economist by training. He is currently serving as Distinguished Fellow, Centre for Policy Dialogue (CPD), Dhaka, Bangladesh, prior to which he served as CPD's Executive Director for ten years. Earlier Dr Rahman had taught at the University of Dhaka for twenty-five years where he was member of the Dhaka University Senate. Professor Rahman was a Visiting Post doctoral Fellow at Oxford University and Warwick University, UK and a Senior Fulbright Fellow at Yale University, USA. His recent research focus has been on Bangladesh's macroeconomic performance, regional cooperation and economic integration in South Asia, trade policy and external sector performance, WTO negotiations and interests of the LDCs, graduation of LDCs and Sustainable Development Goals. He has published widely in Bangladesh and abroad. Professor Rahman has served as a member of various national bodies set up by the Government of Bangladesh including Free Trade Agreement Committee, Core Committee on Connectivity, Regulatory Reforms Commission, National Coal Policy Review Committee and WTO Advisory Committee. Professor Rahman was a member of the Panel of Economists for the Sixth and the on-going Seventh Five Yea r Plans of Bangladesh.

Naing Swe Oo

Dr Naing Swe Oo is a graduate of the Myanmar Defence Services Medical Academy. He secured Diploma in Political Studies from Yangon University, Fellowship in Hepatology (Moscow) from Moscow State University, Diploma in Genetic Medicine (Moscow) from Moscow State University and Certificate in Diving Medicine (Malaysia). He also holds an M BA and doing PhD in business management from Aldersgate College, Philippines.

Neelam Deo

Ambassador Neelam Deo has served as the Indian Ambassador to Denmark and Ivory Coast with concurrent accreditation to Niger, Guinea, and Sierra Leone. She has also served in the Indian embassies in Rome, Bangkok and Washington D.C., where she liaised with the U.S. Congress, the State Department, and the National Security Council on strategic issues. Her last assignment was as Consul General in New York from 2005 to 2008. During the course of her assignments in the Ministry of External Affairs, she held the position of Joint Secretary for the divisions dealing with Bangladesh, Sri Lanka, Myanmar and the Maldives. At different times over the course of her career, she has dealt with Bhutan, South East Asia and the Pacific, as well as countries in West Asia and North Africa. She is an invited speaker on strategic issues and India-U.S. relations at numerous think tanks and universities, in India, Europe and the United States. Apart from her articles and commentaries written exclusively for Gateway House, Neelam occasionally writes for mainstream publications, and is a frequent commentator for television news channels. She has a Master's degree from the Delhi School of Economics and serves on the Editorial Advisory Board of the Indian Foreign Affairs Journal. She is also a member of the boa rd of Oxfam India and is a trustee of Breakthrough (a human rights organization). She is an independent director on the boards of Mahindra CIE Automotive Limited, Mahindra Defence Land Systems, and Mahindra Logistics.

Palitha Kohona

Dr Palitha Kohona is MD, Hairong Investments International Pvt Ltd (Sri Lanka).

Dr Palitha Kohona, a Sri Lankan born diplomat, was the former Permanent Representative of Sri Lanka to the United Nations (UN). Until August 2009 he was the Permanent Secretary to the Ministry of Foreign Affairs of Sri Lanka and was also the former Secretary-General of the Secretariat for Coordinating the Peace Process. He was also a member of the Government delegation at the talks held in February and October 2006 Geneva, Switzerland with the LTTE. He led the Government delegation to Oslo for talks with the LTTE. He is a citizen of both Sri Lanka and Australia. He is now the MD of Hirong Investments International, Sri Lanka, and a Member of the Board of SIBA, Kandy.

Early life and education Dr Kohona, who hails from Matale, received his secondary education in Sri Lanka at S. Thomas College, Mount Lavinia. He obtained a LLB (Hons) at the University of Sri Lanka, a LLM from the Australian National University on International Trade Law and a Doctorate from Cambridge University, UK, for the thesis 'The Regulation of International Trade through Law,' subsequently published by Kluwer, Netherlands. He is also an Attorney-at-Law, Supreme Court of Sri Lanka. He is a Honorary Professor at Utah Valley University, USA.

Diplomatic career Dr Kohona was the Secretary, Ministry of Foreign Affairs of Sri Lanka from 2006 to 2009. Ambassador Kahana was the Permanent Representative of Sri Lanka to the United Nations in New York from 2009 to 2015. During this period he was elected as the Chair of the UN GA Sixth Committee (Legal) in 2013. He was the Co Chair of the UN Working Group on Biological Diversity Beyond National Jurisdiction, Chair of the UN Committee on Israeli Practices in the Occupied Arab Territories, the Chair of the Indian Ocean Committee and the Vice President of the UNCLOS Regular Process. He was a member of the delegation to the UN General Assembly in 2006 and 2008. He has led official level delegations to a range of countries on bilateral and multilateral matters. Previously he was the Secretary-General of the Government Peace Secretariat (2006) during which time he participated in two rounds of peace negotiations with the LTTE in Geneva and led the delegation to a round in Oslo. Prior to that he was the Chief of the United Nations Treaty Section in New York from 1995 to 2006. He worked closely with ESCAP in developing the Euro-Asian road and rail treaties. At the UN he was responsible for introducing major managerial innovations and was awarded the UN 21 PIN for superior performance and efficiency. He managed the computerisation of the UN treaty database which contains over one million pages of information and which now receives over 1.5 million hits per month from around the world. The UN treaty collection consists of over 50,000 bilateral treaties registered with the UN Secretariat and over 500 multilateral treaties deposited with the UN Secretary General covering the spectrum of international interaction. The hand books pertaining to the treaty practice of the Secretary-General were prepared under his guidance. He also initiated the UN treaty training programme as part of an outreach programme for familiarising countries with the UN treaty collection. He also initiated the UN Treaty Event, now held during the General Assembly, which has become a regular feature of the UN calendar. Given his proactive approach to UN reform, he was assigned to the results based budgeting spearhead group and to a range of other groups working on Secretariat reform. He was the leader of the UN legal delegation to North Korea at the invitation of the DPRK Government, in 2005.

Prior to joining the UN, Dr Kohona was with the Department of Foreign Affairs and Trade of Australia. His last position there was as head of the Trade and Investment Section of the Department. Previously he was assigned to the Uruguay Round negotiating tea m of Australia with specific responsibility for the institutional mechanism and the dispute settlement unit. In 1989 he was posted to the Australian Permanent Mission in Geneva with specific responsibility for environmental issues. In Geneva he chaired the negotiating group that developed the compliance mechanism under the Montreal Protocol to the Convention on the Ozone Layer and was a member of the Working Group on the liability mechanism under the Basel Convention on Hazardous Wastes. In 1988, Dr. Kohona led the Australian delegation to the UNCTAD Trade and Development Board.

He returned to Sri Lanka on the invitation of President Mahinda Rajapakse and served as the Secretary General of the Secretariat for Coordinating the Peace Process (SCOPP) from April 2006 until January 2007.

Philip Kuntjoro Widjaja

Prof. Dr. Philip Kuntjoro Widjaja Surabaya holds current positions at various organizations:

Centra l Boa rd of PSMTI—Indonesian Chinese Clan Society Federation, as Vice Chairman for Institutional Relations Affairs.

Central Board of LIT—Institute of Indonesian China for Cultural Economy, as Vice Chairman of Board of Supervisors.

Central Board of Mapanbumi—Pandita Council of Buddha Maitreya Indonesia as Chairman for Department of organization.

Central Boa rd of IARC—The Indonesian Association for Religion and Culture, as Secretary General.

Central Boa rd of Walubi—Indonesian Buddhists Association as Council of International Relations.

East Java Boa rd of Walubi—Indonesian Buddhists Association as Chairman.

National Board of PIM—Movement for Great Indonesia, as Vice Chairman.

Central Boa rd of IRC— Inter Religious Council of Indonesia as Chair of Presedium Board.

IBC—International Buddhist Confederation, as Global Outreach committee member.

ACRP—Asian Conference of Religions for Peace, as Executive Committee and Governing Boa rd.

WCRP—World Conference of Religions for Peace, as Indonesia Chapter.

Ma Chung University, as Skate Holder, Director and Head of the supervisory board.

USIN DO—US Indonesia Council on Religion and pluralism, as Executive Committee of Indonesia Chapter.

Lecture at some State and Private Universities for Management, Cultures, Religions, Interfaith, Politic and National Defense.

Share Holder/Commissioner for several companies, i.e.: Chemicals and Pharmaceutical Industries.

Pinak Ranjan Chakravarty

Ambassador Pinak Ranjan Chakravarty joined the Indian Foreign Service in 1977, after a brief stint in the State Bank of India as a Probationary Officer. He holds a Masters Degree from Delhi University in Physics and Astrophysics. He has served in Indian Diplomatic Missions in Cairo, Jeddah, and London. He was Consul General of India in Karachi from 1994-1995; [he was declared persona non-grata and the Consulate was closed by the Pakistan Government]. He also served as

Counsellor/Minister, DCM at the Indian Embassy in Tel Aviv from 1995 to 1999 and Deputy High Commissioner at Dhaka from 1999 to 2002.

At the Ministry of External Affairs (MEA), he served as Deputy Chief of Protocol, Deputy Secretary/Director in the Americas Division and Deputy Coordinator, SMRC Summit Secretariat, 1995. He was the Chief of Protocol from 2002 to 2006 after which he was nominated as Ambassador to the Philippines but later shifted to Bangladesh, where he served as High Commissioner from 2007 to 2009. From 2010-2011 he served as Ambassador to Thailand.

He was Special Secretary (Public Diplomacy) before he was appointed Secretary (Economic Relations) in MEA. He retired from service in September, 2013.

Currently, he is a Distinguished Fellow at the Observer Research Foundation, one of India's leading think-tanks, where he supervises the West Asia Programme, Bangladesh affairs and ASEAN-related issues.

During his career in the Indian Foreign Service, he has dealt with a wide range of Political, Trade, Economic, Press, Information, Cultural and Consular issues. As High Commissioner to Bangladesh, he was instrumental in pursuing the Grid Connectivity agreement which has led to transfer/sale of Power to Bangladesh. He also drafted the initial concept proposal for the Land Boundary Agreement which solved the un-demarcated border, Enclaves and Adverse possessions.

As Ambassador to Thailand, he coordinated negotiations for setting up the framework for establishment of the BIMSTEC Secretariat, negotiations on FTA, Civil Aviation Agreement and other bilateral agreements.

He has negotiated, inter alia, nuclear and IPR issues with the USA du ring his stint as Director [Americas] in MEA. When posted in Israel, he handled India's crucial defence ties which led to acquisitions of sensitive technologies and hardware.

As Secretary [Economic Relations] in MEA, he coordinated Trade, Economic, Investment related negotiations with various countries. He was the Sherpa for BRICS negotiations and supervised India's Lines of Credit to various countries. He was a Member of the Board of Directors of the EXIM Bank in his capacity as Secretary [Economic Relations] in MEA.

Amb Chakravarty is regular contributor to newspapers and publications on international issues and India's foreign policy. He has published over 115 articles which include book chapters and reviews. He lectures on foreign policy at various institutions in India and abroad. Born in Lucknow, Uttar Pradesh in India, he spent his schooling years in Dehra Dun, thereafter obtaining a post-graduate degree in Physics and Astrophysics from the University of Delhi. He speaks Hind Bengali, English and Arabic.

PK Singh

Lt Gen PK Singh was commissioned as a 2/Lt in the Indian Army in 1967 and retired as an Army Commander (C-in-C) in 2008. His academic qualifications include MSc; M Phil and Post-graduate Diploma in Business Management. He commanded a Brigade in Nagaland/Manipur, an Infantry Division (RAPID)' during Op Parakram, a Corps in Punjab and the South Western Command.

He took over as Director of the United Service Institution of India in January 2009. He is a member of the Governing Council of the Indian Council of World Affairs, New Delhi, and also member of the International Advisory Board of the RUSI International London.

His articles/chapters have been published in the "Oxford Hand book of United Nations Peacekeeping Operations", 2015; in the Bureau of the Asian Research, USA, "Asia Policy No. 19—January 2015"; in the book "The China-India Nuclear Crossroads" published by Carnegie Tsinghu Center for Global Policy 2012; in "Global Security: The Growing Challenges" by the Center for Strategic Decision Research, USA, 2010; and in "Global Security: The Risks of Strategic Surprise" by the Center for Strategic Decision Research, USA, 2011-12.

His monograph, "Afghanistan Beyond 2014: From Rhetoric to Reality, An Indian Perspective", was published in 2014, "Peacebuilding Through Development Partnership: An Indian Perspective" in 2016 and "China-Pakistan Economic Corridor (CPEC): Connecting the Dots" in 2017. He has co-edited four books, "Comprehensive National Power—A Model for India"; "Civilian Capacity Building for Peace Operations"; and "USI Strategic Yearbook 2016 and 2017."

Prabhat Singh

Mr Prabhat Singh is MD & CEO, Petronet LNG Ltd. since September, 2015. He is an Engineering graduate from IIT, Kanpur, and having around 36 years of relevant experience in the Hydrocarbon Industry both in MNC (British Gas) and Maharatna PSUs (GAIL, NTPC, EII) etc. He is a vastly experienced professional having worked his way up in diverse areas including Project Planning, Execution & Management, Exploration & Production, Training & Organizational Reforms and Business Development Marketing.

Mr Singh has been Director of Marketing of GAIL (India) Limited and also served as (i) Chairman of Ratnagiri Gas and Power Private Limited (RGPPL) erstwhile Dabhol Power Company and during his tenure has commissioned the 5 MMTPA LNG regasification terminal at Dabhol and (ii) Chairman of GAIL Global Singapore Pte Ltd. (GGSPL)—a global trading arm of GAIL at Singapore, which is currently creating value & managing India's pioneering efforts towards global LNG business. Mr Singh has been instrumental in putting the country on the world gas map, India being one of the first countries to have sourced LNG (based on Henry Hub) from the US. His major contribution has been the execution of world's longest exclusive LPG pipeline from Jamnagar to Loni. The project was recognized by Asian Development Bank as the "Best Managed Project" of the year. He was also instrumental in ushering in the "Open Access Common Carrier

Principle" in India. Prabhat is one of the core contributors to the concept of gas pooling for power & fertilizer sector which is under successful implementation. Mr Singh is instrumental for successful negotiations in the various International Contracts.

Mr Singh has also been a member of National Auto Fuel Policy of MoPNG & member of the Governing body of Rajeev Gandhi Institute of Petroleum and Technology, Raibarely. IIT, Kanpur honoured him with Distinguished Alumnus Award in November, 2016 for his professional excellence. Times Ascent presented him a CEO with HR Orientation Award in February, 2017. Today, He is recognized as a visionary professional in the Industry for having a great business sense with a human touch & excellent communication skill.

Prabir De

Dr. Prabir De is a Professor at the Research and Information System for Developing Countries (RIS), New Delhi. He is also the Head of ASEAN-India Centre (AIC), RIS. Dr De works in the field of international economics and has research interests in international trade and development. He was a Visiting Fellow of the Institute of Developing Economies (IDE-JETRO), China; Asian Development Bank Institute (ADBI), Tokyo; and Visiting Senior Fellow of United Nations Economic and Social Commission for Asia and the Pacific (UN ESCAP), Bangkok.

Dr. De has been conducting policy research for the Government of India and several national and international organisations. Dr. De has a Ph.D. in Economics from the Jadavpur University, Kolkata, India. He has contributed several research papers in international journals and written books on trade and development. His recent publication includes "Myanmar's Integration with the World: Challenges and Policy Options" (Palgrave Macmillan, 2017). He is also the Editor of South Asia Economic Journal, published by Sage.

PS Sahai

Ambassdor Pramjit Sahai is Post-graduate in Political Science from the Panjab University, Chandigarh Campus in 1961; Worked as Research Fellow, Public Administration Department and Part-time Lecturer at PU Evening College during 1961-62. Joined Indian Foreign Service in 1963. Du ring a span of 37 years of service, was posted to diplomatic missions at Moscow, Washington DC, Singapore, Lusaka, Lilongwe, Aden, Stockholm and Kuala Lumpur. Had worked as Under Secretary in the Ministry of Foreign Trade, New Delhi and Minister (Commerce) and Director General (Supplies) at the Embassy of India, Washington DC. Served as India's Ambassador/High Commissioner to Malawi, Lesotho, Yemen, Sweden, Latvia and Malaysia. Since Superannuation in 2000 has been academically involved in the study of India's relations with South, Southeast and Central Asian countries, and in the areas of Cultural, Consular, Diaspora, Economic and Public Diplomacy.

Presently, Faculty Member, Diplo Foundation, Malta and Principal Advisor, CRRID, Chandigarh. Has edited a number of Books and contributed articles for other books.

Rajat Nag

Dr Rajat M. Nag is concurrently a Distinguished Fellow at National Council of Applied Economic Research, Delhi and Emerging Markets Forum, Washington DC. He is a Distinguished Professor at Beijing Normal University, China and serves as Chair, Act East Council of the Indian Chamber of Commerce. He is also on the Boards of several organizations.

Dr Nag was the Managing Director General of the Asian Development Bank (ADB) during 2006-2013.

Dr Nag's keen interest is in working to enhance regional cooperation in Asia and bridging the gap between the region's rich and the poor.

He holds engineering degrees from IIT, Delhi and the University of Saskatchewan, Canada. He also has a MBA from the University of Saskatchewan and an M.Sc (Econ) from the London School of Economics.

Dr Nag was awarded Doctor of Laws (Honor is Causa) by the University of Saskatchewan, Canada in May, 2016.

Rajiv Bhatia

Ambassador Rajiv Bhatia IFS (retd.) is Distinguished Fellow, Gateway House. He is a leading member and supporter of Kalinga International Foundation (KIF). He is Chair of FICCI's Core Group of Experts on BIMSTEC as well as Chair of FICCI's Task Force on Blue Economy.

As Director General of the Indian Council of World Affairs from 2012-15, he played a key role in strengthening India's Track-II research and outreach activities. He is a former ambassador/high commissioner to Myanmar, Mexico, Kenya and South Africa. He served as Consul General in Toronto, Canada. As Joint Secretary in Ministry of External Affairs, he managed India's relations with Bangladesh, Sri Lanka, Myanmar and Maldives.

A prolific columnist, he regularly contributes research articles to a variety of publications—on South Asia, Southeast Asia, Africa and the Indian foreign policy. Mr. Bhatia was Senior Visiting Research Fellow du ring 2011-13 at the Institute of Southeast Asian Studies, Singapore. He holds a Masters degree in political science from Allahabad University.

His book India-Myanmar Relations: Changing contours (Routledge 2016) received critical acclaim.

Rizal Abdul Kadir

Dr Rizal Abdul Kadir, is Deputy Director-General Maritime Institute of Malaysia. Dr Rizal started his career in the oil and gas industry, before moving into legal private practice, and subsequently worked within the government sector as a Research Fellow with the Maritime Institute of Malaysia. Dr Rizal graduated in 1992. He has since also qualified as a Lincoln's Inn Barrister-at-Law of England & Wales, Advocate & Solicitor of the High Court of Malaya, and as an Associate of the Chartered Institute of Arbitrators, UK. He holds advanced degrees in Public International Law and International Relations. His doctorate from the University of Sydney, Australia researched overlapping maritime claims and produced a thesis entitled Joint Development and the Law of the Sea. Dr Rizal remains actively involved in research, in addition to his present function as Deputy Director-General of the Maritime Institute of Malaysia. He currently researches, writes, and speaks on issue areas in the Law of the Sea, Public International Law, and International Relations.

RK Dhowan

Admiral RK Dhowan is an alumnus of the National Defence Academy, the Defence Services Staff College and the Naval War College, Newport, Rhode Island, USA.

His illustrious career began with being adjudged the 'Best Cadet' and winning of the coveted 'Telescope' du ring his sea training onboard INS Delhi. He was commissioned in the Navy on 01 Jan 75 and went on to bag the 'Sword of Honour' for his course. He was baptised in the art of navigation when, as a young Lieutenant armed with a sextant and the keen eyes of an enthusiastic navigator, he sailed from the port of Riga in the Baltic Sea to the shores of Mumbai. With the induction of the Sea Harrier jump-jets into the Navy, he was selected to undergo the Sea Harrier Direction Course at Yeovilton, UK. His tenures at Indian Naval Air Squadron 300 and the aircraft carrier Vikrant shaped the future of direction specialisation in the Navy.

Important staff assignments held by the Admiral at Naval Headquarters du ring his distinguished career include Deputy Director Naval Operations, Joint Director Naval Plans, Assistant Chief of the Naval Staff (Policy and Plans) and Deputy Chief of Naval Staff.

The Admiral has commanded three frontline warships of the Western Fleet—the missile corvette Khukri, the guided missile destroyer Ranjit and the indigenous guided missile destroyer Delhi. He also had the proud privilege of commanding the Eastern Fleet as Flag Officer Commanding Eastern Fleet.

Besides serving as Indian Naval Advisor at the High Commission of India, London, he has also served as Chief Staff Officer (Operations) of the Western Naval Command (based at Mumbai) and the Chief of Staff at Head quarters Eastern Naval Command (based at Visakhapatnam) and subsequently had the distinction of commanding his almamater, the National Defence Academy, as the Commandant. The Admiral assumed charge as the Vice Chief of the Naval Staff in Aug 11 and was subsequently promoted as the 22nd Chief of the Naval Staff of the Indian Navy on 17 Apr 14. He retired from the Navy on 31 May 2016 after a distinguished career of 42 years in uniform.

On 25 Nov 16, Admiral RK Dhowan (Retd) took over as the fifth Chairman of the National Maritime Foundation (NMF), New Delhi, which is India's premier maritime think tank. The Foundation has benefited immensely from his vast experience in the Indian Navy in general and in specific, formulation of a wide range of maritime strategic publications such as IIN Maritime Cooperation Road map (2014), IN Space Vision (2014), Indian Navy in the 21st Century: Maritime Security for National Prosperity (2014), IN Maritime Capability Perspective Plan (2015), IN Maritime Infrastructure Perspective Plan (2015), IN Indigenisation Plan (2015), Science and Technology Road map (2015), Ensuring Secure Seas: Indian Maritime Security Strategy (2015), Indian Maritime Doctrine (updated 2015), Maritime Heritage of India (2016) and United Through Oceans: International Fleet Review 2016. In his new role as both the practitioner and promoter of broader maritime thinking and fresh strategic perspectives, the Admiral has been lecturing extensively at all leading military colleges, think-tanks and academia in India, as well as at various apex-level institutions abroad, articulating his views on how the maritime strategic landscape has been changing in the world and the leading role India as a resurgent maritime nation would play in the Indo-Pacific region. Under his visionary articulation, the National Maritime Foundation is presently embarked on the mission for the development of strategies for the promotion and protection of India's maritime interests, harnessing the 'Blue Economy' and their advocacy to all stake-holders, both governmental and non-governmental.

S.D. Muni

Professor S.D. Muni is Professor Emeritus at the School of International Studies Jawaharlal Nehru University New Delhi and Distinguished Fellow (Hon.) at the Institute for Defence Studies and Analyses, New Delhi. For nearly forty years, he taught, conducted and supervised research, in International Relations and South Asian Studies at Jawaharlal Nehru University (1974-2006), National University of Singapore (2008-2013), Banaras Hindu University (1985-86), and University of Rajasthan (1972-73). He served as India's Special Envoy to SE Asian countries on UNSC Reforms (2005) and represented India's Minister of External Affairs at the 50th Anniversary celebrations of the Paris Peace Conference, held in Phnom Penh, Kam puchea. He also served as India's Ambassador to Lao People's Democratic Republic (1997-99). Prof. Muni was nominated to the first ever constituted National Security Advisory Boa rd of India du ring 1990-91. He was the founding Executive Member of the Regional Centre of Strategic Studies, Colombo, Sri Lanka, and also served on the Executive Council of the Institute for Defence Studies and Ana lyses (IDSA), New Delhi, India. In 2005 he was bestowed with 'Sri Lanka

Ratna', Sri Lanka's highest national honor for a foreign national. The Institute of National Security Studies Sri Lanka, Colombo, offered him affiliation as Honorary Distinguished Fellow in 2016.

At the Jawaharlal Nehru University, he held the prestigious Appadorai Chair of International Politics and Area Studies, and was Chairman of the Centre of South, SE and Central Asian Studies in the School of International Studies. In October 2014, he also received the "Life Time Achievement Award" from Shri Venkateshwara University, Tirupati, A.P., and was also honoured by Delhi University, Delhi, in March 2017, for his contribution to India-Nepal Relations. He has been sitting on selection committees for appointment of Vice-Chancellors and Faculty members in various Universities. He was invited to address the UN Special Committee on Indian Ocean as a Zone of Peace at Soch then as part of the Soviet Union, in 1985. Author and editor of nearly thirty books & monographs and more than 200 research papers, Prof. Muni was also the founder editor of two prestigious quarterly Journals in India, The South Asia Journal (Subsequently renamed as South Asian Survey launched by Indian Council for South Asian Cooperation), and Indian Foreign Affairs Journal (For Association of Indian Diplomats). Prof. Muni has travelled extensively.

Sabyasachi Dutta

Mr Sabyasachi Dutta is founder Director of the Asian Confluence, India East Asia, Center headquartered at Shillong, Meghalaya in North East India. The "Asian Confluence", is a pan regional initiative to promote an open space for cultural and intellectual exchanges towards creating better understanding of the Eastern and North Eastern region of India in the larger context of India as an emerging power in South East and East Asian geopolitics. Through research, training and advocacy programs, the Asian Confluence provides an opportunity for civil society to enhance people to people contact between India and her neighbours and also encourage a better understanding of the cultural and socio-political issues of the region that actually are the driving force behind India's "Act East Policy". At the heart of the project are initiatives that encourage people to people exchange such as, promoting research and interest in the region through educational tourism, cultural tourism, creation of "out of the box" livelihood generation by promoting leadership and entrepreneurship programs, eco-friendly products and services and impetus to green industries aimed at economic development by forging a network of civil society organizations working on similar objectives. Sabyasachi continues to facilitate cultural programs, exchange programs, talks, discussions and symposia with scholars and leaders of culture and thought, from India and abroad and The Asian Confluence has established itself as a premier organization in the North East with several successful initiatives to its credit such as the "Intelligent Third Space", the NADI Asian Confluence River Festival and the Young Scholars Forum.

Sabyasachi brings a unique combination a experiences to push this initiative: A deep and insightful stint of rural development in the North East and Eastern India where he set up a chain of 80 primary schools using the model of community participation propelled by youth leadership; A successful career spanning 12 years in the Silicon Valley, California USA in cutting edge technology, innovation and entrepreneurship, having held important positions in large corporations such as SONY Corp as well as successful startups, and he hold several patents; He is a long time avid student of Indian Culture, Philosophy and Public policy and International relations.

Shankari Sundararaman

Professor Shankari Sundararaman is Professor of Southeast Asian Studies and currently Chairperson at the Centre for India-Pacific Studies, School of International Studies, Jawaharlal Nehru University. She joined the Jawaharlal Nehru University in 2003. Prior to this she worked as a Research Officer and Research Fellow at the Institute for Defence Studies and Analyses (IDSA) from 1997 to 2003. She was a Visiting Fellow at the Asia-Pacific College of Diplomacy (APCD) at the Australian National University (ANU), Canberra from May to July 2005, where she worked on the trilateral relations between India, Indonesia and Australia. She was also a Visiting Fellow at the Centre for Strategic and International Studies (CSIS), Jakarta in 2006-2007. She is the author of several journal articles, chapters in books as well as a book titled Cambodia: The Lost Decades.

Shreerupa Mitra

Shreerupa Mitra writes on UN affairs, human rights, health, humanitarian aid, World Trade Organisation, oil politics and energy diplomacy. She has previously worked with the United Nations Development Programme and the USAID and has also taught at the National Law University of Odisha. She is a sociologist by training from the Delhi School of Economics and the University of Chicago. Ms. Mitra is the Executive Director of a New Delhi-based think tank called The Energy Forum

Siti Kaprawi

Siti Zaleha Kaprawi has been working in the artistic and creativity fields for more than three decades. Gained her BA Honors in Communication Media in 1989 from the Kent Institute of Arts & Design, United Kingdom. She is dedicated to publications and events related to Culture, Food & Tourism. Culinary is her passion (although she is not a Chef). She has compiled, photographed, layout and designed few cook books and other titles. Won the World Gourmand Book Award in Paris in 2013 for her "Flavours & Colours of Brunei Darussalam" cookbook.

Her business and creative abilities have come originally from her strong family mind-set. Siti is constantly transforming...

Founders of two Companies: 1) ASTERA CONSULTANT: Design, Publications and Event Organisors 2) EKOKAMPUNG Enterprise: Community-Based Ecotourism; Creating Products & Culinary related Activities & Events.

Somboon Chungprampree

Somboon Chungprampree (Moo) is a Thai social activist working for Peace and Justice in Asia. Even as a University student, he was involved in the student movement in Thailand, which focused on Sathirakoses Environmental Justice.

Since 1997, he has worked in different positions with key Tha V Regional V International civil society organisations.

Nagapradipa Foundation, a Thai Non-governmental Organisation established in 1968.

Program Director of Spirit in Education Movement (SEM), focusing on empowering Civil Society in Burma, Laos PDR, Cambodia and) Thailand.

Co-manager of the School for Well-being Studies and Research, and Co-committee of the Wongsanit Ashram.

Presently, he is serving as Executive Secretary of International Network of Engaged Buddhists (INEB).

He is a civic leader and serves on the Board of a number of international and national foundations. He has a great interest in photography.

Sonu Trivedi

Dr Sonu Trivedi is working as Assistant Professor in Department of Political Science, Zakir Husain Delhi College, University of Delhi since 2006. She was a student of Political Science at Lady Shri Ram College, University of Delhi and completed her PhD from School of International Studies, Jawaharlal Nehru University. Shewas a Visiting

Fellow at Institute of Asia Pacific Studies, Chinese Academy of Social Sciences, Indian Council of World Affairs (2014) and a Visiting faculty at IIM, Indore (2015-16). She has also undertaken major research projects funded by UGC and ICSSR and has widely travelled in the region and has done extensive field work in Myanmar, the core country of her research focus. She has been following political developments in Southeast Asia since more than a decade and has contributed extensively by means of articles and research papers to newspapers, magazines and journals on the current political developments and the critical changes taking place in the country. She is also the Convenor of the research cluster on Southeast Asia-The Southeast Asia Research Group at Department of Political Science, University of Delhi.

Suthiphand Chirathivat

Professor Suthiphand Chirathivat is Executive Director, ASEAN Studies Center Chairman, Chula Global Network Chulalongkorn University, Thailand.

Prof Suthiphand Chirathivat is professor emeritus of economics at Chulalongkorn University. He is also executive director of ASEAN Studies Center and chairman of Chula Global Network. He was Dean of Faculty of Economics, Chairman of the Ph.D. Program in Economics, Chairman of Economics Research Center and Center for International Economics at Chulalongkorn University. His academic interests involve the issues related to international trade, investment, finance, regional integration and development, and emerging issues in Asia in relation to the global economy and society.

Swarnim Wagle

Dr. Swarnim Wagle is an economist who served as the 24th Vice-Chair of the National Planning Commission (NPC) in the Government of Nepal. He led the NPC from August 2017 to February 2018, prior to which he served as a Member of the Commission for 28 months at two different periods between May 2014 and August 2017. Dr. Wagle worked as an international development professional for more than 15 years on policy assignments in over 20 countries, most recently as Senior Economist at The World Bank in Washington, D.C. At the United Nations Development Program (UNDP), he co-authored the 2013 Human Development Report titled "The Rise of the South." From 2002 to 2007, he co-led the Asia-Pacific Trade and Investment Initiative.

Dr. Wagle holds a PhD in Economics from the Australian National University, an MPA in International Development (MPNID) from Harvard University, and a B.Sc. (Econ) from the London School of Economic s.

U Khin Maung Nyo

U Nyo became Chief Editor and Advisor to local Economic and Business Journals until 2014. He delivers public lectures at the Universities, Ministries, National Defense College, Chamber of Commerce and academic institutes. More than 60 books (in Burmese) on education, economy, business and youth development were already published.

U Nyo regularly appears in national and international media, which includes BBC, VOA, RFA, and DVB among others on economic and education issues of Myanmar.

U Nyo is also Senior Research Fellow at Centre for Economic and Social Development, Senior Adviser at Myanmar Institute of Strategic and International Studies.

In 2014, he founded Myanmar Economic Association as Chairman and Vice Chairman in 2016.

He is also a member of National Minimum Wage Committee in 2017. Participated as Advisor to the Government Group at 2nd Peace and National reconciliation Conference 2017.

Some research works in English already published includes:

Myat Thein and Khin Maung Nyo: Social Sector Development in Myanmar: The role of the state in ASEAN Economic Bulletin 16, No. 3 (December 1999)

Khin Maung Nyo: Myanmar's response to the Global Financial Crisis 2008 in Ruling Myanmar: From Cyclone Nargis to National Elections Edited by Nick Cheesman, Monique Skidmore, Trevor Wilson, ISEAS 2011

Khin Maung Nyo: Taking stock of Myanmar Economy in 2011 in Myanmar's Transition: Openings, Obstacles, and Opportunities, Edited by Nick Cheesman, Monique Skidmore, Trevor Wilson, ISEAS 2012

Khin Maung Nyo; THILAWA SEZ: Opportunity Beckons in Frontier Myanmar 15 Oct 2015

Khin Maung Nyo; Myanmar's Transition to Democracy in Comparative Politics in ASEAN in MSC-NIDA 2015

Udai Bhanu Singh

Dr. Udai Bhanu Singh is Senior Research Associate and Coordinator of the Southeast Asia and Oceania Centre, Institute for Defence Studies and Analyses, New Delhi. He studied in Delhi at St. Stephen's College (BA Honours and Masters in History) and School of International Studies, JNU (M.Phil and Ph.D). He specializes on Southeast Asia with special attention to Myanmar. He joined IDSA in 1993. He has co-edited three books:

Delhi Dialogue VIII: ASEAN-India Relations: A New Paradigm (Pentagon Press, New Delhi, 2018);

Delhi Dialogue VII: ASEAN-India: Shaping the Post-2015 Agenda (Pentagon Press, New Delhi, 2015);

Delhi Dialogue VI: ASEAN-India: Vision for Partnership and Prosperity (Pentagon Press, New Delhi, 2015).

Dr. Singh earlier authored *ASEAN Regional Forum and Security of the Asia-Pacific* besides contributing to journals and chapters in books. He has participated in Track-2 and 1.5 dialogues with Myanmar, New Zealand and Australia. He contributes to the media and has delivered lectures at academic and defence institutions in India and abroad.

V Suryanarayan

Prof. V. Suryanarayan is one of India's leading specialists in South and Southeast Asian Studies and combines in his teaching and research specialization in history, political science and international relations. Educated in Ernakulam, Mumbai and New Delhi, he specialized in international relations at the doctoral level and received his PhD from the Indian School of International Studies. He has taught in the affiliated colleges of Bombay University; Indian School of International Studies, New Delhi Marathwada University, Auranga bad and North Eastern Hill University, Shillong. For more than twenty years he was associated with the Centre for South and Southeast Asian Studies, University of Madras, first as founding

Director and later as Senior Professor. Prof. Surya narayan was Visiting Professor, University of California, Los Angeles; Columbus College, University System of Georgia; Peradeniya University, Sri Lanka and School of International Studies, Jawaharlal Nehru University, New Delhi. He was the first professor of Maritime Studies and Research, Calicut University. A Chair Instituted by the Naval Head Quarters, New Delhi. He was associated with the Mahatma Gandhi University, Kottayam as the first Nelson Mandela Professor for Afro-Asian Studies. He is currently associated with the Asian College of Journalism, Chennai in its adjunct faculty.

Since his retirement Suryanarayan is associated with two think tanks in Chenna the Center for Asia Studies and Chennai Centre for China Studies, He was the Convenor of the Chennai Chapter of the Society for Indian Ocean Studies for many years.

Prof. Suryanarayan was associated with the Area Studies Programme of the University Grants Commission, New Delhi for several years and was a member of UGC evaluation team to several universities.

Prof. Suryanarayan was a member of the National Security Advisory Board of the Government of India for one term. He was a member of the International Monitoring Team which monitored the Presidential election in Sri Lanka in 1999.

Prof. Suryanarayan has delivered several important lectures. Mention should be made of 1) Presidential address in Section IV (Countries other than India) in the Gaya session of the Indian History Congress; 2) Prof. DD Kosambi Memorial lecture in the University of Goa; 3) Dr. Chandran Devenesen Memorial Lecture in Madras Christian College, Tambaram; 4) Bhaktavatsalam Memorial Lecture in the Department of Politics and Public Administration, University of Madras; 5) Comrade Padmanabha Memorial Lecture in Colombo; 6) RR Sivalingam Memorial Lecture in Colombo; and 7) Convocation address in the Southern Zone of the Indira Gandhi Open University.

A much sought after speaker he used to regularly speak in the National Defence College, New Delhi. He has also spoken in the Defence Services Staff College, Wellington and in the College of Combat, Mhow.

Prof. Suryanaryan has written extensively on contemporary South Asia and Southeast Asia. His books, monographs, chapters in edited volumes and occasional papers have received critical acclaim both in India and abroad. He has contributed articles to the Hind u, Frontline and the New Indian Express.

V.S. Seshadri

Ambassador Dr V.S. Seshadri was a member of the Indian Foreign Service and served as India's Ambassador to Slovenia (2007-2010) and to Myanmar (2010-2013). Prior to that he served in India's diplomatic missions in Nairob Brussels, Tehran, Bangkok and Washington DC. He was also on deputation to the Ministry of Commerce (1999-2003) of India as Joint Secretary in charge of WTO matters.

After his retirement, Dr. V.S. Seshadri has written several articles and papers on Myanmar and international trade issues. He also served as Vice-Chairman of Research and Information System for Developing Countries (RIS) from 2014 to 2017. Presently he is associated with the Confederation of Indian Industry as the Senior Adviser, Trade and International Policy.

Vo Xuan Vinh

Dr. Vo Xuan Vinh is the Deputy Director General, Institute for Southeast Asian Studies (ISEAS Vietnam), Vietnam Academy of Social Sciences (VASS), Hanoi. He joined Institute for Southeast Asian Institute as a researcher since 2004. He successfully defensed his PhD thesis on ASEAN in India's Look East Policy in 2011. He has conducted various research on security, politics and international relations in Southeast Asia, and India's Look/Act East Policy. He has presented his research papers on the South China Sea disputes in India and countries in Southeast Asian since 2009. He is now leading a two year project on maritime security in Southeast Asia. Vo Xuan Vinh is the author of books, monographs, chapters and research papers on issues of geopolitics, maritime security, politics and international relations in Indo-Pacific, and India's Look/Act East Policy. Many of his publications are on the South China Sea dispute and India's engagement in Asia-Pacific.

Index